Masters of the
Art of Command

Books by Martin Blumenson

Breakout and Pursuit
The Duel for France: 1944
Anzio: The Gamble That Failed
Kasserine Pass
Sicily: Whose Victory?
Salerno to Cassino
Bloody River: The Real Tragedy of the Rapido
Eisenhower
The Patton Papers: 1885–1940
The Patton Papers: 1940–1945

Masters of the
Art of Command

Martin Blumenson
James L. Stokesbury

Illustrated with Maps

HOUGHTON MIFFLIN COMPANY BOSTON 1975

Library of Congress Cataloging in Publication Data

Blumenson, Martin.
    Masters of the art of command.

    Includes index.
    1. Military biography. 2. Military history.
3. Leadership. I. Stokesbury, James L., joint author.
II. Title.
U51.B58   355.3′3′0922 [B]   75-19020
ISBN 0-395-17212-8

W 10 9 8 7 6 5 4 3 2 1

The authors are grateful for permission to reprint the following:
    From *Army* Magazine the chapters entitled: "Baum," "Kingston,"
"Anderson," "Saxe," "Thomas," "Devers," "Clark," "Iberville," "Crook,"
"Liddell Hart," "Patton and Montgomery," "Patton," "Command at Kasserine," "Eisenhower," "Coalition Command," "Military Obedience,"
"Stone," "Relieved of Command," and the maps entitled "The Route of
Task Force Baum" and "Hwachon Dam." Copyright (c) 1963, 1964, 1965,
1966, 1967, 1969, 1970, 1971, 1972, 1973 by the Association of the
U.S. Army.
    From KASSERINE PASS by Martin Blumenson, published by Hough-
ton Mifflin Company, 1966, the chapter entitled "Daubin," material
included in "Command at Kasserine," and the maps entitled "Tunisia"
and "Sbeitla."
    From *American History Illustrated*, February 1967, the National His-
torical Society, the chapter entitled "Woodfill."
    From U.S. Naval Institute *Proceedings*, December 1957, the chapter
entitled "Hitler versus His Generals." Copyright © 1957 by the United
States Naval Institute.

For Elizabeth Stokesbury
and J. Orin Oliphant

Acknowledgments

In addition to the acknowledgments given on the copyright page, we wish to express our gratitude to James Hodgson, co-author of "Hitler versus His Generals," for permission to reprint that chapter.

Our debt to individuals is especially great, and it is a pleasure for us to thank particularly the staff of the Acadia University Library, Dean A. H. MacLean, Mrs. Barbara Van Dyke and Mrs. Mae Ann Stevens; Miss Blanche Gregory, Mrs. Ruth K. Hapgood, and, for help far beyond the call of duty, L. James Binder.

MARTIN BLUMENSON
JAMES L. STOKESBURY

Preface

THE GENESIS of this work was in the spring of 1970. It came about as the result of a request from the Program Chairman of the Humanities Association at Acadia University: Would Professor Stokesbury and I make a joint presentation on Napoleon and Patton as military commanders?

The idea intrigued us. We knew quite a bit about these historical figures, and we thought that a comparison of the men and their times would be fruitful and instructive. We agreed to give the lecture. Posters announcing the event appeared on campus, placed on bulletin boards and tacked on trees, and the two of us worked on our talks.

The appointed evening finally arrived. It was a balmy night, prematurely warm, and I remember thinking, as I walked to the hall, that the weather was simply too nice for students and faculty members to attend another lecture, even on a subject as fascinating as ours. Only a handful of friends and faithful followers would be there. Stokesbury felt as I did.

We were surprised. The turnout was exceptionally good. All the seats were taken; folding chairs had to be brought in. Everyone listened to us with what seemed to be rapt attention. More reassuring was the question and discussion period immediately afterward, which was lively and long. The conversation about these brilliant and complex military men continued over the inevitable coffee and cookies.

When the two of us met the following day, we marveled at the interest that had been displayed. Was there really, we asked ourselves, an audience for this sort of thing? Did people actually want to know how commanders functioned in war, how leaders directed men in battle?

We wrote to L. James Binder, Editor in Chief of *Army* magazine, and proposed a series of articles on masters of the art of command. His response was enthusiastic. With this encouragement, we collaborated on several pieces. Our aim was to show how certain military professionals met the challenges of their times. What were their problems and how did they solve them?

The following essays elaborate this theme. They are not a systematic treatment of the subject; they are meant to show how some commanders acted. Most of the persons described are important and well known in the history of warfare; others are obscure. No matter what the case, the point that emerges is that command is an art to be mastered, a craft that requires specialized knowledge, a well-developed intuition, high intelligence, and the ability to reason. The process of motivating human beings and controlling impersonal forces during a clash of arms is extremely complicated and difficult, and successful practitioners of the art of command have been a special breed of men, distinguished by strength, will and flair.

They are to be found in the following pages: men who operated at different levels of command — young lieutenants learning their trade, and crusty and battle-hardened generals dominating their scenes. Some essays are biographical sketches that seek to illuminate a particular period as well as a particular man. Others are concerned with the general problems of command in specific contexts, for example, the restraints imposed by coalition warfare.

The exercise of command depends on two essential elements: authority and responsibility. Without these, there can be no command. A commander must have the right, within his sphere of activity, to decide all questions pertaining to his functions, to direct all those individuals who are subject to his orders, and to expect obedience from his subordinates. He must also be ready to accept full credit or blame for his acts, whether they lead to success or failure.

These two conditions define the state of command, but there is an additional circumstance. Each commander occupies a certain position according to an established hierarchical system. Even as he commands in a specific area, he is under the command of a superior officer. Lieutenants serve under a captain, generals commanding divisions are under the direction of a general at the next higher level of command, the corps. In the United States, the President as commander in chief stands at the top of the pyramid. Yet even his exercise of authority and responsibility is subject to the approval of the ultimate power, the American people.

The art of command has been practiced throughout the ages. If the principles have changed but little, the problems incident to particular times and places have undergone some transformation. It is the historical framework within which individual commanders have operated that concerns Professor Stokesbury in his introduction, and he has illuminated this subject with marvelous clarity and verve. His essay explains how the changing nature of warfare has imposed both special opportunities and limitations on those who mastered the art of command.

— Martin Blumenson

Contents

Maps

Masters of the
Art of Command

Introduction

MILITARY LEADERSHIP, the art of command, has always been a subject of intense interest. That one man should be in a position to play God, that his decisions will govern the lives of hundreds of thousands, perhaps millions, of men naturally fascinates us. This combination of human resources and superhuman responsibilities engages our sympathy and wonder. "War is an impassioned drama," and no element of it is more dramatic than the command decisions that mean life and death for lesser — or better — men, and perhaps survival or disaster for states and empires. We want to know what decisions a leader makes, what choices he has available to him, and what there is in his own past and environment that influences his actions.

What we should really like to have is some formula for producing success, and if humanity were reducible to science, or if history repeated itself exactly, we might find one. But since man is the one creature who defies wholly quantifiable terms, since each historical event, no matter how similar to one of the past, is still unique, there is no formula, and therefore no science. What rules there are provide an adjunct to the art of command, and we study that art and its practitioners to ask why one man wins, another loses. What makes one man a great leader, another just a name on the rubbish heap of history? What is the art of command, and who have been the masters of it?

There is a traditional image of the great commander. We see him as knowledgeable in his profession, experienced, bold, brave physically and morally, an impressive man of decision and action. One can think of a stereotype of military greatness, a combination of

Hannibal, Napoleon, Robert E. Lee, and George S. Patton, Jr.;
put all these together, though, and the result is a sort of military
superman, unreal and unsatisfactory. Napoleon and Lee, for example, had in common almost no characteristic except military genius.
A catalog of the virtues necessary for greatness becomes so all-
inclusive as to be meaningless, with the single most essential element
impossible to ferret out, and we are still left with one man an un-
accountable genius, the next an obvious dud.

Much that determines whether a man gets marked as one of
history's great commanders depends on himself, and perhaps more
does not. There are both internal factors, personal and professional,
over which a man has some limited control, and external ones —
time, space, and environment — over which he has even less.

Field Marshal Montgomery of Alamein tried to deal with the internal springs of greatness in a book called *The Path to Leadership*.
The things he mentioned went beyond the superficial criteria that
come immediately to mind. It was so obvious as not to need stating
that a man must possess what we usually consider the human virtues.
Some, of course, are more important than others; a man burdened
with modesty is not likely to succeed in an assertive business, though
generals such as George H. Thomas provide an exception to that
rule. A degree of human sympathy is vital, but too much of it is
fatal; a general must know not only how to save the lives of his men,
but also when to expend them, and to what purpose. Even more crucial, he must have the courage to do so knowing that the balance
sheet will be drawn up only after the fact. The power to decide on an
action, and the strength to see it through, are probably the most
fundamental qualities of a great soldier.

After he had considered the requisite personal characteristics, Montgomery then described less tangible attributes, such as sincerity and
the belief in one's cause, and, in effect, the personal rectitude of the
leader. There is a good deal of truth in saying these are necessary;
men may differ passionately about the gods they worship — otherwise there would be no wars — but the initial belief must be there.
Skeptics and cynics do not make great leaders of men. Napoleon was
a skeptic about religion, but not about France, and France was the
cause in whose name he enlisted the loyalties of his soldiers.

The professional qualities needed by a great general are a little easier to define because they are less likely to be as elusive as personal attributes. It should be axiomatic that the great soldier must have a profound understanding of his business, a thoroughly professional training and background — though it must be admitted that this has not always been the case, and before our own complex period some of the greatest soldiers started out as raw amateurs; Benedict Arnold, Nathanael Greene, Cromwell, and a couple of Napoleon's marshals come to mind as men who gained their military education almost by intuition. But once more such men have been the exception rather than the rule.

Knowledge and training can be acquired by most career soldiers, but there are still the personal and professional attributes that single out the generals from the regimental officers and determine which man ends his career as a colonel and which as a general or field marshal. One of the most important of these is the ability to see the situation through the eyes of the enemy; Napoleon called this "seeing the other side of the hill." To a certain extent, this ability is intuitive, but more of it can be acquired than might at first seem possible. Napoleon remarked that he never looked at a position without asking himself, What do I do if the enemy appears there, or over there, or from this quarter, and what will *he* do in such case?

Even if a soldier possesses all the personal and professional skills we think he needs for supreme command there is still no guarantee that he will come to rank among the military immortals. There are as many external forces at work on his career as there are internal ones, and over these he has even less control.

The most significant is simply the factor of time and space, or the point in history that a soldier happens to occupy. His career has to fit in with the general stream of events; the past is full of nameless men who were just a bit too young or too old for their moment. Hindenburg was already in retirement when World War I broke out, but not everyone gets the second chance that he got. Marshal Bugeaud was one of France's greatest soldiers, but he was just short of his baton when Napoleon fell; he spent the rest of his life in little colonial campaigns, and his name is known only to specialists. If any given war had broken out ten years earlier, or ten years later, than it did, it would have produced a different crop of leading names. Montgomery, to paraphrase him again, remarked that Britain always started her wars with a disaster because she was never prepared for them; therefore the commanders going into a war were always vulnerable, and the best thing to be in the British Army at the beginning of a conflict was a colonel or perhaps a brigadier — high enough to step into command when the scapegoats for peacetime policy were axed, not high enough to fall in the general cleanup.

One can see this kind of thing easily in the United States Army. Ideally, for World War II, a soldier would have graduated from West Point about 1912, had service in France in World War I as a company or battalion officer, taken the right courses and done the appropriate tours during the interwar years, and been a brigadier general or senior colonel in his mid-forties when World War II broke out. With that sequence he could hardly avoid a place in the history books; whether it was a good or a bad place would depend more on personal qualities, but the time sequence itself would be highly desirable.

Other factors are a bit more subtle. A very influential one is the changing nature of the state and society. The degree of social mobility available to a soldier is an important determinant in his career and the levels to which he may rise. Revolutions point this up more clearly than anything else, for they juxtapose the immobility of one type of society with the mobility of another. None of the American commanders of the Revolution would have risen far without it; two of the most senior, Gates and Charles Lee, had already left the British service as middle-grade officers because they lacked the opportunity to rise higher. Several of Napoleon's marshals were serving in the ranks of the French army when the revolution there broke out; probably none of them would have gone past sergeant major under the old regime. Under the new they got batons, dukedoms, and more; Murat and Bernadotte became kings. In other countries there were minor variations, but things ran along more or less similar lines. The British system, for example, was ostensibly more open than that on the continent, but only if one already belonged to the acceptable classes; a Sir William Robertson's rising from private to Chief of the Imperial General Staff was unique, and even in World War II the British preserved what North Americans regard as artificial distinctions; a flying officer and a sergeant pilot might do the same job, but one was an officer and gentleman, the other not quite. It was still easier to reach the top of the ladder if you started from halfway up instead of at the bottom.

Such class-consciousness can, of course, work both ways. Some of the best soldiers of the French army of 1789 were thrown out of it, and even guillotined, because they had noble antecedents. Before the revolution you had to prove nobility for a commission; during it you had to prove common birth. So though a man may not be able to choose the bed to be born in, that bed can have a great effect, positive or negative, on his career.

In the same way politics plays its role as a determinant. Field Marshal Sir Garnet Wolseley of the British Army was a first-rate soldier, but what really made his career was the fact that he was about the only first-rater who happened to be a Liberal. That party, though openly anti-imperialist, found itself involved in a frontier war every time it came into office, and its answer was always to unleash Wolseley. The same factor, operating in reverse, had all but ruined Sir John Moore two generations earlier. It was much more subtle than the Stalinist purges of the 1930s in Russia, or the pressure Hitler put on his generals to conform, but it had more or less the same results.

A part of playing politics is playing press agent, and the great general is likely to be his own best reporter. Caesar never looks better than when modestly recounting his own deeds, in the third person, which set a style for the next two thousand years or so. Napoleon wrote his own bulletins and impressed nearly everyone but his soldiers, to whom the phrase "to lie like a bulletin" was a commonplace. In modern times, with our communications revolution, a general's relations with his press corps are as important as those he maintains with his superiors. If he can be appropriately flamboyant, in some way that catches the public fancy, and can get along well with the correspondents, he is well on the road to glory. We like to think that history is the final judge here, the great arbiter of reputations, but usually history is the preserve of specialists, and the image fixed in the popular mind lasts a long time.

Another influence that is to a large extent beyond the control of the soldier is the technology of his period, or the state of the art of war at any given time. The soldier, like everyone else, has to work with what he has. This is true both in the broad sense of the development of science and technology, and in the narrow sense of what is available to the practitioner in a specific situation. There have been periodic fluctuations in technological development, so that one man will go down in history as a great innovator, another as a man who carried an established set of conditions to near perfection. The failures, of course, are those who have a major transformation handed to them and refuse to take advantage of it. It may be a change of technology, such as the tank; or of military organization, such as Louis XIV's army or the Prussian general staff system; or of the whole social structure, such as in the French Revolution. In each of these examples those who looked steadfastly backward were swept away by the future.

Finally, but not least significant in a man's career, there is simply the factor of luck, or fate, or whatever one chooses to call it. Who can tell how many great commanders of the future were slaughtered in the opening weeks of 1914? In the most basic sense, one has to live to make the grade. Even here, of course, there are exceptions. We call General Wolfe great because he took Quebec, dying in the process. Had he lived, he might well have proved to be less a master of the art of war than we generally consider him to be; more than one general has redeemed faulty dispositions and won fame by a suitably glorious death. Unfortunately it is a trick that can be done only once in a career. For the most part, as Napoleon said, it is better to be a lucky man.

II

The art of war has had a basic continuity from its earliest appearance until the advent of the railroad. For roughly those four thousand years man did the same things in the same way, responding to the very real physical limitations on what he could actually accomplish. In this time technology changed very little, social organization less, and man not at all. With minor adjustments that built on one another, the great commander of one era could have fit easily into another. Today we are so used to mass society, and especially mass transportation, that it is difficult to remember the limitations under which earlier peoples labored.

The marching man in the Hittite armies moved at the same speed as his later counterparts in the armies of Frederick the Great. He could carry about the same weight of material — sixty pounds was his limit for any length of time — and he required the same amount. This was true as well of the cavalryman, though in those four thousand years the cavalry had one major development: the stirrup was introduced in India, perhaps as early as the first century of the Christian era. This enabled the mounted horseman to turn himself into a more effective form of shock weapon than he had formerly been. Other than that, horses went at about the same speed as they had done before and demanded the same amount of care.

The limitations of animal transport remained a major feature of the period. There was always the problem of how fast a draft animal could go and how much rest it required. One example will serve to illustrate the problem for the entire period. Wellington's army during the Peninsular War was perhaps the most highly developed eighteenth-century army, fighting a war that had not, at least under the conditions that prevailed in Spain, been outdated by the French Revolution and Napoleonic concepts. Under normal conditions, whatever they might be, Wellington's soldiers could march about fifteen miles a day; this allowed time for meals — two a day — breaking camp, a degree of foraging, and all the other things necessary to an army on the move. The march was usually accomplished in the morning, the troops moving out about seven or eight and stopping soon after noon. This seems to us fairly slow, but in fact the troops could march faster than the animals could pull their supply wagons and impedimenta. The train of the army was tied to the speed of oxen or bullocks, and they could go only about twelve miles a day without breaking down; even then they needed a day's rest every fourth day. The oxen could therefore go thirty-six miles in four days, though the soldiers could march sixty miles in the same time; or the soldiers could outrun their supplies by a day and a half every four days. Wellington was thus tied to his train, his army moving at the pace of the slowest unit. It was true that the British were not good foragers and found it difficult to live off the land. General Foy, who fought them, remarked that a French battalion would live well where a British company would starve. Still, it was the British who won the war, and Foy was forced to concede, "The British infantry is the best in Europe," before adding, "Fortunately, there is not much of it."

Wellington's pace was essentially the same as Marlborough's, a century before him. For that matter it was the same as the Romans', eighteen centuries earlier. No commander could overcome these limitations, and the great soldier was not the one who fought against them, but the one who could take advantage of them for his own purposes.

Similar limitations were placed on the size of armies by the availability of supplies in any given area. Throughout history armies have tended to fight the same campaigns over and over again. Northern Italy was always a battleground, and so were the Low Countries. There are very good reasons for this, as one can see by superimposing a transportation or communications map over one showing population or agricultural production. Once again, until the advent of the railroad and the internal combustion engine the possibilities of human and animal motion put very real restrictions on what could be done and where.

As early as the classical period generals knew that about twenty thousand men was the largest number that could be kept together and handled as an integral force, without starving themselves by eating up all the food in the area they could reach. More than that number had to be so dispersed for logistical reasons that they became tactically uncontrollable. The Roman response to this was the consular army. Usually a consul was given two legions, about 5000 men each, in addition to their nonlegionary auxiliaries, another 5000 each. This 20,000-man force became the standard Roman field army.

Of course there were armies in greater numbers than this, but the problems of controlling them were immense. When Wellington marched up out of the Peninsula in 1813, he had about 80,000 troops; but they marched by four distinct routes and traveled for all practical purposes in corps of 20,000 each. The contemporary French answer to this difficulty was the *corps d'armée,* again running to about 20,000. In Napoleon's later years a sort of gigantism overtook him, resulting in such things as the unwieldy mass he took to Russia — and everyone knows the results of that.

Climate placed similar obstacles in the way of what soldiers could do. As long as armies depended on animal transport they could operate only in seasons when animals could eat. If an animal had to carry his own food as well as his payload, the payload was of necessity so reduced as to make the whole effort more bother than it was worth. The same thing was true of the men, and during the Seven Years' War the French generals lamented that they were tied down in their operations to the problem of making ovens to bake bread for their troops. While the Prussians had developed an iron oven to be carried about on a wagon, the French were still building brick ovens, using them, abandoning them, and then repeating the process all over again. During the later eighteenth century, as the depot system reached its ultimate development, generals were able to push their operations farther and farther into winter weather. They would pause between the start of the rainy season, that is, the advent of mud, and the coming of heavy frost; then they would operate again in the winter, pausing a second time for the spring thaw and mud. But the results of this were problematical, and the whole depot system was being discarded before anything definitive was decided on the question of winter campaigns.

There were of course significant developments in this period. Social and technological change became increasingly apparent in early modern Europe, and caused corresponding changes in war and generalship. But each new advance brought new problems in its train. It is certainly true that artillery became a major factor on the battlefield, and its development had profound social ramifications, such as the decline of feudalism, to which it contributed, but all it did to the problems of military transport was to increase them. One of the chief obstacles of the Blenheim campaign for Marlborough was how to move his guns; he eventually did it by boat, barge, and sledge. As for small arms, it was not until the mid-nineteenth century that they became sufficiently useful to change the rules of the game. A British officer of the early part of the century could seriously advocate a return to the longbow, as being faster, more accurate, and farther ranging than the miltary musket then in universal use. Today he seems rather like one of his contemporaries, an admiral who went about with a pocketful of acorns, planting them here and there so that in another century Britain would still have the oak needed for her ship timbers. Both were a bit out of date; neither could know that at the time.

Notwithstanding these assorted technological limitations, and equally important social ones, there were many aspects of preindustrial warfare that were familiar later. Even in ancient times highly sophisticated military systems existed, and when these are examined they prove remarkable both for elements of modernity and for their longevity. States such as the Hittites and Assyrians, mere names today, lasted for many centuries, far longer than we have.

The military system of Egypt was unique in one particular way: it never lost a war. Few other states can claim to be as fortunate, but then few have been so blessed by geography. Surrounded by seas or deserts, the Egyptians were in a thoroughly isolated position, and their homeland was all but immune to invasion. Their only real point of contact with outsiders was across the isthmus of Suez and up into Sinai. As the Egyptian state matured and was consolidated, it pushed its frontier into this area, and the border campaigns of Egypt were fought in Palestine. The pharaohs led their armies personally in war, and the god-king reported back to Egypt what he wanted to have happened rather than what might have actually taken place. He was therefore as fortunate in his public relations as in his military geography.

In 1294 B.C. Ramses II, with an army of Numidian mercenaries, marched on the Hittite stronghold of Kadesh. Planning to capture the city before the Hittite field army could come to its relief, he pushed ahead too rapidly and got himself cut off and surrounded. Though he slightly outnumbered the Hittites, they possessed iron weapons and the formidable three-man chariot, and the Egyptians were very hard-pressed. By his personal leadership Ramses at last managed to cut his way free of the trap, and he counterattacked when the enemy took time to loot the Egyptian dead. Ramses then succeeded in driving the Hittites under the walls of Kadesh, but he failed to take the city, which held out for seventeen more years. Home again after the campaign, Ramses announced a great victory in cutting his way clear of the encircling Hittites, conveniently forgetting that his own presumption had put him into the trap to begin with, and that the object of the campaign had been to capture the city. But whatever his merits, or lack of them, as a general, Ramses knew his business as a politician and propagandist.

Some of the approaches of the Assyrians are even more familiar. As a state they traditionally suffer from a bad press, but the degree to which they were any worse than other preclassical empires is highly problematical. They differed in several important respects from their predecessors and contemporaries. They were really the world's first military society, in the sense that their long struggle for survival — they were plainsmen with no natural frontiers — turned them into a people whose primary business was war. Additionally, they were the greatest empire builders the world had yet seen, and their rule provided for their subjects a greater degree of order and security, over a larger area and for a longer time, than had any state before them. Finally, they discovered the use of calculated terrorism as an instrument of policy, a discovery we tend to regard as belonging to our own time. The Assyrian rule was relatively benevolent to those who were already subject, or who willingly accepted their rule. But rebels and other resisters were dealt with in such a way as to *décourager les autres.* Cities were razed to the ground after being taken; there were wholesale decapitations; women and children were systematically massacred. The bombing of Rotterdam would have been an act readily understandable to the ancient Assyrians, and they would no doubt have agreed with Napoleon's admonition to his generals in the Vendée: it is better to appear ruthless and kill a thousand than to be falsely lenient and then have to kill ten thousand as the price of that mistake. Assyria was always on a war footing and — until she was swamped by her enemies — produced a string of first-class generals, all with unpronounceable names.

It is fashionable today to regard the United States as a second Rome. A recent Canadian anthology of essays on Americans is entitled *The New Romans,* and Americans are seen as big, brash, noisy, self-confident, and materialistic, bursting with energies that are often misdirected. In such comparisons the cultured and sophisticated Greeks — or Europeans — come out ahead, an example of the way literature is used to compensate for the vagaries of history. Whether such a comparison is valid — and its validity is apt to depend on the vantage point of the beholder — certain elements of the Roman military and social order suggest parallels with our own day. The development of the Roman army, especially the reforms of Marius, should be of interest to Americans trying after more than a generation of conscription to revert to an all-volunteer army.

War, of course, depends on much more than fighting. Livy, the chief authority for the Second Punic War, said that Hannibal invaded Italy in the hope of detaching Rome's recent enemies from alliance with her so that he could crush Rome's rising power before it was consolidated. He failed to do so, in spite of his ability to defeat army after army and to live in Italy practically as he pleased for twenty years. The general of today, so often fighting in concert with, or in support of, allies of different races and backgrounds, may well ask himself what magic the Romans had: How could they hold their allies to them after two decades of wasting war and near defeat? Hannibal may have been the most interesting figure of the long contest, but it was the solidity of the Roman system, the essential validity of it, that won the war.

The famous Carthaginian provides us with another example of a great commander who in the end proved to be a failure. Winning battle after battle, he eventually lost his war, a sort of early Robert E. Lee who could not be everywhere. Yet his defeat has not harmed his reputation; it may in fact add to his fascination as a master of war.

The Dark and Middle Ages perhaps offer least to the student's knowledge of the art of command and the elements of military greatness. In western Europe, tactics, strategy, and above all military organization were at such a low ebb that the search for useful military lessons becomes all but fruitless. In the east, of course, the Byzantines produced both a remarkable system and some of the world's greatest generals and theoreticians: Maurice, Heraclius, Leo, and others. Gibbon did the Byzantines a great disservice when he casually remarked that their virtues were accidental, their vices inherent. There were also the great invasions out of Asia, but these inspired so much more terror than enlightenment that little positive was learned from them; it was left to later generations to marvel at the generalship of Genghis Khan and his successors.

As for Europe itself, research has shown that these periods were not wholly barren, and that there was more evolution of weapons and technique than one might have thought. The element of leadership, of course, as distinct from the science of war, is worthy of study in any context, and if recent work has downgraded Richard the Lion-Hearted, it has balanced that account by rehabilitating poor Richard III, Shakespeare's "Crookback Dick."

With the reappearance of the state as the primary political organism at the end of the Middle Ages and through the Renaissance, we enter a period that is most familiar to us. Modern history has generally been seen in the context of the nation-state and of the relations of different parts of the state to each other, as well as of different states to one another. Here we arrive once again at an era full of possibilities for the study of war and particularly of generalship and leadership. And here at last we reach an era in whose complexity we can discern the beginnings of our own time.

Through the later stages of the Renaissance it was the Spanish and the French who were regarded as the great practitioners of warfare. Their ascendancy was almost universally acknowledged, with the exception of the periodic appearances in Sweden of such meteors as Gustavus Adolphus and later Charles XII — this was before the days when Sweden had discovered the utility of remaining neutral and selling to both sides.

When the Spanish became preoccupied with their own troubles, which were legion, the French produced the first real monarchical army of the nation-state. Not least of the elements that made France dominant in Europe and the world was the army of Louis XIV, imitated by all his rivals and foes so that it eventually became the pattern for all to follow. The leading figures in its development were the Marquis de Louvois, Louis's war minister from 1668 to 1691, and a brilliant galaxy of soldiers, the most notable of whom was the Vicomte de Turenne, in 1660 marshal general of France.

The reforms that Turenne introduced have become so familiar that they hardly seem very revolutionary today; that is a measure only of how important they have been for every army since the seventeenth century. It was the French who first brought their field commanders to heel, turning generals from potential rivals of the crown into servants. One of Turenne's most startling innovations, and the one most resented by those on whom it was practiced, was his assertion of royal control over the officer class. His was the first real establishment of a hierarchy of command in modern times, the absolute sine qua non of a military force. He and Louvois together insisted on the primacy of the War Ministry over the field officers, and they made it stick by denying supplies to those who refused to carry out their instructions. It was a basic change; it was also so radical that it took generations to gain full acceptance.

Nevertheless, by the opening of the eighteenth century the monarchical army on French lines had assumed a form recognizable to us, an army of all arms, formed on the regimental system, directed by a

War Ministry, and serving, with more or less effect, the needs of its parent state. It arrived just in time for the first of the great succession wars, and the appearance on the stage of another figure whose problems merit study.

Since 1945 students are apt to regard the Duke of Marlborough as an ancestor of Winston Churchill; before 1940 Churchill liked to regard himself as a descendant of "the great Marlborough." The two had really many points in common: both were leaders, in name or in fact, of their country during a time of great crisis, and both were forced to deal at length with the problems of coalition warfare. Marlborough often complained that his allies, the Dutch, caused him more difficulties than his enemies, the French. The war was fought in Flanders, and the Dutch were hurt more by winning than the French were by losing, so perhaps they deserve sympathy beyond what Marlborough was wont to display. In any case, the point remains that one need not confine himself to the present for examples of the possibilities and problems of coalition warfare.

If Louis XIV and his ministers succeeded in bringing their generals under control and asserting the primacy of what was a sort of civilian control over the professionals — even though Louis liked to think of himself as a soldier, he was not very professional at it — there was a reverse side to this coin as well, and all through the eighteenth century French generals suffered from what they regarded as excessive interference by the home government with their operations. The opening stages of any campaign the French waged were fought out in Versailles, as each of several factions among the court party jockeyed to make certain that its man was given command of the army in the field. In fact, seen in this light, one might say that some of the most successful French generals of the eighteenth century — in terms of achieving their objectives — were not the soldiers at all but their loyal female champions at court. It was a pity the ladies were not as astute in their choice of protegées as they were assiduous in pushing their claims. One result of the whole business was that even the best of the French generals had to fight in the field while looking over their shoulders to guard against rivals' undercutting them at home. Every move was subject to a long-distance scrutiny that was almost invariably hostile; there were always more men on the outside trying to get in than there were on the inside. No general fights well when he is constantly afraid that the order for his relief is already on its way to him.

While Europe went on its way fighting its stereotyped set-piece battles and sliding down the slope to bankruptcy and revolution, soldiers overseas were innovating and adapting to new conditions forced upon them by terrain and different enemies. The activities of Iberville or Robert Rogers foreshadowed the type of warfare perfected in World War II by the Long Range Desert Group, Wingate, and Merrill. The little hit-and-run colonial campaigns taught anew intriguing lessons about surprise and mobility, lessons that formal soldiers have had to relearn in every war, and that, as can be seen in a myriad of examples, they failed to learn at their peril.

The American Revolution, whatever may be said of its different strategical combinations — and there were some that were remarkably fruitful as well as some that were almost equally stupid — raised for the first time in modern history the problem of dealing with citizen-soldiers, a far different type from the unimaginative and stolid professionals then in vogue in Europe. Americans who came off their farms or out of their little towns as embodied militia were accustomed to speaking their minds. Their officers were usually local men of property; sometimes they were chosen because they were natural leaders of their communities, sometimes just because they were well known. A man might do anything and be well known in his town, and Washington was appalled at Cambridge to find one militia officer still practicing on his men his trade of town barber. Neither he nor his men saw any incongruity in this, but such men were not disposed to give unquestioning obedience to such officers. They had to be led, not driven, and they had to be shown why it made sense for them to go through the maneuvers desired of them. For those men, far more than for European soldiers at the time, generalship had to be supplemented by leadership.

No one yet has really improved on Baron von Steuben's formula for training citizen-soldiers or, for that matter, on his characterization of the difference between North Americans and the soldiers he had commanded in Europe. To one of his old colleagues he wrote, "You say to your soldier, 'Do this,' and he doeth it; but I say to my soldier, 'This is why you should do this,' and *then* he doeth it."

With the French Revolution the citizen-soldier, and in his train the mass army, reached Europe. On August 23, 1793, the Committee of Public Safety decreed universal conscription, and the nation in arms was born. Most of Europe was already at war with the revolution and the rights of man. Now French soldiers, in the name of liberty, equality, fraternity, or in the name of the Emperor Napoleon, would march roughshod over those ancient monarchies and enter triumphantly every capital from Lisbon to Moscow. Before that tide would recede Europe would have to learn to use against the revolution the weapons of the revolution. The autocrat of all the Russians would have to pose as the friend of man, and Austrian archduchesses would have to kiss peasants as an enlistment bounty.

The cast of brilliant soldiers thrown up by the French Revolution has never been surpassed, and it is to be hoped no one will ever again have occasion to try to match it. Carnot remains the personification of what a war minister should be, as Napoleon is the personification of what a commander should be. Much of the success was due to genius and personal magnetism, which one either had or did not have, but much also was the product of study and concentration, which Napoleon was the first to admit. He had no use for the mind unformed by study, and acknowledged that he himself was a great picker of brains and assimilator of other men's ideas. Militarily, indeed, it has been pointed out often enough that all the elements of Napoleonic warfare existed before Napoleon; his genius was to combine them and make them work. The fascination he excites seems eternal, as over a quarter of a million different book titles attest, with more being added every year. Writers never seem to tire of pointing out, or students of analyzing, the lessons of Napoleonic warfare: how he rose, or how he fell. No one has yet improved on his handling of troops, his dispositions, his insights into how a battle or a campaign would develop, his masterly sense of timing. Ultimately, to cite A. J. P. Taylor, he provides the greatest lesson of all, that man cannot be God.

III

Napoleon's genius carried the art of war to a peak just as the pre-industrial period was ending. The next few generations would see and deal with a new set of conditions, and generals would have to apply different solutions to age-old problems.

The most distinctive feature of the developing industrial period after 1815 is the concept of mass. With the Industrial Revolution and the population growth of the nineteenth century came mass production, mass society, and the mass army. In 1812 Napoleon took a quarter of a million Frenchmen to Russia, not to mention his allies and his satellites; that strained his empire to and indeed beyond, its limits. Yet by 1872 the peacetime strength of the German army was set at nearly half a million men, and several million could be mobilized for war.

For the soldier or military student the most important material factors of the period, as always, were weaponry, transport, communications, and the changes in them. Within the space of a long generation the flintlock musket, which had been the standard weapon of the soldier for more than a century, gave way to the modern magazine-fed rifle, and battle ranges changed accordingly. The modern breech-loading artillery piece and the machine gun would soon come to dominate the battlefield. The game of war, with its rules worked out to a nicety through a long period of stability, had to be revised to meet the new situation. With hindsight we can see how desperately soldiers clung to older notions of what could and could not be done. Against all the evidence of the Franco-Prussian and the Russo-Japanese war, theorists continued to insist that soldiers could always take ground and that the machine gun was a highly overrated weapon.

They learned to use the new means of transport. The railroad and the steam engine were too important to ignore, and gradually such mundane things as rail junctions and coaling stations for ships would assume a great importance on the military maps. But the truth is that none of these things had the liberating effect that might have been hoped for them. Rail junctions were no more important than road junctions had been before and were just as hard to take or defend; if the steamship liberated sailors from the caprices of the wind, it made them even more dependent on the availability of coal dumps.

The same was true of new modes of communications. The telegraph and then the wireless provided as many new problems as they did possibilities. Virtually the first British commander to fight tied to a cable line was Admiral Sir Beauchamp Seymour, who bombarded Alexandria in 1882 during the rebellion that culminated in the British take-over of Egypt. Seymour's difficulties were pathetically amusing

— he tried to cope with the telegraph that told him what he wanted
to hear or what he did not want to hear or, worst of all, nothing.

All of these difficulties, so trying to commanders laboring under
them, were no more than a small part of larger transformations occurring in society. Industrialization, nationalism, liberalism, and
above all the vast increase in numbers of people and things made for
a reordering of procedures. The monarchs, the Church, and the
landowners tried to keep or to revert to the status quo after 1815,
but in the long run society had to be reshuffled to meet the new forces
at work.

The new era was of course different but by no means divorced
from its past; it turned out to be neither the anarchy the conservatives
feared nor the utopia for which the liberals hoped. The problems of
war and peace, economics and politics, life and death may have been
seen in new dimensions, but they were the same old problems. The
perfectibility of man, so fondly if distantly glimpsed by the eighteenth-
century philosophes, appeared as far away as ever. A mass society
began to emerge, but man in the mass showed himself no wiser than
the autocrats who had previously ordered his existence. Representative or responsible government hardly prevented states from going
to war. Poor old Napoleon III with his gallstones desperately wanted
to avoid the Franco-Prussian War; it was the mob outside that kept
chanting "To Berlin!" The problems of producing and distributing
wealth became, if anything, worse than ever, for the machine gave
men more potential for amassing wealth and also for sinking into
poverty.

It had been hoped that the machine age would free man from his
apparently endless round of toil; instead, man became a slave of his
machine. The farmer who had labored from dawn until dusk now
became the slum dweller who labored from before dawn until after
dark. Liberal progress in the direction of a more humane attitude
toward one's fellows was slow and halting. Not until the latter part
of the nineteenth century did laws begin to make an inroad on
society's disregard for the individual, and by that time the liberal
impulse itself was in danger; most of the great humanitarian legislation of the period was enacted by governments that were either conservative or openly autocratic. Progress toward a society in which
each man might live a full life was desperately slow. By 1900 the
times were out of joint in a variety of ways.

One offshoot of mass society was the mass army. The French Revolution and Napoleon had moved toward the concept of the nation in arms. Now, with industrialization, it would be necessary to move again, to the concept of the nation at war where, finally, all the citizens would be combatants in one sense or another. The nation could demand much more from its citizens than the monarchy had ever been able to demand from its subjects. It took half a century to make the transition. After 1850 soldiers too began to play the numbers game.

The Franco-Austrian War of 1859 is often thought of as the last of the old-style wars, when commanders were still doing their best to imitate Napoleon, and the campaign has often been dismissed, more or less justly, with the aphorism, "The war of 1859 was fought by armies of 1809 using the tactics of 1759." After that, new generations of commanders were appearing on the scene, and the changes of contemporary society were becoming too profound to ignore.

To North Americans the Civil War marked the great watershed of military development in this era. Both sides utilized railroads for logistics and communications, and rail lines and terminals became major objectives of strategic development. The North mobilized something over two million men; the South something under. The second wartime generation of commanders, Thomas, Grant, Sherman, Lee, those who had matured through the war itself, proved themselves as masterly as any of the Europeans in the traditional art of war and as much at home with the ramifications of new developments. By the twentieth century German students were acknowledging that "it is the campaigns in America we must study."

This was not apparent at the time, however, and the great Chief of the German General Staff, Helmuth von Moltke, remarked scornfully that "a conflict of armed mobs chasing each other around the brush" was of no interest to professional European soldiers. Part of this attitude on von Moltke's part was the result of his having discovered one of the most fundamental answers to the problems of modern warfare. If the Americans were in their amateurish way the first to fight a mass war with a mass army, the Prussians were the first to come up with an intelligible way to organize that army; von Moltke brought to fruition the development of the general staff system. His concepts gave rise to the form of military organization that was best suited to the developing conditions of society and technology.

There are probably few institutions in history that have been as thoroughly misunderstood in the popular mind as the German General Staff. It has usually been associated with the stiff Prussian drill of the lower ranks, and regarded as a sort of robot instrument for making war; or, alternatively, it has been thought of as some evil plotting machine seeking an opportunity to unleash war and destruction on unsuspecting neighbors. In practice it was neither of these things, but was fundamentally an autonomous but still integral part of the German army, which was able to inculcate a similarity of outlook into the members of the German officer class and provide for the evolution of an appropriate military doctrine; it was both the brain and the nervous system of the army. It reached definitive development in the Wars of German Unification, so by the 1870s the various necessary elements of the modern army in a developing industrial society were all present.

Different states of course reacted to the new conditions in different ways; each had its own national peculiarities and preferences, and some did well with them and others did poorly. In the half century before World War I the various military forces of the different powers made their contributions to the general development of the art of war and preserved their idiosyncrasies.

In the American Civil War the Union developed what would or could be a model for the future. Von Moltke was right in characterizing it as an armed mob, but it was so only during its early stages. In 1861 the Union Army was an organization of recruits learning how to be soldiers and do close-order drill; by 1862 it was a group of soldiers learning how to be an army; by 1863 it was an army with a group of officers learning how to run it and fight with it; and by 1864 it was probably the best army the world had ever seen. It is no historical slight to the Confederacy to say that it, in contrast, started the war with a magnificent conglomerate of individuals, and ended it the same way; it was perhaps the world's greatest "natural" army, but it did not go through the evolution the Union Army did, and since northern industrial society represented the society of the future, it is that evolution with which we are here concerned. While the Confederate Army remained a group of highly skilled individualists, the

Union Army became a machine, a sentient, reasoning machine. Dating such a generalization is hazardous, but one might say that the army reached that stage in 1863, at Chancellorsville and Chickamauga. Ironically, both of those battles were crushing defeats for the Union, and yet D. H. Hill, a Confederate general, later said that the Southern soldier never fought after Chickamauga as he had before it; he still had all the old skill and doggedness, but his *élan vital* was gone. With a deep folk intuition, he knew he had met something beyond his experience and that he was not going to win this war. What he had met was a machine army; it still lacked the directing brain that could handle it — otherwise Chancellorsville and Chickamauga would not have been defeats — but what was significant was that this army could survive these defeats and not panic or be routed beyond recovery. Probably no other army in the world could have done that. The Prussians suffered much less at Gravelotte and St. Privat, and their tactical position was not nearly as serious; yet whole corps collapsed into masses of fugitives, and had the French been led by anyone but Bazaine they would probably have won the war then and there.

It took a little longer to develop the men who could handle this army than to develop the army itself, but, with the advent to high command of the leaders who had matured through the war, the machine gained direction and purpose. Lincoln recognized that, and he never interfered with Grant as he had with McClellan or Pope. The army had found its head at last, and the world's first modern military machine reached full growth.

Of course, once the machine had fulfilled the purpose for which it had created itself, it destroyed itself. With the end of the Civil War the United States disbanded its army, laid aside its military experience, and reverted to its peacetime pursuits. The Americans were so preoccupied by other matters in the latter part of the century that military affairs did not loom large on their horizon, and subsequent military development was left to the Europeans.

On the continent the mantle of Napoleon seemed to have settled firmly on the shoulders of the French army. Even though it had finally been defeated, there was still no doubt that France was the true repository of military glory. The Second Empire in particular was fond of its soldiers, and Napoleon III, in reality the most pacific of men, was forced by the legend of his forebears to play the role of great commander. It was a role for which he proved singularly inept.

In a way it was appropriate that the shade of Napoleon hovered over the encampments of France, for theirs was an army of the past. Their *armée du métier* was a volunteer long-service professional corps. Its officers derived their active experience from Algeria, where they learned their trade in frontier warfare; it made them brave, self-reliant, and somewhat contemptuous of the schoolroom. Most of them came up through the ranks and they were confident that hard fighting and a sort of peasant cunning were what a soldier needed; there was a definite anti-intellectual tendency among these officers. They represented quite the antithesis of what was going on in Prussia.

It is this antithesis that gives the Franco-Prussian War its interest for the military student. Just as in its way the American Civil War was a struggle between the spirits of rampant individualism and voluntary collectivism, the Franco-Prussian War was also a struggle between conflicting ideologies, at least military ones. The French reflected the time-honored concept of the professional long-service army, relatively small but extremely proficient in the details of its trade. The Germans more truly represented the nineteenth century and its burgeoning industrialism; they turned out short-service conscripts like nails or ashtrays, not as good qualitatively as the finely finished French product, but overwhelming in mass.

Were the difference between the two systems only that, it would probably not be worthy of any great note. Unfortunately for France, the difference was more profound. For von Moltke had discovered how to make his large war machine function; the French confined their interest to the platoon tactics of Algeria. Men who wrote books or thought theories were suspect. If one had ambitions, he became a military politician, not a military thinker. There was no French equivalent of the Prussian General Staff, and the fine but truncated French army fought its war without a head. From the opening battles on the frontiers, the French lost the initiative through their own lack of higher direction, and the decay grew progressively worse with successive setbacks, reaching its nadir at Sedan and the disgraceful surrender of Metz.

It was obvious to professional observers that the German army was the wave of the future. The army that paraded triumphantly through the Arc de Triomphe, that loudly proclaimed its new emperor at Versailles, this was the model to be copied. The professionals of course preferred to forget the amateurish struggles of the French to relieve Paris, to raise new armies out of the ground, and to keep the war going. Interest in that would have to wait until later. It was perhaps diverting for German units to watch the remains of France's regular army storm Paris, to put down the Commune and its hungry workers who refused to surrender and wanted to fight to the death for their vision of the *patrie;* it was diverting, but it was of no interest to real soldiers. Not yet, anyway. For a couple of generations it would only be ragged socialists who took their children to see the wall of the *fédérées,* the unofficial shrine in Père-Lachaise cemetery where the last of the Communards were shot down. The idea of people's war did not disturb the thoughts of colonels who were still busy building elaborate fantasies on the continuing value of horse cavalry.

The lessons Europeans drew from the Franco-Prussian War were exactly the ones they wanted to draw: the army of the future would be a mass army, with a cadre of professionals to serve as the hard core, fleshed out by huge reserves when war broke out. Conscription for short service, and a long term in a compulsory reserve would provide the masses. A general staff would function as the brain, the directing intelligence, of this immense machine. France was out; Germany was in. In the 1870s Britain gave up the shako and introduced a variety of the *pickelhaube.* The United States abandoned the French-style kepi of the Civil War, and adopted a spiked helmet for full dress. Military fashion and military theory were both highly imitative.

Now that the Germans had shown the way the rest of the powers made their obeisance to the new system. Even the defeated French adopted the mass conscript–general staff approach, though they continued to prefer to leave their field commanders a great deal of latitude — after all, one of them might turn out to be a Napoleon. The Grand Quartier Général never reached the degree of completeness as a system that the Prussian original did.

The British went through perhaps the most peculiar evolution of all; in many respects it was a consequence of their unique position. With Britain unencumbered by foreign alliances, British soldiers studied European and American wars, and the War Office did its somewhat feeble best to prepare the army for a war fought in the European style. The problem was that the wars Britain had to be prepared to fight were not the wars actually fought, and while staff officers and students pored over the Civil War and the Franco-Prussian War, their own operational experience was far different, acquired in the Sudan or South Africa or on the Indian frontiers. Few officers ever got to command much more than a brigade in the field, and theoretical military development was almost totally divorced from practical development. It was not until after the turn of the century that Britain set up a general staff, and even then the commanders did their best to ignore it. Men like Kitchener, who knew everything about the empire and little wars fought at the end of long lines of communications, regarded a general staff as some sort of foreign affectation, and continued to use their staffs largely as Wellington had used his. The one real contribution of the British Imperial General Staff was its plan to enlarge the army by using the territorial forces, and Kitchener immediately scrapped that on becoming secretary of state for war in 1914. No matter what was said by such writers as Spencer Wilkinson, the "Brain of an Army" had not developed very far in the British Army before World War I.

If the Europeans, in various ways according to their national predilections, were adapting to the new forms necessitated by technological and social change, they also found that their ideas were imitated in the emergent non-European world. Any country with some pretensions to military power had to follow their path. The Turks reformed their army with the aid of German advisors — von Moltke the elder himself had spent some time seconded to the army of the sultan — and their navy with British advisors. Who had the strongest hold became apparent in 1914 when Turkey sided with the Central Powers and set the stage for the Dardanelles campaign.

Probably the most notable of the non-European powers to assimilate the new ideas was Japan, and the military observers in the Russo-Japanese War noted the copying of Prussian organization and tactics. Having decided to go western, the Japanese did so with a vengeance, and their own peculiar brand of intense patriotism coupled with their ability to adopt and adapt foreign forms made a formidable combination, as the Russians were the first, but not the last, to discover.

The lesser powers followed suit, and all over eastern Europe and Latin America the smaller states had their Prussian armies and their British navies; events like the Chilean Civil War in the 1890s often pitted one against the other. By 1914 the pattern was well developed, and soldiers everywhere could predict what the great war — which would never really come, of course — would be like: huge masses of men would be mobilized according to a strictly devised timetable; the operational plans would go into effect; there would be a great clash along the frontiers, in which the fastest mobilizers would win the initiative. The losers would be caught in disarray, would progressively fall apart, and then it would be all over; a triumphal march through Paris, or Belgrade, or Berlin, or wherever, and that was it.

In Russia a retired railroad millionaire became interested in warfare and had another vision. He said that after the initial battles soldiers would go to earth, the spade would become as important as the rifle, men would be unable to carry ground, and the world would fight to a state of exhaustion. All he underestimated was the degree of tenacity mass man would develop, but that minor flaw mattered little because no one listened to him anyway; his name was Ivan Bloch, and what could a Polish-Russian Jew know about soldiering?

So in June Princip shot his archduke and in Austria they decided it was time to finish with Serbian fly bites before they were bitten to death. The powers spent July sending each other nasty telegrams signed "fraternally yours," and in August they all marched off to the great adventure. The chance had finally come to prove how well they knew their business.

Bloch was right, the professionals were wrong. World War I, the Great War, became a vast slaughter of the innocents, in which neither side could or would turn off the tap of blood. War became total war as the emotions and passions of the masses were fully engaged. Artillery and the machine gun proved dominant on the battlefield, and it soon became apparent that the armies had lost their ability to maneuver. After the battle of the Marne and the race to the sea, the possibility of a war of motion was lost in the west, and the armies settled down to monotonous trench warfare, in which the ordinary round of death and dirt was enlivened only by extraordinary periods of more death and dirt. The western front became a great battle of attrition. In the east there was more room to maneuver; there was, in fact, so much of it that neither side was able to force a decision. In France they measured their gains in yards; in Poland in miles; but in neither place could a mortal blow be delivered. There was a surfeit of leadership — for men could be led but hardly driven to the sacrifices they made. Generalship, by contrast, proved patently inadequate. The vast changes in society and technology of the preceding half century were too great to be easily assimilated or mastered, and the commanders of World War I seem to be a group of men struggling to control forces far beyond their power to manage.

The Allies tried various expedients to break the deadlock. They attempted to force the Dardanelles, and failed. They bought Italy, but the Alps were stronger than the Italians. They lopped off pieces of the German empire, but that proved indecisive. They employed a naval blockade, but the Germans proved too resourceful for it to have immediate effect.

The Germans had fewer alternatives available to them. They tried for knockout blows on either front, and could not quite manage them. They tried different levels of submarine warfare, but by waffling probably threw away this one real chance to win the war. Then they too settled down to a stalemate; strategy had become a matter of who could take the more punishment.

It should have been apparent to a rational person that the traditional forms of warfare were ineffective. Weapons of defense had developed to the point that mobility was no longer attainable; contrary to popular opinion it was possible to break the enemy's line; what was impossible was to get through that break with enough force and mobility to exploit it and win a battle — or a war. In this situation there were perhaps three alternatives: they could fight until one side or the other collapsed; they could develop weapons or techniques that would restore mobility to the battlefield; or they could make peace.

The last of these proved impossible. The wartime governments, which, truth to tell, did not do too much very well, did one thing with exceptional success: they aroused and engaged the passions of their people to such an extent that a negotiated peace, or a peace without victory, became inconceivable. When Lord Landsdowne suggested it in the British cabinet in 1916 he was brushed aside; when he tried to suggest it publicly in 1917 the *Times* refused to print his letter;

the *Daily News* finally did so, and the result was that Landsdowne was mobbed by angry Londoners, who considered him a traitor. The mass had adopted William the Silent's alternative to surrender — to die on the last dike. Of course, the more emotions were aroused and the more blood that was spilled, the harder peace became to obtain anyway. You could hardly spend a couple of million men for some fly-dirtied corner of empire, so the war aims had to be raised to the level of abstract generalities — making the world safe for democracy, or things like that. To that extent the world's greatest war, begun for very little, ended being fought for nothing, or at least nothing that could be achieved by military means.

The second alternative was the development of weapons and techniques that would restore mobility, and by that make victory possible. This was of course tried, but its progress was too slow for a generation of men. The landship — carefully disguised with Churchill's camouflage term "tank" — came into service at the Somme in 1916, but did not reach any degree of effectiveness until 1917 at Cambrai. The airplane made similar progress, remarkably rapid in a peacetime context, too slow in war. Superiority oscillated from one side to the other. But by 1918 the Allies were for the first time developing useful mobile weapons, with the tank and with aircraft such as the Sopwith Snipe designed for ground-support operations. Few of the other alternatives proved of much value; poison gas, for example, was almost as deadly to its users as to the enemy.

The Germans were the most successful with new techniques, as opposed to new weapons. They finally broke the impasse of trench warfare early in 1918 by Hutier tactics, using small groups of shock troops to reinforce success rather than to batter ineffectually at enemy strong points. They scored some remarkable tactical success with these in their spring offensives, but they were too little and too late, wasted on points that were strategically useless — a notable failure of their higher generalship — and then swamped by the belated tide of arriving Americans. It was a very near thing. So was their submarine offensive, but that too was contained, this time both by new techniques — the convoy — and new weapons, like the improved mines that allowed the Allies to stretch their confining wall across the entire North Sea from Scotland to Norway.

Given the failure of this development also, the only remaining alternative was to fight until one side or the other collapsed. This was what the combatants did, but even Bloch had underestimated the punishment they would undergo for some shred of victory. The war was estimated to have cost $123 million a day for the first three years, and then $224 million a day for 1918. All the belligerents together mobilized over sixty-five million men, and in killed, died, wounded, prisoners, or missing, had casualties of over thirty-seven million, or 57 percent. Austria led this dismal parade with a casualty rate of 90 percent, but Russia and France were close behind with about 75 percent. The war left behind a continent of old people, young children, and widows. What the prewar socialists called the proud tower of European civilization lay in ruins.

IV

By 1939 certain of the social and technological developments that had been taking place through the 1914–18 war were nearing fruition. Not all of them by any means were positive trends. The irrational had come of age in the arts and to a certain extent in the sciences; psychology was replacing philosophy, will replacing reason. In politics mass man had found his Rousseau-ist Legislator in Hitler, Mussolini, and Stalin. It was significant that Spengler could preach the decline of the West and be hailed as a prophet, albeit of doom. War, depression, and revolution were the orders of the day, and after the agonies of World War I there were alternate cycles of frenetic gaiety and dark hopelessness. Russian leaders proclaimed the imminent demise of the capitalist system and did their best to help it along, in the intervals they could spare from removing each other.

Not that western society appeared to need a great deal of help toward its own destruction. Western Europe and North America, in their own ways, showed signs of having lost their bearings and being deep in what Arnold Toynbee would call a "time of troubles." It is a sad reflection on the period that the only western leader really capable of dominating his time was Adolf Hitler. Any profound look at the social and political scene of the twenties and thirties would tell one there was legitimate cause for alarm.

In the realm of military technology things were being done to restore mobility to warfare, and in effect to make wars winnable again. On land the tank and the airplane would be the keys to the new combination, at sea the submarine and the aircraft carrier. It is important, however, to realize how little these weapons had actually been advanced since 1918. For, in fact, they did not develop nearly as much in the twenty years between wars as they were to do in the six years of World War II. We who are accustomed to think in the developmental pace of the Cold War years should remember that there was far less pressure to move before 1939 than there has been since then.

One result of this slow change was that the new weapons were basically untried, with only a speculative potential and with a still very limited performance, by 1939. The last of the biplane fighters were still in service in Britain, Italy, and Russia in the early years of the war; in the United States Navy the first monoplane was the disastrous Brewster Buffalo. The famous Grumman Wildcat was only the second, and production deliveries of it started after the war in Europe was already a year old. Development of the bomber was almost equally slow; the biplane Hawker Hind was still in service in Britain at the time of the Munich crisis. Looking back now, it is almost impossible to reconcile the brightly painted wood and canvas airplanes with the fear they inspired just before the war, yet they carried the promise of future destruction. Roughly the same may be said of the other new weapons. Compared with their descendants by the end of the war, they were really all in their infancy at the start of it.

There were two notable results of this slowness. One was that the advocates of the new warfare, the Douhets, Severskys, Harrises, Fullers, Guderians, De Gaulles, tended to be prophets not necessarily listened to. They were not exactly without honor, but they were putting forth theories as yet to be conclusively proven; if they themselves were true believers, their hearers often remained unconvinced. The fact that the war would prove them correct could hardly be known in advance. Their brain chldren remained to a large extent embryonic, and it would take both the experience, and the spur, of the war itself to make these weapons effective.

The second result was that, since these weapons were ambiguous and unproven, they could be disregarded by the traditionalists among the military services. It was thus possible for perfectly sane men, among the most knowledgeable and respected in their professions, to downgrade the new weaponry. In both the Royal Navy and the United States Navy the submarine took a back seat between the wars; after all, it had been beaten in the Great War. The French continued to insist that the tank was no more than an infantry support weapon. They had already succeeded in disregarding the existence of the undefended Belgian frontier, and after that it was a small matter to turn the same blind eye to the tank. Having won the last war, they knew all about how the next one would be fought.

In Germany it was different, and perhaps the greatest service the victorious Allies performed for Germany was to force her disarmament; it enabled her to start afresh after the war, and new weapons, new materials, new doctrines, could be considered with a more or less open mind. Not, of course, that it did them that much good in the long run. It is ironic that we tend today to think of the Germans as the epitome of military endeavor in this century, a reputation to which their track record hardly entitles them.

In the early years of World War II, the prophets were proven correct. Those armies that were able to readjust to the new methods and weapons survived; those that did not went under. Sometimes survival depended on time, geography, and just plain luck as much as on anything else.

Poland was the prime example of a country that lacked time, geography, and luck. All the Poles had was courage, and the Great War had already shown that that was neither a rare nor a decisive quality. It would no more stop a machine-gun bullet than a lance would stop a tank. The German blitzkrieg was a new type of war, and Poland became simply its testing ground. Large armored columns, headed by tanks, supported by dive bombers and fighters, followed by motorized infantry, cut huge swaths through the Polish plains, encircling the Polish troops and rounding them up or wiping them out by the thousands. The whole job took only four weeks, and the last of those was needed solely because the Poles persisted in believing two fallacies: that Warsaw could be defended by loudspeakers playing the music of Chopin, and that their allies would live up to their promises and come to the rescue. For a second time Poland disappeared from the maps of modern Europe.

To the outside world the new war machine of Hitler's Germany looked fantastic, unbeatable. There were problems, of course, and the Germans knew that behind those armored spearheads was a chaos of dog-tired troops and scrambled communications. But then, Napoleon had had the same kind of disorder in his rear areas as he marched on Vienna in 1805 and 1809; it did the enemy no good if he was too paralyzed himself to take advantage of it. And anyway, it was the Germans who learned from the mistakes of the campaign; no one else was left around to profit by it.

When their turn came the French went the same way the Poles had. They had hoped to sit behind the Maginot Line and let the Germans batter themselves senseless; all through the thirties they had been unable to resolve the problem of Belgium, and in the end they tried to ignore it. So when the blitzkrieg opened in the west, the Allies fell right into the trap. They rushed forward honorably to defend Belgium and Holland, and were cut off by the German breakthrough in the Ardennes. The Allies never recovered their equilibrium, and the rest of the campaign became a heart-wrenching series of lost opportunities, initiatives taken too little and too late. Mentally, the British and French generals still moved the way their men did, at a foot-soldier's pace; they never caught up. The British ended up penned in against the Channel and being evacuated in one of history's most dramatic mass escapes. "You British always run for the sea," a French general told them — but it was not Britain's fault that France had an outdated military doctrine and technique. In six weeks France paid the price for her pride, her politics, and her complacency.

However, there were things that even the German blitzkrieg could not achieve. Tanks could not cross the Channel, "the greatest anti-tank ditch in the world," as De Gaulle called it. So Great Britain got a second chance. Argument still rages, and no doubt always will, as to whether the Germans could have gotten across. They decided against it. Their first, and perhaps their greatest, mistake of the war — aside from starting it — was to think they could achieve the destruction of Britain by strategic bombing when they did not have a strategic air force. In 1940 they had a first-class tactical air force, but it was not up to a strategic objective; in the Battle of Britain they overreached themselves. Their frustration in the west would be at least partly responsible for their second greatest mistake — attacking Russia. Hitler had the same problem Napoleon had had; he chose the same solution — and he met the same end.

As the British were protected by water, so the Russians were by space. Here too the Germans nearly overwhelmed their opposition, but the Russians survived. In a sense, they got not only a second chance, but a third chance. In 1939 they had a group of senior generals who were most notable for their political reliability and the fact that they had survived the Stalinist purges of the thirties; their military competence was called into severe question not by Germany, but by Finland, who played a very successful David to the Russian Goliath. The opening of the Russo-German phase of the war saw Russia get her second chance to improve her forces, and, of course, she was nearly defeated again; only her vast spaces and the longed-for arrival of winter saved her this time. But she too lived to fight on, and thus the Germans were once more faced with their old military nightmare, the major war on two fronts.

Of all the nations, the Americans were the luckiest. If the Channel was an effective antitank ditch, how much more so was the Atlantic. When one recalls that it was only in 1940 that the United States began military conscription in peacetime, that for the next two years we billed ourselves as the "arsenal of democracy," and then remembers the beating we took in 1942 as a result of what was still a monumental unpreparedness for war, one can see how truly fortunate we were. We benefited not only by distance, but by Europe's experience as well, and some of our best military hardware was the result of specifications based on what the British had learned.

The great crisis came in 1942; by the next year an unstable equilibrium was gained, and by 1944, as American, Russian, and British manufacturing capacity became fully developed, the struggle at last reached a stage of total modern warfare, with whole peoples and their productive capacity dedicated to creating a war machine. The Anglo-American campaigns in France, the Russian in eastern Europe, will probably remain the penultimate examples of war waged by fully industrialized society. By this time, under the stress of total war, twentieth-century man had developed the industrial capacity to put his armies on wheels or wings, to feed, clothe, and sustain them; he could mobilize the entire manhood of a nation for warfare; he had developed mass armies and provided communications systems to run them and generals who could handle them. The nation in arms had become the nation at war, capable of fighting to the death, and suffering or inflicting total destruction. Photographs of Rotterdam, or Cologne, or Stalingrad tell the tale: war as an extension of politics had been carried to its ultimate conclusion. It had become the negation of politics.

At this point, of course, society also reached a plateau of generalship. A quarter century has not been sufficient to settle the dust of partisan argument. Discussion still rages over Eisenhower's versus Montgomery's views of strategy, or Patton's leadership as opposed to Montgomery's. It is safe to say that with the passage of time the great army commanders of World War II will come to form the same sort of constellation in the military galaxy as the marshals of Napoleon.

Having reached this near-perfection of physical destruction, society had only one more path to follow. In 1944 men had achieved a point where by utilizing all the works of man it was possible to destroy all the works of man. By 1945 the first step was taken on the final path, the possibility of destroying man himself. On August 8, 1945, an atomic bomb was dropped on Hiroshima. The nuclear age had begun.

The advent of nuclear power presented men with intriguing possibilities and problems. It changed the framework within which the art of command might be exercised, but neither as drastically nor as unprecedentedly as had at first been anticipated. On the one hand it made it possible to destroy all one's enemies, but on the other it raised the possibility that one might be destroyed in turn. The result was the somewhat overdramatized "balance of terror," which none of the nuclear powers dared upset too obviously.

What really happened was the creation of a duality of force; on one level, the superpowers, locked into an ideological view of cold war, and on another level, a series of small wars that all parties desired to keep localized. The situation was somewhat analogous to that of Britain in the nineteenth century, fighting her frontier wars but still trying to stay prepared for events in Europe if a major war should break out. In other words, it was a return to limited war, in the style of both the eighteenth and nineteenth centuries. And if the application of overwhelming brute force was ruled out — as it was — what was needed was a return to the arts of generalship and leadership, exercised against an ever-shifting background of domestic and international politics and world opinion.

In late 1946 war broke out between the returned French forces in

Indochina and the communist-nationalist forces of Ho Chi Minh and Vo Nguyen Giap. For four years the war went along sporadically, with neither side able to gain much of an advantage. The French failed to assess the true nature of their opposition and fought their war in a fashion that was already outdated, based on European concepts of war that were not really applicable in Southeast Asia. By 1950 the conflict in Indochina had become intensified, with the Vietnamese receiving more overt assistance from the Chinese and the French effort being increasingly supported by the United States.

Seen against the continuing crisis of the Cold War, it was easy to regard events in the Far East as part of the "international Communist conspiracy" that was for Americans the omnipresent devil of the fifties, and the French were happy to accede to this view of things in return for the aid and comfort of the stronger power. French generals toured the United States selling politicians the idea that this was one big fight, and American aid and advisors began flowing to Southeast Asia.

By 1954, however, after a new American administration had temporarily dampened down its Asian difficulties, the pressure was stepped up by the communists in Indochina, and there are French authorities still who tie their defeat at Dien Bien Phu indirectly to the changed United States policies since 1952. Whether that is truth or simply convenience, the Americans became more overtly involved in Indochina during the closing days of the campaign, and the possibility of direct intervention was seriously considered in Washington. It seems ironic today to think that it was turned down because it might eventually involve the commitment of United States military forces to direct action in the area.

Here, in any case, was a major war fought against the backdrop of nuclear power. Neither of the belligerents, of course, had its own nuclear capability, but the ally of one had it and chose not to use it. The lessons to be learned from the Indochina War were therefore time-honored ones; parallels for study would be found not in the writings of the nuclear war theorists. One learned more about how to fight guerrillas from the British operations in South Africa against the Boers than from anything being done contemporaneously with the Indochina War itself. If anything, the war was a lesson that leadership and the arts of generalship were more important than any amount of brute force a state could employ — or could not employ. Nuclear power did not weigh very heavily in a war of small unit actions; the old skills of soldiers and officers mattered more.

In February of 1948 a communist-led revolt began among the Chinese population of Malaya. The British responded to that by the proclamation of a state of emergency and the undertaking of low-level antiguerrilla operations. An unsatisfactory state of equilibrium existed until 1952, when the British troops, about 45,000 strong, began a coordinated operation to put down the rebels. This lasted for five years or so, while the government forces pursued a classical policy of antiguerrilla warfare: harass the enemy, deny him rest and sanctuaries, gradually whittle him down. By 1957 the emergency was all but ended, and it was declared officially over in 1960, twelve years after it had begun. The British task was rendered somewhat easier than it might have been by the fact that Malaya is a peninsula, and by the fact that the movement was not really an indigenous one, being confined largely to the Chinese immigrant population. The communist losses were slightly over 10,000; the British somewhat under 5000. The country had been kept in turmoil for a decade.

Neither of these wars in its earlier stages deflected the newer military thinkers from their preoccupation with nuclear power and the delights of strategic airpower. There were plenty of other crisis areas in the world, and both the Indochinese and Malayan operations were relatively small and distant from the center of things. Then in June of 1950 the North Koreans invaded South Korea.

The South Korean army, which was little more than an internal police force, was quickly ruined. The American advisory troops stationed in Korea were all but overrun, shocked violently out of the lethargy of a nearly peacetime mentality, and suddenly, in this hitherto unimportant corner of the world, the Cold War had become hot. Because of the fortuitous absence of the Russians from the United Nations, the United States was able to have North Korea branded an aggressor and to obtain token support from the other nations of the UN. For the most part, however, the Korean War was fought by the United States and the Koreans themselves.

It was a very curious war; action against the regular armies of North Korea and, later, of China was the nearest thing since World War II to World War II itself. In this sense the war was one soldiers could understand and cope with. Yet in other respects the war was similar to the limited wars of the eighteenth or nineteenth centuries. Senior commanders such as MacArthur, who had spent their entire lifetimes in the era of total war and total victory, found themselves frustrated and eventually infuriated by the necessity of waging a limited war for limited, or even undefined, objectives. For it appeared that the atomic bomb, the ultimate weapon of total war, had neither carried war to that final totality — for no one dared use it — nor prevented war altogether — for man was still man. What it had done was necessitate a return to the warfare of the pre-total-war era. Strategy, tactics, and generalship were just as important as ever — witness the Inchon operation, one of the most brilliant strategic coups in warfare. Leadership was perhaps even more important than it had been before, with the need to turn conscript soldiers into professionals in a war of whose meaning they were either totally uncertain or downright skeptical. The old arts of command had in no way been obviated by the new — unusable — level of weaponry.

Throughout the fifties and early sixties the United States found itself involved in an endless argument about what kind of military forces it needed and where its money should be spent. The air force insisted that the strategic bomber force was the answer to all problems, tending to neglect the political fact that no one dared use it. The navy kept pressing its case for better carriers and better submarines, arguing that its nuclear capability submarines were essentially an invulnerable deterrent and that its carriers and amphibious forces presented the widest spectrum of mobility and crisis capability. Army spokesmen tried to convince the public that their service was as important as it had traditionally been, and pointed to Korea as a lesson of what might happen if the army were reduced to dangerous levels. The problem was that there was not enough money to provide all things for all men, and military leadership went to the public and the politicians to seek popular support for their projects.

The same kind of trial was experienced by other countries. The French had no sooner gotten out of Indochina than they became involved in a war in Algeria. The situation there was so chaotic, with so many sides to it, as to be totally insoluble to the satisfaction of everyone, or even of anyone. For eight years the French army fought another small unit war dedicated to proving the proposition

that Algeria was really a part of France. In the end they finally won
it. By means of cordoning off Algeria from its neighbors, dividing
the country up in a *quadrillage* system, resettling many of the natives,
and harrying the guerrillas unceasingly, the French army succeeded
in doing what it had been unable to do in Indochina. Unfortunately
for the army, and for France, the strain of this victory proved too
great for the fabric of the republic. Just as its army was winning,
the parent state collapsed; the result was Charles de Gaulle and the
gift to the Algerians at the conference table of what they were unable
to win on the battlefield. And the result of that was the revolt and
breaking of the French army. It is perhaps a truism that only to the
peril of both can an army become either divorced from, or stronger
than, the society that creates it.

As Algeria was to France, so very nearly was Vietnam to the
United States. In 1954 when the French evacuated Indochina, the
United States, at that time fully caught up in the Cold War and
thinking in terms of containing communism, became the residual
legatee of the troubles in Southeast Asia. The situation grew into a
major war, which no one could foresee, control, or, it seemed, end.
As the war grew, as the United States bombed North Vietnam and
committed ground troops to the area, the morass became deeper and
deeper. American politicians had in fact asked their military forces
to achieve an end unobtainable by military means: the democratiza-
tion of Southeast Asia. The soldiers responded by saying that this
desired end was always just a little bit further off, and if they could
have a bit more matériel, a few thousand more men, they would
deliver the victory; it is, after all, the task of soldiers to achieve the
aims ordered by their governments. The results of this imbroglio
were a greater and greater degree of frustration, the creation of a
governmental situation with important constitutional implications —
the matter of the very survival of our system of checks and balances
— and a questioning by a large segment of the American population
of the integrity of their government and institutions.

The full import of the Vietnamese War on the United States has
not yet, of course, been measured, and it will probably be years before any profound assessment of its effects can be made. History is
like the trail a man leaves behind him in the snow. Far behind him
it is blown in and almost obscured by the wind; the nearer the man,

the sharper the trail. But then in front of him is only blank whiteness, and the next step has yet to be put down.

Through this long trail of military events run several constants. The student of war must always recognize the various external factors, the effects of geography, climate, weather. Some elements in the military equation change; at different times society has ordered itself in different ways, and the Assyrians, Carolingians, Prussians were the products of different social orders, with differing senses of values and of the aims and ends of their societies, which made them react in different ways to their problems. Technology too has changed, introducing new factors, presenting new opportunities, and new problems, for the exercise of military force.

Yet if there is one thing that the following essays show, one underlying theme to these selections about the great, the near-great, and the all-but-forgotten, it is that the art of command has changed less than one may believe at first glance. The skills of the soldier and the officer, of the newest "military manager" of modern armies, are not startlingly different from those of Sulla, the most ancient in this collection. The soldier's operations, his genius, his mastery of the art of war — if he has it — all the forces that he can command are still at the mercy of all the forces he cannot command. The problems of the military art have changed quantitatively more than they have qualitatively. The question of leadership still has its fascination, and the great masters of the past still speak to the potential masters of the present and future. As Thucydides said many centuries ago, in a remark that sums up both the lessons of the art of command and all our striving:

> By labor to win virtue, that is the lesson which we have learned from our fathers, and which you ought not to unlearn, because you chance to have over them some trifling advantage in wealth and power; for men ought not to lose in the time of their wealth what was gained by them in the time of their want . . .

—James L. Stokesbury

P A R T I

The Young Soldier at Work

GENIUS MAY BE BORN, but generals are made. Only a few individuals are Austrian archdukes or Russian grand dukes at birth and destined at once for high military rank. Most masters of the military art have to start somewhere near the bottom and work their way up. Marlborough was a cadet under Turenne. Napoleon opened his career as a lieutenant of artillery. If George Washington appears to step full-grown into the historical limelight as commander in chief, it is because his long service as a colonial officer in the British wars against the French is usually overlooked.

Some young soldiers move up the ladder quite rapidly because of the exigencies of time and fortune. George B. McClellan enjoyed a meteoric rise in the Civil War, thanks to judicious press agentry, his own genuine talent, and the desperate need of the federal government. But McClellan shot up so quickly that he lost his balance. He traveled around Washington with a large and ostentatious escort guard, affected a pose designed to make him resemble Napoleon, and talked of his willingness "to become a dictator to save the country and then to perish by suicide to preserve her liberties."

Actually a first-rate trainer of troops and an excellent administrator, McClellan was deficient in the principal duty of the soldier — he refused to fight. Although he proved to be a skillful tactician when forced into battle, as, for example, at Malvern Hill, he was unable to bring himself to take the risk of losing the army he had raised. For a while his troops loved him for that, but even they came to prefer victories more, and after Antietam they became disgusted with him and were ready for a change.

Only a genius can leap directly into high command and be successful, for there is much to learn in the military art. It is far better that the solid practitioners come up gradually and absorb the skills required at successive levels. On the other hand, a month of combat teaches more than years of peacetime duty. Admiral Sir Cyprian Bridge at the end of the nineteenth century castigated what he called "the cancer of a long peace," for it fostered faulty methods, pedantic procedures, and the spirit of the parade ground, which are usually the first casualties in wartime. The army of France became far more adept in the decade of revolutionary wars than the army of Prussia in the two generations of peace following Frederick the Great, and a single day of battle at Jena and Auerstadt proved that conclusively.

Although we think of soldiering as a highly specialized and distinct occupation, few professions are actually exposed to as wide a variety of activities as the military. The officer has always to be a leader, but at different levels he is a tactician, a strategist, an administrator, a diplomat, a businessman, an organizer, a manager, sometimes a theoretician, perhaps even a moralist and philosopher. Before World War II, American businessmen were generally contemptuous of officers' skills, but afterward they discovered that employing retired military men as managers and administrators paid off.

A young man contemplating a military career hardly sees himself as a retired general and chairman of the board. He imagines himself, rather, as remaining everlastingly young. By an altogether human inversion, older officers like to regard themselves as young again, too. This may explain in part why platoon leaders write about grand strategy and why generals dwell on the tactics they put to use when they were lieutenants.

Small units exhibit a similarity that transcends time and geography. In the platoon or company that is properly brought up and led, a feeling of mutual confidence pervades, a fellowship, kinship, camaraderie. This sense of trust may sound very vague when talked about and therefore seldom is. Yet the very real feeling of belonging to a group is what keeps veterans' organizations together. It is what makes soldiers say that combat was "pure hell, but I wouldn't have missed it for the world." The unarticulated common bond among men in uniform — not only of shared danger but also of social cohesion — is one of the great attractions of service life, undoubtedly as precious in Roman times as in the twentieth century.

Small unit actions are also very much alike, no matter when they occur. Military artists of the eighteenth century could always envisage the whole of a great battle, and they never bothered to describe the details, the activities of the smaller units and individual troops. For Louis XIV or some other commander, watching from a hill, the battle unfolded in majesty and pomp. How different for the soldier! If he was lucky, he could see the knapsack in front of him, the man on either side, and the regimental colors in the distance. Under fire he did without the colors.

In more modern times the soldier gets even less than that. A closeup view of a bush or the side of a ditch or a fence to be crossed and maybe a furtive glimpse of his fellow squad members here and there; this is what he sees. As Bill Mauldin had Willie say, "After the war I'm gonna be an expert on all types of European soil."

Generals and newspaper correspondents may talk of the big picture, but soldiers in small units rarely, if ever, have any idea of what is going on elsewhere and why. Someone at a higher level may make a mistake or act from false information and may thereby kill young soldiers, but no one down there will know the reason. At the squad, platoon, and company levels, everything appears to take place in a vacuum. Soldiers work in a void. What really matters to them is the mutual dependence among individuals in the same situation. The most striking factor of the small unit action is immediacy.

Junior officers too tend to resemble each other. This may be more true in the modern times of mass production than in earlier periods, when young men could purchase a commission or join the profession of arms in various unstandardized ways. But add or subtract a mustache, change the hair style and the uniform, and the lieutenant of Korea or Vietnam looked much like his counterpart of the Indian-fighting army on the Great Plains. They learned the same things, the most important of all being how to lead men, and they had the same problems. Their outstanding hallmark was their youth, along with the self-confidence, or the appearance of it, that went with youth.

This is quite possibly the most insidious characteristic of war. Despite the horrors, despite the destruction, despite the loss of life, men seem to like, and even to desire, combat. The reason may be more fundamental than the philosophers think: in war everyone is young.

Woodfill

GENERAL PERSHING called him "the outstanding soldier of the AEF."
President Harding and his secretary of war were flattered to be
photographed with him. Congress adjourned in his honor. Members
of the Senate and House gave him a banquet. New York City paraded
for him. The stock exchange, when he came to visit, suspended its
frenzied business activity for all of three minutes, a most unusual
token of admiration. He commanded instant recognition and immediate respect. Wherever he went, crowds cheered.

A common soldier of uncommon valor, he was a boy from the
backwoods, Daniel Boone reincarnated. He fought insurrectionists in
the Philippines, stalked and bagged bears and other big game in
Alaska, developed along the Mexican border the quick reflexes
needed to kill rattlesnakes, and performed an exceptional act of
heroism in France.

With little formal education — he had completed only the fourth
grade — he personified the American virtues of simplicity and
natural wit. When Marshal Foch came to the United States after
World War I and met Samuel Woodfill, he said he was happy to meet
the first soldier of America. Woodfill replied that he was happy to
meet the first soldier of the world. The response was probably apoc-
ryphal, but it was in character. It touched the American people, for
it was fitting that a simple, rustic fellow display thus the modesty and
grace so admired by his countrymen. The real folk heroes, according
to American legend — at least in an earlier generation — are intuitively well mannered. They are usually farm boys, fresh as a hayseed,
who can mingle with the dandies, sophisticates, and city slickers and
invariably outpoint them.

Awarded the Congressional Medal of Honor for exceptional heroism far beyond the call of duty, Woodfill also wore the Purple Heart. The French government, by presidential decree, made him a Chevalier in the Legion of Honor. In the Grand Hotel at Brest a French admiral pinned the Croix de Guerre with palm on his blouse and kissed him on both cheeks. The King and Lord of Montenegro, as he was styled, presented him with the Croix de Danilo. The Italian government gave him the Croce di Guerra. He had earned the Philippine Campaign Medal, the Mexican Border Service Medal, and the World War I Victory Medal with battle clasps for the campaigns of St.-Mihiel, Meuse-Argonne, and the Defensive Sector. He captured the imagination of the public. He was feted, wined, and dined. He had his portrait painted. He had his exploits recorded in the pages of Sunday supplements. And suddenly he passed into obscurity. Like the old soldier in the song from which General Mac-Arthur quoted, he faded away. A splendid soldier and exemplary man whose training, experience, and conduct in life carried him inevitably toward the moment of his supreme act of valor, he is virtually forgotten today.

Born in Bellevue, Indiana, near the Kentucky border in 1883, Samuel Woodfill learned to shoot a rifle when he was so small he had to rest the muzzle of his piece on a fence or stone wall. He tried to enlist when the United States declared war against Spain, but was turned down because he was too young. Several years later, in 1901, when the army called for volunteers to help subdue the Filipino insurrection, he again took the train to Louisville, and this time he joined up.

Woodfill spent three years on Leyte, Samar, and Luzon, qualified as an expert rifleman and sharpshooter, and became acquainted with the virtues and vices of a soldier's life overseas, the deadly monotony interspersed with the sudden thrill of danger. He came to know by observation rather than by personal participation — he was an abstainer and something of a loner — the drinking, gambling, and women that were usually part of soldiering. Woodfill apparently had little to say but was well liked by his comrades. He contracted malaria, dysentery, and the dengue, but lost no days of duty for bad behavior or venereal disease. "Honest and faithful service," his company commander, Captain Robert Alexander, wrote in his official personal file.

Returning home after his tour of duty, Woodfill found Indiana dull. He re-enlisted for Alaska, the newest frontier. During his eight years at Fort Egbert, he strung telegraph and telephone lines in the north country and patrolled immense regions of frozen and largely un-explored land to help maintain law and order among the Indians and prospectors. He developed into a quiet and self-sufficient person. Photographs taken of him at the time give an impression of reserved aloofness and strength. His officers characterized him in their efficiency reports as "excellent, a model soldier." After another short visit home he re-enlisted, and in 1914 his unit was transferred to Laredo, Texas, for service along the border. For three years Woodfill campaigned against Pancho Villa's bandits in the stifling heat of the southwest. Having advanced to the grade of sergeant, he was termed by his commanders a "steady and reliable noncommissioned officer."

It was hardly surprising, therefore, when the United States went to war against Germany in 1917 that Woodfill became an Emergency Officer. As a second lieutenant, he reported to Gettysburg, Penn-sylvania, and was placed in command of a rifle company, Company M, 60th Infantry, being organized as a unit of the 9th Brigade, a component of the 5th Division.

Sam Woodfill married Lorena Blossom Birchfield during his Christ-mas leave, was promoted to first lieutenant after the turn of the year, and took his company to France. In the summer of 1918, together with the rest of the division, he and his men trained for combat. In September they moved into the St.-Mihiel sector. Though they saw no actual front-line duty, they learned to recognize the sounds of warfare, to live in trenches, to take cover in shellholes, and to become acclimated to the constant presence of death.

After American, British, and French troops had reduced and flattened the salients along the line stretching from Switzerland to the English Channel, Marshal Foch, the Supreme Allied Commander, launched the last great offensive of the war. The U.S. First Army attacked in the Argonne Forest, just west of the Meuse River and Canal. The objective was the Sedan-Mézières railroad, fifty-three kilometers away. Several German defensive lines blocked access to the railroad. The first consisted of the trenches along the front. The second was a series of lateral strongpoints. The third was part of the much-vaunted Hindenburg Line which, in the Meuse-Argonne region, passed through the village of Cunel. Against these field fortifications Woodfill would gain his fame.

As Foch's great drive opened on September 26, 1918, the 5th Division, in First Army reserve, was receiving and training newly arrived replacements who, in the words of the division historian, "had never seen a hand grenade, who knew not the 'manual of the gas mask,' who had not learned the endearing qualities of the Springfield [rifle]."

Designated the III Corps reserve, then ordered to relieve the 80th Division on an active front along a narrow sector near the village of Cunel, the 5th Division's 9th Brigade moved up on October 11. The sector, about halfway between Verdun to the south and Sedan to the north, was several miles west of the Meuse. It had been the scene of terrific fighting, and countless shells had churned the open ridges, ravines, and slopes of the Argonne. Woods once dense with tangled underbrush resembled a disaster area struck by a hurricane. Villages were wrecked and ruined. The front reportedly ran along a lateral road connecting the villages of Cunel and Brieulles, four kilometers apart. A kilometer or so ahead of the road, in a small wood known as the Bois de la Pultière, was supposed to be located a line of surveillance, or outpost line.

When officers of the 9th Brigade reconnoitered the ground they were about to take over, they discovered that the actual front line was not along the Cunel-Brieulles road but to the south of the villages. If an outpost line existed, and no one was quite sure it did, it was probably located along the road. The relieving officers nevertheless agreed to transfer the troops. As soon as the departing units had gone, the brigade would drive forward and establish the front line where it was thought to be and where it was expected to be.

The brigade completed the relief during the night of October 11, the units deployed in "the familiar formation, regiments in line" — the 61st Infantry on the right, the 60th on the left — "battalions echeloned in depth." Leading the 60th into the front was the 3d Battalion. The advance element of the battalion, Woodfill's Company M, marched through a dark and eerie landscape of shell-pitted fields and broken woods as German guns threw shells into the area.

On the morning of October 12 the brigade was in place, and soon after daybreak the commander of the 3d Battalion, 60th Infantry, ordered Woodfill to advance, along with the leading company of the 61st Infantry on his right, to positions north of Cunel in the Bois de la Pultière. Woodfill extended his company in a long skirmish line through the woods, the men about fifteen paces apart with rifles at the ready and bayonets fixed. Hidden from the Germans by a low-hanging, early morning mist, the troops moved forward under an occasional hostile shell and burst of machine-gun fire. Woodfill walked up a narrow-gauge railway cut, and as he and his men emerged into a clearing, the fog lifted. German machine guns immediately opened fire. The men of Woodfill's company hugged the ground. Within minutes, artillery rounds joined the machine-gun bullets. Several men were hit.

Here was the vital moment of challenge and decision. To remain in the clearing was to subject his men to injury and death. To go back was to admit failure. To go forward was the only practical solution. But to do so required eradicating several well-camouflaged machine guns in the woods beyond the open ground. Woodfill was the most experienced man in the company and the best shot in the outfit. He signaled his troops to follow him, and plunged ahead, determined to knock out the machine guns and get his men moving forward again.

What happened next is a story shaped and elaborated by many people. The men close to Woodfill saw him take off toward the German machine guns. Presumably some who followed him were close enough to see what took place. Several days later four men, at least two of them virtually illiterate, signed typewritten affidavits stating what Woodfill had done. His battalion commander, deciding that the company commander's achievement merited an award, reported this to his superior at regiment, who passed it on to the appropriate officer at brigade, who in turn informed the proper officer at division headquarters. In the process, the account of Woodfill's heroism was undoubtedly twisted, perhaps deformed, probably inflated. The officer at division headquarters who was charged with writing citations for awards had to know exactly how such papers must be worded to receive the approval of higher headquarters, where they would be carefully reviewed. Following certain standard rules, using well-understood military "canned language," he wrote a short narrative description of Woodfill's exploit. Woodfill himself was undoubtedly interviewed soon after the event. In later years he told and retold what had happened. He wrote it for the War Department at least once. Somewhere along the way, he himself fixed and solidified the main features of the experience. Newspapermen and war correspondents wrote colorful accounts of his action. And that distinguished personality, Lowell Thomas, who wrote Woodfill's biography ten years afterward, presented an exciting and convincing tale.

When Woodfill reached his decision to clean up the machine-gun nests barring his company's advance, he was in a cleared field. To get to the woods concealing the enemy weapons, he would have to cross 150 yards of open ground. First he unhitched his pack and hid it in a nearby bush. Then he jumped to his feet, ran toward a shellhole, and threw himself into it as a hail of bullets thrashed about him. Crouching, he listened to the sound of fire to try to discover where the enemy gunners were located. Bullets seemed to be coming from an abandoned stable to his right front, from a machine gun straight ahead but hidden by shrubbery, and from a church tower in the village of Cunel, two or three hundred yards away to his left front. Woodfill could see no one in the church tower, but he raised his rifle and discharged a clip of ammunition — five rounds — into a small window. The enemy fire ceased. He turned his attention to the stable. Noticing that a board had been removed from the gable end of the structure, he aimed at the hole and let go another clip. The enemy fire stopped.

Now there was the machine gun directly to his front. But it was completely concealed from Woodfill's sight. He dashed for another shellhole ahead and dropped into it under a hail of bullets. When the fire subsided, he crawled out toward the woods. Lying on his stomach, stretched as flat as he could get, his arms extended to pull, his toes digging into the ground to push, he inched forward across the field to the cover of a small knoll. There he rested, listening intensely to locate the German machine gun.

Once sure of its location he crawled around the knoll to a country lane, probably the Cunel-Brieulles road. He slid into the muddy roadside ditch. Crawling through the mire but carefully keeping his rifle dry, he reached a place he estimated was close enough for him to see the enemy machine gun. He took out his automatic pistol and laid it on the lip of the ditch. Then he slid his rifle slowly over the edge, placed the butt against his shoulder, and raised his head gradually. He almost ducked back in astonishment. Thirty feet away was a clump of bushes and sticking out of the shrubbery was the muzzle of a machine gun.

The sight elated him. This was how he had stalked bears in Alaska. But his every shot would have to count. Unless he struck the mark cleanly, he would be obliterated by return fire. He closed his eyes for a moment, then searched out the Germans in the bushes. It was difficult to distinguish the fieldgray German uniforms. By squinting, Woodfill discerned a camouflaged helmet and the outline of a face. It was the gunner, and he was firing short bursts in an almost idle manner.

Woodfill shifted his rifle slightly, aimed, and squeezed off a round. The German helmet and face disappeared. Only then did he notice that the German gunner had been standing in a small entrenchment behind the gun. When he dropped, another man in the trench shoved him aside and took his place. As he reached his hand toward the trigger of the machine gun, Woodfill aimed and fired. The German fell. A third soldier pulled the fallen man away and stepped forward. Woodfill dropped him. When a fourth man did the same, Woodfill eliminated him too. A fifth man in the gun crew tried to escape by crawling away, but Woodfill disposed of him. When a sixth German left the position on a dead run, Woodfill was somewhat surprised. Since he had used up his clip of rifle ammunition, he killed the last enemy soldier with his pistol. Later that morning, members of Woodfill's company found the pile of Germans, the tops of their heads blown off.

Fearful that other Germans had spotted him, Woodfill leaped from the ditch and ran into the woods. He stumbled against, and almost tripped over, a man sprawled on the ground. The man sprang to his feet and grabbed Woodfill's rifle. Woodfill snatched his pistol from his belt and fired. The German dropped. Woodfill then saw that the man was an *Oberleutnant*. He ripped off the shoulder strap and stuffed it into his pocket as a souvenir. Searching the body, he found a Luger and put it in his pocket.

By this time some of his own men were crawling forward cautiously. Woodfill signaled them with a wide sweep of his arm to move more quickly. To provoke them into a more rapid advance, he trotted on through brush and around trees, occasionally dropping to the ground when a shell screamed overhead, sometimes creeping when machine-gun bullets flailed the air near him. Dashing from one point of cover to another, he came upon another machine-gun nest.

As he crouched in a patch of thistle, he saw that a crew of five men occupying a shallow dugout served the gun, their heads and shoulders in plain sight. Woodfill aimed his rifle and nailed them, one after another in quick succession. Before he could reload his rifle, three German boys appeared, bringing ammunition to the machine-gun position. Woodfill raised his empty weapon and the three young soldiers lifted their hands high and shouted, *"Kamerad."* After taking their pieces he sent them to the rear, sure that several men of his company would escort them back to battalion.

Woodfill was now deep in the woods, well on his objective. But he saw no place to stop and establish a defensive line. Continuing his advance, he found a third machine gun, placed on the edge of a trench, with the gunner standing behind the weapon. Woodfill could just see the top of his head. He aimed and fired, and the gunner fell. When another man tried to take his place Woodfill shot him. Three more times he repeated the process.

No sooner had he knocked out the crew than a wave of artillery shells swept through the area. Woodfill ran for the shelter of the trench. He jumped and landed beside two crouching Germans. One leveled a Luger at Woodfill, who had his own pistol in hand and fired first. The German doubled up and fell. The other German was reaching for a rifle leaning against the wall of the trench. Woodfill squeezed the trigger of his pistol a second time. It failed to fire. Throwing it down, he grabbed a heavy pick and brought it down with all his might on the German's head. Noticing that the other soldier had regained his pistol, Woodfill swung the pick and dispatched him in the same manner.

Woodfill's men were coming up, and they entered the trench two and three at a time. In an hour the trench was full of Americans. But the position seemed dangerous to Woodfill. Lacking contact with friendly forces on his flank, he seemed far out in front of the line. Furthermore, German fire was coming in steadily. He sent a runner back to battalion asking for reinforcements. Instead, his commander ordered him to withdraw several hundred yards. Woodfill had cracked the Hindenburg Line, but no one else had been able to do the same.

In the afternoon he led his company out of the Bois de la Pultière and back to the Cunel-Brieulles road. There he established a line of skirmishers. That was his last day of combat. Exhausted and suddenly sick, he turned himself in to the medics. In later years there would be some question whether he was wounded that afternoon. He said — but only long afterward, for he made no claim that was recorded by the medical authorities at the time, though the medics may have been at fault — that he received a small shell fragment in his left leg and furthermore that he was gassed: his eyes, nose, mouth, and throat, he declared, were slightly burned. The medics ordered him evacuated to a base hospital in Bordeaux. When he recovered, the war was over.

The Medal of Honor he won by his gallantry on October 12 was conferred personally by General Pershing. On a Sunday in February 1919, at 3:30 P.M., before a large crowd of high-ranking American, British, Belgian, French, and Italian officers gathered in the quadrangle of the chateau that housed Pershing's General Headquarters at Chaumont Woodfill and sixteen others received the award. The presentation was followed by a buffet supper, where toasts were drunk, jokes were exchanged, and, best of all, in Woodfill's words, chicken was eaten "sans mess kit." Among those present were the well-known Generals Liggett, Bullard, McAndrew, Summerall, and, most gratifying of all, Major General Robert Alexander, the first company commander Woodfill had served under in the Philippines.

Woodfill returned to duty in Luxembourg as a captain in the Army of Occupation, but the excitement was gone. He went back to the States in July, was mustered out, then re-enlisted as a sergeant in order to complete his years of service for retirement.

Two years later, the elaborate preparations for the burial of the Unknown Soldier in Arlington Cemetery in Washington, D.C., brought Woodfill his greatest glory. To select outstanding servicemen to act as pallbearers, the War Department screened 3000 citations for valor and chose 100 names that were shown to General Pershing. He made the final choice of three to represent the army: Sergeant

York, Colonel Whittlesey of the Lost Battalion, and Samuel Woodfill. It was then that he termed Woodfill the outstanding soldier of the AEF. It was then that Woodfill was taken to the White House, banqueted by members of Congress, photographed, cheered, and applauded. When the ceremonies and tributes were over, Woodfill returned to his outfit and served out his enlistment. He retired in 1923 as a master sergeant. He had completed twenty-two and a half years of actual service, of which more than ten and a half years counted double for foreign duty, giving him a total credit of over thirty-two years for his retirement pay. With a monthly pension of $138, he settled down with his wife on a farm in Indiana.

He emerged from obscurity briefly in the early 1920s. A newspaper reporter in Indianapolis discovered that Woodfill was about to lose his farm because he was unable to continue paying his mortgage. A public subscription raised enough money to enable Woodfill to retain his land. Meanwhile Mrs. Woodfill had embarked upon a campaign to increase her husband's retirement pay. She corresponded with congressmen and other influential people. In the late 1930s, she wrote also to Mrs. Franklin D. Roosevelt. She wanted Woodfill to be promoted to his wartime rank of captain and retired at once at that pay rate. The difference was only about eleven dollars per month, but prestige was involved. Yet all the bills — and at least eight were introduced into Congress on Woodfill's behalf — failed, primarily because the army opposed establishing the precedent of setting a monetary value on heroism.

After his retirement Woodfill worked as a night watchman at a steel factory, then took a job with the State of Kentucky to help disabled servicemen compile evidence for collecting compensation. He was again a guard at the steel works when the United States entered World War II. Six months later, in June 1942, someone in the War Department — was he acting on a suggestion made by General Pershing? — decided to recall Sergeants York and Woodfill to active duty. Both men responded, but York failed the physical. Woodfill, five feet ten and one-half inches tall, 168 pounds in weight, with light brown hair and blue eyes, was in good health. He lacked the required number of teeth, but the War Department gave him a waiver. On July 1, 1942, after his wife had died, Sam Woodfill came on active duty as a major.

Assigned as lecturer to the Replacement and School Command of the Army Ground Forces, Major Woodfill toured the country, visiting training centers to talk to recruits. His subject was a recital of the act that had earned him the Medal of Honor to impress on the young soldiers the importance of physical endurance, mental conditioning, thorough knowledge of American weapons, and confidence in those weapons. For a year he traveled extensively, giving an average of two lectures per day. The officers who rated his performance judged him to be "superior" both as lecturer and leader. "Frank, neat, generous, earnest, practical, well-read, and determined to obtain superior results" was the description of him in one appraisal. "Courteous, dignified, helpful, bold, quick-witted, energetic, and reliable," read another.

In August 1943, having reached and passed the statutory retirement age of sixty, Major Woodfill was released from active duty. He returned to Indiana and a small apartment in the town of Vevay. A year later he wrote to The Adjutant General in Washington. In the neat handwriting and somewhat stilted language of those who have learned to write late in life, he inquired, courteously and with dignity, why he had received no retirement pay since the termination of his last tour of active duty. He was sure that the matter was simply an oversight. But he had been living, he informed the War Department, on his personal savings. The stoppage had been a simple administrative error, and the monthly payments, together with a lump sum of accumulated back pay, were mailed to him.

On August 13, 1951, someone found his body in his apartment. An autopsy disclosed that he had died three days earlier of organic heart disease. He died as he had lived — quietly. And quietly he was buried in the family plot in the local cemetery.

Shortly thereafter, a newspaperman in Madison, Indiana, wrote a series of articles about Woodfill and suggested that a monument be erected to his memory. A congressional inquiry attracted the attention of the Pentagon. As a result, the army, on October 17, 1955, re-interred Major Woodfill with full military honors in the Arlington National Cemetery. He lies there today less than thirty yards from the grave of General Pershing. Had he been able to choose, he would have liked that location.

Daubin

A GOOD SOLDIER is supposed to believe that he is part of the best platoon in the best company of the best battalion in the best regiment of the best division in the army.

Second Lieutenant Freeland A. Daubin, Jr., really believed this about the platoon of tankers he commanded in Company A of the 1st Battalion in the 1st Armored Regiment of the 1st Armored Division of the United States Army. To Daubin they were the best — bar none.

He felt lucky to be in the outfit. From the moment he joined, he knew he belonged. He could conceive of no other assignment where he would have felt so much at home. Everything pleased him, the individuals from the division commander on down, the *ésprit* of the team, and especially the light M-3 tanks he worked with — what a really great piece of equipment.

The division trained for more than a year before going to the United Kingdom in the spring of 1942. In the early autumn, the 1st Battalion of the 1st Armored Regiment, along with other units, moved to Scotland. The tankers put in several weeks of hard work to waterproof their vehicles, then went to the Firth of Clyde and boarded stubby, converted oil tankers flying the white ensign of the Royal Navy.

For twenty days, escorted by five armed trawlers, the men cruised the sea toward an unknown destination. They came ashore on November 8 at Oran, Algeria. During their short period of quasi-combat, as Daubin called it, they accomplished their missions with an exceptional verve and efficiency.

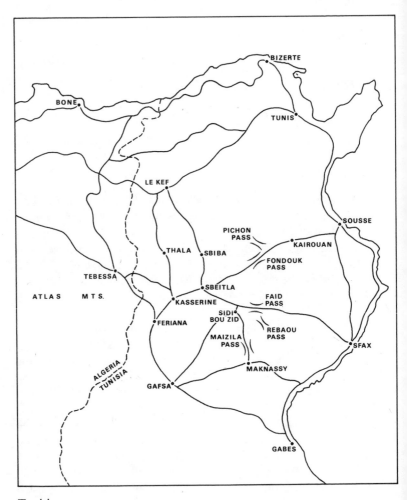

Tunisia

The men had never lacked self-esteem. Now, like any body of troops experiencing a dashing and easy victory, they began to think quite highly of themselves. Self-confidence was desirable and healthy, but self-adoration led to carelessness. Seeing themselves as invincible heroes, they forgot that the French who had opposed them had been understrength, underequipped, and undermotivated. Really, the invasion had been simple, the battles nothing more than skirmishes, and the outcome never in doubt.

To puncture swelled heads, the battalion commander, Lieutenant Colonel John K. Waters, called his men together. "We did very well against the scrub team," he said. "Next week we hit German troops. Do not slack off in anything. When we make a showing against *them,* you may congratulate yourselves." Congratulations, then, the men concluded, were only a week away.

The battalion moved to Tunisia, some men traveling by rail — their tanks and other tracked vehicles tied to flatcars — the others riding in or driving the wheeled vehicles. The trip through that peculiar land fascinated Daubin. French colonial troops who guarded key bridges, tunnels, and mountain passes waved at the Americans who passed. Daubin always waved back.

Joining Anderson's First Army, which was stabbing toward Tunis and Bizerte, Waters' battalion was to work closely with a British lancer regiment equipped with Crusader and Valentine tanks. In contrast with these, the American M-3 looked puny. But that was only the appearance, the men told themselves. The M-3 really packed a wallop. After months of range work, field maneuvers, action at Oran, constant maintenance, and loving care, the men were proud of their light tanks and had affection for them.

Love had not come at first sight. The M-3 was too ungainly, too awkward, to inspire immediate admiration. The tank seemed as tall as it was long, with a chopped-off look that made it appear almost incomplete. The turret where the commander stood was extremely cramped. It could be rotated but only manually. Perched on the forward edge of the flat top deck, it reminded Daubin of a hatbox about to fall from the top shelf of the hall closet. Protruding from the turret was the 37-mm. cannon. Thin and needlelike, it resembled the bill of a woodpecker. But it was supposed to be a pretty good weapon, and the men believed in its prowess.

On hard ground the M-3 handled beautifully. It was agile and fast. Its 250-horsepower continental eight-cylinder radial air-cooled engine gave a high horsepower-weight ratio. Soft ground was something else. The eleven-inch track was too narrow for adequate flotation. Only fourteen tons in weight, the M-3 became hopelessly bellied in places where tanks four times heavier romped through with ease.

When the tank was buttoned up, the driver and bow gunner peered through narrow slits protected by prisms. The tank commander was even worse off — he looked through tiny peepholes in the so-called pistol ports along the sides and rear of the turret, and his forward vision depended on a low-powered telescopic gun sight. It was normal for a tank commander to go into battle with the overhead hatch open, for it was necessary, though risky, to raise his head out of the turret to see what was happening.

Very much aware of the deficiencies of the M-3 in visibility and flotation, the men had a great and abiding faith in the 37-mm. cannon. They were also confident that the 1½-inch armor plating on the front gave adequate protection against small-arms fire and high-explosive shell fragments.

Because of their beliefs and their unbounded enthusiasm, they would have protested the relegation of the light M-3 tanks to secondary and screening missions. They expected and usually received the same combat assignments as the better armed and heavier armored medium tanks. Why not? They were tankers too, descendants of the dashing cavalrymen of derring-do, and they believed passionately in the doctrine of seeking out and destroying enemy armor. They could hardly wait to carry out the deep and furious thrust into the enemy rear and the fight to the finish of tank against tank.

As they looked forward eagerly to meeting the enemy, they heard and passed on some really wild rumors: the invasion had thrown the Germans and Italians into a panic; ten thousand enemy troops were being evacuated every day from Tunis and Bizerte; the only enemy armor in Tunisia consisted of a few obsolete panzers; most of the enemy forces were supply troops, rear-echelon types armed with rifles. What a cinch it would be to knock them off.

When the battalion bivouacked and the officers assembled for orders, a single fear was prevalent — the Germans might escape before the troops could punch their one-way tickets to Valhalla. Waters had a bemused grin. He had received a quaintly phrased mission. His battalion was to establish what the British called a "tank infested area" about one hundred square miles in extent. How to accomplish the infestation? That was left to his imagination.

Operations would go on a shoestring. The battalion had no artillery support — only its own mortar and assault gun platoons. Maintenance would be the responsibility of the troops — no ordnance shops were nearby. Infantrymen were simply not present. Air cover would come from a single understrength squadron of Royal Canadian Air Force planes brought forward hurriedly without ground crews; the pilots themselves would arm and repair their planes, fill by hand the bomb craters in the wheat fields and highways they would use as runways, and fly their ships on whatever fuel they could scrape together.

The center of the assigned infestation area was about thirty miles away, and at first light on the clear, crisp morning of November 25, the vehicles started out, winding over goat tracks and sheep paths, past upland Arab shepherds that made Daubin think of biblical figures.

As the column descended into a valley, the men noticed about two dozen German planes in the distance, several ME-109 fighters covering a group of JU-88 bombers. When two Spitfires appeared and engaged the Germans, the men cheered as a Jerry fighter went down in flame. They became still when they saw a Spitfire trailing smoke, the pilot gliding down to try for a level landing. In silence they watched the Spit disappear behind a hill. They listened. The jarring crash and the explosion left no doubt.

Company A located enemy troops in a farmhouse that was actually a substantial stone and plaster fort built for defense against marauding Arab bandits. Connecting several buildings that formed a rectangle about a large tree-planted courtyard was a thick wall with loopholes for muskets and a fighting parapet. The ground was flat; the only possible places for concealment would be the knee-high vineyards.

A firefight started. Mortars, assault guns, and tanks hammered away at the farm, but the shells only brought down terra-cotta tiles from the stoutly beamed roof.

Daubin's tank was quickly put out of action. Armor-piercing machine-gun bullets damaged his 37-mm. tube. When he examined his machine later, he found many small projectiles embedded in the armor plates, which gave his tank the appearance of a three-day growth of beard.

In the midst of the firefight came sudden shouts — "Here they come. Take cover." A plane popped over a hill and buzzed low over the company. The roar of the plane was followed by a small earthquake and a shower of dirt clods. The JU-88 had laid an egg and was gone. Everyone felt foolish.

The plane had evidently tested the company's air defenses, for soon afterward a swarm of aircraft swooped over the valley.

With a glow of pride, Daubin noted that all the light machine guns designated for antiaircraft defense in his platoon were manned. With a shock of horror, he realized that the antiaircraft weapons were not worth, as he said, a tiddley damn. The gun, in his words, was a misconceived abortion. Mounted on a spring-up cradle bracketed to the backside of the turret, it had metal belt boxes so loose that, despite the cardboard shims, the vibration worked loose every fifth or sixth bullet. The weapon jammed so frequently that it was useless. It could be loaded with a belt from inside the tank immediately before use, but air attacks were over and gone in a twink, too fast for prior loading.

Worst of all, the gunner was as exposed to aircraft as a fireplug to every passing dog. So far as Daubin was concerned, there was only one practical thing to do during an air attack: stand on the back deck of the tank *à la* Humphrey Bogart, raise a clenched fist, and curse the Luftwaffe.

As the aircraft streaked over the valley in a long column, the lead plane peeled off and headed toward the tankers at five hundred feet. Forget the noise of the strafing guns and the screaming brakes, Daubin said. The sight alone of a Stuka diving — the flexed appearance of its dihedral wings, its nonretractable landing gear thrust forward like the talons of a pouncing eagle — is enough to turn sporting blood into plasma.

If the men had had heavy machine guns adequately mounted, they could have talked back. But there was only one such gun in the company — on the command half-track — and its thin chatter hardly interrupted the German monologue.

Nine times the planes came over, fifteen of them, a mixed flock of ME-109s, Stukas, and twin-engined JU-88s. And when they were finally gone, the troopers of Company A picked themselves off the ground and discovered that one man had been killed and a few were slightly wounded. Not a single tank had been put out of commission.

The firefight against the farmhouse continued. But it was no go. Toward the end of the afternoon, Company A withdrew.

Company C, as Daubin learned that evening in the bivouac area, had also had an exciting day. The tankers had blasted several Volkswagens out of the road without even slowing down. They littered a village with the debris of destroyed trucks and motorcycles. They wiped out a guard detachment at a bridge.

Feeling that the Germans were by then alerted to their presence, they took to olive groves for cover and moved cautiously forward. When the olive trees petered out, the lead tank breasted a ridge to see what was ahead.

Down below was an airfield packed with parked planes. Fat geese on a pond.

It was too good to be true. But it was no mirage.

The company commander formed a line of foragers. Over the rise and down on the airfield charged seventeen light tanks, like cavalry troops of old. Enjoying themselves in a wild orgy of destruction, some tankers blasted the planes with high-explosive shells, riddled them with canister, set them afire with tracer bullets, while others physically crushed lined-up ships by running over tail assemblies.

Frenzied pilots trying to get their planes up and away taxied into each other or scudded off across the field with a tank in hot pursuit. Two got away. Eleven were destroyed.

The tankers turned their attention to hangars and shops, destroyed twenty-five more planes, and set gasoline stocks on fire. They lost two men, killed when the planes that had gotten off the ground strafed the field.

That evening the companies of the battalion came together and made camp. The troops looked forward to a Thanksgiving feast of British Compo mutton stew with hardtack biscuits. But first they had to gas up their tanks, replenish their ammunition stocks, check their weapons and engines, camouflage their vehicles, dig foxholes, and put out guards. They were highly conscious of the absence of artillery, infantry, and air support and well aware of how isolated they were from friendly forces.

Then they ate their rations and drank their concentrated British tea. They smoked leaves rolled in toilet paper, swapped their experiences of the day, and griped about how the base troops in Oran and Algiers had the soft life — they were having a meal of turkey, sweet potato, and cranberry sauce, and they were smoking cigarettes made of real tobacco.

The major test that Waters had warned about came several days later. Company A was in bivouac on a hill on one side of a pass, Company B on the other. The tanks were snuggled into the slope of a small ridge that overlooked the main road fifty to one hundred yards away. A mile distant was the walled farm that remained in German hands.

It was a bright, clear morning. The company commander was at the battalion headquarters. Daubin was sitting on the command half-track and chatting with the maintenance officer and the first sergeant, when a lookout yelled, "Movement on the road!"

"Where?" someone shouted.

"Near the fortified farm."

Daubin looked through his GI binoculars and could see little. The sergeant handed over a set of powerful French naval glasses he had picked up in Oran. Through these Daubin made out a column of dust. Raising the clouds of sand and dirt were large vehicles, each mounting a long protrusion that resembled the boom spar of a sailing ship.

He felt the excitement rising within him. What was a German engineer unit of mobile derrick equipment doing on that road? The machines were about to blunder into the company positions. They could be easily ambushed.

Several high-velocity shells came screaming in and dispelled the illusion.

Daubin gulped. Those were not engineer vehicles. They were German tanks, Mark IV Specials. The boom spars were long-barreled 75-mm. rifles. The Germans had apparently picked up movement in the company area and were approaching to make contact.

The men jumped to. Camouflage nets were jerked down, bedding rolls and musette bags tossed out, engines warmed. All extraneous gear — all the stuff that gets collected — was jettisoned. Cranked up and ready to roll, the troops awaited the return of the company commander from battalion headquarters. While waiting, they watched a brilliant attack by the assault gun platoon — three snub-nosed 75-mm. howitzers mounted on half-tracks. Through a thinly planted olive grove, the guns moved in wedge formation across the valley floor to intercept the German tank column. About one thousand yards from the Germans, as they emerged from the olive trees into open ground, they halted. Section leaders quickly set out their aiming stakes by pacing and got their guns parallel; in a few seconds, all had ranged in with the center gun; then all three opened up, each firing ten shells as fast as the gunner could yank the lanyard.

Of the thirty rounds fired, all against the lead tank, many hit the target directly and all were close. Figuring they had disposed of the lead tank, the gunners quickly shifted fires against the second and third tanks in column.

The hail of high-explosive shells stopped the Germans. But after an instant of hesitation, the panzers moved out of the dust and smoke unharmed. Seeing their tormentors, the tankers sent screaming bolts of steel that missed the American guns.

Realizing the futility of further action by the assault guns, Waters called them back. The gunners threw smoke shells at the German column and, while the tankers were temporarily blinded, executed a classic disengagement without the loss of a man or gun. The assault guns had only scratched the paint of the German tanks. But they had given the battalion time to mount an attack.

Waters ordered Company A to close diagonally against the German right flank, while Company B fired on the left flank and rear. The company commander having raced back, Company A boiled down the hill with Daubin's platoon on the right. Normally the company had seventeen tanks, but only twelve were in operating condition that day. Daubin had three instead of four tanks in his platoon. All headed for the column of what turned out to be thirteen Mark IV panzers.

Before emerging from the scattered olive trees that grew on the slope, Daubin spied an Italian light tank crawling along the valley floor several hundred yards off the German flank. He halted to dispatch this enemy. Two armor-piercing shells stopped the Italian cold. One round of explosive set him afire — "brewing," the British called it.

Daubin's crew cheered. "Look at the Ginzo burn!"

Their elation vanished when they noticed several tanks of Company A burning too.

In his state of high excitement, an irrelevant thought crossed Daubin's mind. A burning tank was an impersonal stage prop brought up from the bowels of hell to decorate a battlefield. The sight exerted a morbid fascination over him, and he watched minutely, observing the phenomenon in detail. A tank that is mortally hit belches forth long searing tongues of orange flame from every hatch. As ammunition explodes in the interior, the hull is racked by violent convulsions and sparks erupt from the spout of the turret like the fireballs of a Roman candle. Silver rivulets of molten aluminum pour from the engine like tears, splashing to the ground, where they coagulate into shining reflecting pools. When the inferno subsides, gallons of lubricating oil in the power train and hundreds of pounds of rubber on the tracks and bogy wheels continue to burn, spewing dense clouds of black smoke over the funeral pyre.

Awareness of wicked rifles swinging toward him interrupted the reverie. The German tankers were disregarding Company B, which pecked away at the rear of the column. Instead, they were giving their undivided attention to Company A, which had swiftly executed the flanking maneuver.

Within gun range of the column, Daubin found partial cover in a small wadi, a dry stream bed that extended the protection of its low bank. Singling out one German tank as his own, he banged away, his cannon popping and snapping like a cap pistol.

Jerry seemed annoyed. Questing about, his turret rotating and turning with it the incredibly long and bell-snouted gun, the German soon spotted his heckler. In a leisurely way, he began to close the gap between himself and Daubin's light tank, keeping his thick sloping frontal plates turned squarely to the hail of Daubin's fire.

The crew of the M-3 redoubled its efforts. The loader crammed what suddenly appeared to be incredibly tiny projectiles into the breach, and Daubin, the commander who was also the gunner, squirted them at his foe. Ben Turpin could not have missed at that range. Tracer-tailed armor-piercing bolts streaked out of the muzzle and bounced like mashie shots off the hard plates of the Mark IV. The German tank shed sparks like a power-driven grindstone. Yet he came on, 150 yards away, then one hundred, and seventy-five.

In a frenzy of desperation and fading faith in his highly touted weapon, Daubin pumped more than eighteen rounds at the German tank that continued to rumble toward him. Through the scope sight, Daubin could see the tracers hit, then glance straight up — popcorn balls, he thought, thrown by Little Bo Peep.

Fifty yards away, Jerry paused. Daubin sensed what was coming and he braced himself. The German loosed a round that screamed like an undernourished banshee. Ricocheting off the wadi bank a trifle short, the shell showered sand and gravel into Daubin's open turret hatch.

How had the German gunner missed? Was he addled? Was his gun useless at such short range?

Impassively, the Mark IV continued to advance. Daubin wondered wildly whether the tanker intended to use his gun tube to pry the M-3 out of its cozy terrain wrinkle. Was he planning to knock Daubin into a corner pocket with a three-cushion shot?

Instead, Jerry pulled to the right and mounted a small hummock of ground. This destroyed Daubin's slight advantage of defilade.

Now the German was only thirty yards away. It was time for Daubin to go. Gracefully if possible. But go. Any way. If he could.

Having made an estimate of the situation and held a staff conference with himself, he decided that he was in a predicament known in the trade as "situation doubtful." A rapid retrograde movement to an alternate firing position was in order. Because his driver was half-buried in the brass of expended shells and unable to receive his foot and toe signals, Daubin crouched behind him and yelled into his ear. He wanted the driver to pull back with all possible speed, to zigzag while backing, and to keep the front of the tank facing Jerry.

"Yes, sir," the driver said clearly, without a trace of excitement in his voice.

Are people calm because they fail to understand what is happening, because they lack imagination? The altogether normal, though unexpected, response encouraged him.

As the driver jockeyed his gears, Daubin began to feel that everything was going to be all right. The M-3 lurched backward and across the wadi, then up the bank. A distinct feeling of relief came over

Daubin. He climbed into his turret and straightened up for a quick look out of the open hatch.

At that moment, death, inexplicably deferred, struck. The slug that was doubtlessly aimed at the turret struck the vertical surface of the armored doors and caved in the front of the tank. The driver was instantly killed.

Blown out of the turret by the concussion, Daubin was thrown to the ground. He lay dazed, only vaguely conscious of the fact that he had been wounded. He saw the bow gunner, blind, stunned, and bleeding, crawl out of the tank and collapse. He watched the loader get out, jump to his feet, and run crazily toward cover until the German tank cut him down with machine-gun fire.

Then he became aware of his M-3. Sheathed in flame, the tank was still moving, backing out of the wadi, continuing to retire. He watched it go, backing slowly, until it was out of sight. The panzer had already turned in search of another victim.

When Daubin could move, he pulled himself painfully into a ditch. As he waited for help, two thoughts kept recurring. How long would it be before a German tank swept past and finished him off with a single obliterating blast? And how was the battalion going to stand up to the Germans with only those measly little tanks and guns?

Captain Ben Cohen, the battalion surgeon, and Father Brock, the chaplain, found him. Heedless of the fires that fell about them, they were cruising around the battlefield in the medical half-track, removing men from knocked-out tanks and picking up the wounded. They lifted Daubin into the vehicle and carried him back to the battalion headquarters area.

While he waited for an ambulance to take him to the rear, he learned that the battalion had destroyed nine of the thirteen German tanks, not by setting them afire as the result of penetrating hits but rather by riddling their engine doors and knocking off their tracks — nibbling at them instead of smashing them.

He did not know, nor would anyone realize until a group of high-ranking officers visited the theater on an inspection tour at the end of December, that the troops had not yet received recently developed and highly effective armor-piercing ammunition. They had been using shells meant to be expended in training exercises.

Daubin learned that his company commander had been instantly killed when an enemy shell put a hole through the turret of his tank. His tank sergeant and devoted companion in combat, an Apache Indian, brought the body to the battalion headquarters area. Then, with tears streaking the dust on his dark face, the sergeant hastily replenished his ammunition and returned to the battle without a word.

Daubin would recover from his wounds, return to his outfit, and fight again in North Africa and also in Italy. But he would never forget his hundred-mile ride to a British field hospital in Tunisia.

There were four patients in the ambulance. One was an *Oberleutnant* whose Mark IV had been destroyed. Since he and the British medical orderly could speak French, Daubin had a brief exchange of conversation with the German, who was sure the Americans would lose the war. Daubin asked him why he thought so. Because, the German said confidently, the Americans built poor tanks.

How poor they were would become quite obvious at Kasserine two months later.

Baum

ON A DARK NIGHT about a month before the end of World War II in Europe, 307 American soldiers set out on a strange mission into German-held territory and vanished. For more than a week no one heard from them. Half a dozen then returned. They came back singly, famished and exhausted. They told a tale that was proud, if curious and sometimes disconnected. Not until later, after United States forces advanced into the area and found additional survivors, did most of what had happened become known.

Officially, the story has never been told. Only a few entries remain in the battle records of the units concerned. General Patton mentioned the incident in his memoirs, but only to cite it as one of the few examples where he failed in combat — and this, Patton explained, because he had accepted unsound advice from subordinates.

After the war was over, vague rumors of the mission and much speculation persisted in the European theater. But only a few persons knew what had really happened. No one knows the whole story. Among those who learned generally what had taken place were several combat historians who interviewed a few survivors shortly after the event and who left an incomplete account of the operation. Captain Kenneth A. Koyen put together an excellent story in a history of the 4th Armored Division he wrote shortly after the war. Still later, German military records that had been collected and brought to Washington revealed more.

The affair revolved about a German prisoner-of-war camp at Hammelburg. The principal place of confinement for captured Allied officers, it had in March, according to Allied intelligence estimates, about 4700 inmates, among them some 1500 Americans. From the best evidence available at the time, though no one could be sure, one of these prisoners was Lieutenant Colonel John K. Waters, a battalion commander who had been captured two years earlier in North Africa. Waters was General Patton's son-in-law.

The expectation of Colonel Waters' presence in Hammelburg provided the reason for the controversy that has surrounded the incident. Was Waters incidental to the Hammelburg affair? Or did he, in effect, cause it?

Putting it another way, did the action have a sound military basis? Or was it the result of a personal interest on the part of General Patton?

The incident took place toward the end of March 1945, when Patton's Third Army was through the Siegfried Line and thirty miles beyond the Rhine River. When the 4th Armored Division crossed the Main River and took Aschaffenburg, the stage was set for the Hammelburg adventure.

Deception is a cardinal principle of warfare. Like a good boxer or halfback, a good general knows the value of a well-executed feint. Ordered to turn his army to the north from Aschaffenburg, Patton had a marvelous opportunity to deceive the Germans. A foray to the east would disguise his intention of swinging to the north.

Forty-odd miles east of Aschaffenburg lies Hammelburg. A thrust to Hammelburg would not only throw the enemy off balance but would also liberate the prisoners, rescuing some from starvation and death and bringing medical care to the sick and the wounded. A month earlier, in the Philippines, General MacArthur had gained considerable publicity by taking the prison camps of Santo Tomas and Bilibid in Manila and liberating 5000 prisoners of war and civilian internees. Similar acclaim would certainly greet Patton's exploit at Hammelburg. He would, he said, make MacArthur look like a piker.

The mission was dangerous. To send troops so deep into enemy territory invited disaster. The unit striking to Hammelburg would be highly vulnerable to German counteraction, could be easily surrounded, and might be quickly destroyed. How much to risk on so chancy an operation? The discussion was serious. But what ensued is not clear from the records. Whether Patton or his subordinates favored sending a large force is still being debated by those who were close to the decision.

The point was this: Should a combat command be dispatched?

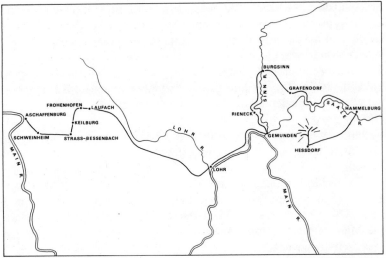

The Route of Task Force Baum

Numbering somewhere between 3500 and 5000 men and about 150 tanks, a combat command was a sizable force that could take care of itself. Or was it foolish to send so large a force? In a hit-and-run affair, would a smaller force have a better chance of success? Fewer vehicles and men would mean quicker movement, a more sudden descent on the objective, a better possibility of escaping detection, greater hope of returning.

The upshot of consideration carried on at various command levels was to settle on the small force. Only 300 men would go — 307, to be exact — and fifty-four vehicles.

The mission was given to the 4th Armored Division, a veteran, hard-hitting unit. The men, many of them from the New York area, had so much self-confidence, such high *ésprit,* that they held Germans in contempt. "They've got us surrounded again, the poor bastards," the soldiers used to say. This was the kind of outfit needed for something like the Hammelburg raid.

Major General William M. Hoge, the division commander, passed the mission to Combat Command B (CCB), headed by Lieutenant Colonel Creighton W. Abrams, one of the great combat leaders of the war. Abrams was a tank officer who, before taking command of CCB, had earned his reputation as commander of the 37th Tank Battalion. He had not forgotten how much another combat soldier had contributed to his success.

In an armored division, operations are frequently carried out by task forces. These are provisional units composed basically of tankers and infantrymen — supported as needed by artillerymen, engineers, medics, and other components — all temporarily joined under a single command to accomplish a particular task. There is nothing standard about a task force. The smaller the job, the smaller the task force, and the contrary.

As commander of many task forces during the campaign, Abrams and his tank battalion had often worked with the 10th Armored Infantry Battalion. The triumphs, then, had to a large extent come as the result of the close work of the tankers of the 37th and the infantrymen of the 10th; on numerous occasions they had proved to be an unbeatable combination. One of the important elements in that partnership was the infantry battalion commander, Lieutenant Colonel Harold Cohen.

There is a marvelous photograph in Koyen's history. It shows Abrams and Cohen standing together, both laughing, beside a tank. They are bareheaded and their hands are clasped about a bottle of wine. Abrams' face is chubby and boyish, Cohen's long and narrow, his steel-rimmed eyeglasses caked with dust. A tall, slim man who managed to be at the same time elegant and tough, Cohen had learned his military trade the hard way. He owned a textile mill in South Carolina, and he might easily have gone into the Quartermaster Corps, there to apply his expertise to army clothing. Instead, he had enlisted in the infantry. After Officers Candidate School, he moved up the commissioned ladder fast. As smart as he was aggressive, he had a knack of looking ahead to contingencies and preparing for them that was invaluable for a commander in combat. For the Hammelburg mission, which would test the ingenuity of the commander and which would require flexibility, instant reaction, and immediate response to a variety of unexpected situations, no one was better qualified to lead than Harold Cohen.

This was Abrams' thought, and he gave Cohen the task. Cohen formed the force for Hammelburg. He assembled a group built around a tank company and an infantry company. The men would ride inside and on the decks of ten medium Sherman tanks and six light tanks, in twenty-seven half-track personnel carriers, seven jeeps, three motorized assault guns, and a cargo carrier called a Weasel. This task force would have punch, speed, and flexibility.

Unfortunately Cohen was unable to lead the force he had created. Bad hemorrhoids aggravated by long jeep rides had acted up all through the campaign, and they were getting worse. Cohen was desperately trying to disregard the pain and discomfort, but on the morning of the day that the Hammelburg mission was to start the medical authorities insisted that he be hospitalized at once. With reluctance, Cohen turned over the job to his operations officer — his S–3 — a captain named Abraham J. Baum.

Like Cohen, Baum was hardly a career soldier. He came from the Bronx in New York City. Before the war he had been in the garment industry; he made ladies' blouses. A brawny type with reddish hair and a pink complexion, Baum looked like a policeman. He was twenty-four years old and anything but subtle. He knew what the war was about, and he was going about winning it in the most direct way he knew. His instincts were right and his training had been thorough. Nine months of combat had hardened him. If he lacked Cohen's finesse, he gave way to no one in the matter of guts.

This was not the only reason why Cohen chose Baum on short notice. Baum knew all about the mission. As Cohen's S–3, he had done the detailed planning for the operation. Though no one asked him — and even if someone had, he probably would have ventured no opinion — he thought the operation somewhat on the foolhardy side. The odds were too great. When he learned that he was to lead the expedition he was flattered. And eager. He liked the direct action of command much better than the paperwork of staff activity.

Baum was given fifteen maps of the Aschaffenburg-Hammelburg area along with his instructions. He was to take his task force by the most direct route, by-passing resistance, to the POW camp, liberate the prisoners, load as many Americans on his vehicles as he could, and return. Other prisoners who were able to walk and willing to try were to set out on foot and get to Aschaffenburg the best way they could.

To give the task force initial impetus, Abrams decided to have CCB take the village of Schweinheim, just east of Aschaffenburg. With the German defense cracked open, Baum would be able to slip through and take off on his long run to the east while the rest of the division, along with the Third Army, turned to the north. Abrams launched his attack on the evening of March 26. It took three hours of fighting for CCB to capture the village and disorganize and disperse, at least temporarily, the Germans defending the area. Around midnight it was time for Baum to take off.

Shortly before Baum's departure, a curious episode took place. One of General Patton's aides turned up. He was Major Alexander C. Stiller. He wanted permission to accompany the expedition. Baum was suspicious. "Why do you want to go?"

"For the thrills and laughs," Stiller said.

Whether this made sense to Baum or whether he thought Stiller was out of his mind is not recorded. But he invited Stiller to ride with him in his command jeep. As Baum explained later, Stiller had no command function and no part in the action except a share of whatever personal hazards were incidental to the mission. Stiller's appearance and his presence with Baum's task force gave weight to the malicious gossip that circulated through the European theater after the war. His excuse for wanting to go along was obviously implausible.

Why, then, was he there? The relationship between general and aide-de-camp being what it is, Stiller realized that the likely presence of Waters at Hammelburg gave Patton a personal interest in the operation quite apart from the military aspect. No one told Stiller to go along with Baum. No one asked him. But Stiller wanted to see whether Waters was at Hammelburg, to help bring him out if he was, or at the least to bring back word of his whereabouts and the state of his health. Yet in a world where emotion and sentiment were rarely displayed, Stiller had to be offhand in his explanation. "For the thrills and laughs" made little sense. What else could he have said without sounding pretentious?

Task Force Baum took off like a shot. Swiftly, the vehicles passed through Schweinheim and out of sight. Now the only news of Baum's progress would come from radio messages, some relayed by a Cub liaison plane flying out to pick up weak transmissions. Brief reports arrived from time to time. On the following morning Baum sent back word to alert the air forces to a target well worth bombing: a troop concentration area. "Tell air," he said, "of enemy marshalling yards at Gemünden." A little after 1000 hours, Baum reported his location near Rieneck. At 1300 he was in Grafendorf. Later in the day came word that he had lost four medium tanks, two officers, some enlisted men.

Then the messages ceased. A final communication came at 0300 on the morning of March 28: "Mission accomplished," Baum reported. After that, silence.

By midnight the men at various command posts in the division area who were listening for some clue to Baum's whereabouts came to a reluctant conclusion. They had to presume that the task force had been destroyed. At that time the division headquarters sent a terse message to its subordinate commands: "No news of Baum."

The tank and infantry battalions that had furnished the men for the task force gave up hard. Not until ten days after the disappearance of Baum and his soldiers, still with no definite word about what had happened, the 37th Tank Battalion finally listed on its morning report seventy-three men and four officers missing in action; the

10th Armored Infantry Battalion morning report showed 209 men and six officers missing in action.

By that time half a dozen men were showing up at scattered places along the front. Coming back into American lines and telling their stories, they confirmed the loss of the task force. One was Technical Sergeant Charles O. Graham who, after the break-up of Baum's command, had wandered through no man's land for more than six days, escaping capture by perseverance and good luck. At last, from a hiding place in a wood, he saw some infantry troops he could not positively identify as Americans. But he was so hungry that he placed his hands behind his head in an attitude of surrender and marched forth to meet them. He found himself quickly surrounded by a small group of suspicious soldiers who held their rifles at the ready.

When he said he was an American they told him not to hand them that crap. He gave his name, showed his dogtags, produced his pay-data card. The men remained hostile. "Probably a German in American uniform," one of them said. "We ought to shoot him on the spot." But Graham finally convinced them who he was. When they asked what army he belonged to, he answered, "The Third." When they wanted to know who the commanding general was, he replied, "Blood-and-Guts Patton. Ever hear of him?"

They turned out to be from the 45th Division, and they took him to the rear. There he had something to eat, his first food in six days: a cup of coffee and a cup of canned pineapple slices. An officer cautioned him to eat slowly. He did, but he still had a bad case of cramps.

Baum himself returned to the 4th Armored Division on April 9, two weeks after he had set out on the Hammelburg mission. Elements of the 14th Armored Division had advanced to Hammelburg in strength on April 6 and liberated the prisoners once more, this time for good.

The interrogation of Baum after his return clarified the action, though some points still remain in doubt. Even the captured German documents that give a picture of the other side of the hill fail to resolve some of the questions. Yet enough is now known to sketch a reasonably accurate account of what happened.

Against very little opposition Baum's column had rushed through five villages in succession: Strass-Bessenbach, Keilberg, Frohenhofen,

Laufach, and Hain. A few German riflemen and *Panzerfaust* (bazooka) gunners in these villages fired at Baum's force, but they were too surprised by the sudden appearance of the American vehicles to do more than shoot in desultory fashion at the rear of the column. Baum's force suffered a few casualties from this fire, but he did not halt. He was not supposed to stop. Nor could he afford to if he was going to get to Hammelburg — and back. If a man was so badly hurt that he was likely to die in a jolting vehicle, he was given first aid and placed beside the road — with a prayer that Germans would find him and give him medical care.

The opening act of the Hammelburg drama gave Baum a pleasant moment of reflection. The speed of his movement was sweeping him past occasional German artillery pieces covering the road before the enemy crews could man their guns.

Beyond Hain — ten miles from Baum's starting point — the road entered a dense wood. In the silence of the forest, the sound of Baum's tank engines and the clank of his tank treads seemed as eerie as the clashing of cymbals by apparitions in a deserted theater. Apparitions or not, what was significant was the absence of Germans. For the first time since he had learned of Hammelburg, Baum began to feel that the operation might almost be practicable. For the first time since he had been given the mission, he began to believe he might really succeed.

Ten miles beyond Hain, on the other side of the forest, just as it was getting light, Baum's task force entered the village of Lohr. The vehicles were barreling along; there was no time for reconnaissance or caution. In the main street of Lohr, a Hansel-and-Gretel village that should have been empty at that hour of the morning, the task force met a German tank unit that was moving slowly in the opposite direction — westward toward the front that Baum had recently left. The advantage was all on the side of the Americans. The Germans had no idea that hostile units might be so close. Before the enemy became aware of the task force, Baum's men opened fire. Without stopping, the task force rolled through the village, blasting the enemy vehicles and destroying twelve. The Germans were able to get off a few rounds, and they disabled one of Baum's tanks.

Continuing, the task force soon came upon a train loaded with antiaircraft multibarreled guns set in concrete. The train was not moving; no one seemed to be around. This was too good a target to ignore. Baum stopped. His men darted from their vehicles and swarmed over the open flatcars, dropping thermite grenades down the barrels of most of the guns and damaging them. A single tank shell put the locomotive out of commission. All this took only a few minutes.

Seven miles beyond Lohr, the task force roared into Gemünden, a fair-sized town. As Baum passed the railway station, he noticed about a dozen trains in the railroad yard, each composed of about twenty passenger cars. The locomotives were panting, steam up, preparing to depart. Neither Baum nor his men knew it, but the trains were to be loaded that morning with a nearby German division, which was to be transported to the front. The targets were tempting, and, as Baum's task force passed, his tankers took pot shots at the locomotives and disabled about half of them.

Daylight had come, and Gemünden was too large a town to slip through. There was an important bridge in the town, but there were enemy soldiers too. Baum lost three tanks to bazooka fire. Rocket fragments wounded him in the hand and knee. He had an uncomfortable sensation that he was about to be trapped.

The bridge in Gemünden was still standing. But German troops were protecting it — too many for Baum's small force to disperse, though his men picked up quite a few prisoners. Baum called for help over his radio. Could CCB get him a few planes to bomb the troops holding the bridge and divert their attention so he could make a dash across the stream? The reply came in the affirmative. But Baum decided he could not wait. He had an infantry platoon dismount and work its way carefully to the bridge. At a signal tanks and men made a run for the structure.

As the lead tank of his column drew near, while two riflemen were already sprinting across, the bridge seemed to leap into the air under the prod of an explosion. When the dust and smoke drifted away, the result was plain to see. The Germans had set off previously prepared demolition charges and destroyed the span. "The Krauts blew the bridge in our faces," Baum later recalled.

This was a serious setback. How to get across the river? Before he could figure that out, he had to get out of Gemünden. A prisoner had given information that a German division being brought to the front had recently arrived in the area. As Baum said later, "Finding the town loaded, I decided it was best to seek another route. We backed out of town and went north." A few P-47s appeared above Gemünden in response to Baum's earlier request, and they bombed and strafed the town, preventing the enemy from pursuing Baum.

From prisoners who were questioned, Baum picked one who seemed to be familiar with the region. After some grilling, the soldier admitted he could get Baum's column across the river at Burgsinn, six miles to the north. Baum took him into his command jeep to make sure there would be no foolishness or trickery. The prisoner knew better than to trifle; the ferocity in Baum's eyes was unmistakable.

On the road to Burgsinn a German staff car suddenly came over a rise and toward the column. Before the enemy inside the car could stop they were not much more than a stone's throw from the muzzle of the gun on Baum's lead tank. Three German soldiers, one of them an officer, piled out of the car and into a pillbox beside the edge of the road. The gunner in the lead tank lazily swished the weapon over, and the menace was enough. The Germans came out of the pillbox holding their hands high in surrender. The officer turned out to be a general. Led to Baum, he began to speak volubly. In German. Baum interrupted. "Who the hell are you?" Another burst of incomprehensible language. But Baum had no time for translation. "Get the son of a bitch up in a half-track," he ordered, "and let's get going."

There was no opposition in Burgsinn. Before Baum's column crossed the river he picked up a civilian to guide him to Grafendorf, seven miles away, halfway between him and Hammelburg. The guide led the task force over a rugged trail that crossed a steep ridge, then descended to another river crossing at Grafendorf.

Had Baum taken the time to interrogate the general he had captured, he might have learned something of the frantic efforts the Germans by then were making to stop his task force. The army commander opposing Patton, General von Obstfelder, was cursing his adversary for having correctly diagnosed a weak spot in the German defenses. Obstfelder's command post near Lohr had almost been overrun by Baum. His units were scattered. He hardly knew where he was going to find any troops to oppose the task force.

Because Obstfelder was unaware of the 4th Armored Division's imminent swing to the north from Aschaffenburg, his greatest worry was that Baum's small task force was the precursor of additional units. He could possibly do something about Baum. But if Baum was spearheading a larger force, Obstfelder had nothing capable of stopping that. Ignorant that his advance was causing consternation as far away as Berlin, Baum swept into Grafendorf shortly before noon. There the task force overran a POW camp and liberated 700 Russians. In a wild frenzy of joy, the Russians immediately raided the town and broke into food dumps and liquor warehouses. The elation was contagious, but Baum had no time to celebrate. To prepare for the last dash to Hammelburg, less than seven miles to the east, he turned over to the Russians 200 German prisoners his men had collected along the way.

Shortly after noon, the armored column approached the town of Hammelburg. Overhead, the men noticed a small German plane. They drove it off with machine-gun fire. The Americans didn't know it, but the damage had been done. The pilot had verified the size and location of Baum's task force. And this information he made available to Obstfelder.

Obstfelder acted, but he would need several hours to erect some sort of barrier against Baum. It was, therefore, "mere coincidence," as the Germans later admitted, that a German assault-gun battalion was entering Hammelburg. Having left the Russian front some time ago, the German battalion was moving westward for service against the Americans. This unit arrived in Hammelburg at the same time as Baum.

The mutual surprise soon vanished, and a firefight began. For more than two hours Germans and Americans exchanged bullets and shells. Though Baum lost three Sherman tanks, five half-tracks, and three jeeps while destroying three German guns and three ammunition carriers, by sheer aggressiveness Baum's force broke through the enemy column and through the town and drove toward the prison camp less than two miles away.

The POW camp was divided into two compounds, one occupied by Americans, the other by Yugoslavs. It was the latter that Baum's force hit first. Because the color of the Yugoslavs' uniforms was similar to that of the Germans', Baum's tankers fired into the camp. Several barracks began to burn. At that point, the presence of Colonel Waters became undeniably clear.

The senior Yugoslav officer asked the German camp commander

to send several Americans out to stop Baum's fire. The German asked the senior American officer, Colonel Paul R. Goode, to carry out the mission. Waters and two others volunteered to accompany Goode.

Together with a German interpreter, the four Americans walked out of the Hammelburg camp by the main gate. With Goode in the lead, Waters and the interpreter following, and the two other officers in the rear carrying a United States flag and a white sheet tied to a pole, the party headed toward the flank of the task force.

As they passed a farmhouse, Waters noticed a soldier. Unable to tell whether the man was American or German, Waters called and attracted his attention. The soldier, who turned out to be German, took one look at the marching men, put his rifle through the barnyard fence, and from a distance of about fifteen yards, without aiming, fired one round. The bullet struck Waters and seriously wounded him. While Waters was being carried to a German hospital in the village, Baum's task force liberated the camp.

With the liberation came the pandemonium of a joyful, almost hysterical, welcome. The freed prisoners climbed aboard Baum's vehicles, pounding their fellow Americans on the back, hugging them, shouting in exuberance. Several hours went by before Baum could restore order.

The Germans in the town of Hammelburg had not been idle. The commander of the gun battalion that Baum had ripped through still had a dozen pieces in working order. Yet he was not quite certain what he ought to do. Should he continue on his way toward the American front as his orders read? Or should he move against Baum?

A German officer who was on leave and spending his vacation in his home town of Hammelburg resolved the uncertainty. He took command of the gun battalion. Believing that Baum would have to return to the American lines and would therefore have to pass again through Hammelburg, this officer set up an ambush.

In the Hammelburg camp, Baum discovered he had liberated close to 5000 Allied prisoners. Of these, about 1500 were indeed American officers. Loading as many Americans as possible on his tanks and personnel carriers, and accompanied by those who could walk and who chose to accompany him, Baum began his return trip to Aschaffenburg. The wild enthusiasm had subsided. All the men were sober and grim, conscious of the dangers that still lay between them and freedom.

The task force did not get far. Scarcely was the column outside the camp when a sharp, flat report sounded. A single shell knocked out the lead tank of Baum's command. The German assault-gun battalion was lying in wait between the camp and the town of Hammelburg.

Hope of taking the prisoners back to American lines disappeared. Without having to be told, most of the men returned silently to camp. For some, confinement had sapped their energies and impaired their health. For most, it was a choice between waiting a few more days for liberation — they knew the war was won — and risking their lives against overwhelming odds without weapons to defend themselves. Sixty-five liberated American officers elected to continue.

To avoid the ambush, Baum turned his task force southwest toward Hessdorf, five miles away. It was late in the evening by then, and Baum's only chance of evading capture by counterforces he was sure were converging on the area was to slip back to the American lines during the night. Close to midnight Baum reached Hessdorf. There he turned north. The tormenting problem of the immediate movement was his need to find bridges or fords over the Main River and its tributaries that lay between him and safety.

Unknown to Baum, Obstfelder had finally gathered together a few units to run down the American raiders. Two miles outside of Hessdorf, Baum's vehicles encountered the first of these forces. A German roadblock consisting of half a dozen antitank guns barred Baum's way. These guns knocked out three tanks and inflicted additional casualties among Baum's men.

Baum pulled back. Discovering a trail leading to the top of a nearby hill, Baum moved to the commanding ground and took stock of his situation. He had slightly more than a hundred men and about sixty liberated officers in condition to fight, three Sherman tanks, six light tanks, and twelve half-tracks. He was dangerously low on gasoline. And he had only a few hours before daylight to make good his escape. If he could get through the German roadblock, he still had about forty miles to go to reach the American lines. But there was no point to sitting on the hill and awaiting destruction or capture. They would try.

Baum issued his orders. The men siphoned gasoline from the halftracks and divided it among the tanks. They then burned the half-tracks. The wounded were placed in a building on the hill, and with brightly colored silk panels used for identifying themselves to Allied pilots the men fashioned a red cross and placed it on the building. Baum sent a radio message stating that his mission was accomplished, and he received acknowledgment of its receipt. Finally, he called his men together and gave them a brief pep talk. With that, he led them down the hill to attempt to break through the roadblock.

No sooner had the men started when they knew it was hopeless. Day was beginning to break and in the dim early morning light they saw the converging columns of enemy forces. Obstfelder had gotten his show on the road.

In addition to the antitank guns blocking the road to the north, self-propelled guns had come up behind the task forces, probably the same ones that had ambushed Baum in Hammelburg, and they were firing. Six large tanks were approaching from the north, while at least a company of infantrymen was moving up from the south. Surrounded, Baum's force was about to be squeezed. In the ensuing firefight, the Germans quickly destroyed the few remaining American vehicles. His tanks gone and the Germans closing in, Baum held a final conference. He told his troops to break into small groups of three or four and try to filter through the Germans to safety. Wishing them luck, he dismissed them.

Only a handful reached the American lines. Baum himself was not so lucky. Accompanied by Stiller and a lieutenant liberated from Hammelburg, he moved off the hill on foot. Bloodhounds bayed in the distance — dogs from the Hammelburg camp that the Germans were bringing up to track down task force survivors. Before Baum reached the bottom of the hill, he and his party were taken prisoner by a patrol. The *coup de grâce* was a bullet fired by a German sergeant, who shot Baum in the thigh, giving him his third wound of the action.

His hand and knee bandaged and his leg bleeding, Baum was not recognized by his captors as the commanding officer. While Stiller was led away by gleeful Germans who believed he had commanded the task force, Baum was herded to a collection point with a large group of former prisoners. They told the guards that Baum too had been an inmate of the camp, and he was evacuated by ambulance to Hammelburg. In the confusion at the camp, he was placed in the ward of the hospital reserved for Serbian prisoners of war, and there a Serbian doctor, assisted by an American medical officer, passed Baum off as a former prisoner. Baum was happy to see thirty-five members of his task force in the same ward and in the same condition.

That evening, just before darkness fell, American pilots saw a convoy of German vehicles approaching Hammelburg. In a field nearby was spread a large white sheet; on it were the letters USPWS — United States prisoners of war. The Hammelburg affair was over.

Having come close to complete success, Baum had accomplished quite a bit. His task force had disrupted the entire Aschaffenburg-Hammelburg area, damaged military trains, destroyed antiaircraft guns, deranged troop schedules, disabled assault-gun units, and provoked general uncertainty and confusion. Who knows what trouble the Germans had with 700 liberated and drunken Russians near Grafendorf?

A relatively small force had achieved this at relatively small cost. According to the final casualty reports, thirty-two men were wounded during the mission, nine were killed. But these do not include the men who refused to report minor wounds. Or the dead and wounded among the Hammelburg prisoners who had opted for freedom. Most of the members of Task Force Baum were eventually accounted for. Some returned after the final liberation of Hammelburg. Some came back after the end of the war. Sixteen are still missing in action.

The roster of Baum's subordinate leaders reads like a typical American roll call. Listen to the names: Lange, Casteel, Moses, Sutton, Hoffner, the infantry officers; Nutto, Wrolson, Keil, Weaver, the tank officers; Sergeant Graham at the head of the assault-gun platoon. And listen to what Baum said: "My enlisted men and officers were tops. There was never an order questioned throughout the whole trip, and not a peep or a squawk out of any of them."

The tribute is well deserved. From a military point of view, the task force compelled the Germans to draw additional troops to the Hammelburg area and thereby helped make Patton's feint successful. The sudden appearance of Americans deep in hostile territory had also weakened further the already deteriorating enemy morale, disclosed to the German high command how woefully inadequate the defenses east of Aschaffenburg were, and underlined the futility of trying to deceive Patton by maintaining a semblance of resistance.

Unwilling to admit that so small a force had brought such consternation, the Germans reported they had destroyed thirteen of fifty American tanks and driven the rest back to the west. A propaganda broadcast boasted of the obliteration of an entire United States armored division near Hammelburg. But German resistance was disintegrating. The Allied armies were driving recklessly forward to overcome and scatter the final opposition. The war would be over in a month.

The end of the war in sight, the Hammelburg mission was virtually forgotten — except for the gossip that persisted in the European theater — the talk that Patton had wanted to liberate Hammelburg in order to rescue his son-in-law. What the gossipers overlooked was the military reason for the action and the solid military accomplishment of the raid. This is what the professional soldiers remember when they talk of Hammelburg.

Kingston

HE LOOKED younger than his twenty-two years. Or perhaps he seemed younger because I expected a man who had a bullet hole in his shirt, a rip in the leg of his pants — torn by a shell fragment — and a bullet crease across the top of his helmet to look tough, hard-bitten, and old. He was boyish. He was too young, I thought, to be the commander I was looking for, too young to have accomplished one of the impressive achievements of the Korean War. How could this lieutenant have commanded captains?

I met him in Korea in the summer of 1951 when I was visiting the 32d Infantry. The regiment had recently come out of the line and was in bivouac for a week or so of rest. I was there for a few days doing some interviewing about an action of interest to my historical section. At the regimental headquarters I came to know pretty well the operations officer, Major Frederick Lash. When I finished my assignment and was ready to go back to Seoul, I went over to the S–3 tent to thank him for his help. That's when I learned about Kingston.

The idea came to Lash as an afterthought. We were shaking hands when he mentioned it. "By the way, Lieutenant," he said, "have you ever heard about Task Force Kingston?"

I never had.

"You might look into it sometime," he suggested. "It's a little on the odd side."

I was curious, but only mildly. Lots of people had good stories. Still, I respected Lash. I had enjoyed his hospitality. And his off-hand, underplayed manner provoked my interest. "What's it about?" I asked. We went over to the mess tent for a cup of coffee, and he told me. He had been the battalion operations officer during the action and had been part of it. The story had its intriguing aspects. It wrote a glowing sentence in the official record of the Korean War. Not many young second lieutenants had that to their credit.

"Where is this guy Kingston?" I asked.

"He's with Company K," Lash said, waving a hand vaguely. "They're bivouacked over the hill there."

I decided I might as well stay another day. "Can I get over there all right?"

"Sure. It's not far."

It wasn't far by an infantryman's reckoning. Lash gave me directions, said he'd put my driver up another night, and telephoned the company I was coming.

My jeep could go only part of the way. Then I climbed a trail up one of those steep Korean hills. If the company hadn't sent a soldier to meet me at the top, I'd have been lost. The soldier guided me down the slope and across a meadow where a baseball game was in progress. We reached a stream, and my guide, being polite, held the swinging footbridge steady as I crossed. On the opposite shore I found myself in a grove of trees, and there Company K had pitched its tents. It was peaceful there that summer morning. Walking through the meadow had been hot, but among the trees it was suddenly cool. The sound of water in the stream didn't hurt the illusion any. Nor did the distant cries of the baseball game.

The first sergeant of the company was sitting outside his tent working bareheaded at a table. He looked young. (I found out later that he was nineteen.) His table was full of mail, and he was printing words and dates across a lot of unopened letters — words like "Deceased," "Missing," "51st Evac. Hosp." I still remember a pile of pink envelopes — I could almost smell the faint perfume. The letters were neatly bound with a piece of string, the top one addressed to a private by his wife who, from the number of letters, had written faithfully every day. Across the face of the envelope the sergeant had printed the word "Deceased" and a date.

The sergeant directed me to the officers' tent. There I found Lieutenant Robert C. Kingston. He was reading a book under a tree, looking for all the world like a kid home from college for summer vacation. He seemed shy when I introduced myself. He wasn't too happy when I asked him to tell me about his task force. But he said he'd try.

We talked most of the day despite some interruptions. It was his twenty-second birthday, and, aside from the other company officers who sat with us from time to time, visitors came strolling in. Even the battalion commander came by to wish him many happy returns. Lash showed up. Everyone had some excuse to explain his being there, such as pretending to be on an inspection trip. It was obvious they had come to pay their respects. The cooks had a cake for him at dinner. After it got dark the company officers had their party for Kingston. They were nice enough to invite me to join them and spend the night. We gathered in the tent where a brand-new bottle of whiskey had been saved for the occasion. Somebody played the accordion — someone had taken the trouble to go all the way to Seoul to borrow it so Kingston could have music on his birthday. It was a pleasant evening.

The sound of voices outside the tent awakened me the next morning. It was quite early, but no one else was in the tent. The officers were outside arguing.

"I'll go," Kingston was saying. "It's my turn to go."

"Why don't you be sensible?" someone asked. "You don't have to go."

"Use your head," someone else said. "You don't have to do everything."

"I'm going," Kingston said.

"What for?" someone shouted. "What the hell are you trying to prove?"

"Shut up," another voice said. "He doesn't have to prove anything. All he's got to do is stay here."

"Listen, Bob," a calm voice said. "It's foolish for you to go out on this patrol. You don't have to. You've only got a few more weeks to stay here. Take it easy. You're practically on your way home."

"I'm going," Kingston said. "Jack is new and he needs the experience. I'm taking him along."

"I'll take Jack," someone said.

"I can go myself," Jack said, "I'm not a baby."

"You're coming with me," Kingston said.

There was sudden silence. Kingston came into the tent. I was up

by then, putting on my boots. He went to his cot and from under-
neath pulled out his helmet, the one with the crease across the top.
He put it on his head, waved at me, and left.

He was gone by the time I got outside. Two of the officers who
had been arguing with him were still there. I asked what was going on.

"The goddam fool," one of them said. "Someone spotted some
Chinks over the ridge, and battalion told us to send a platoon up the
valley to clean them out. Kingston says it's his turn to go. So
he went."

"No one could stop him?" I asked rather uselessly.

They didn't bother to answer.

"Imagine," the other officer said. "Imagine getting it in a rear area
like this."

I was suddenly miserable. I went down to the mess tent and had
some coffee. I had planned to leave right after breakfast, but I
couldn't. All morning long I sat outside the tent brooding. I fussed
with my notes, but all I could think of was how Kingston was pushing
his luck. A hole in his shirt, a shell fragment through his pants, a
crease across his helmet.

The hours dragged interminably. The shade under the trees was
somehow gloomy. No one was playing baseball in the meadow. The
first sergeant was sitting at his table outside his tent, and for some
ungodly reason he was wearing his helmet. He didn't look nineteen
years old anymore.

I finally saw the troops coming down the slope of the hill just
before noon. They straggled across the meadow. They looked tired,
beat. I searched among them for Kingston. I couldn't find his figure.
Or Jack's.

Putting my notes away, I hurried down to the company headquarters. The men came across the swaying bridge and headed for
their tents. A solitary figure walked toward the headquarters to
check in. It was Kingston's platoon sergeant. I was sure the worst
had happened until I noticed the first sergeant — he wasn't wearing
his helmet. Someone was singing in the mess tent. A couple of
soldiers were tossing a baseball back and forth as they headed toward
the meadow. The grapevine had been working. I should have known
everything was all right even before I saw the two men coming down
the hill.

Kingston and Jack were late because they had first reported in at battalion. The platoon had rounded up one Chinese. No one had been hurt. Lunch was a cheerful meal. I departed soon afterward.

I still didn't have the whole story on Task Force Kingston, but after seeing him and the effect he had on the people around him I was determined to get it. It took me several weeks to look into the official records of the campaign and to find the people who could supply a few missing pieces. By then I had a pretty good idea of Task Force Kingston, what it had done, and why it was unique.

The time was late November 1950. The North Korean army had been defeated and its remnants were streaming north in retreat. The United Nations troops were in pursuit, advancing toward the Yalu River, the northern boundary of Korea. General MacArthur, who liked impressive terms, named the movement a "compression envelopment," which didn't really mean anything. The war, then called a police action, seemed about to end. Reaching the Yalu was a formality, like rounding the bases and touching home plate after hitting the ball out of the park. The troops talked of being home by Christmas, or at least in Japan. They didn't know yet about the Chinese communists.

The Buffalo regiment of the 7th Division — the 17th Infantry — was driving north to the Yalu along a main road leading to the village of Hyesanjin, the last community this side of Manchuria. Fifteen miles to the west the 3d Battalion of the 32d Infantry was moving along a parallel road leading to Singalpajin. Once at the Yalu, the 17th was to march west from Hyesanjin to Singalpajin, the battalion of the 32d was to push westward to meet marines coming north from Chosin Reservoir.

This was the plan, but it was never used. Chinese troops were massing, and they were about to disrupt more than these local arrangements. No one knew this, however, when Second Lieutenant Kingston was called to the battalion command post on the evening of November 21, 1950. The place was Wondokchang, thirty-two miles south of the Yalu. From Wondokchang the road runs north for ten miles to Samsu, twelve more to Yongsong-ni, and finally ten more to Singalpajin.

The 3d Battalion, besides being temporarily short one rifle company that was guarding a power plant, was operating all by itself. Forty-four miles north of the regimental headquarters, it was alone in enemy territory and somewhat in a vacuum. No one had much information about friendly neighboring forces. No one knew much about enemy forces that might be nearby. Though beaten, though streaming north to sanctuary in Manchuria, the North Korean troops had a way of turning to fight when cornered. They were still dangerous and, though a major offensive was out of the question, their deadly weapons were ambush, the unexpected trap, the sudden flank attack.

Reluctant to plunge ahead into the unknown, the battalion commander gave Kingston the mission of spearheading the advance. Kingston was to reconnoiter and, if possible, take Samsu. To help Kingston and the thirty-three men in his platoon, the battalion commander gave Kingston seven tracked vehicles (from the 15th Anti-aircraft Artillery Battalion). Kingston's command thereby became a task force. The vehicles were half-tracks. Four of them mounted twin-forties — two rapid-fire 40 mm. guns. Three had quad-fifties — four caliber .50 machine guns tied together. Designed to fire at planes, the guns were nevertheless effective against targets on the ground. They put out a tremendous volume of fire. They were practical also because the men of Kingston's infantry platoon could ride on the carriages that mounted the guns. The vehicles and their crews were commanded by a first lieutenant named Allen. Though Kingston was a second lieutenant and therefore junior to Allen, Kingston commanded the task force. This seemed odd, but the rationale was not: Allen's function was to support Kingston; the guns were in support of the infantry.

Of the three enemies in Korea — the weather, the terrain, and the North Koreans — the weather was probably the worst. If the sun was shining, the temperature in winter might get up to 20 degrees below zero; 30 and 40 below were more normal. The troops wore everything they could manage to get on — woollen long johns, two pairs of socks, cotton pants over woollen trousers, pile jacket over woollen shirt, parka with hood, trigger-finger mittens with woollen insert, scarves around their heads under their helmets to protect their ears. Anyone who was sitting or standing was usually stamping his feet to keep them from getting numb.

The cold affected equipment. Motors had to be started every hour and run at least fifteen minutes. Men had to shoot their weapons periodically to be sure they worked. They had to build fires in empty 55-gallon drums and put them against mortar base plates to keep the metal from crystallizing and snapping. Artillery shells did not always detonate completely when fired.

Living, simply keeping alive in the cold, was enough of a job without having to worry about the terrain and the enemy. Yet these too were dangerous. The ground was covered with snow, a dreary landscape almost bare of growth. Streams were frozen so thick the ice could support tanks. The single road to Samsu was narrow. It wound through mountains, across the face of cliffs, along the edge of a gorge. A skid could mean death.

Across the road the North Koreans had rolled boulders down from the hills. Kingston's vehicles were able to get past four of these rock-slides — by maneuvering around them or pushing the rocks aside. A fifth obstacle near a destroyed bridge caused some trouble. The column had to back up several hundred yards to a place where each vehicle could plunge off the side of the road. Each in turn teetered uncertainly for a second or two before dropping off the embankment and skidding into a frozen field. The column crossed the field, then a frozen creek, and finally found a place where the vehicles could get back on the road. But first some timbers from the bridge had to be used to make a ramp. All this took time. Whenever the vehicles halted, men had to be sent out to the front and flanks as outposts. Kingston's task force spent all day moving the ten miles to Samsu.

Still, no enemy troops had been seen. Not until the task force was within sight of Samsu did the first hostile fire sound that day. Several shots rang out in the town. Kingston immediately halted the vehicles, told the infantrymen to dismount. They waited, listening for more evidence of the enemy's presence. Only silence. So they slipped into town, a village of about fifty houses, bombed-out, burned, bullet-riddled. The place was deserted, without a living thing, not even a dog. The shots? The bodies of four civilians lay in the schoolyard, probably murdered on Kingston's approach.

Waving in the vehicles and setting up an all-round defense of the town, Kingston radioed battalion that he was there. Soon after dark, trucks carrying the rest of Company K and battalion headquarters arrived in Samsu.

That night the operations officer, Captain Lash, called Kingston into the command post. "You'll continue your advance tomorrow," Lash told him.

"How far?"

"All the way."

Kingston's face showed his surprise. "The Yalu?"

Lash nodded. "Think you can make it?"

Kingston grinned. "Are you kidding? Sure I'll make it."

It was no choice assignment, and it wasn't going to be easy. For the next three days Kingston's task force started from Samsu toward Yongsong-ni each morning and had to turn back each afternoon. The reasons were the same: terrain, weather, and North Korean troops. The road was narrow, with a cliff most of the way along the right side, a drop-off to a river on the left, high ground on both sides giving the enemy the opportunity to keep the task force under surveillance and fire. The weather stayed cold, and the men were miserable. Rockslides, defended roadblocks, sudden fusillades of fire obstructed the task force. Snow flurries kept planes from flying in support. Ice on the road kept the vehicles to a crawl. Artillery shells from Samsu seemed to have no effect on the enemy.

Darkness came early on the third day, and the drivers had to use their blackout lights to get back to Samsu. The men were suddenly tired, disgusted with an operation that seemed to be getting nowhere. Kingston found himself swearing under his breath.

He reported in to battalion headquarters, where he saw the battalion commander. "No casualties, but we lost a quad-fifty. It tipped over into a ditch."

"You didn't leave anything in the quad-fifty, did you?"

It was a routine question, but Kingston flared. "What the hell do you think I am?" He recovered at once. "I'm sorry, sir. We stripped it — ammo, spare parts, gas, the works."

There was a silence between them before the colonel spoke. "You all right?"

"Yes, sir." He nodded to add emphasis. "Just mad."

"You want to try it again tomorrow?"

"You bet I do, Colonel."

"You need anything else?"

He had already gotten more troops added to his task force: a jeep mounting a machine gun; a tank belonging to the 7th Reconnaissance Troop; a squad, then a platoon, from the 13th Engineer Combat Battalion under a first lieutenant named Donovan; a forward observer, Lieutenant Trotter, from Battery C, 48th Field Artillery Battalion, whose job it was to direct the fire of howitzers emplaced at Samsu; a tactical air control officer, Captain Jiminez, whose job was to bring in planes to bomb and strafe.

But Kingston asked for and received another tank, more jeep-mounted machine guns, some mortars. This brought his command to more than a hundred men. With this strength he blasted through on the following day to Yongsong-ni, a collection of thirty houses, most of them burned. But it took a firefight, an air strike, and several casualties to get the troops through the town.

Kingston reported his arrival to battalion by radio. "I'm going on," he told Lash.

"Watch your step. We just got some intelligence information; there's about a battalion opposing you."

"You want me to stop?"

"No, but be careful. I've just sent you up some heavy mortars."

"Can you send me more troops?" He meant infantry.

"Not right now. Maybe later."

About a mile beyond Yongsong-ni the road ascends. The incline starts gradually, becomes increasingly steep. It rises finally to a mountain pass, a defile overshadowed by high ground on both sides.

At the bottom of the rise the task force ran into North Korean fire. Rifle and machine-gun bullets swept the road, wounding several men, among them Lieutenant Allen, the antiaircraft officer.

From the ditches where the infantry took cover, from the carriages where the crew members huddled behind their guns, the men of the task force put out a tremendous volume of fire. The tanks blasted the high ground at almost point-blank range. Yet the North Koreans refused to give way. It was difficult to see the enemy troops, the elusive figures behind boulders. Mortar shells began to drop in and around the Americans; some artillery came in. But it was impossible to locate their positions.

"Trotter!" Kingston shouted. "Get some shells up here."

Trotter was already on his radio, calling for artillery support.

"Jiminez!" Kingston roared.

"OK, OK," Jiminez yelled back. "I'm getting the planes now." His radio operator had been wounded, and he had taken over the squawk box.

The arrival of the heavy mortars was heralded by the appearance of Captain Harry Hammer, who commanded a platoon. He had loaded his men and weapons into trucks at Samsu, then drove on ahead in his jeep. At Yongsong-ni, hearing the sound of gunfire, he walked on to find Kingston taking shelter behind one of the twin-forty carriages. Hammer crouched beside him. "I have seventy men and four mortars on the way up," he told Kingston.

"Set them up," Kingston said, "and get some shells up here."

Hammer hurried back to Yongsong-ni to speed the movement.

The mortars didn't help. Neither did an air strike by four Corsairs, which gave such close-in support that one bomb showered dirt over a few of Kingston's men. A small stone cut his lip. Sending Sergeant Wayne O. Wood and a squad of men to outflank enemy positions on high ground turned out to be an impossible maneuver. Enemy machine guns cut them down.

Kingston yelled to his own machine gunners to keep working. He noticed Sergeant Templin firing his jeep machine gun even though he lacked cover, Sergeant Emerick working his 60 mm. mortars from the ditch. Despite the fact that every man in the task force was shooting, the opposition was too strong. "I'm breaking off," he told Lash over the radio. "I'm taking too many casualties." He was bitterly disappointed; he had not fulfilled his promise. But to keep at it didn't make sense at the price he would have to pay. Though it was ticklish work to disengage, Kingston at last moved his men back to Yong-song-ni, where he organized defensive positions.

Not long afterward, more reinforcements arrived. Lash had sent up a rifle company and an artillery battery for attachment to the task force. The rifle company posed a problem. It was Company I, and the commander not only outranked Kingston but was an infantryman too. Though Hammer and Jiminez were also captains, their position under Kingston could be rationalized by the fact that they were in support of Kingston's infantry, but the infantry captain did not exactly fit that category.

"Kingston," the company commander informed him, "I'm taking command of the troops in Yongsong-ni."

This was usual practice.

"OK, Captain," Kingston said. "You're the senior commander in town. You're the commander of Yongsong-ni."

Cold, tired, angry, Kingston was spooning a supper of cold beans out of a can. His cut lip hurt.

"How about the task force?" Kingston asked. "You also in command of Task Force Kingston?"

"I suppose so. You have any objections?"

"What did battalion say?'"

"They said to come up and reinforce you."

An incoming shell crashed into the wall of a building nearby, the sole wall of the building still standing before the shell demolished it.

"Hammer," Kingston shouted, "get your men on that."

A few more rounds came in from a single gun; then the fire ceased. No one was hurt. The only damage was to a tire on a truck, shredded by shell fragments.

Later that evening, as Kingston huddled around a bonfire with several of his men, the rifle company commander came by. "Want to talk to you," he told Kingston.

They walked off a few yards from the men. "Listen," the captain said. "As far as I'm concerned, this is your task force. You have the mission. I'm here to reinforce you, and I'll support you. You need anything, you let me know."

Surprise kept Kingston silent a moment. "You sure you want it that way?"

The captain was sure.

"Thanks," Kingston said. Then his voice became crisp. "I'll tell you what I think we ought to do. Much as I want to get there, I think we ought to rest the men tomorrow. Let them write some letters home, clean their weapons, get some sleep, three hot meals. I'll check it out with battalion. Is that OK with you?"

The captain nodded. "Fine. Go ahead."

Since battalion had no objections, the men got their day of rest. The only activity came from the artillery and the heavy mortars, which put out some harassing fire.

The following morning Kingston gathered his vehicles and his platoon of riflemen together to lead the advance. Company I would follow on foot. Before the column started, two more officers showed up. One was a major from the Buffaloes, the 17th Infantry — no one in the task force ever found out his name; his job was to "coordinate" the contact at Singalpajin. The other was Captain Ed Wild, battery commander of the howitzers supporting Kingston; officially he was there to "coordinate" the forward observers, but really all he wanted to do was spit in the Yalu.

Kingston's impatience to complete his mission and cover the ten miles to the Yalu was obvious. And contagious. It spread to the men of the task force, now numbering around three hundred men, including the anonymous major, three captains, and several first lieutenants.

The day of rest had worked wonders. The men were in high spirits. "Let's go!" Kingston shouted, waving his arm in a wide forward motion and springing aboard a quad-fifty carriage. The vehicles rumbled forward, the crews firing an occasional few rounds to keep their weapons in working order, the infantrymen shooting from time to time to keep their rifles operating. No enemy fire came from the mountain pass. Part way through the defile, two dead North Korean soldiers lay in the road, one on a stretcher. Three engineer soldiers, after checking the bodies to be sure they were not booby-trapped, rolled them out of the way.

At the top of the pass, across eight miles of bleak countryside, lay the Yalu River gorge and the cliffs of Manchuria, clearly visible. Though he still could not see the river itself, Kingston had a feeling of elation.

The task force reached a small destroyed bridge, and the vehicles halted while the engineers set about to repair it. Some men set fire to haystacks in a nearby field to keep warm. At one of the fires a hand grenade fell out of someone's pocket and rolled into the flames. The explosion killed one man, wounded eight. Among those wounded was Trotter, Kingston's forward observer. Captain Wild radioed back to his battery to tell Lieutenant Jim Hughes to get forward as fast as he could.

When the bridge was repaired, the task force continued without incident until the road ended at a gap. The road there was notched into the face of a cliff, and North Koreans had demolished part of the ledge. This was serious, for it meant a long repair job for Donovan and his engineers. The vehicles were immobilized. Impatient to keep going, Kingston consulted with the rifle company commander. No enemy troops were in sight. There was a good chance that the way to the Yalu was open. "I'll take my platoon down the cliff and strike cross-country," he told the captain.

"Fine, I'll come with you."

Along with him came his forward observer, Lieutenant Robert Stein; Hughes, Kingston's forward observer; Wild, the battery commander; and the unknown major. Descending the cliff to a wide plain, they picked up the road again. It was a small force now, for casualties over the past few days had drastically cut the size of Kingston's platoon. He placed seven men under Sergeant Vanretti in the lead to act as point. Then came Kingston and the group of officers. Following were eight men under Sergeant King, a cool, level-headed type.

They walked a few miles toward the cliffs of Manchuria, toward the Yalu gorge and the river they still could not see. Around a curve in the road they came upon the village of Singalpajin. The road ran through a large flat field bounded on three sides by a loop of the Yalu gorge. Along the left side of the road a row of undamaged houses marked the outskirts of town. Vanretti held up his hand to signal halt. He sent four men to the first house to make sure it was empty. Kingston waved King forward and directed his men to the right of the road to cover Vanretti and his group. The first two houses were unoccupied. Everyone was moving forward when a volley of rifle fire suddenly descended on Kingston's group. A bullet wounded Stein in the arm. Stein, Wild, Hughes, and the company commander dived into a drainage ditch alongside the road. Kingston remembered having passed a small culvert; he sprinted back and jumped into it. The major followed.

When the fire subsided, Kingston raised his head from the culvert and yelled to King to deploy off the road into the field on the right. Even as he shouted, the four officers burst from the ditch and sprinted to the first house. Stein was holding his left arm. Bullets kicked up the snow around them, but they made it to the house and disappeared inside. What the hell! Kingston said to himself. Then he figured they needed the shelter to fix Stein's wound. He noticed the major's face. The officer was gritting his teeth in pain.

"What's the matter?" Kingston asked.

"Sprained or broke my ankle."

A soldier from Vanretti's group crawled down the ditch to the culvert to find out what Kingston wanted done. Kingston told him to help the major to the rear. Both men crawled off. Kingston inched forward to get in touch with Vanretti and the point.

He found Vanretti and his five men taking cover in the ditch. King's men meanwhile were coming forward on the other side of the road, moving one at a time in short rushes. The enemy seemed holed up in the fourth house of the town, a building larger than the rest. It was perhaps forty yards away.

"What'll we do?" Vanretti asked.

"I'll get King to cover us," Kingston said. "You take two men and work your way up on the left of the house. The rest of you men cover them from here. When you're in position, Vanretti, I'll run straight at them and try to get their attention. You move in on them. Thirty minutes ought to do it. But be sure to wait for me."

Vanretti nodded. He pointed to two men and started crawling out of the ditch, across the field. The two men followed. Kingston sent a man across the road to tell King what to do, and rifle fire soon started to beat against the house. Kingston crawled down the ditch to get out of the line of fire of his own men.

When thirty minutes had passed, Kingston leaped out of the ditch and started running, heading straight for the house. He had a grenade in his right hand, his rifle in the other. He whooped and yelled as loud as he could. Out of the corner of his eye he could see Vanretti and the two men with him spring to their feet and run toward the house. The crust on the snow was hard. Though it supported Kingston at first, the crust cracked as he picked up speed, then broke. The faster Kingston tried to run the deeper his feet sank through the crust. He felt he was moving at a walk, his feet floundering in the snow. Vanretti too seemed to be walking, painfully slowly. Kingston's breath came in large gasping sobs. His eyes stung from tears brought on by the cold, and he closed them for a few seconds as he ran. He heard the whang of bullets close to him. Having covered half the distance, he felt he could go no further. He was breathing in great aching gasps. With what seemed to him his last ounce of strength, he flung the grenade toward the house. He was watching it arch through the air when something hit him hard on top of the head, spun him around, knocking him down.

When Kingston opened his eyes, Vanretti was bending over him.

"You're all right," Vanretti was saying in a gentle, imploring voice. "You're all right. You're going to be all right. You got to be all right."

He noticed that Venretti was holding a helmet with a bullet crease across the top.

"You're all right, Lieutenant," Vanretti urged. "You're going to be fine."

Kingston sat up, blinking his eyes, still not altogether coordinated.

"We got them," Vanretti said. "That grenade came in perfect."

"Anybody hurt?"

"Not a one; nobody."

"How many were there? In the house."

"Five. We got them. We thought they got you."

A body of troops came walking around the curve in the road. It was Company I, which soon cleared the rest of Singalpajin. Not many North Koreans were there. The bulk of the battalion that had opposed Kingston at the defile had apparently crossed the frozen Yalu into Manchuria.

During the day everyone managed to get to the edge of the gorge to look at the frozen sheet of ice that was the Yalu. Several men, among them Wild, descended to the river bank to spit into the river.

Once the road on the cliff was repaired, the vehicles descended into town. The troops set up camp for the night. Hearing the sound of motor convoys across the river in Manchuria, they discussed the rumor that Chinese troops were entering Korea to oppose the United Nations forces. It was November 28, and they did not know that the Chinese had already intervened in the war. The marines had already been hurt at Chosin Reservoir.

The next morning a radio message from battalion informed the troops at Sangalpajin that plans had been changed. They were not to wait for the Buffaloes. Instead, they were to return to Samsu. A general withdrawal from North Korea was underway.

During the grim days of retreat that followed, the fact that Task Force Kingston had reached the Yalu seemed like an incredible dream of small import. No one congratulated the men or their leader. Yet of all the American units that had tried to get to the Yalu, only two made it — the 17th Infantry and Task Force Kingston. The Buffaloes arrived there first and got the publicity. All Task Force Kingston got was a sentence in the official record. And the satisfaction of having completed the assigned mission. Behind the accomplishment was the personal triumph of a twenty-one-year-old second lieutenant.

I met Fred Lash again several years later, this time in the Pentagon. He was a lieutenant colonel. After making known our mutual pleasure at the encounter, we retired to a coffee bar for a few minutes. The talk turned to Kingston.

"Did he make it home OK?" I asked.

Lash assured me that Bob Kingston had gotten home to Brookline, Massachusetts, all right.

The mention of a particular place startled me. For the first time I realized that aside from what Kingston had done in Korea, I didn't know much, if anything, about him. "It never occurred to me," I told the colonel, "to ask him where he was from. Or anything about himself."

He shrugged. "Why should you? I don't know much about him myself."

"Tell me something," I said. "Maybe you can clear up something that has always bothered me."

The colonel waited.

"Tell me about the command setup on Kingston," I said. "Part of it never quite made sense."

He smiled. "It *was* odd. It was a peculiar command setup."

"Hammer told me no one ever questioned the fact that Kingston was the boss. But really, when you sent Company I up to Yongsong-ni, didn't you mean for the company commander to take over?"

Lash laughed. "That's a low blow. Officially, according to the records, we put the company commander in command of the task force. But since the task force had already been in existence about a week and was being mentioned in the situation reports, the periodic reports, and the journals, we didn't change the name of it."

"Well, who was in command the last day when the troops reached the Yalu?"

"Officially? Or actually?"

"I guess you've answered it. All right, tell me why you sent Company I up to Kingston? Why not Company K? K was available, wasn't it?"

Lash laughed again. "You've hit one of my darkest secrets. But

I'll tell you. I figured that if Kingston's company came up to reinforce him, he would revert to being simply a platoon leader in that
company. But since Kingston's platoon was not an organic part
of Company I, Kingston had a good chance to remain in control."

"You figured it would work like that?"

Lash was modest too. "Well, maybe not so clearly as that."

"But it worked."

"Yes, it worked out fine. Any command situation works out fine
when you have good men."

"You don't mean just Kingston."

"I mean the commander of Company I too. He was a good officer,
and he deserves a lot of credit."

"Hammer, Allen, Donovan, and the rest of them also, I suppose."

"Right," Lash said. He paused for a moment before adding
thoughtfully, "But mostly Kingston. The others crystallized around
him."

I didn't know whether "crystallized" was exactly the right word,
but I certainly understood what he meant.

Anderson

AN UNEASINESS floated in with the fog. On the high sandbar — an island in the river bend where the tents of the corps headquarters stood in neat rows — everyone was irritable. The Korean hills that loomed over and pressed against the command post had never looked more ominous.

It was early April in the first year of the Korean War and spring had yet to come in 1951. Winter winds still whipped downriver near Hongchon, tugging at tent ropes, but failing to dispel the mist or the edginess. When a sudden hint of warm weather melted some of the snow and sent water down the mountains, the current picked up speed around the sandbar, the channels on both sides deepened, and the fords became dangerous. It was then that the anxiety took on a name: Hwachon Dam.

The dam was in a mountainous region of steep-sided and trackless peaks, an area so rugged that the contour lines on the maps resembled thumb prints. Among the hills an elongated spot of blue marked the existence of a large inland lake, a reservoir nestled gracefully among the partially wooded slopes rising abruptly from the water. The natural curves of the shoreline contrasted sharply with the short, straight lip of the dam. Air photos taken on the infrequent days of clear weather were like picture postcards. The majestic and serene heights, the still mirror of the water, and the white spume splashing over the dam's concrete spillway could have been, say, a scene in the Rocky Mountains. One of the largest dams in Korea, it holds back the Pukhan River and creates a lake thirteen miles long and a mile or so wide. The trouble, back in April 1951, was that the dam and the reservoir lay in enemy territory and the river flowed down the middle of what was then the IX Corps area.

All across the Korean peninsula the Eighth Army was grinding forward slowly. In the central part, the IX Corps had fought north to Hongchon, then another twenty miles to Chunchon. Now, along a single avenue, the only road of consequence, the troops were going still another twenty miles, across the 38th parallel into North Korea. Ten miles above the parallel, at the shore of the reservoir, they would be at Phase Line Kansas, a place marked by a slash of grease pencil across the map. There they would pause. Some units that needed rest would be replaced, roads would be improved, ammunition and other supplies would be accumulated, and preparations made for another push.

Stopping temporarily at Kansas would leave Hwachon Dam, as well as the reservoir, in the hands of the Chinese communists. If the enemy released the water held by the dam, they could send a flood roaring down the Pukhan River, gouge a channel down the middle of the corps, wash away bridges, command posts, supply dumps, and other installations, break the corps in two, and separate and in some places isolate the troops in each portion.

The dam is a straight-line, overflow type, 275 feet high, with a spillway 826 feet long. Eighteen gates at the top control the water level in the reservoir, and the same number of penstocks at the bottom run dynamos for electric power in peacetime. When gates and penstocks are in the closed position, they restrain a top depth of thirty-two feet of water.

My first reaction was an alarming thought: opening the gates, it seemed to me, would send a wall of water rushing down the center of the corps like a tidal wave. Not quite. The gates are massive doors, six by ten yards, each weighing several tons. Even if the central power system is working, which it was not in 1951, it takes almost an hour to lift a gate all the way. By hand, it requires about ten hours. Thus, water released would flow out gradually. Once out, it would spread across low areas. The depth of a flood would vary according to the width of the river channel at any particular point. The worst that might happen was a rise of ten to twelve feet, which was bad enough. It would rip out bridges, cover the Chunchon plain with at least a foot of water, back up and swell the tributary streams, and hamper — perhaps halt — the operations of the corps.

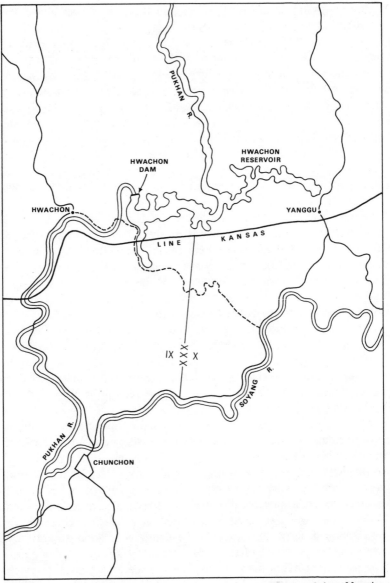

Hwachon Dam

Civilians said that the level of the Pukhan River was well below normal for that time of the year. The reason: only a trickle of water was escaping from the reservoir. Pilots who flew over the dam reported the spillway gates closed. Were the Chinese then planning to use the water in the reservoir as a weapon? Were they raising the water level in order to inundate the corps by opening the penstocks and gates?

Lieutenant General Matthew B. Ridgway, who then commanded the Eighth Army, was aware of the dams in Korea. A month or two earlier, he had asked particularly about Hwachon Dam. What would happen if he had it destroyed by air bombardment? The answer persuaded him to leave the structure intact. The reservoir and dam gave water and electric power to the capital city of Seoul. There was no point in ruining the mechanism that would fall into the hands of the United Nations forces after the troops moved beyond Kansas.

More immediately alive to the danger of Hwachon Dam was the IX Corps commander, then Major General William M. Hoge. He had a suggestion. If the Chinese released the water in the reservoir, he could send a small group to the dam to close the gates, then blast shut the machinery — the mechanical hoists that raised and lowered the heavy doors. With the gates thus fixed in the closed position, any surplus water would flow over the dam, and there would be no possibility of artificial flooding. Once the army advanced past Kansas and took permanent possession of the dam, it would be easy enough to repair the damage.

Ridgway liked the idea. He told Hoge to go ahead, but cautioned him to keep casualties to the fewest. Hoge was sure he could do the job with few losses. His combat command of the 9th Armored Division had captured the Remagen bridge during World War II, and he knew how to make a lightning thrust. There was no reason why Hwachon Dam should be tough. Especially since one of the U.S. Army's great combat outfits had reached Phase Line Kansas just below the structure: the 1st Cavalry Division. Cavalry solely in name, for its horses were long gone and the division was composed of infantrymen. A decade and a half later in Vietnam, with helicopters and other new equipment, these soldiers would be known as cavalry of the sky.

Telling the division commander to be ready to immobilize — his word — the dam, but only if the Chinese threatened to release the water in the reservoir, Hoge gave him a company of Rangers. One hundred skilled soldiers trained for rapid and hard-hitting movement, the Rangers would be perfect for a raid to knock out the machinery. By joining these elite troops to the first-rate division, Hoge formed a team that was bound to succeed.

While the Rangers were moving by truck to Kansas, their commander drove to division headquarters. He had studied the map, and he had a notion of how best to carry out the task. A quick hit-and-run affair was just the sort of thing his men were good at. They were saved for special assignments, and Captain Dorsey B. Anderson was confident they could do this one too. He went to see the division G–3, a young lieutenant colonel named John Carlson, who planned the combat operations. If it became necessary to get up to the dam, Anderson suggested, his Rangers could cross the reservoir in boats during the night. They could slip to the dam under cover of darkness and knock out the mechanical hoists before the Chinese knew they were there.

"Where are we going to get the boats?" Carlson asked. It was a rhetorical question. Getting the boats was none of Anderson's concern. "That's an awful lot of water to cross. If you blast the dam during the night, you'll have to come back during the day. You'd be sitting in the middle of the lake in full view of the Chinese."

Anderson agreed. But he still thought that crossing the water was the best way to get to the dam.

"No," Carlson said. "We have to figure out something easier."

While he searched for a solution to the problem, Anderson visited a nearby dam. No one knew for sure, but the experts believed it was similar to Hwachon. In case Anderson had to destroy the machinery, he wanted to know in detail how to do it. Looking over the concrete structure, he became familiar with the mechanism and saw how to blow the cogs on the power wheels that controlled the floodgates. At Hwachon Dam, in each of the eighteen winch hoists where exposed gears meshed, his men would have to apply thermite grenades directly to the teeth, then tamp them properly to insure a good burning effect. The Rangers, therefore, would have to hold the dam several hours in order to close the gates and make sure the demolition charges did the job.

As the Rangers took a brief refresher course in the use of explosives, Anderson flew over Hwachon Dam in a light plane. The ground, he told me later, appeared even more rugged than he had anticipated. But he had one consolation: he could discern no enemy positions around the structure. Even without Chinese opposition, the Rangers would find it difficult enough to get over the terrain. The hills that seemed clothed in grandeur when viewed from the air would cause only anguish to men walking across the dizzy slopes and around the jagged, contoured heights. If his men had to cross the reservoir in boats, they would have to traverse about a mile of ground between their landing site and the dam.

But perhaps a reservoir crossing would be unnecessary, for Carlson had decided that it would be too dangerous. He favored an overland attack — without frills, nothing fancy. In getting to Kansas, the division had had no easy time, but the Chinese, when attacked aggressively, had pulled back even from well-organized defenses. Why should an advance beyond Kansas be different? The dam was probably lightly held, and it could be easily overrun and its sluice gate mechanisms quickly destroyed. One of the division's three regiments, the 7th Cavalry, was directly below the dam, and if General Hoge gave the green light, it could go around the edge of the reservoir, grab the dam, and let the Rangers walk in and blow the power wheels.

A minor problem intruded: the division was about to turn over its part of the front to a relieving marine division. Once the transfer was completed, the troops would leave Kansas and travel far to the rear for a well-earned rest. Getting a break from combat for a week or two, they would go through the semblance of a training program, but mostly they would sleep, loaf around, have hot meals, see some movies, and a few would manage a pass to Seoul. The relief would take place on two successive nights, starting on the evening of April 9. Just in case Hoge ordered the raid to Hwachon Dam, Carlson scheduled the division's departure so that the 7th Cavalry would be the last to leave Line Kansas.

Since a rise in the Pukhan River would trigger Hoge's decision to go to the dam, close watch over the water level was kept at three measuring stations.

In the dark and early morning hours of April 9, as interrogations of prisoners of war would later reveal, about twenty Chinese soldiers and five Korean civilian employees of the power plant began to open the gates of Hwachon Dam. Using auxiliary engines to lift some, they opened others manually. By daylight they had raised two gates completely open, lifted two of them three-quarters of the way, and opened six slightly. Had they been able to raise additional gates, they probably would have done so.

Before American pilots — who made daily inspections when weather permitted — could fly over the dam and discover the open gates, a surge of water struck the first measuring point along the Pukhan. At 0700 the river began to rise, and the level rose by four feet in fifteen minutes. Downstream at the second station, the river began to rise an hour later, and by 1000 the stream was eighty-six inches — more than seven feet — above normal. Farther downstream, at the third station, the Pukhan jumped seventeen inches in the ten minutes after 0930, twenty-seven inches during the next twenty minutes, and climbed steadily to just over seven feet by 1230.

By opening ten of the eighteen gates, the Chinese released enough water to wash away one American treadway bridge supported by pontoons and to require the corps to disconnect four others to avoid their loss. All were major installations, and they would have to be replaced, raised, and lengthened — a tedious, time-consuming task.

As soon as Hoge learned that the Pukhan River was rising, he told the 1st Cavalry Division commander to get to the dam, shut off the flow of water and put the machinery out of order. There was plenty of time to do so before the division left Kansas. Most of the units were leaving that night, but the 7th Cavalry was scheduled to go into reserve on the following night, the tenth. Major General Charles D. Palmer, who had taken command of the 1st Cavalry Division on February 5, was preparing to turn over his front to the marines. So far as he was concerned, the relief took precedence over Hwachon Dam. Passing on Hoge's instructions, Palmer's G–3, Carlson, instructed the 7th Cavalry to go beyond Kansas "if possible."

The 7th Cavalry transmitted the mission, along with the ambiguity, to one of the three battalions. "Be prepared to be relieved tomorrow" — April 10 — read one message. Then another: "Go up there [to the dam] if possible, stay there, do not get cut up, but do not withdraw unless necessary. If you can close locks, do so. If not sure how to operate and likely to damage, leave them alone. Destroy machinery if necessary to pull out."

Somewhat puzzled but expecting light resistance, the battalion commander, Lieutenant Colonel John W. Callaway, sent one of his three rifle companies into attack at noon. The Rangers were just behind and ready to go forward to close the spillway gates and destroy the machinery. Callaway's troops barely moved beyond Kansas before striking well-concealed but active Chinese defenses. The company commander was killed almost immediately, and the advance came to a halt.

When Callaway received a report that the men were unable to move because they were suffering heavy casualties, he went forward to get the details first-hand. The ground was so rough that it took him all afternoon to reach the riflemen. It was dark by the time he arrived. He discovered that the report of high losses was exaggerated. Two men had been lost: the dead commanding officer and a severely wounded soldier.

Judging the terrain to be too broken for proper control during the night, Callaway held off further attack. He made sure that his troops would be ready to resume the effort in the morning. Then he decided, he told me, to return to his headquarters. Perhaps word had come that the whole Hwachon thing had been called off; perhaps the relief of the division was going on as scheduled.

Several Korean laborers were carrying the wounded man to the rear, and Callaway joined them. The trip was slow, for the night was pitch black and the trail to the aid station crossed several cliffs. It wasn't easy to keep the litter of the wounded man steady and level. The exertion turned out to be in vain; he died en route.

Back at his command post around 0100 on April 10, Callaway learned that most of the division was leaving Kansas. But his own attack was still on, so he ordered his troops to get to the dam after daybreak. The decision to continue the attack had been reached earlier that evening by Hoge, who told Palmer to go on up and get the dam.

General Palmer and Carlson discussed the possibility of sending the Rangers across the reservoir in boats. Since Callaway's thrust had uncovered strong resistance, Carlson still believed it was too dangerous to cross a mile of open water. It was also too complicated. Much simpler was Callaway's overland effort, particularly since the division was to complete the relief as scheduled — that is, during the night of the tenth. The loss of two men in Callaway's assault company indicated that the attack had probably bogged down because of the death of the commander rather than the strength of the Chinese opposition. If the troops continued to press forward, they would surely drive the enemy from the approaches to the dam, scarcely two miles ahead.

Hoge's understanding was quite different. He expected the Rangers to cross the reservoir that night, and this he told Ridgway.

When Hoge visited Palmer on the morning of the tenth, he learned that Callaway's second attack, like the first, had gotten nowhere. Running into murderous fire, the troops made no progress beyond Kansas. In the process, six men were killed, twenty-seven wounded.

Where were the Rangers? Hoge asked.

Palmer explained. An operation across the lake hardly seemed worthwhile. Two of the regiments, along with the engineers and other elements, had already gone to the reserve area. Only the 7th Cavalry remained in the line, and it was due to leave that night. Getting involved in the complications of an amphibious assault might delay the relief.

Hoge's normally flushed face turned a deep, tomato red. "I want you to stop fooling around," he told Palmer. "What I want is a bona fide attempt to take the dam."

As Hoge was applying the whip, the Chinese were closing six gates of Hwachon Dam. Why they did so was a mystery. But the result became noticeable around noon. The water level of the Pukhan, which had remained about six feet above normal, started to subside. The danger of flooding began to diminish.

What now? Was there any point in continuing the attack?

Hoge's answer came early that afternoon. He had changed his mind. The marines were to take over from the 7th Cavalry during the night, thus completing the division's relief.

Colonel William A. Harris, Commanding Officer of the 7th Cavalry, was delighted. He had deep affection for the men entrusted to his care. They had fought over extremely difficult terrain for several months, and he knew how worn out they were. Telling his three battalion commanders to terminate their operations at 1700, Harris authorized them to start walking their men to the rear that evening. They would meet the trucks that had brought the rest of the division to the reserve area and that were coming back now to pick up the 7th Cavalry. In the battalions, a carefree, holiday mood took over as men began packing their gear and loading their vehicles for the move into reserve. Most of the company commanders sent weapons carriers filled with equipment to the rear.

Exactly at 1700, Harris received word that Hoge had changed his mind again: there would be no relief until the Hwachon gates were knocked out. The decision might have seemed like personal pique on the part of Hoge. Not only was the river level falling; the reservoir had lost so much water that only a moderate amount, a volume of no further consequence to the corps bridges, was flowing through the four gates that were still open. No one knew exactly how much water was left in the reservoir, for the weather had turned rainy and foggy, and aerial observation was impossible. But an estimate of the volume of water that had passed over the dam indicated that the level in the reservoir was low — so low that what was being held back could no longer be destructive.

Why then was Hoge insisting on shutting the gates? Because the Chinese could play a vicious game. They could build up the water in the reservoir, then release another flood. If they got hold of some portable electric generators to work the massive doors, they could harass the corps quite easily. Furthermore, the rainy season lay ahead. If the Chinese released the water during a heavy rainfall — and a rise in the Pukhan River as high as eighteen feet, simply from a heavy downpour, was a matter of record — they might wash out even high-level bridges. Thus, despite the absence of an immediate danger, a long-range menace persisted.

This bothered Hoge, but what bothered him more, he later said, was his feeling that the halfhearted thrusts toward the dam had stirred up the enemy. The division had frittered away time and resources and had dissipated the advantage of surprise. Commanders had been more interested in being relieved than in getting to the dam. If Hoge allowed the relief to be completed as scheduled, if he assigned the Hwachon Dam mission to the marines — who would need at least a couple of days to settle in — he would lose more time. He would enable the Chinese to prolong their game with the water and also to improve their already strong defenses. In the interest of speed, the 1st Cavalry Division, specifically the 7th Cavalry, had to take care of the gates.

Palmer and Harris were sick with dismay. Scheduling a unit's relief, then giving it a combat assignment, takes the heart out of its people. No one about to be relieved wants to move into attack. Everyone would be looking over his shoulder toward the promised relief and rest. But there would be neither relief nor rest until the machinery was knocked out.

Since the overland route to the dam seemed fruitless, Palmer and Harris decided to send the Rangers across the water. Coming ashore about a mile from the dam, the Rangers would make a quick run to seize the installation, close the gates, smash the hoisting machinery, and be gone as quickly as they had come. To divert the enemy's attention, Harris would launch two diversionary efforts, each by a battalion. His third battalion would be ready to cross the reservoir if the Rangers needed help.

The plan was fine, but the decision to carry it out could not have come at a worse moment. Not only was most of the division far to the rear in reserve; almost all of its trucks were tied up in this movement. Everyone would have to scramble at the last minute to get the equipment and supplies required for the combat operation.

The news that the Rangers would cross the reservoir that night came as a distinct surprise to Captain Anderson, the Ranger company commander. It was rather short notice for a complex operation of this sort, he felt, and somewhat late; by the time all the troops and equipment were assembled, only a few hours of darkness would remain. But he made no protest. His men were ready. The relief had no effect on them. They would be pulled out of the front as soon as they completed their mission.

After sending word for the men to be marched to the embarkation point on the shore of the lake, Anderson met his executive officer and his three platoon leaders there about 0230 on the morning of April 11. As he gave them his final briefing, he had a feeling of pride. He had a good outfit. All four of his lieutenants were young men who looked like college students; deceptively mild in manner, they had the assurance of professionals. The sergeants were a few years older. They knew their business too. Everyone in the company, Anderson reflected, was tough but avoided braggadocio. His men had no need to tout their abilities.

Anderson told his subordinate officers that no one knew how many Chinese defended the dam. The resistance stirred up by Callaway — in particular the number of Chinese mortars firing — had led to the conjecture that the enemy troops in the area outnumbered the Rangers. For that reason, the latter were to paddle across the water, using no motors unless they were discovered. Their best hope of reaching the dam lay in an approach utilizing stealth and surprise. To add firepower, about twenty machine gunners and mortarmen of the 7th Cavalry would accompany them. From the near shore of the reservoir would come supporting fire. Artillery would also be available.

The artillery actually in support of the Rangers consisted of thirty-two pieces, all 155-mm. and 8-inch howitzers. These large guns would be firing at their longest limits of effective range. The 155s would be shooting from about nine miles away; the 8-inch howitzers from around ten miles. Firing at extreme ranges was not good, for the longer the distance the broader the dispersal of shells at the target. It also wore out tubes more quickly. But the pieces were unable to come closer because of the paucity of roads around the dam. The 105-mm. howitzers, the artillery workhorses, which usually fired at a range of about five and a half miles at most, were unable to come far enough forward to shoot at all. The virtue of using 105s was their higher rate of fire, and this the Rangers would lack.

His instructions delivered, Anderson supervised the issue of additional ammunition to the men. They moved to the shore of the reservoir for embarkation. It was cold, and a damp fog blew in off the water. Tension began to build among the troops.

Near Chunchon, at 1st Cavalry Division headquarters, a hard-working major named Dayton F. Caple was spending a sleepless night. He was the G–4, who looked after logistics. Frantically, he was trying to collect equipment and supplies needed for the operation and to get them forward. His first thought was to find at least six DUKWs (amphibian trucks) to carry the Rangers across the reservoir. Less than a week earlier, the division had obtained a dozen for crossing the swollen Pukhan River above Chunchon; once across, facing no other water obstacles on the way to Kansas, the division got rid of them. As a matter of fact, Caple had let them go that very morning, sending six to the marines and six to the division on the immediate right in the adjacent corps. Though he acted at once to call them back, the absence of roads in the forward area held up the movement of the DUKWs.

Realizing that he probably would be unable to have DUKWs at the embarkation point in time for the Rangers to cross, Caple tried to get boats. An assault boat — made of plywood, weighing 410 pounds, powered by an outboard motor or paddles, and usually handled by three trained soldiers — was standard engineer equipment normally used in constructing a pontoon bridge. Early that month, to cross the Pukhan above Chunchon, the division engineer had procured forty assault boats and a dozen outboard motors. But when the Hwachon operation was ordered, the equipment was gone. Boats and motors, along with the trained operators, were moving with the engineers into the reserve area. A radio message got twenty boats and some motors started back. Ten, somehow, wound up on the wrong side of the Pukhan River. The bridge was out, and the boats had to be rerouted in a long detour. They reached the embarkation site shortly before noon on April 11 — too late for the Rangers to use. Fortunately, the other ten had arrived in time, but barely so.

The trouble was the roads, or rather the lack of them. A fair highway led north from Hongchon, but shipments destined for the Rangers had to diverge at Chunchon and follow a road into the area of the adjacent corps. The road soon petered out and became a wagon track. Choked with boulders, the trail was so tortuous, narrow, and rocky, and had such steep gradients and so poor a surface that trucks were unable to negotiate it. All equipment and supplies had to be transferred to jeeps, and even jeeps in four-wheel drive had trouble gaining traction. Finally, four miles short of the reservoir, the trail ended. Equipment and supplies had to be transferred again, this time to the backs of Korean laborers.

Throughout the night of April 10, as an army of American soldiers and Korean workingmen pushed and hauled trucks and jeeps and trailers and manhandled matériel across the mountains, another army of road-builders blasted rock, filled craters, and tried in other ways to improve the surface of the route. Despite the congestion, ten boats, ten motors, 180 paddles, and twenty air mattresses were brought to the embarkation site. The air mattresses were an inspiration. They substituted for life preservers. Caple had found a cache of life belts near Hongchon, but was unable to learn how many were there. He sent an officer by light plane in a hazardous night voyage to get at least 150 if possible, and a truck to haul them forward. The officer found plenty of life belts and talked someone into lending him a truck and a driver. But it was well after daybreak, well after the Rangers had departed, when he arrived at the reservoir.

Ten boats, some with outboard motors, were assembled at the embarkation point before dawn on April 11, but one had a hole in the bottom and was useless. Since each boat could carry ten men, some Rangers would have to wait until boats returned from the far side of the reservoir for a second trip. In each boat was an infantryman who would be responsible for bringing the craft back after the Rangers clambered out on the far shore. Lacking trained operators, the 7th Cavalry had sent out a call for volunteers, asking infantrymen who had some kind — any kind — of experience with boats and motors to come forward. A lieutenant who knew something about motorboats because he had done a little fishing on vacations found himself in charge of twenty soldiers who were willing to take the Rangers across the reservoir. Their valor was as great as their inexperience. Though a certain degree of confusion and disorder was to be expected in an operation of this sort, particularly during the hours of darkness, the milling around at the shore of the reservoir contributed to the venture a sense of improvisation and uncertainty.

Lieutenant Michael D. Healy's platoon got into three boats to make the initial excursion. Healy had a "killer" element of ten men armed with knives, axes, grenades, pistols, and carbines who were to eliminate quickly and quietly any enemy troops at the landing site, a demolition group responsible for placing explosives at the dam, and a squad carrying automatic rifles and machine guns. Pushing off at 0345 and guided by compasses, the men paddled across the smooth lake. The noise of the activity at the embarkation site soon slipped away, and they found themselves swallowed in an immensity of darkness and quiet broken by the splash of oars and an occasional sigh of exertion.

Forty-five minutes later, the first boat scraped the bottom of a rocky bank. Healy jumped out and pulled the craft up on the shore. The men got out. After giving his medical aid man a flashlight with a blackout cover to guide the other boats in, Healy, together with five men, verified the absence of Chinese troops in the immediate landing area. When the rest of the platoon was ashore Healy left two men at the inlet as guides and took the others up the sharp incline of a finger ridge that led to the base of a mountain peak.

On the other side of the reservoir Lieutenant Joseph W. Waterbury's platoon, together with Anderson, the forward observers, and the machine gunners, stepped into the remaining six boats when Healy's men were about fifty yards out in the water and disappearing from sight. They reached the landing cove as the sky was showing the first signs of light. Anderson led this contingent up a parallel finger ridge and met Healy at the base of the height. He quickly organized the seventy-odd men for the advance up the steep slope of the mountain. With Healy's platoon in the lead, Anderson's command group immediately behind, and Waterbury's platoon following, the Rangers started up the hill. The climb was difficult. Except for the slap of canteens against thighs and the scuff of shoes on the bare and rocky ground, the mountainside was quiet.

Out in front of the rest Healy and five soldiers were about a hundred yards from the top when they heard shouting. Looking up, they saw, through the heavy morning mist, the indistinct figures of about half a dozen men on the crestline waving in welcome. It was impossible to tell whether they were enemy troops or members of the 7th Cavalry who had managed to get to the dam overland. Waving back, Healy's men continued to climb the hill. Behind them Sergeant George E. Schroeder, who was walking with the forward observers, heard the shouting, glanced up, and thought that some Rangers had already reached the hilltop. Why were they so noisy? Was the dam already captured?

The men in the lead covered another fifty yards up the slope when the increasing light of the morning revealed that the troops on the top of the hill were wearing the Chinese quilted uniform. But as long as they kept waving and shouting in a friendly manner, the Rangers continued. Maybe the Chinese wanted to surrender.

A burst of machine-gun fire shattered the illusion. All hope of gaining surprise and reaching the dam undetected vanished as everyone on the slope fell flat. But not before two men were hit. The radio operator accompanying a forward observer was killed instantly, and another man got several bullets in the leg.

Sergeant William V. Goolsby, medical technician, was lying on the ground just as flat as he could stretch when he heard the wounded man call for help. The enemy shooting had picked up in volume as rifles and another machine gun joined the clatter, and Goolsby had no desire to move. The wounded man called again. Forcing himself to lift his head, Goolsby saw where he was. Telling himself the distance was not far, he crawled, cautiously at first but with rising confidence, to the side of the soldier. After pulling him into a small gully that gave protection from the firing, Goolsby bandaged the leg, which was bleeding profusely. Because the man was in shock, he helped him to his feet, then supported him as he limped down the hill to the landing site. There they waited for the boats that would bring the last platoon across the reservoir.

On the slope of the mountain Rangers in prone positions began returning the enemy fire. Forward observers called in mortar and artillery rounds, which dropped up ahead in slow cadence. Healy, accompanied by his group of five, crept toward the top of the hill, trying to locate the enemy weapons. Behind them several men fired a recoilless rifle, whose roar was as loud as a clap of thunder and whose backlash was as potent as a jet engine's. After they got off several rounds, one enemy machine gun fell silent. Shifting to the left, the men tried to search out the other machine-gun position, but in vain. Halfway up the hill, a sergeant had his troops assemble two machine guns and lay down grazing fire to cover Healy's advance. Before the guns could expend a mere three boxes of ammunition — 750 rounds — some Rangers, to the sergeant's astonishment, were at the top of the hill.

At the ridge line Healy raised his head several times to draw fire so that the other enemy machine gun could be spotted. When Healy saw where the position was, he and his group moved off without command, creeping to within grenade distance. Two men had dragged their machine gun up the hill, and they opened covering fire while Healy and his lead scouts threw grenades and assaulted the Chinese machine-gun nest. As they knocked out the gun and killed the crew, other Rangers rose to their feet and charged up the hill, shooting while they screamed to bolster their courage. A dozen Chinese troops fled across a draw and disappeared.

It was now 0615. Two and a half hours had passed. Light had come. The Rangers had taken their initial objective and were about half a mile from the dam. They were winded from the ascent, but they began at once to dig foxholes. Ahead, obscured by the morning fog and a jumbled mass of peaks, was the dam, and some of the men who listened thought they could hear the distant gush of water falling over the spillway. Behind them and off to the right and left, covered by a colorless carpet of mist that turned the reservoir into an immense void, was the lake, separating them from their friends. On the mountain top where they were now perched, they felt as though they were in limbo.

Schroeder spread a bright red silk panel on the hillside. If pilots came over to bomb and strafe the enemy after the morning mist lifted, they would know, by the colored cloth, where the Rangers were. About that time it started to rain. The rainfall would be light and intermittent, but the sky would remain covered throughout the day. There would be no air support for the Rangers.

Two boats, each paddled by a single crewman, had returned to the embarkation point after carrying Rangers across. Since the noise of the weapons on the far shore indicated that the Rangers had been discovered, there was no reason to remain quiet. The men tried to start the motors in order to get the last platoon, Lieutenant James L. Johnson's, more quickly across the water. Neither motor would start.

Two of Johnson's three squads paddled across the reservoir between 0600 and 0700. They were guided into the landing site by Goolsby, who was waiting to send the wounded man back. Johnson and his troops unloaded the boats, ascended one of the finger ridges, climbed the peak, and made contact with Anderson. It was close to 0800. At the cove Goolsby placed the wounded man into one of the craft and helped the crewman shove off for the return trip. He was tempted, he later admitted, to join them. He watched the boat for a few minutes and saw the wounded man, apparently dissatisfied with the rate of speed, pick up an oar and start to paddle.

Walking up the hill, Goolsby found everyone digging foxholes. Some mortar rounds were coming in, mostly white phosphorus, and two men had been burned, though not seriously. He treated them, then started to dig a hole for himself.

At the embarkation point, where two more boats had returned, the final squad of Johnson's platoon, the company executive (Lieutenant John S. Warren), and six Korean carriers with a load of ammunition climbed aboard. The motors started, and they quickly powered the men across the reservoir. As the craft headed for the landing cove, the morning mist lifted. The Rangers were hardly surprised when enemy fire came from their left front. As machine-gun bullets stitched the water around them, they turned to the right to escape. When more shots came in, they tried a third landing site. Another burst of fire convinced them they would be unable to get ashore without losing men and, probably even more important, the ammunition. Both boats returned.

On the far shore the enemy fire that had dissuaded the two boats from landing prompted Anderson to a decision. If he moved the Rangers inland and toward the dam, he explained afterward, he thought he might be cut off from the beach by Chinese troops coming in on his flanks. If, instead, he extended his line to the left and seized another hill overlooking the shore, he would not only secure his exit but also facilitate subsequent landings that would bring him reinforcements and ammunition. Anderson sent Johnson and his men through Healy's platoon and along a finger ridge toward the hill knob he wanted. Johnson had scarcely started when the shrill zing of machine-gun bullets and the whine of mortars sounded. Projectiles peppered the ridge and stopped his advanced. His men took cover, falling to the ground and burrowing their heads beside a rock outcropping and trying to hide in the all-too-short and scraggly brush.

Fifty or sixty Chinese troops charged in from the right front. They reached grenade distance before being beaten back. This attack, Anderson said later, was merely a ruse to draw the Rangers out of position. For immediately afterward a mass of what seemed like several hundred screaming, bugle-blowing Chinese soldiers poured down from the right and threatened to overwhelm the Americans. Making no effort to use covering fires, the Chinese bore directly down against the Rangers.

No one could remember — or, if he could remember, tell — precisely what happened during the next thirty minutes. This was the place in a man's story where his voice would falter, where he would lower his gaze uncomfortably, where his fingers might nervously pluck an escaping thread on a shirt seam or brush an imaginary spot of dust from his trousers. This was the nightmare the men barred from their immediate recollections. No one was sure any longer exactly what he had done, how he had reacted, what he had seen, or even how long it had lasted. Everyone preferred to ignore or to leap quickly across this terrible abyss between life and death, this awful span across which they had come unscathed.

"After it was over," they would say. Or, more formally, "When the attack was repulsed." Or perhaps, "After the Chinese were driven back."

It was still too close to them, too frightening to bring back, too near the edge of insanity. Not until much later would they feel safe enough to recall fragments of the wild melee, snatches of the madness, and they would then improvise and embroider colorful but carefully controlled designs on the tapestry of violence.

Schroeder thought he threw grenades for half an hour, then remembered that he had had only two. Healy talked about the bugles. Johnson tried to describe the appearance of a Chinese soldier falling when struck. One Ranger said he was thinking of home.

Goolsby saw a man get hit, the mortar fragment practically tearing off his arm. He crawled over and found the soldier unconscious. Treating him for shock, Goolsby tried to inject albumin into his veins, but the vessels had collapsed, and the soldier died almost at once from loss of blood. Another man was wounded in the lower part of the stomach, and Goolsby tried to give him albumin, but the hill was too steep. All he could do was to wrap him in the field jacket of the dead soldier and keep him warm. There was no way of getting him off the hill. He saw another Ranger, who had propped himself up in an exposed position to fire his automatic rifle, get struck in the head. The man toppled over backward, his body convulsed for a moment in a mute cry of agony; he was dead before he hit the ground.

"Let me put it this way," Anderson said, trying to explain what took place. "The approaching Chinese were so densely packed and so close that my pistol was more effective than a machine gun."

Waterbury had his radio damaged by a rifle bullet. He sent a runner to tell Anderson he had to pull back. As the soldier departed, crawling through the sparse brush toward the company headquarters, a grenade sailed through the air and exploded, knocking Waterbury down, half-conscious, and sending him rolling down the hill. He had no idea how far he tumbled or how long he lay where he came to a stop. Dimly he realized that some Rangers, men of his own platoon, were running wildly off the peak and toward the landing site.

"About twenty men broke and fled," Anderson later said candidly. "It happens occasionally when a platoon leader is knocked out of action."

The Rangers finally drove the Chinese off. A lieutenant named Forney, who brought in artillery fire, and the 4.2-inch mortar observer, worked beautifully together, the latter compensating for the slow rate of artillery shelling. The man calling in the fires of the 81-mm. mortars was too nervous to get his rounds on target; his radio operator had been the first to be killed shortly after the landing.

When the Chinese attack died down and the survivors had pulled back, Anderson checked his troops. They still held about 400 yards along the ridge line. But they were just about out of ammunition. They had half a box of machine-gun bullets, only four rounds for the recoilless rifle, two clips of pistol bullets, and about two clips per rifle, and thirty rounds per carbine. They were out of automatic rifle clips and grenades. Since the strength of the Chinese ruled out an advance to the dam and since the lack of ammunition made his positions untenable, Anderson radioed the 7th Cavalry for permission to return across the reservoir. He was told to stay. He would soon be joined by a rifle company, which was on its way across the water. Unless the infantrymen arrived quickly, the Rangers would be unable to withstand another Chinese attack. Anderson instructed his men to fix bayonets. Those who had no bayonets attached knives to their weapons.

The time was about 1200 on April 11. It seemed much later.

While the Rangers were crossing the reservoir that morning, the 7th Cavalry launched its two diversionary attacks. One battalion sent an assault company to cross the Pukhan River. Under a rain mixed with sleet, the men descended a steep slope to the water, sliding and slipping on the thin layer of mud that barely covered the rock core of the hill. They planned to cross on several footbridges thrown up several days earlier, for the rugged ground prevented them from carrying boats to the river's edge and the current was too swift to allow them to paddle across on air mattresses. At the bank of the river they discovered that the water level had risen and washed out the bridges. All they could do — even though they saw no enemy troops — was to fire across the stream, call in artillery shells, and hope that the threat they had mounted had kept some Chinese away from the dam.

The other battalion, Callaway's, attacked for the third day and ran into the same enemy pillboxes. An officer who had been with the marines at Iwo Jima later said that the Chinese put out more mortar fire than the Japanese ever had. A sergeant who had fought in Europe said that the Siegfried Line defenses were the only comparable positions he had ever seen. Lacking air support because the bad weather kept the planes on the ground, with attempted precision artillery fire making no impression on the fortifications — the pieces were too distant for pinpoint accuracy — and deprived of the help of tanks because there were no roads, the battalion tried to divert attention from the Rangers and lost twenty-eight men, three of whom were killed.

As early as midmorning Colonel Harris, the regimental commander, concluded that the two attacking battalions would have little success. Because the Rangers had been discovered, he judged they would need reinforcement. He decided to send his third battalion across the water. One company of that battalion had already marched to the embarkation site, and shortly before noon Harris ordered the 200 men across. By this time the ten other assault boats sent by the division engineers, as well as the life preservers, had reached the shore of the reservoir. Climbing into the craft, the infantrymen tried to get the outboard motors started. None worked. It was early afternoon before the first boats departed. Warren, the Ranger executive, who had been unable to get across earlier, accompanied the infantry to show the way.

Half the distance across the water, the men ran into a volley of mortar shells. One boat was hit and damaged slightly; one soldier was wounded, not seriously. Continuing to paddle, the men reached the far shore. They beached their craft around 1330, and immediately positioned guards around the landing site and awaited the arrival of the rest of the company.

When Warren stepped out of his boat he met Waterbury, who had tumbled down the hill and who was still dazed. He felt vaguely guilty because he was not badly hurt — a cut on his hand was bleeding slowly and his legs wobbled. He wanted to take some boats to a beach directly below the Rangers to get ammunition up the hill more quickly and also to help evacuate the wounded. Warren assured him that he would look after the ammunition and casualties, then helped him into a boat that was about to return across the reservoir. As Waterbury was being transported back, the last squad of Johnson's platoon, the Korean carriers, and a load of ammunition appeared at the inlet. Soon afterward the rest of the infantry company arrived.

When Anderson saw the final contingent of his own force and the company of infantry approaching, he felt pretty good. With 300 Americans on the hill and plenty of ammunition, it would be difficult, if not impossible, for the Chinese to dislodge them. Not only that. Now they could get started toward the dam. It was about 1600.

An hour earlier General Palmer, 1st Cavalry Division commander, had telephoned the 7th Cavalry to learn how things were going. Colonel Harris, the regimental commander, was cautiously hopeful. He thought there was little chance of taking and holding the dam that day, but he believed it might be possible to get three companies of infantry — in fact, the whole battalion — across the reservoir. That would enable the Rangers to get to the dam during the night and blast the machinery. Around daybreak, all the troops could get out. How did that sound? That sounded all right to Palmer, and he gave his OK. Then he telephoned Hoge to pass on the information.

To Hoge, the corps commander, the dam appeared to be defended in surprising strength. What were the Chinese up to? Intelligence had failed to estimate anywhere near the correct numbers of Chinese around the dam. In addition to the unexpected opposition, Hoge revised his understanding of the terrain. What he had originally conceived of as separate compartments were in reality interconnected areas. Seizing the dam required the capture of a sizable parcel of ground around it. Taking that much real estate demanded at least an entire division. Since two-thirds of the 1st Cavalry Division had already left Kansas, he would have to use the marines. But if he sent the marines forward in a full-scale attack, he would have to commit more troops to cover their flank. He would be getting involved in a major attack beyond Kansas, which was unauthorized. And Ridgway had said he wanted few casualties.

Hoge had to admit that the operation was getting out of hand. Since the flow of the Pukhan River had dropped off, even though the level remained relatively high, he decided there was no special need now for haste in taking the dam, no sense in being stubborn. He told Palmer he would recommend calling off the operation. Unless, of course, the Chinese resistance suddenly disintegrated. If the Chinese abandoned the dam, the Rangers might as well knock it out.

Palmer called back Harris and passed along Hoge's thinking. Well, what did Palmer want him to do? Harris could call off the operation any time he wished.

He needed little urging. But he could not blindly end the action. He had made an investment. Perhaps it was worth hanging on to a little longer. He reviewed the situation. To take the dam, he estimated, he would need to send two more rifle companies across the reservoir. Since there was no fast way of getting them across the water, together with ammunition and other supplies, the positions established half a mile from the dam might be swept away during the night. For, obviously, the Chinese would attack in strength after darkness fell. Since the weather had killed any air support, and since the artillery assistance was not the best, he began to doubt that the losses being suffered were worth the goal. To prolong the operation was simply asking too much of the troops.

Come on back, he radioed. He wanted the Rangers to pull out first, covered by the infantrymen.

Anderson had three reactions in quick succession. First he was shocked: Why call it off when there was a good chance now of getting to the dam? Next he was angry: What was the point in getting men killed for nothing? Then he relaxed: He had not the slightest desire to question the order. When he put out the word to his men, he could almost hear the collective sigh of relief. No one wanted to spend the night on the wrong side of the reservoir.

Since any withdrawal from a forward position is a ticklish operation — troops are vulnerable when they move — Anderson asked for smoke, the artificial haze put out by smoke pots, generators, or artillery shells. "Negative," came a voice over the radio; no smoke was available.

Caple, the division G–4, had tried to obtain smoke. He needed at least 200 smoke pots to provide effective cover, but the forward supply points were out of stock. After much telephoning, he found twenty-five smoke pots at a depot near Wonju, eighty-five miles from the dam, and about the same number near Suwon, just as far away. Both places were at least sixteen hours by road to embarkation sites, and only fifty smoke pots were worse than useless. Looking for smoke generators in the immediate area of the reservoir, Caple found absolutely none. When he phoned the artillery, he learned that there was a shortage of smoke shells.

In some desperation Caple telephoned the corps G–4 for help. Instead of getting in touch with the corps chemical officer, who controlled smoke munitions, someone in the corps G–4 section called the corps ordnance officer. Someone in that staff office also forgot that smoke came from chemical supply, and he phoned the army ordnance office in Pusan. From there a telephone call went to Tokyo asking that smoke pots be airlifted from Japan. Only the corps chemical officer semed to know that there were plenty of smoke pots in Korea — at a chemical dump near Hongchon — but he had no idea that anybody needed them.

During the night of April 10, word came from Pusan to the corps ordnance officer, who notified the corps G–4: a C-54 plane would fly from Japan in the morning and arrive at Hoengsong at 0900. Perhaps only a C-54 was available — there was no way of telling in Korea. But if smoke pots had been loaded into a C-47 plane, someone should have known that they could be landed at the smaller airfield at Hongchon, twenty miles nearer the ultimate destination.

Major Caple sent a truck to Hoengsong during the night to meet the plane. The driver was there in time, but the plane failed to arrive. The weather had turned bad over Japan, airfields were fogged in, and the flight had been canceled. There was no smoke to cover Anderson's withdrawal.

Since the Chinese remained strangely quiet, Anderson brought his men down the hill and safely to the cove. He sent a boat to an inlet closer to the hill, where Goolsby was waiting with the casualties. Using pine branches and field jackets, Goolsby had fashioned makeshift litters. They were difficult to keep steady and level as they were carried down the steep slope of the hill. The dead men kept falling off. The wounded men groaned constantly. Goolsby decided to carry only the man with the stomach wound. This took considerable exertion on the part of six strong Rangers. The dead were dragged and rolled down the hill to the water.

Anderson made sure all his men were embarked before he set off. He reached the original embarkation point at 2030. Soon after he came ashore, he noticed several amphibian trucks. Somewhat idly, for he was too tired to be indignant and he knew nothing about the condition of the trail across which they had come, he wondered why the DUKWs had arrived so late.

The Rangers had to walk several miles to trucks that were waiting to take them back to Hongchon. Not until they climbed wearily into the backs of the vehicles and settled down did the tension start to lift. Only then, as the trucks moved off slowly in the darkness, did they begin to relax. Most of them found that their legs were trembling. Or their hands when they tried to light a cigarette. A few stifled sobs. Several were sick. No one spoke.

For the Rangers the Hwachon adventure had all but ended. Ninety-eight soldiers and five officers plus six Korean carriers, had crossed the reservoir. Two men were dead, and the man with the stomach wound would die on the following day. Eleven others had been wounded, and one was injured, having broken his leg in a fall. The few infantrymen who had accompanied them had lost one man killed and wounded one.

Up on the hill across the reservoir, soon after the Rangers pulled out, about sixty Chinese attacked the infantry company. The riflemen beat them back. They estimated they killed about forty-five, but the figure was no doubt exaggerated.

The infantrymen had little sense of victory. They were filled with trepidation. The departure of the Rangers had removed all the boats from the far shore. Suppose the Chinese attacked again and drove them from the hill. How would they get off the beach? Except for an occasional mortar and artillery shell dropping in, the hill remained calm. Just before darkness the boats returned. The men moved quietly off the height.

At the cove, while half the company formed a perimeter and stood guard, the others dug foxholes around the beach. When these were completed, half the men departed. Those who remained were gnawed by the anguish of insecurity. Again there were no boats to take them off. It was well after dark by then. The day-long rain had soaked the soldiers' uniforms. A raw wind drove a sleeting rain that had a cutting edge. Enough boats had returned by midnight to take everyone off. Making a final check to be sure that his men had left nothing for the enemy, the company commander was the last to shove off.

In the pitch black darkness, the troops guided their boats toward the flickers of flashlights that Harris, despite the danger of provoking enemy artillery, had ordered shown. The last elements of the company returned to the original embarkation point at 0130 on the morning of April 12. They noticed Korean carriers still bringing supplies and equipment into the area.

A total of 193 officers and men of the rifle company, in addition to twelve machine gunners, had crossed the reservoir to reinforce the Rangers. All had come back. Three men were wounded. No one was killed.

Exactly six hours earlier General Hoge had sent General Ridgway a message. "Attempt to seize Hwachon reservoir unsuccessful," he wrote, "due to strong obstinate enemy resistance."

Callaway's battalion, in the three days his troops had tried to reach the dam overland, had lost ten men killed, fifty-six wounded.

Long after the operation was called off, equipment and supplies continued to arrive at the shore of the reservoir. The matériel had been dispatched in case the action lasted another day or two. Three bulldozer crews worked almost forty-eight hours without sleep to help open the trail. On the morning of April 12 more than twelve hours after the Hwachon Dam venture had come to an end, a road had been made passable for trucks all the way to the embarkation point. At that time, thirty-five assault craft, twenty motors and trained mechanics — all rounded up by Caple from a variety of sources — finally reached the site. By then, enough ammunition, gasoline, oil, and other things had been delivered to guarantee adequate support to the crossings.

Twenty-four hours later, on the morning of April 13, the IX Corps transportation officer got a phone call from Hoengsong: a truck was needed to move 221 smoke pots that had just been landed at the airfield for immediate delivery to the 1st Cavalry Division. Having no idea what this was all about — the 1st Cavalry Division was out of the corps area and in reserve — but knowing that smoke was a chemical responsibility, he advised the chemical officer. He was in the dark too, so he checked with the corps G–4, who told him why the smoke had been ordered. Furious, and rightly so, because no one had consulted him, the chemical officer arranged to have a truck pick up the pots and haul them to the chemical dump, where he already had a surplus on hand.

The circumstances of the Hwachon operation might have been the subject of an inquiry, particularly since there was a lull all across Korea as the troops settled into Kansas. But an entirely unrelated development had overshadowed the raid. On April 11, at the height of the action, came the startling news that President Truman had relieved General MacArthur and was replacing him with General Ridgway. As Ridgway flew to Tokyo the events at the dam fell into obscurity.

Soon afterward the reason why the Chinese had put up such strong resistance at the dam became clear. They had been using the broken terrain to gather and conceal equipment and supplies for a gigantic build-up. On April 22 they launched the first phase of an overwhelming spring offensive. They drove the Eighth Army off Kansas, and in a week forced the United Nations troops back thirty miles. When the situation became somewhat stable again, the forward line of IX Corps was just ahead of Hongchon.

By then the Hwachon Dam foray was ancient history. Few would remember the futile incident unless to remark that men sometimes die for the inconsequential. The corps had carried out an attack as a precaution against a danger that never materialized.

But who knows beforehand whether an imagined menace will become real? Who knows until afterward when the expenditure of men will lead to a decisive moment of triumph on the battlefield?

The Hwachon Dam operation turned out to be an insignificant gesture. Except, of course, to the thirteen Americans who died, to the seventy who were wounded, and, no less, the unknown enemy troops who were killed and hurt. Meaningless, except also to those who suffered the dread of dying. And to all of us who agonize with them.

PART II

Some Masters of the Art

By the time the young soldier has become a senior commander he has been exposed to a wide variety of experiences. He has matured; he knows how to exercise his craft. He has an understanding of the needs and desires that motivate men. He is more or less aware of the reasons for, and the results of, warfare.

In most modern armies the senior commander has a background that combines a judicious blend of formal schooling and practical responsibility. At different levels of school he has learned his trade for the middle levels of command. If he is judged competent for additional responsibility, he is sent to colleges where he will be prepared for the higher reaches. And finally, if he is good enough, he attends institutions that deal with the esoteric areas of the civil-military and the politico-military. In between his periods of attending school he is putting the lessons of the classroom to use, refining and reshaping his ideas and his attitudes in the practice of his art.

In print this sounds highly formalized and even somewhat stereo-typed. In actuality the range of the military experience is so wide as to defy categorization. Officers meeting at the Command and General Staff College have had such divergent careers that they seem to belong to different professions. What makes the military system work is the similarity of methodology, or, in military terminology, doctrinal background; what gives the system its vitality is the diversity of practical experience.

The process of military education has not always been so fully developed. In ancient Rome the higher commanders were drawn from the Senatorial class. They might come to high responsibility with almost no experience in the practicalities of soldiering. Those who actually ran the army were the long-service professionals, senior centurions who were more or less analogous in background to the present-day warrant officers, but enjoyed much greater prestige and authority than their modern counterparts. The arrangement worked surprisingly well for a long time in Rome, but in the end the regulars realized that they were calling the tune, and they took over the government and the state with disastrous consequences.

In early modern times an aspiring soldier learned his trade by going where the action was. There he attached himself to one of the contemporary big names. During the Renaissance, Italy was the place to visit, not so much for its art as for its battles. The French, Spanish, and Germans all made sport of Italy, and if a young officer could show that he had acquired his training on the staff of Gonzalo de Córdoba, who was known in his own day as "the Great Captain," he could easily pick up a commission in a prince's army. Germany during the Thirty Years' War was another great nursery of soldiers, and many commanders in the English Civil War had done their apprenticeship, even to "trailing a pike" in the ranks, with the Protestant or Catholic forces that were ravaging the North German Plain.

A definite change in where to get an education — although not how — occurred on May 19, 1643. On that day at Rocroi the French general Condé, who was twenty-two years old, defeated the Spanish army of 18,000 foot and 8000 horse. By wiping out 17,000 of the finest infantry Europe had known since the days of Rome, Condé destroyed forever Spanish hegemony on the continent. Rocroi, together with the naval Battle of the Downs four years earlier, ruined Spain far more conclusively than the Armada, so beloved by English writers, half a century before.

After Rocroi, if a young man wanted a military education, he went to France to get it. Not that "the Great Condé" conformed to the pattern he had set. He himself had been schooled in the Jesuit College at Bourges.

The beginnings of more formal military education date from the end of the eighteenth century and the early nineteenth. Napoleon went to Brienne, the equivalent of a modern state-subsidized military preparatory school. After that he studied at the somewhat moribund Ecole Militaire in Paris. Later he was so sensitive to the value of a military education that he reinvigorated the military college and moved it to St. Cyr just outside the capital, where Madame de Maintenon, wife of Louis XIV, had established an institute for girls. A tune that the girls sang when the king came to visit is now better known as "God Save the Queen."

Napoleon set up other military institutions of learning, such as the Cavalry School at St. Germain, and these developments were in line with the trends of the time. The Americans established West Point and the British Sandhurst in 1802, and the Prussians had military colleges antedating them. The days would soon be gone when an intelligent sergeant major could double as a field marshal. Soldiering had become a profession that required special education.

The trouble with teaching, as they say, is that nothing worth knowing can be taught. All the schooling in the world is insufficient unless it is backed by experience and judgment, and everyone knows of individuals who have been educated beyond their intelligence. It takes a combination of diverse qualities to make a competent officer, and something more than that to develop the great leaders of the profession.

Perhaps the most notable trait of the master of the military art is that his record transcends the limitations of his own time and space. His operations may illustrate, or subvert, the principles of war — for it is only a master who dares deliberately to break the rules and who can succeed in defiance of them. However he manages his affairs, he must dominate the events instead of being overwhelmed by them.

An interesting similarity among many practitioners is that they were neither innovators nor possessed of a gimmick. They were masters more by the solidity than by the flamboyance of their performance. Such men are not likely to become household words; they are more like the fullback who is always good for five yards than the halfback who goes the length of the field once a season. Most of them achieved fame when the art of war had reached one of its periodic plateaus, that is, when the weapons and equipment, as well as the formations, were generally the same in all armies. Sulla, it is true, introduced offensive field fortifications, but, by and large, great commanders were those able to defeat others who had equivalent or better forces. All faced and overcame severe limitations on their resources and on their freedom of action. For the great general in the final analysis is the one who solves the greatest problems and surmounts the greatest difficulties.

In Sulla's time the standard army was made up of infantrymen, using sword and shield, in addition to supporting cavalry and various auxiliaries. This combination was so well adapted to the conditions of warfare that it lasted for several centuries. It is still possible to argue that deficiencies of the parent society rather than intrinsic failings in military technology and organization caused the demise of the system.

Maurice de Saxe and Robert Clive lived at another time when all military forces were similarly organized, armed, and handled. In their day soldiers moved freely from one army to another and transferred their allegiance as they wished. War was regarded as the game of kings, and men fought, in Southey's words, "because their governors fell out."

In many ways this was a rather attractive period. The evils of war for the civilian population, at least in western Europe, had been somewhat lessened by the newly established system of supply depots, which restrained pillage. And Frederick the Great could remark that a good war was one that did not disturb the civilians. He had more practical reasons for saying this than delicacy of feeling. Frederick wanted his civilians untouched by war because they were the productive elements of society; if left alone they would increase not only production but especially the taxes that kept dynastic armies in the field.

There were other mitigating factors. The strict delineation of social classes, the formal manners of the privileged, and the general inefficiency of weapons technology made war more colorful and less bloody than it had been before or would be again. Prevailing military modes laid emphasis on the art of maneuver. Generals — particularly Turenne, who was the greatest exponent of this idea — hoped they might so badly outmaneuver their foes as to force a surrender without fighting a battle. Unfortunately the commmanders were usually unsuccessful in achieving this aim, and some battles were bloody indeed. The casualty ratios would be thought completely outrageous for modern formations, which, if more highly complex, are correspondingly more delicate. In the twentieth century, losses of 20 percent were considered enough to make a formation combat ineffective. In contrast, at Freeman's Farm, the first battle of Saratoga in 1777, the British 62d Regiment suffered a loss of 83 percent of its officers and men.

By the time of George H. Thomas the form of warfare that had existed for more than a century was coming to an end. Substantial changes were occurring in society and technology, and the nature of warfare was at the edge of another great transformation. Yet Napoleon would have understood Thomas' maneuvers, and he would have been delighted by them. So would Saxe.

World War II also represented a peak of warfare and generalship, for the great practitioners thoroughly understood the technical means available for the waging of war. In contrast, the military leaders in World War I, who had much the same technology, had been unable to assimilate and adapt the new means of waging war, and the generalship was, as a consequence, inferior.

The highly developed art of generalship that emerged in World War II spawned many great commanders, but the struggle was so immense in scope that all but a very few have been virtually forgotten. Some soldiers who receive a footnote in the history of World War II would have been the subjects of legends in the days before men could write.

Sulla

It HAS OFTEN BEEN SAID that Rome conquered the world three times: by the supremacy of her arms, her law, and her Church. The military historian is likely to maintain that the first of these was the most important. Without the power of armored might, the other two conquests probably would not have taken place.

Despite the long periods of turbulence and strife in Roman history, the study of Roman military history is apt to leave one slightly puzzled. In so renowned a military nation, one would expect to find a series of great soldiers developing the art of war from one height to the next. Yet it is difficult to find leaders of genius. A few come immediately to mind, but very few. One thinks of Caesar, of course, but one wonders whether his military feats were exaggerated by his flair as his own press agent. Scipio Africanus is well known for his defeat of Hannibal. Few others are popularly remembered.

It would appear that the Romans won their campaigns by superior discipline, training, and morale, which may be other names for a degree of proficiency and stubbornness unequalled in the ancient world. Basically, the Roman commanders seemed to be solid practitioners rather than men of fiery brilliance. In this galaxy Sulla deserves to be better known.

Lucius Cornelius Sulla was born in 138 B.C. He was a member of the distinguished family of the Cornelii, one of the leading Senatorial families of the Roman republic. His life spanned a half century of upheaval when the republic was edging toward collapse, when fights among political factions were becoming the order of the day, and when the stability that had so long marked the Roman state was about to disintegrate.

When Sulla was a young man, the army, which had always been important in the life of Rome, was about to become dominant. The army as an institution had undergone a significant change, and Marius, soon to be consul, gave the army its distinctive cast. Before Marius, soldiers had to be citizens and landholders; their primary loyalty was to the state. Now, they were often landless men; they owed their allegiance to their leaders. Eventually faction would become war, Roman armies would fight Roman armies, and in the end the republic would give way to the empire.

As often happens in history, it was an external threat that brought the internal one to a climax. About 113 B.C. Rome was menaced from the north and the south at the same time. In Gaul, two Germanic tribes, the Cimbri and the Teutones, swept toward the Alps, a horde of 300,000 fighting men, with wagons, wives, and children. Across the Mediterranean in Africa, a war broke out in Numidia where a new king, Jugurtha, either defeated or bought every Roman general sent against him. For five years these threats loomed over Rome. Then Marius was elected consul. He went off to Africa and defeated Jugurtha. Most of the military victory was the work of Sulla, who held the subordinate rank of quaestor under Marius. The Jugurthine War brought Sulla some small prominence, enough to excite the jealousy of Marius.

Marius next campaigned in north Italy. Again Sulla seconded him. The combination triumphed. The Romans destroyed the Teutones at Aquae Sextiae, where the legions slew over 100,000 men. At Vercellae in 101, the Romans wiped out the Cimbri.

Marius was hailed by Rome as the savior of the state. As he began to dominate affairs in Rome, he had no reason to doubt Sulla's support, although Marius regarded him as his potential rival. Sulla passed his time governing various provinces of the empire, chiefly in the East.

In 93, when the subject Italian states rebelled against Rome in the War of the Allies, commonly miscalled the Social War, the two commanders cooperated once more to defeat the rebels. During three years of campaigning, 300,000 men were slain, and central Italy was transformed into a wasteland. When an uneasy peace settled over Italy, Marius, now at the ripe age of sixty-nine, retired, ostensibly leaving the field to Sulla.

Not until 88 B.C. did Sulla have the chance to display his qualities as an independent commander. He received the appointment to command an army being prepared to fight against Mithridates of Pontus in Asia Minor. Assuming his post in southern Italy enthusiastically, he trained and treated his men well, in the process attracting and maintaining their unswerving loyalty.

His first action was directed not against the enemy, but rather against his own government. For the Assembly in Rome had fallen under the influence of demagogues and populists. Distrusting the aristocratic Sulla and feeling that his army should be commanded by a man of the people, the Assembly decreed his deposition. When Sulla received the news, he marched on Rome. He surrounded the Forum with his troops, killed the popular leaders, and reinstated the aristocratic party. Then having set matters to rights, he set off for the East to carry out his original mission.

This was the time that the expanding power of Rome was overcoming, one by one, the last successor states of the great Hellenistic civilization in the eastern Mediterranean. Mithridates VI Eupator, King of Pontus, had gradually brought much of Asia Minor under his control. He then moved into Greece, where he posed as the liberator of the Greeks from Roman domination. In 88, while Sulla had been occupied at Rome, Mithridates marched into Athens and ordered the killing of all Italians in the Greek peninsula.

When Sulla and his army reached Greece, the Pontic general Archelaus held Athens. Sulla besieged the city and its port of Piraeus. In the midst of the siege, Sulla learned that his enemies had regained control of Rome. They left him to rot, sending neither funds nor reinforcements to him. To finance his campaign and hold his army together, he confiscated funds from nearby Greek cities.

Finally, in March 86, he attacked Athens, and his soldiers stormed their way into the city in spite of the numerically superior Pontic army. Archelaus retired to the north while the Romans rewarded themselves with the traditional pillaging and looting.

Eventually, Sulla followed his foes into Boeotia. The two armies met at Chaeronea, where Philip and Alexander had conquered Greece two and a half centuries earlier. Sulla had but 30,000 men; his enemies numbered about 110,000 troops and ninety chariots. To offset his inferiority, Sulla undertook what has been called "the first known offensive use of field fortifications." His men dug trenches to protect their flanks from the enemy cavalry. They threw up palisades along their front to counter the chariots, which were a reversion to an older form of warfare, largely gone out of style.

In the battle, the Pontic and Greek cavalry attacked the flanks, and the Romans, fighting from their trenches, drove them off with little trouble. The chariots then came up against the palisades, and the Roman arrows and javelins were highly effective. As the wounded horses recoiled through the Mithridatic phalanxes, they threw the units into confusion. Sulla immediately launched his counterattack with his heavy infantry. He broke the Pontic formations. As the Pontic army began to collapse, Archelaus withdrew what he could.

After retreating six miles to Orchomenus, Archelaus pulled his men together and halted Sulla's pursuit. For a time the two armies eyed each other while both tried to regain their strength. In this effort Archelaus was the more successful. He received reinforcements both from the Greeks and from King Mithridates, but to no avail. Trusting to the superior discipline of his men and to the use of further field fortifications, Sulla triumphed once more.

In the battle of Orchomenus, the Pontic forces again opened with a cavalry attack, this time strong enough to dent the Roman formations. Sulla personally rallied his men and led them forward in a counterattack. Skillfully he turned this into an envelopment. The result was a complete rout of the enemy army. The whole Pontic control of Greece was destroyed.

Sulla then crossed the Hellespont and invaded Asia Minor in search of King Mithridates. He encountered, instead, a rival Roman army, which the popular party at home had sent out to defeat him. This army was under Lucius Valerius Flaccus, and Sulla did his best to ignore him. Flaccus was murdered by his lieutenant, Fimbria, who assumed command and stood aside while Sulla made a compromise peace with Mithridates. Sulla appealed to Fimbria's army to join him, and when the army decided to do so Fimbria committed suicide. Having thus in one way or another solved his eastern problems, Sulla sailed with about 35,000 veterans for Rome. He arrived at Brindisium in the early summer of 83, determined to settle many scores.

Rome was in the midst of fantastic confusion. After Sulla's departure for the East four years earlier, power had fallen again into the hands of Marius and a lesser supporter of his, Cinna. They had indulged in proscriptions, massacres, and executions to consolidate their hold on the government and the country. Then the aged Marius died. Cinna became sole dictator, and he ran the state as he chose. Learning that Sulla was on his way home, Cinna raised an army by levy and marched south to meet him. Instead of giving battle, Cinna's men killed him. The consul Caius Norbanus took Cinna's place.

Marching north, Sulla met this army near Capua at a place called Mount Tifata, overlooking the Volturno River — a battlefield where American troops would defeat Germans just over 2000 years later. Sulla's veterans contemptuously cut the Roman levies to pieces, then settled into Capua for the winter.

From Capua, Sulla negotiated for a peaceful solution to the problem of who should rule Rome and how. The talks were unsuccessful: Sulla remained committed to an aristocratic form of government, which would preserve the traditional dominance of the Senate; the popular party insisted on a more democratic form of government. Both would turn out to be impossible. The Senate would prove too corrupt to wield power, and the idea of popular rule would eventually sour into an untrammeled dictatorship.

In any event, Sulla reluctantly marched on Rome in the spring of 82. An army composed of raw recruits and commanded by the son of Marius blocked his way, but Sulla's men brushed them aside easily. Marius' son fled to the city of Praeneste, but he ordered all the leaders of the Senatorial party in Rome to be killed. The democratic forces obeyed him, then upon Sulla's approach, evacuated the city. Sulla moved in unopposed and took over.

He was not quite yet safe home. The remnants of the democratic forces still in being were joined by an army of 100,000 Samnites who marched up from the south for a replay of the old Social War. Sulla, controlling 50,000 men, met them at the Colline Gate, on the inner wall of the city. The battle opened in the late afternoon and lasted through the night. It was a murky, cut-and-thrust melee in the suburbs. At the end of the slaughter, one of the bloodiest affairs in Roman history, Sulla was completely victorious. He took about 6000 prisoners, had them surrounded and executed. He then had their heads taken to Praeneste. This was a convincing argument for the city to surrender. Young Marius committed suicide and his head was nailed up in the Forum.

Sulla had now triumphed and gained power by the most basic and primitive means — the elimination of his enemies. The Senate made him dictator and he set about to rehabilitate the Roman constitution, trying to restore Senatorial supremacy.

His first act was to proscribe about 5000 people, and there was terror throughout Italy as his men tracked down and executed his potential foes. He next had the Senate pass retroactive laws legitimizing everything he had done. Then he had a whole series of laws issued, designed to prevent a recurrence of the dictatorship Sulla himself possessed. Known as the Cornelian Laws, they were intended, among other things, to preserve the independence of the Roman judiciary. Sulla finally pronounced an edict outlawing armies in Italy itself. With that, he disbanded his own legions and settled his soldiers on state lands. To everyone's surprise, he retired.

Sulla lived two more years as a private citizen, enjoying quietly the normal pleasures of that depraved society. His retirement was surprisingly peaceful, but, then, all his enemies were dead. He died as the result of illness.

Will Durant summed up his career in these words: "It was said of him that he was half lion and half fox, and that the fox in him was more dangerous than the lion. Living half the time on battlefields, spending the last decade of his life in civil war, he nevertheless preserved his good humor to the end, graced his brutalities with epigrams, filled Rome with his laughter, made a hundred thousand enemies, achieved all his purposes, and died in bed."

He wrote his own epitaph: "No friend ever served me, and no enemy ever wronged me, whom I have not repaid in full."

Though as bloody-minded and as brutal as any of his contemporaries, Sulla has generally received better grades from posterity. His surrender of power has tended to make historians regard him somewhat more indulgently and favorably than they have assessed his rivals, Marius and Cinna.

He was, in fact, a strange mixture of qualities. Sallust has left us a portrait of the man — he had bright blue eyes in a white face with red blotches. He was a *bon vivant,* and Sallust adds, "He lived extravagantly, yet pleasure never interfered with his duties, except that his conduct as a husband might have been more honorable." He was a keen reader of Greek and something of a connoisseur of art works, which he looted avidly and consistently. He loved soldiering and the army, and he was thoroughly at ease on the various levels of his professional competence.

As a military man, he is difficult to assess, as is any soldier who moves out of the realm of military affairs into the world of politics. Dupuy remarks that, as a practitioner of warfare, Sulla was essentially a second-rate soldier whose opponents were the same. It is true enough that, except for his innovation of the offensive field fortifications, he made no major changes in the military art in his period. Military technology had reached one of the aforementioned plateaus with the Roman legionary infantry, and most of the armed forces fought within the same general system, except for Archelaus' outdated chariots.

Yet neither was Napoleon much of an innovator. He was a genius who carried another existing system to the point of perfection. This is hardly to suggest that Sulla was the equal of Napoleon, but rather to highlight the fact that within any military context it takes a gifted man to be uniformly successful against those who possess the same tools.

Judged simply by his record, then, Sulla would have to be regarded as a very efficient commander. The fundamental problems of his day were to instill and retain the loyalty of one's troops, to maintain their discipline and morale. In every campaign and battle he fought, Sulla brought his men to the field better prepared in these respects than his foes. In every battle he fought, these factors, coupled with his superior handling of men in combat, enabled him to defeat potentially overwhelming numbers.

He played useful subordinate roles in the Jugurthine War and the war with the Cimbri and Teutones. He was one of Rome's two successful generals in the Social War. He defeated his rivals before going to the East. He won the First Mithridatic War, at least to the extent that Rome would allow. He triumphed in the Civil War.

Having at last become dictator, he had the good sense to retire. Thus he could, with justice, add to his name the surname "Felix" — Sulla the Fortunate, Sulla the Happy, an outstanding and thoroughly successful soldier of his age.

Saxe

THE CIRCUMSTANCES of the birth, life, and death of Hermann Maurice de Saxe were illustrious and exceptional, to say the least. He was born on October 28, 1696, the first of 354 acknowledged illegitimate children of the elector of Saxony who was later also king of Poland and who was known, with good reason, as Augustus the Strong. He became marshal general of France, one of the great soldiers of the eighteenth century and also one of the great theorists and innovators of all time. He died at his chateau of Chambord in 1750, shortly after a troupe of actresses visited him, from what his doctor called *"un exces de femmes"* and what his biographer called "an end only a shade less glorious to a Frenchman than death in action — a very acceptable second-best."

Unfortunately for young Maurice, his birth came within a few days of that of the legitimate heir to his father's throne. Noble bastards were by no means unacceptable in polite society, but Saxe had to make his own way in the world. He started early, entering the Saxon army as a cadet at the age of twelve.

His introduction to the military came at a field army review. At Luetzen, where Gustavus Adophus, King of Sweden, had fallen eighty years before, General von der Schulenburg presented Saxe to his battalion, kissed him on both cheeks and proclaimed:

I should like this battlefield to be a happy augury for you. May you inherit the spirit of the great man who died here. Let all your actions be inspired by his gentleness, severity, and justice. Never relax discipline in the slightest degree, even when prompted by friendship. Above all, be sure that your personal conduct is above reproach, for that is the only way to insure respect.

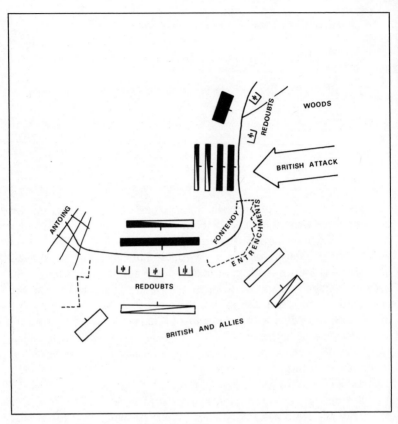

The Battle of Fontenoy, May 11, 1745

On the following day the Saxon army broke camp and marched off to war. Schulenberg joined the Duke of Marlborough and Prince Eugene of Savoy, who were assembling forces for an invasion of France.

Saxe's baptism of fire came in 1709 at Malplaquet, the bloodiest battle of the War of the Spanish Succession. In that contest, Louis XIV entrusted his last reserves to Marshal Claude de Villars, who lost the battle, but inflicted such casualties on his opponents that he won the war. After the fight, Villars wrote to his sovereign, "Sire, should God grant your enemies another such victory, they are surely destroyed."

Saxe brooded on that battle for twenty years. How well he had learned the lessons of that engagement would become apparent in 1745 at Fontenoy, where Saxe, now fighting for the French, won the last great victory of French arms before the revolution.

Maurice took part in four campaigns, and when the War of the Spanish Succession ended in 1714 he was in command of a cavalry regiment. Looking for more action, he set off with Prince Eugene to fight the Turks. With the Austrian imperial army, Saxe went down the Danube and campaigned to expand the Habsburg control into southeastern Europe. He spent several years there and thoroughly learned his trade.

That war having burned itself out, Saxe returned to Paris. He had now seen warfare at first-hand, and he settled down to study it. For a time he lived on the fringe of royal society. He existed by his wits, an unemployed professional soldier out of place in peacetime. He read widely, had numerous love affairs, ran into debt, and drifted.

In 1725 his reputation as a soldier brought him the offer of a throne. Accepting it, he reigned over the Duchy of Courland for four years, struggling constantly against Russians and Poles. Lack of funds finally forced him to abdicate. Back in Paris in 1730, he was again without a job. During these inactive and seemingly useless years he conceived and wrote his treatise on warfare, the work that lifted him above his times and established him as a military thinker.

In 1733, when the War of the Polish Succession opened, Saxe was appointed a lieutenant general in the French army. In 1734 he distinguished himself at the conquest of Philippsburg, the great Habsburg fortress, by driving off a relieving force under his old tutor Eugene. Saxe's future seemed bright, but to his chagrin the war came to a close. Once more an unemployed soldier, he relieved his boredom by dissipation and debauchery.

The War of the Austrian Succession in 1740 changed all that. Saxe was now ready to become France's foremost soldier. He first commanded the French forces moving into Bohemia. With his usual skill and luck, he launched a surprise assault and stormed the city of Prague. Capturing a fortified city in the eighteenth century without the painstaking intricacies of siege warfare was a minor miracle. But keeping his troops from raping and plundering was even more miraculous. The citizens were duly grateful and rewarded him handsomely for holding his men in check. Louis XV named him a marshal, remarkable testimony from a Catholic monarch to the military prowess of an illegitimate Lutheran Saxon.

Marshal Saxe was at the height of his powers in 1745. Louis XV nominally commanded the French army in the Low Countries, but his duties consisted of such matters as selecting the daily password. Saxe was really in command. Moving against British-Dutch forces led by the Duke of Cumberland, Saxe besieged the city of Tournai. Cumberland led an army to relieve Tournai, and Saxe met him at Fontenoy.

At the head of 50,000 men, the flower of the French army, Saxe took up positions and awaited the attack of 50,000 British and Dutch. He established two wings, one at a right angle to the other. He placed his reserve in the center behind the angle. Ahead of his front line he built redoubts, a technique learned from his experience at Malplaquet and from his study of Poltava, where Peter the Great had defeated the Swedes in 1709. The opposition battered against these redoubts for hours and finally broke through. Cumberland penetrated the French main line too. But he had by then lost half of his battalions, and when Saxe committed his reserve, he drove the British and Dutch from the battlefield.

Saxe was ill from dropsy during the battle of Fontenoy. Too feeble to mount a horse, he commanded from a litter. Louis XV, together with his entourage, had withdrawn from the scene of carnage, but after the action subsided he returned to congratulate his commander. At the point of exhaustion, Saxe waved languidly to the heaps of dead and wounded. "And so you see, sire," he said, "the fruits of victory."

There were other fruits as well. The British retreated and the

French picked up towns and fortresses all over the Netherlands. In the following year, proving that Fontenoy was no accident, Saxe beat the Allies at Roucoux. Two years later, bringing the war to a close he took the great fortress of Maastricht.

By then he was marshal general of France, the first to hold the title since Henri Turenne, who had been killed more than a half century earlier by a cannon ball at Sasbach. Saxe accepted the high rank with the words, "You have made me the equal of Turenne; it but remains for me to die as he did."

He died instead in the strikingly beautiful chateau of Chambord along the Loire that Louis had given him to occupy for as long as he lived. To the last, his appetites for women, wine, and war remained great. Just before he died he said, "I see that life is but a dream; mine has been a beautiful one, and a short one."

The eighteenth century was, with a few exceptions, an era of "indecisive decisions." Had Maurice de Saxe been no more than a conventionally successful professional soldier, he would now be left to the antiquarians. Yet it is precisely because he recognized the military shortcomings of his day that he continues to be known not only as a great practitioner of the art of war, but also as one of its foremost theorists. As he studied the campaigns and captains of the past, Maurice was infuriated by the sterility of combat. He concluded that the military system of the time needed a thorough overhaul.

Armies were raised from the dregs of society, the economically useless, men who would desert at a moment's opportunity. Logistically, armed forces were tied to the speed of advance of a bullock — less than nine miles a day. Tactically, they maneuvered in closely disciplined and rigid formations. Technologically, their weapons were inferior in firepower to the medieval longbow. Strategy was a matter of taking towns, and towns were traded back and forth when one side or the other went bankrupt and had to make peace. War was a sport of kings and as formal as a minuet.

The distillation of Maurice's thought was a slim volume appropriately entitled *Mes Reveries* (*My Dreams*). He told the reader: "I wrote this book in thirteen nights. I was sick; thus it very probably shows the fever I had. This should supply my excuses for the irregularity of the arrangement, as well as for the inelegance of the style. I wrote militarily and to dissipate my boredom. Done in the month of December 1732."

It was indeed a peculiar work. Thomas Carlyle, who delivered snap judgments with an air of finality, called it "a strange military farrago, undoubtedly written under the influence of opium." A more balanced assessment was Captain Sir Basil Liddell Hart's. He said of Saxe: "As a military thinker and prophet his outlook was so original, his expression so unfettered by convention, that his writings enjoy a perennial freshness and appeal to the modern spirit of scientific inquiry."

Above all, Saxe brought a fresh mind to the problems of war. He found warfare a process suported by "custom and prejudice, confirmed by ignorance." He proposed — in almost every aspect of military endeavor — changes that were startlingly new when brought into existence generations later. Without being an "ideologue," as Napoleon called one who was filled with impractical ideas, Saxe offered a complete reform of warfare.

Technologically, he wished to have less cumbersome cannons and muskets, weapons that were breech-loaded, and he pushed for improvements. He invented a small artillery piece termed an *amusette* that gave close support to the infantry; the combatants in the American Revolution would call them "galloper guns," and Napoleon would add them to his battalions in his later years when the quality of his troops declined.

Saxe disliked the uniforms then in style. They were designed primarily for show rather than for fighting. It was not so much the colors to which he objected; they were useful for identification and they supplemented the identifying flags each unit carried in action. Rather, Saxe was bothered by cross-belts, which constricted a soldier's chest and cut his breathing. He detested the manner of carrying the sword, which banged about the legs and tripped men. He had distaste for hats that blew off in the breeze and disintegrated in the rain.

Far ahead of his contemporaries, Saxe recognized the extent to which material conditions affected soldier morale. He wanted troops to eat in regular company messes. This would provide them with hot food. It would also strengthen the sense of identification of each man with his unit and his companions. He wanted soldiers when in barracks to sleep in beds, not to be billeted in taverns or assigned two and three to a stall in a barn as was the custom.

The best way to improve armies, he felt, was to make the military profession attractive. He deplored trickery and kidnaping, the usual methods of obtaining men for the ranks, and he advocated a system of conscription that would make every young citizen liable for military service and make his obligation an honor to fulfill. Not since the Romans had this view been advanced. Although the idea was unacceptable in the eighteenth century, it was adopted several generations later, and the Duke of Wellington would write that the French soldiers were of better stock and in better health than his own.

Once he had his soldiers, Saxe proposed to treat them well. His attitudes on discipline, drill, and tactics came to fruition in the Napoleonic era. A strong disciplinarian, who believed that everything was possible with steady and well-trained troops, he was anything but a slavish drillmaster. He wanted to have his men able to march well. "The foundation of training," he wrote, "depends on the legs and not the arms. All the mystery of maneuvers and combats is in the legs, and it is to legs that we should apply ourselves. Whoever claims otherwise is a fool."

Tactically, Saxe favored skirmishers and light infantry. He sought to deliver attacks in column, that is, in depth. He distrusted volley fire, for he was convinced that men required to hold their pieces until commanded to shoot would have poor aim.

He tried to remodel his army into smaller units. Most forces marched in two or three "wings," with infantry on one road, cavalry on another, and guns on a third. To bring two opposing armies to battle required virtually a mutual agreement by the commanders. To make armies flexible, Saxe advocated what led to the modern divisional system. He argued for units of combined arms. He saw the advantages in units composed of horse and foot operating together. This led the French, a generation later, after the Seven Years' War, to employ light infantry formations consisting of mixed horse and foot elements. Instead of having regiments known by the names of their colonels, Saxe would give them unit numbers, which would provide continuity and raise morale. Each man would have a unit insignia, and Saxe went so far as to suggest marking a soldier's regimental number indelibly on his hands.

When he dealt with cavalry, he was eloquent in his scorn. Cavalry was useless, he said, because "of the love we have for fat horses."

He wanted his cavalry to be pared to the bone, horse and man alike, for only then could they endure privation and have the stamina to conquer. In his own day, cavalry tended to be gorgeous and heavy to the point of immobility. Saxe wished his troops to be light and rugged, ready to scout and to pursue the vanquished, for he recognized that a devastating pursuit truly gathered in the fruits of victory.

His thoughts culminated in his observations on generalship. Describing the virtues needed by a general, he said: "The first of all qualities is courage. Without this the others are of little value, since they cannot be used. The second is intelligence, which must be strong and fertile in expedients. The third is health."

Describing a general's duties, Saxe wrote:

> The functions of a general are infinite. He must know how to subsist his army and how to husband it; how to place it so that he will not be forced to fight except when he chooses; how to form his troops in an infinity of different dispositions; how to profit from that favorable moment which occurs in all battles and which decides their success.

To be able to do all this well, a general had to keep himself from becoming immersed in unimportant details. The routine had to be left to subordinates. Nor should a commander become so carried away by excitement that he throw away his ability to direct. Saxe cited a battle where Marshal Villars lost his temper, seized a pike, and plunged into the midst of the fighting. Villars performed prodigies but was defeated. What he had done was best left to the sergeants. Finally, a general always had to be aware of the importance of morale. As Saxe knew well, not all men were brave and, if a general wished success, even the bravest soldiers had to be willing, even anxious, to fight the enemy.

Mes Reveries was published in 1757, twenty-five years after Saxe wrote it and five years after he died. To us, and probably more to his contemporaries, the book recalls the man: creative, bold, aggressive. To a large extent, the teachings of Saxe were overshadowed by the career and accomplishments of Frederick the Great, who was responsible (along with others before and after him) for the dictum, "God is on the side of the big battalions." Until 1918 soldiers generally believed and accepted that statement. Only afterward did they appreciate what Saxe had said: "It is not the big armies that win battles; it is the good ones."

Clive

HE SEEMED hardly prepared for military service, this unstable melancholy man; hardly destined for fame and glory. Yet events conspired to place him in the right situation at the right time, and through force of character and innate ability he became "the first and greatest of the English *conquistadores.*" A valiant and inspiring leader in combat, he was a military administrator and statesman as well. This combination of qualities enabled him both to win an empire on the battlefield and to hold it together at the political seat of power. He was no less a manager than a tactician, no less an organizer than a strategist. No soldier could desire more than these virtues.

Robert Clive was born in Shropshire, England, in 1725, of an old and established family. His father was a member of Parliament for many years. He himself was an unruly youngster, showing aggressive rebelliousness, extreme moodiness, and alternating periods of high spirits and inner depression. Because of his temper, he attended, and departed from, several schools in quick succession. Finally, since education failed to interest him and boyhood pranks got him into trouble, the family enrolled Clive at the age of eighteen as a bookkeeper-clerk in the East India Company.

At this time three European states were exploiting India — Portugal, which had passed its peak and was now restricted to several small areas; France and England, which were just beginning their great battle for political and economic domination of the subcontinent. The ancient Mogul Empire was disintegrating, and British and French traders, who inevitably became involved in local quarrels, found that their technology and discipline transformed them from auxiliaries to principals, from hangers-on to masters.

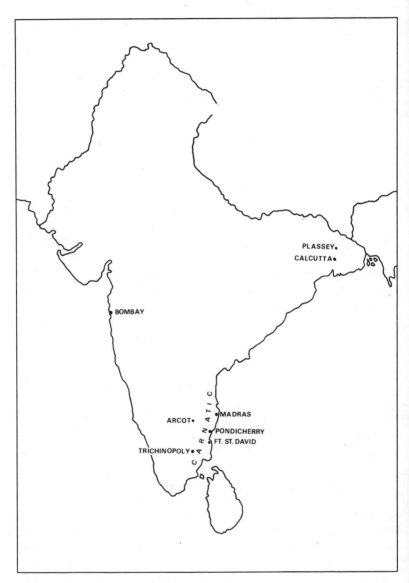

India in the days of Robert Clive

The competing instruments, the French Compagnie des Indes and the British East India Company, were remarkably alike. They were business organizations sustained by the capital of private investors. They received the support of their governments in the form of naval and ground forces. Both had the prerogatives of near-sovereign states, with their own private armies to maintain order and diplomatic representatives to maintain relations with native states. In their search for profit and power, both nurtured and manipulated indigenous conflicts.

As a civilian member of the company at the lowest level, Clive was sent to Madras, the headquarters of operations in southeast India. Perhaps the climate and the boredom exacerbated his bad temper; he fought duels and twice attempted suicide. Between bouts of melancholia and overexuberance, he discovered the books of the governor's library, a sizable collection of historical volumes, including military writings, and the hours Clive spent reading during three years gave him the education he had earlier rejected.

Now twenty-one, he was about to find his vocation. The larger setting was the growing Anglo-French rivalry. The immediate impulse was the War of the Austrian Succession, which sent a tremor beyond the dynastic struggle in Europe to the imperial conflict on the fringes of the civilized world. In previous wars between their countries the rival companies had remained neutral. Now the British refused to do so. As the European enemies met in combat in Bengal, the Deccan, and the Carnatic, the French marched on Madras and forced the British to surrender.

The British population of the station was interned, but Clive and others escaped just before the capitulation. Suddenly aroused by the reality of the imperial confrontation, Clive volunteered for military service. Since he was of a good family and had the proper social status, he was offered and accepted a commission as an ensign. In this capacity he campaigned against the French, participated in several battles, and distinguished himself at Pondichéry, the main outpost of the French empire. He thereby learned the trade of soldiering, and it fascinated him.

When the Treaty of Aix-la-Chapelle temporarily ended the hostilities, Clive continued his military career in the service of the company. He was appointed a captain of commissary, his task to supply provisions to the troops. In that position, as was customary at that time and place, he began to "shake the pagoda tree," that is, to make his private fortune. Though the accumulation of money interested and enticed him, the recurring clashes between the French and British East India companies brought him back to active campaigning.

Each company sponsored and supported different candidates for the post of nawab, or native ruler, of the Carnatic. The company that succeeded in establishing its prince in power would obviously benefit from the resulting trade concessions. In 1751 the simmering rivalry boiled over into open war. Chanda Sahib, the French choice, marched an army of his native troops to Trichinopoly, the capital of the British nominee, Mohammed Ali, who, with his own native forces and a small British garrison, found himself surrounded and besieged. If the British were to maintain their prestige — already lower than that of the French — and the credibility of their support, they would have to march to the rescue.

Unfortunately for British aspirations, Major Stringer Lawrence, the commander of the armed forces in the area, was temporarily in England on leave. In this situation, Clive offered to lead an expedition overland to break the siege of Trichinopoly. It was an arduous task, but there appeared no other choice. The company officials made available to Clive 200 European and 300 Indian troops, and three small cannons. With this miniature army, Clive moved quickly, not to Trichinopoly, but to Arcot, the capital of Chanda Sahib. Taking the city, Clive sought to divert the enemy's forces from Trichinopoly, a classic example of Liddell Hart's "indirect approach."

The diversion succeeded. Chanda dispatched his son Raja Sahib at the head of 10,000 men to Arcot, where they occupied the city and invested the fort in which Clive had taken refuge. The state of siege lasted for fifty days. It reduced Clive's combat effectives to 120 Europeans and 200 Sepoys, but they managed to hold the fort's mile of ruinous walls.

Finally, Raja Sahib assaulted, his men driving a herd of elephants ahead of them. The animals, their heads armed with iron plates, were supposed to batter down the gates of the fort and let the troops swarm in and overwhelm the defenders. Instead, the elephants panicked when they come under Clive's musket fire. Turning and stampeding, they disrupted the attack. Raja mounted a second assault, this time without the elephants, but it failed too. The entire attack had lasted an hour, and at the end Raja had lost 400 men, Clive half a dozen. This feat of arms broke the Raja's campaign against Arcot. His native forces lost heart and dispersed. Although Chanda's forces continued to besiege Trichinopoly, Clive's victory electrified the British at Madras, and they sent reinforcements to Arcot.

Emerging from the city, Clive waged mobile warfare against the French and their native troops, trying to mop up the rest of Raja's forces. Major Lawrence returned to India, raised and assembled more troops, and, with Clive's help, lifted the siege of Trichinopoly.

These campaigns broke the power of the French in the Carnatic. The victories were more moral than physical, but now the British had the ascendancy. A truce in 1754 established Mohammed Ali as nawab, and the Treaty of Paris nine years later confirmed his power and that of his supporters, the British.

Meanwhile, reports of Clive's brilliant capture and defense of Arcot had traveled to Europe. Clive became well known as a warrior, and when he returned home in 1753, at twenty-eight, he was called by the prime minister, William Pitt, a "heaven-born general." The company voted to present him with a sword worth 700 pounds sterling, but he let it be known that he would refuse the gift unless Lawrence received a similar honor.

Clive ran for Parliament, but when he lost the election he decided to return to India. Commissioned a lieutenant colonel in the British Army rather than in the company forces, he was appointed governor of Fort St. David, a stronghold near Madras. He sailed for India in 1755 at the head of several hundred replacements.

On the way to Madras, the ships transporting Clive put in at Bombay. The authorities there were impressed with Clive's reputation and with the troops accompanying him. They asked if, before continuing his voyage, he would take action against a band of pirates operating in the area. Clive assented, planned an assault on the pirate stronghold, the port of Gheriah, and then led his troops against it. His attack was successful, and he destroyed the pirate haven.

Clive reached Fort St. David in June 1756, the same month that serious trouble broke out in Calcutta. The nawab, Suraja Dowlah, sometimes called Siraj-ud-Daula, besieged Calcutta, which had been established by the British and had become the most valuable trading center in Bengal. Suraja quickly seized the town and plundered it. Most of the English population escaped by fleeing aboard ships in the harbor, but one hundred and forty-six persons were captured and herded into a small underground cell used for prisoners and called the Black Hole. Only twenty-three would eventually emerge alive.

On receiving news of the outburst, Clive organized a relief expedition composed of 900 European and 1500 Indian troops under his command. Transported by Admiral Sir Charles Watson's fleet, Clive sailed from Madras in October. Because of contrary winds, it was December before they reached Bengal. The troops debarked a short distance below Calcutta and invested the city while Watson bombarded it. Forcing his way in, Clive liberated the handful of English prisoners still alive and then went on to clear the city.

The complete defeat and punishment of Suraja remained to be accomplished. In February, at the head of a force numbering 600 British soldiers, 500 sailors, and 800 Sepoys, with seven guns, Clive met and routed the nawab's army of 34,000 men, fifty elephants, and forty cannons. This decisive victory restored peace and the British East India Company's privileges.

The peace was temporary. The French remained strong, and Suraja seemed attracted to them. Clive determined that both the nawab and the French must be destroyed. He planned his campaign carefully. First, he struck the French settlement of Chandernagor. He sent warships to bombard the town while he opened siege operations. After some spirited fighting, Clive overran the place. This not only hurt the French, but it also eliminated a threat to Clive's lines of communication. With his supply line from Calcutta now secure, Clive marched inland in search of Suraja. He found the nawab near the village of Plassey.

Suraja had an army of more than 50,000 men, infantry and cavalry, entrenched behind the Bhagirathi River. Supporting these troops were fifty-five guns manned by professional French artillerymen.

Clive had 1100 European and 2100 native soldiers and ten guns. He also had the nawab's second-in-command, Mir Jaffir, in his pocket, having bribed him, though the man had not yet delivered. Clive crossed the river without hesitation and took up his position in a mango grove. The nawab's force, formed in a semicircle, moved to surround Clive. Suddenly a violent rainstorm swept the field. The French gunners, who had been firing, stopped because their powder was wet. When the nawab ordered a cavalry charge, his horsemen reached the British positions before Clive's men, who had just had time to cover their powder from the rain, drove them back with heavy casualties.

Clive advanced his forces toward the nawab, who then launched an infantry attack. This too was repulsed by the steady fire of the British. Clive moved in for the kill and swept the nawab's army from the field. As his troops scattered and fled, Mir Jaffir and his followers came over to Clive's side, this being their only contribution to the battle. The French gunners fought valiantly as long as they could.

The battle of Plassey made Clive and the British company masters of Bengal. Suraja was assassinated a few days later, and Clive's hand-picked ally, Mir Jaffir, was installed as the new nawab.

Now firmly established with the reputation as one of the leading soldiers in the world, Clive was appointed by the company as governor of Bengal in 1758. For two years he enhanced the authority of Mir Jaffir, led minor military expeditions against the French, made money for the company, and pocketed a fortune for himself.

With the company's affairs prospering and his own health in decline, Clive returned to England. He received an Irish peerage, a knighthood, and a seat in Parliament.

Five years later the company's position in India had deteriorated and was approaching bankruptcy because of mismanagement and graft. Some writers have attributed part of the company's decline, at least indirectly, to Clive, asserting with some justice that it was increasingly corrupted by his conquest. In any event, Clive was asked to go out to Calcutta as governor and commander in chief. In two years he restored fiscal discipline, curtailed legal and administrative abuses, and reorganized the army.

With the company again enjoying prosperity, Clive departed. But in the absence of his firm control, corruption once more became common and debilitating to the company's general financial position. When in 1772 the East India Company was forced to appeal to the British government for subsidies to save it from collapse, Clive's enemies in Parliament charged that he was responsible.

There was a long trial, which finally exonerated Clive. Parliament voted the resolution that, although he had personally enriched himself during his years of service — a practice that was accepted so long as the amassing of wealth was neither too blatant nor too avaricious — he had rendered "great and meritorious services to his country." Clive himself, after enumerating the opportunities placed in his way for personal profit, burst out: "By God, Mr. Chairman, at this moment I stand astonished at my own moderation!"

Despite the verdict of not guilty, political opponents continued to attack Clive's personal integrity. Physically exhausted and sick, tormented again by the extreme moodiness and depression he had suffered in his youth, not yet fifty years old, he committed suicide in 1774.

Slightly above average height, erect and with a commanding presence, Clive had "a certain rough-hewn, almost elemental force and a tireless energy." He died at the peak of his maturity and on the eve of the American War of Independence. It is intriguing to speculate on what he might have done in the American Revolution. His performance in India was more than sufficient to place his impress on his age. He had checked the French ambitions in India while extending British power, and his achievements, both military and administrative, laid the foundations for British rule for the next two centuries. He was unquestionably one of the greatest soldiers of his day and one of the great natural soldiers of all time. Untutored by formal military education, uninstructed except by the realities of the situation in which he found himself, he acted boldly, grasped victory, and with it "the brightest jewel in the British crown."

Thomas

BY-PASSED and overlooked during the Civil War centennial orgies a decade ago, George H. Thomas is finally, a century after his death, being belatedly recognized as one of the great soldiers of United States military history. This would hardly have surprised Slow Trot, as his contemporaries called him; indeed, he would have found it entirely typical.

A ponderous, deliberate man, Thomas could never be rushed. General U. S. Grant once relieved him of command for refusing to act before he was ready. Yet his sense of timing was always vindicated. The despair of hurry-up seniors and subordinates alike, he struck like a hammer at the right moment. Slow as he was, fame came even more slowly. It has never really caught up with his talents.

George Henry Thomas was born in Southampton County, Virginia, in 1816, the descendant of Welsh, English, and French Huguenot settlers. As a young boy he studied at the local academy, then began to read for the law. Appointed to the Military Academy, he graduated in 1840, twelfth in a class of forty-two that included William T. Sherman and Richard S. Ewell. To classmates he was Old Tom, the first of a formidable list of nicknames delineating the eccentricities of his character.

His career as a young officer carried him to the southern and western frontiers. As a second lieutenant in the 3d Artillery, he went on field service in the Seminole War. He participated in operations for two years and earned a brevet promotion for gallantry in action. The list of his associates reads like a *dramatis personae* of the Civil War. For many students today, the intrinsic interest of the army's history

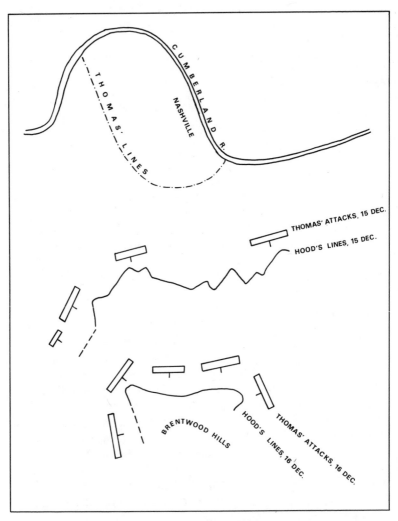

The Battle of Nashville, December 15–16, 1864

from 1820 to 1860 lies in the coming conflict, and their interest consists of watching future great men mature in out-of-the-way posts and campaigns.

After several years of garrison duty in the south, Thomas received his first lieutenant's commission in 1844. Not long thereafter, together with most members of the small U.S. Army, he was off to Mexico, attached to Braxton Bragg's battery of artillery serving with Major General Zachary Taylor. (Bragg would become a general in the Confederate Army.). Thomas followed Bragg and Taylor through the Mexican War. He was breveted captain for heroism at Monterrey and major for bravery at Buena Vista.

After Mexico came more service in Florida, then a three-year tour at West Point as instructor in artillery and cavalry. By this time Thomas had his regular captaincy. He next spent a year at Fort Yuma, in Arizona Territory.

In 1855, giving up the red stripe of the artillery, he accepted an appointment as major in the newly raised 2d Cavalry. The regiment, later renumbered the 5th Cavalry, was a breeding ground of generals. Albert Sidney Johnston was the colonel, Robert E. Lee the lieutenant colonel, William J. Hardee (who had studied at the French cavalry school at Saumur and was to write the famous book on tactics) was the second major. Other officers were George Stoneman (later a Union general) and John B. Hood, Fitzhugh Lee, and Earl Van Dorn, all of whom would be distinguished generals of the Confederacy.

Thomas joined his regiment at Jefferson Barracks, then went down with it to Texas for garrison duty along the Mexican border. For four years he did much exploring and mapping; his experience as an artilleryman proved to be useful in surveying and drafting. During one of his exploring missions through unknown territory Thomas was hit in the face by an Indian arrow. To recover from his wound, he was granted twelve months of leave on November 1, 1860. He returned to the east.

Before the year was out, the Union had split apart. A Virginian by birth, Thomas had married in the north. Like so many fellow officers, he faced the agonizing decision of which government to serve. Unlike so many of his colleagues, Thomas renounced his loyalty to his state and accepted the broader loyalty to his country.

Despite suspicion in some quarters over his being a Virginian, Thomas rose rapidly in the expanding Union Army. Returning to active duty in April 1861, he became a colonel a month later. He commanded a brigade in the early, groping attempts to make war in the Shenandoah Valley, and then was sent to organize and train new troops in Kentucky.

In November he took command of the 1st Division of the Army of the Ohio. Two months later he had the distinction of winning the first battle in which federal troops were well handled. At Mill Springs (also called Fishing Creek) in Kentucky, on January 19, 1862, Thomas severely defeated Major General George B. Crittenden's Southerners and drove them out of the southeastern part of the state.

The forces on both sides were still gathering strength and flexing their muscles in 1862. No clear-cut strategy had as yet emerged, particularly in the western theater, and the armies flailed wildly and stumbled in their efforts. During that summer Thomas served under Major General Don Carlos Buell, under Major General Henry W. Halleck, and under Buell again, in operations in central Kentucky that were largely indecisive. In September, when Buell was relieved a second time for ordering a retreat and Thomas was instructed to replace him, Thomas declined the command. He argued that Buell, having made his dispositions, had again ordered an advance; his removal, therefore, was invalid. This argument provoked some consternation in Washington. The government and the high command, apparently applying standards in Kentucky that they did not apply in Virginia, expected instant success. Furthermore, although Thomas' sense of ethics, justice, and loyalty to his commander should have been regarded as exemplary, the War Department's version was colored by Thomas' Virginian origins.

A month later, when Buell was succeeded by Major General William S. Rosecrans, Thomas protested this too. His ground for complaint was that Rosecrans was junior in rank to him. President Lincoln, who sometimes became impatient with the military mind at work, responded by antedating Rosecrans' commission and making him senior to Thomas. It was not to be the last mistake Lincoln would make in selecting commanders.

Having made his protest and been answered, Thomas settled down as a loyal subordinate in command of the XIV Corps of the Army of the Cumberland, as it finally came to be called. He played a major role in the battle of Stones River (or Murfreesboro) at the turn of the year. Indeed, he was the chief reason why Rosecrans could claim a victory there, and Rosecrans received the thanks of Congress for his skill.

Through the early months of 1863, while Grant in the west was moving toward Vicksburg, Rosecrans dithered his way toward Chattanooga. The city was of immense strategic importance, but Rosecrans dallied. Even Halleck, who was not noted for speed, tried to get him to act. The only result, as Halleck put it, was "heavy expense for telegrams." Finally, however, Rosecrans moved. He brilliantly maneuvered Bragg out of Chattanooga, then walked into a trap. This was the occasion that would make Thomas' name.

On September 19, Bragg with 60,000 men pounced on the 65,000 troops Rosecrans had dispersed along the banks of Chickamauga Creek. The blow hit Thomas. He withstood it while the rest of the Army of the Cumberland moved to support him. The next day the Confederates came on again — westerners and Lieutenant General James Longstreet's men from Virginia. When a gap opened in the federal line because of misunderstood orders, the Rebels promptly drove into it. The whole right wing of the Union Army collapsed, and Thomas' corps was bent back in horseshoe form. Rosecrans and his headquarters were carried away in the rout. Although the Confederates turned their attention then to Thomas, they battered in vain against his weary soldiers. All through a long summer afternoon the gray columns came on, but without success. At the end of the day Thomas had earned the name that is forever attached to him: the Rock of Chickamauga.

Some Southern commanders maintained that Chickamauga broke the heart of the Confederacy as Vicksburg broke its back. After Chickamauga they would never again regard Union troops with the comfortable sense of superiority that so often in the past had carried them to victory against heavy odds.

The Union learned something too. The army finally realized the value of George H. Thomas, who was promoted to brigadier general in the Regular Army, as distinct from the U.S. Volunteers (which in later wars was called the Army of the United States), and who was appointed commander of the Army of the Cumberland. The day the order elevating him to the command was read out on parade, his troops broke ranks and mobbed him ecstatically. The rear-rank private had long known what Washington had just discovered.

It was perhaps unfortunate for Thomas' career that, just at the point when he reached independent command, the Union forces at last gained an overall leader. Had Thomas not been so scrupulous in his earlier respect for Buell, he might well have ended up in the chief command. As it was, Grant was now designated for that post.

Thomas, holding on to Chattanooga and under siege by the Rebels, was ordered to hold the city at all costs. He replied that he would do so until his army starved. It was already close to starvation, but Thomas managed to hang on for almost two months. After being delayed by bad weather, relief arrived in November. Yet it remained for Thomas to provide most of his own salvation. When Sherman's troops were unable to seize Lookout Mountain, Thomas converted his holding attack into the main effort. He took the objective in a frontal assault. A considerable feat, it was but a prelude, for the next day his men scaled and seized the supposedly unassailable heights of Missionary Ridge. That brought the battle to a victorious close.

As 1864 opened, the war began to move toward a climax. Grant went east to pursue Lee to the death. In the west, Sherman took over-all command, with Thomas, Joseph Hooker, and John M. Schofield under him. Instructed to cut the Confederacy in half again, Sherman eventually did so. He became so obsessed with this part of his mission that he allowed the western Rebel armies to escape him.

During Sherman's advance on Atlanta, Thomas' Army of the Cumberland provided well over half of the numbers in Sherman's forces, made every offensive move, and broke the last stand of the Rebel defense at Peachtree Creek near Atlanta. The bluecoats of his command were the first troops into Atlanta.

Thomas then suggested that his army should march for the sea. Instead, Sherman went that way. Thomas was left to face the Confederate Army of John B. Hood, who had slid westward after the fall of Atlanta. While Sherman disappeared into the heart of the Confederacy, Thomas held Nashville. Hood marched north, and in early December he besieged Thomas' army.

Hood's plan was rather rudimentary. When Thomas emerged to attack his siege lines, Hood would counterattack and defeat him. Exactly how remained to be seen.

Thomas proposed to oblige by attacking, but only when he was ready. First, he made it his business to see that his cavalry was properly mounted. This took time and Grant fumed. He himself was stalled before Petersburg and the government was demanding action. Grant ordered Thomas to mount a full-scale offensive at once and then directed Schofield to replace him. Before the order could be carried out, Thomas was ready and the order was rescinded. Then came the blizzard and with it more delay. There were also complaints about his leadership and even the old hints questioning his loyalty. Grant sent Major General John A. Logan to relieve Thomas. But before Logan arrived, Thomas moved. On the first day he drove Hood's men out of their entrenchments and routed one corps. On the second day he broke up two more of Hood's corps. The Confederate Army of Tennessee disintegrated as a fighting force.

Chased by Union cavalry into Mississippi by Christmas, Hood asked to be relieved of his command. He was accommodated, and the war in the middle states was all but over by the end of the year. Thomas received the thanks of Congress for Nashville and promotion to major general in the Regular Army.

After the war, Thomas remained for some years in command of the region he had fought over. He administered justly and wisely. When in 1868 President Andrew Johnson sent his name to the Senate for promotion to the brevet grades of lieutenant general and general, Thomas believed the move to be a political one. Seeing it as an attempt to clip Grant's wings — that is, to offset Grant's political ambitions — Thomas declined. His grounds were that his postwar service did not merit such promotion, and that it was too late to be acceptable as a reward for war service.

Urged also that year to run for the presidency, he refused that as well. Grant ran instead. It might have been better for the subsequent reputations of both men, and of the presidency, had Thomas become President instead of Grant.

In June 1869, Thomas took command of the Military District of the Pacific. He died there on active service on March 28, 1870.

A splendid physical figure, Thomas stood six feet tall and weighed 200 pounds. He wore a full beard in the fashion of the day and was always neatly dressed. He was extremely conscious of the appearance of his troops, and he often remarked that the fate of a battle might depend on the condition of a belt buckle. He was also extremely solicitous of his troops' welfare. Although Sherman stripped his army to the bone for the advance to the sea, Thomas insisted on taking his supply wagons with him. His troops loved him as they did few other generals in the Civil War, especially on the Union side. They came to cherish even his peculiarities. His nicknames were legion but none was unkind. To the Army of the Cumberland, he was their own "Pap" Thomas, who would take care of them.

He did, too. Grant was sometimes called a butcher. Sherman made wasteful frontal assaults. Even Lee can be faulted for a few costly and fruitless attacks. This cannot be said of Thomas. There is no instance in which he ever threw away the lives of his men, expending them in useless battle.

If that were his only claim to fame, it would be sufficient to mark him from most generals. But there was more to him than that. Throughout the war, Thomas evinced a high degree of competence. He was a major contributor to the success of operations wherever he fought.

To some extent, the area where he operated militated against his fame. The campaigns in the middle states have always been regarded as a sideshow. Popular interest has rather been riveted on the great struggle in the east between the Army of the Potomac and the Army of Northern Virginia. Secondary interest has gone to the west, to the epic attempts to control the Mississippi, culminating in the great operations against Vicksburg. Only late in the war did the central area gain prominence, and then it was dominated by Sherman's Atlanta campaign and his march to the sea.

In spite of the secondary nature of Thomas' region, the central theater was a vital one, and Thomas' role was of major significance. Had he not been present to bolster such second-raters as Buell and Rosecrans, the middle states might have been lost. When Sherman arrived, Thomas provided the central boss of the shield around which Sherman wove his arabesques. Sherman himself put it more succinctly, saying once, "I wish Old Tom were here. He's my off-wheel horse." His dependability, coupled with Sherman's fiery genius, provided an almost unbeatable combination. Yet later, when Sherman had left for Savannah and no longer eclipsed him, Thomas alone directed and managed a classic battlefield operation at Nashville.

Steady and even-tempered, courteous and gentlemanly, Thomas never departed from the highest standards of public and personal conduct. Unswerving in his devotion to his country and to his duty, unsurpassed in his professional performance, Thomas was the personification of generalship in a period in United States military history that is notably distinguished for the quality of its leaders.

Huebner

CLARENCE RALPH HUEBNER personifies what will power, native intelligence, and natural aptitude — helped by luck and hard work — can do in the way of fashioning an outstanding military career. He started with two years of high school, four years of business college, and six years in the enlisted ranks; he retired after forty years of service as a lieutenant general, having been military governor of Germany and commander in chief of United States Forces in Europe. Of all the great American soldiers of the twentieth century, including many far better known to the public, none better exemplifies the fundamental strength of a citizen army in a democratic society — the career open to talent.

Like many middle-western Americans, Huebner was destined to make his mark fighting against his ancestral homeland. He was born of German Swabian stock; his grandfather had come to the United States immediately after the 1848 revolutions. In Germany he had protested against the practice of conscription and the renting out of German soldiers as mercenaries. In America he joined an Illinois volunteer regiment and served in the Civil War for his adopted country. This made him eligible to homestead, and after the war he took his family in two covered wagons to Kansas, where he became a successful farmer.

Young Clarence took a roundabout path to his own future career. He grew up in comfortable circumstances, went for eight years to the one-room schoolhouse in Bushton, and then went on to two years of high school. He then attended a business college in Grand Island, Nebraska, where he became an expert accountant, stenographer, and typist. These skills enabled him to obtain a position as a court reporter for the Chicago Burlington & Quincy Railroad. By the time he was twenty-two, he was a moderately successful young man with no place to go. His response to his situation seemed rather impulsive, even quixotic, in the thoroughly civilian and peaceful United States of 1910: he enlisted in the army.

For the ranks of the small and purse-starved Regular Army, Huebner was something of a catch. When he finished basic training at Fort Logan, Colorado, his company sergeant tried to keep him there because of his typing and administrative skills. Fortunately he escaped and reported to the 18th Infantry at Fort McKenzie, Wyoming, for field soldiering. Later he went down to the old southwest, to San Antonio and Galveston, and Douglas, Arizona. At these quiet frontier posts, while the world drifted on toward a war no one could imagine, he served as company clerk, mess sergeant, and supply sergeant. He was one of his regiment's most efficient soldiers, the best rifle shot, the most neatly dressed, the most attentive. He was also the regimental court reporter for every court-martial.

Huebner's intelligent devotion to duty soon attracted the attention of his officers, and he was asked whether he wanted to take the examinations for a commission. He was certainly interested, but his formal education seemed altogether deficient. However, officers from the regiment coached him, and with the help of Ephraim G. Peyton, William C. Rose, Wait C. Johnson, and Oscar W. Griswold — the latter would command a corps in World War II — Huebner passed his tests and was commissioned a second lieutenant of infantry in 1916. The first night he wore his bars, his company commander took him to the officers' club for dinner, where he was toasted and given a symbolic welcome by all the regimental officers. It was a scene that would probably have been possible in no other army in the world at that date, with the exception of the French.

Two months after his commissioning, Huebner was sent to Fort Leavenworth to attend the Infantry Service School. He completed the course in April 1917, just as America declared war against Germany. A month later he was on his way to France, in command of a rifle company of raw recruits in the 1st Division. All the United States had in those early months was manpower, and she threw it into the war so lavishly that it nearly swamped her small Regular Army. Huebner was promoted to captain for his new command, but it took months for the papers issued in Washington to catch up with him.

Landing in St. Nazaire with his green company, Huebner was given a few months, which he used feverishly to turn his men into soldiers. In November they took over a quiet sector of the line from the French at Lunéville, south of Nancy.

By the end of 1917 the Russians were collapsing. That winter the Germans were able to move men from the eastern to the western front, and the static conditions in France were soon to crumple under the impact of the German offensives of 1918, hammer blows aimed at winning the war before the Americans could make their weight felt on the field. Entering real combat as the war became mobile again, the Americans would have a far different experience from that of their exhausted allies. A generation later, when the defensive-minded French were collapsing, Huebner would be training units once more for mobile warfare.

In March of 1918 Huebner's company went into the Beaumont sector north of Toul. He himself was wounded and reported killed in action, but both he and his troops performed like veterans. A month later the recovered Huebner was again at the head of his company in the Cantigny area. When his battalion commander was killed he took command of the unit and performed the actions that brought him the Distinguished Service Cross:

> For three days . . . he withstood German assaults under intense bombardment, heroically exposing himself to fire constantly in order to command his battalion effectively, and although his command lost half its officers and 30 percent of its men, he held the position and prevented a break in the line at that point.

Promoted to major in June, Heubner was shifted to the Aisne-Marne front, where he was again wounded, and again cited for gallantry, this time near Soissons, and awarded the Oak Leaf Cluster to his Distinguished Service Cross.

Once more he recovered quickly, and returned to his command in time for the battle near Saizerais, action around Beaumont, the St.-Mihiel attack, and the Meuse-Argonne offensive. In October 1918 he was promoted to lieutenant colonel and given command of the 28th Infantry. Some of the majors in his regiment had been captains before the war, when he had been a sergeant.

Huebner's overall services in the Great War brought him the Distinguished Service Medal. He was one of the very few men to win this and to be twice awarded the Distinguished Service Cross. His gallantry, proficiency in command, and his rapid rise in grade made him a man to be remembered, one who had passed the test of courage. He was noticed by General John J. Pershing, who later sent him to Leavenworth somewhat ahead of his time — he was an honor graduate there — by Summerall, who pushed him toward the Army War College, by John L. Hines, who, when he was Army Chief of Staff, befriended Huebner. Hanson Ely and Frank Parker praised and helped him, and he drew favorable, and subsequently useful, notice from George C. Marshall. War service in France would be to the World War II generals what the Mexican War had been to Civil War generals. It was fortunate that Huebner had his; after the Armistice he served in Germany for a year on occupation duty, then returned to the United States in 1919, and a year later, with the rest of his contemporaries, reverted to his substantive rank of captain.

From the peaks of 1918, the U.S. Army descended to the quiet valleys of the twenties — and then to the deserts of the Depression. In these years Huebner matured his talents, attended his courses, and did his regimental duty. He was a member of the Infantry Board and served in the Office of the Chief of Infantry and with the 19th Infantry Regiment in Hawaii. In 1940 he was a colonel, and was posted as Chief of the Training Branch of the Office of the War Department General Staff; here he had much to do with the formation, organization, training, and indoctrination of armored units, then part of the infantry. In that year, when the United States began its first great peacetime expansion of the armed forces, and when German tanks were ripping the heart out of the French army, this was a crucial position.

Immediately after Pearl Harbor Huebner was named to command the Infantry Replacement Training Center at Camp Croft, South Carolina. He was soon brought to the Office of the Chief of Staff as a brigadier general, where he again attracted the favorable notice of General Marshall. He served for a year as Director of the Training Division of Army Service Forces headquarters in Washington, and for that tour of duty later received the Legion of Merit. His citation read:

By his outstanding ability and devotion to duty he contributed materially to the solution of the complex training problems of the United States Army.

Now a major general, Huebner was assigned in March 1943 to the North African Theater of Operations. He was scheduled to become Eisenhower's G–3 at Allied Forces Headquarters in Algiers, but instead he was named Deputy Chief of Staff to the British general Sir Harold R. L. G. Alexander. This appointment was made because of a sense of dissatisfaction in United States quarters over Alexander's handling of American troops. Formerly commander in chief of the British Middle East Theater, where he and Montgomery, his subordinate, had defeated Rommel at El Alamein and chased him across Libya, Alexander was appointed to serve under Eisenhower as the commander of the Allied ground forces in Tunisia. He assumed that command just at the height of the disaster of Kasserine Pass, and thus got an unfortunate introduction to the fighting qualities of the American soldier.

Seeing the new troops in a most unfavorable light when compared with the veterans of the British Eighth Army, Alexander was loath to give the Americans significant missions. During the planning for the Tunisian campaign he assigned them a decidedly subordinate role. It finally took a stern protest by Eisenhower to rectify the situation, as a result of which both the Americans and British shared the victory.

Huebner joined Alexander's staff to prevent further favoritism based on nationality and to provide a genuinely Allied outlook. The tacit understanding was that Alexander would consult with him before issuing directives concerning the United States units in his area. Huebner did not last long in this position. He embarrassed Alexander by coming in his quiet way to dominate the entire staff, and more particularly by being party to a certain incident.

It concerned the Sicily campaign, which had been planned so that Montgomery's Eighth Army could drive up the east coast of the island in the main effort to the strategic objective, Messina, while Patton's Seventh Army had the subsidiary task of protecting Montgomery's left flank. This in itself the Americans regarded as degrading. Then shortly after the invasion Montgomery talked Alexander into giving him the use of a road that had been reserved for Patton's forces. As a consequence, the 45th Division, on the Seventh Army's right flank, was squeezed left behind the 1st Division, then fighting its critical action around Gela.

The movement was difficult and could be dangerous; it seemed wholly unnecessary and it cut short the beginning of a decisive American drive into the interior. At best Alexander's action appeared to be thoughtless; at worst it was a deliberate slight to the Seventh Army.

There were protests from the United States commanders who were concerned, and Patton, Huebner, and Albert C. Wedemeyer went personally to see Alexander. The first two were part of the regular chain of command and were therefore constrained to moderation in their complaint. Wedemeyer, however, was in a particularly strong position. An important member of Marshall's Operations Division and close to the Chief of Staff, he happened to be in the theater on an inspection trip at the time of the invasion of Sicily. Since the 45th Division was participating in its first action, Wedemeyer went along to help. In an emergency he took command of a regiment and led it for several days, then became for a while assistant division commander.

Wedemeyer thus had first-hand and full knowledge of what the loss of the road meant to the 45th Division's operations. He was soon returning to Washington and would report to Marshall, who could take up the matter with the Combined Chiefs of Staff, so he was in a position to speak forcefully to Alexander about this instance of breaching Allied cooperation and mutual confidence. As unity among allies was the only thing more fragile than unit boundaries, Alexander acknowledged his failure to consult with Patton or Huebner before making his decision on the road. He said that he would do so in the future, but that this order would have to stand.

As a consequence simply of having been present at the conference and witnessing Wedemeyer's confrontation with Alexander, Huebner was placed in an impossible situation. Before long he was supplanted by Lyman L. Lemnitzer, who would remain with Alexander for the rest of the war. Subsequently, and to a large extent because of the performance of United States troops in Sicily, Alexander's exercise of command became completely impartial — Eisenhower would call him "broad-gauged." But Huebner was out of a job.

This turned out to be a lucky break. Huebner was free for reassignment at a time when Eisenhower, Patton, and Bradley were becoming dissatisfied with the way that Terry Allen and Theodore Roosevelt were handling the 1st Division. These two officers had built the unit into a magnificent outfit that had performed in outstanding fashion in North Africa and was now doing an equally good job in Sicily. But in their effort to develop morale and instill *ésprit,* they had gone perhaps too far, and discipline had deteriorated.

Early in August, after the taking of Troina in a week-long, hard-fought battle, the division was pulled out of the line for a rest. Allen and Roosevelt were both reassigned — they would again do outstanding jobs — and Huebner became the commander of the 1st Division.

It was a difficult task, for the men revered their former commanders and resented the newcomer who quickly abolished the informality of his predecessors. Within a brief time, however, Huebner had overcome this handicap, won the affection of his troops, and placed his own stamp on them. They were shaped once again into a cohesive, top-notch, and highly disciplined unit. So successful was Huebner that in England the 1st Division was selected to join the D-Day landings, and he commanded it, along with two regiments of the 29th Division, going ashore at Omaha Beach.

This was where the landings were the hardest. Allied intelligence had discovered, too late to change the invasion plans, that the strong German 352d Division had moved into the Omaha Beach area. The resistance of these troops almost prevented the Americans from getting a foothold.

On D-Day Huebner's men were along a single strip of sand and shingle, pinned down by severe enemy fire, when he decided to go ashore himself. It was already 1600, and it looked as though the Omaha landings were about to be marked a complete failure. The crew of the landing craft taking Huebner to the beach was nervous and when the boat grounded the bow door jammed. Huebner clambered over the side. A machine gun raked the boat; he jumped into the water, fell into a hole, and went way under. The tide washed him to more shallow water, and he managed to get to dry ground.

He later said that this was the most critical moment of his life. Unless his men could get off the beach and into the interior, Omaha would be a tragic disaster.

Somehow his appearance on the beach worked magic. His assistant division commanders, Willard G. Wyman and Norman G. Cota, and all the regimental commanders had been trying to get their men forward. Suddenly, with Huebner himself on the scene, things began to improve. How can one explain the way a single man's presence will galvanize a large-scale movement into successful activity? This is the intangible quality of leadership at work, what the soldier's entire life points toward, and seldom has it been displayed to clearer advantage. For his work that day Huebner later received the Oak Leaf Cluster to his Distinguished Service Medal with the statement:

> The success of the greatest amphibious operation in history against a strongly fortified and almost impregnable coastal barrier was in large measure due to the organizing ability, foresight, indomitable determination and inspiring leadership of General Huebner.

By virtue of night attacks, and the fact that they had practically destroyed the 352d Division, Huebner's men quickly expanded the Omaha beachhead to Caumont. After shifting to the St.-Lô area, they took part in Bradley's Cobra operation and helped start the breakout that raced across the Selune River, and, on Huebner's initiative, took the strategic town of Mortain. J. Lawton Collins quickly approved Huebner's move, telling him only to be sure to get the high ground at Hill 317. Huebner's reply was, "I already have it." Because he did, the German counterattack at Mortain was stopped dead.

The 1st Division was in at the kill at the Argentan-Falaise pocket; then it sped across the Seine into Belgium and at Mons encircled another large German force. It fought in the fierce battle for Aachen, and then, close to exhaustion, in the bloody struggle for the Huertgen Forest. Throughout these operations Huebner continued to display his professional competence, and was the logical choice, by January 1945, for command of the V Corps. In that new command his first accomplishment was the taking of the Roer dams, the key obstacle that had kept United States forces from closing up to the Rhine. He then took the corps over the Rhine and across most of Germany to the Elbe.

A few days before the end of the war in Europe, V Corps was

transferred from the U.S. First Army to the Third, just as Patton got the green light for a drive into Czechoslovakia. Huebner remarked, "I'll give us about twelve hours before General Patton calls up and tells us to attack something." It was less than twelve minutes before the phone rang, and Patton was asking Huebner, "where the hell" he had been since Sicily. "I'm sure glad you're back with me again," he added. "I want you to attack Pilsen in the morning. Can you do it?"

There was only one answer to that: the V Corps moved out and took Pilsen. Although Huebner was sure he could go farther and take Prague as well, Patton lacked the authority to continue moving east, and for the V Corps the war ended in Pilsen.

After returning to the United States with his corps headquarters for redeployment to the Pacific, Huebner was appointed Army Ground Forces G–3. Then in 1946 he became Chief of Staff, United States Forces, European Theater. His next assignment was as military governor and commander in chief in Germany, so for a time he was virtual ruler of the homeland his grandfather had fled a hundred years before. His final assignment was Commanding General, United States Forces, Europe.

In these last years of his service in Germany, Huebner found that the administrative skills he had learned so long ago were still of value. He eliminated the dangerously slack postwar discipline, instituted a model training program, abolished segregated Negro units and integrated black troops into all formations, improved the educational offerings of the army's schools in Europe, and took effective action against the black market.

He retired in 1950, one of the best-loved officers ever to wear the uniform of the U.S. Army.

Among the finest young combat officers of World War I, Huebner grew to become one of the outstanding division and corps commanders of World War II. He combined decisiveness and aggressiveness with a sure tactical touch. He demonstrated unsurpassed leadership in training and in battle; he probably brought up — trained, educated, and developed to maturity — more young officers who themselves became generals than any other single commander. He was, in the highest sense of the term and in the genuine tradition of the United States Army, a leader of men.

Devers

A SOLID PERFORMER who contributed more than his share to the Allied victory in World War II, Jacob L. Devers has never received the public recognition due him. Honored immediately after the war by those who understood and appreciated his achievements, he has fallen into an unmerited obscurity.

One of the very few Allied army group commanders in World War II, he operated immediately under Eisenhower on the same level as Bradley and Montgomery. Yet he failed to attract the public attention and acclaim generated by these officers. Bernard L. Montgomery reached Britain's highest military grade of field marshal, and Omar N. Bradley received the American equivalent, five stars of General of the Army. Devers remained a four-star general.

He successfully directed two armies throughout the campaigns in western Europe, from the invasion of southern France to the end of the war. Yet his subordinate army commanders, Jean De Lattre and Alexander Patch, are better known. He was a theater commander operating directly under the Combined Chiefs of Staff, but other commanders of combined and joint forces, for example General Joseph W. Stilwell and General Sir Harold R. L. G. Alexander, attracted more headlines.

Why has Devers been almost unknown to the general public? For one thing, he eschewed the sensational. Never flamboyant, quiet, rarely wrong in his judgment, he seldom sparked controversy. Uninterested in publicity, he lacked the flair that made people talk about him. He was, in short, poor copy for the war correspondents, who preferred to haunt the tents of the more colorful and articulate generals, individuals who provided good stories and who thereby became familiar through the press to the people back home.

Another reason why Devers failed to gain a significant place in the public esteem stemmed from the nature of his service. He always seemed to be in a sideshow, somewhat apart from the main action. The invasion of southern France, which he directed, could hardly compete with Normandy. His earlier command of the European theater was during a time of operational inactivity, for he was charged with the build-up for the cross-Channel attack while Eisenhower engineered and executed the successive offensives in North Africa, Sicily, and southern Italy.

When Eisenhower was transferred to England in January 1944 to prepare for the Normandy invasion, Devers was shifted to take Eisenhower's place in the Mediterranean, but without Eisenhower's prerogatives. A British officer, General Sir Henry M. Wilson, succeeded Eisenhower as Supreme Allied Commander. Devers became his deputy and the senior American commander in the theater. By then, the Mediterranean theater had become a distinctly secondary front.

Still another reason for Devers' relatively inconspicuous position in the American mind was his misfortune to be in the Mediterranean during the Rapido River operation, the Anzio landings, the Cassino and Monte Cassino attacks, all of which were controversial. Although he could hardly be blamed for these events, he became, somehow, part of them.

In contrast, the success of the 1944 spring offensive in Italy was ascribed to Alexander's direction; the blinding feat of the French in traversing the mountains to the gates of Rome was regarded as General Alphonse P. Juin's accomplishment; the final triumph at Anzio was given to Lieutenant General Lucian K. Truscott, Jr.; and the victorious entry into Rome belonged to General Mark W. Clark. These too were part of Devers' work, and he rightfully should have shared in the glory.

Something else that may have diminished Devers' fame was the perpetual dissatisfaction of the French, who worked under his tactical direction in France, Germany, and Austria. They were troublesome allies, inordinately sensitive and proud, burning to redress their earlier defeat, and Devers had difficulty keeping them reined in tightly. They later said that he prevented them, by his allocation of resources, operational zones, and objectives, from achieving the victories for which they thirsted in order to wipe out the disgrace and the shame of their surrender in 1940.

Like Eisenhower, Devers made coalition warfare work, but in some respects his was a more difficult coalition and he rarely made it run with the sure smoothness that characterized Eisenhower's technique. Perhaps even Eisenhower would have been able to do little better than Devers in his situation, pushed as he was by the political ambitions of Free French leader, Charles de Gaulle. Certainly Eisenhower too had less success with the French on the operational level — as seen in the liberation of Paris. Still, it was probably a matter of chance that made Devers look inept beside Eisenhower in this aspect of generalship.

Finally, ironically, according to Charles B. MacDonald in his superb book, *The Mighty Endeavor:*

> One top American failed through no fault of his own to make the close-knit [first] team [working with Eisenhower]. This was . . . Jakie Devers, who needed all the charm of winning smile, protruding ears, and boyish features to hold his own in a company where he lacked the full confidence of the chief. Somehow Devers' and Eisenhower's path had touched only tangentially. Devers was, instead, George Marshall's man . . . Arriving by way of southern France rather than Normandy, Devers and his 6th Army Group were Johnnys-come-lately, poor relations from out of town, strangers to the established family.

Devers suffered because Eisenhower knew him little and could never warm up to him. Despite this handicap, Devers discharged duties of awesome responsibility during the war and carved a remarkable niche for himself among the commanders of World War II.

A native of the rich farming area of York, Pennsylvania, Devers entered the Military Academy at the age of eighteen in 1905. He won his letter in baseball; perhaps significantly, he was a pretty good infielder with the glove, not so good with the bat. He attained no cadet rank, probably because he seemed to have little aspiration toward responsibility. He did reasonably well in his academic subjects, although he seemed never to study, and graduated thirty-ninth in a class of about 100. The general impression Devers left with his classmates was of a rather lazy person and his class yearbook twitted him for this trait.

His class of 1909 had among its members several future generals besides Devers. George S. Patton, Jr., would command the Seventh Army and later the Third Army in Europe, Robert L. Eichelberger would command the Eighth Army in the Pacific, William H. Simpson the Ninth Army in Europe, Edwin F. Harding a division in the Pacific, and John C. H. Lee the Services of Supply in Europe. Devers would outrank them all in terms of command responsibility.

Commissioned as a second lieutenant of field artillery, Devers served in the western states with artillery units for three years. He then was an instructor at West Point for four years, after which he was transferred to Schofield Barracks, Hawaii.

Eight months after Congress declared war in 1917, Devers returned to the United States. Instead of being sent to France, he was ordered to Fort Sill, Oklahoma, for duty as an artillery instructor. Shortly after the war ended, he took command of the 1st Field Artillery stationed on the post. By then he was a colonel, but he had missed the combat in which so many of his young contemporaries had made their marks.

Devers went overseas in 1919 and for several months served in the Army of Occupation in France and Germany. Then, reduced in rank, along with all the Regulars who had gained temporary promotion during the war, he was sent to West Point as an instructor in field artillery tactics. After five years at the Military Academy, he attended the Command and General Staff College, completing the course as a Distinguished Graduate.

Following various artillery assignments at Fort Sill and a tour of duty in the Office of the Chief of Field Artillery, Devers graduated from the Army War College, finishing his formal military education and becoming qualified to hold high command. He had further service with the artillery and again at West Point, where he was graduate manager of athletics.

During the interwar years Devers attained a reputation as an outstanding horseman. He participated in horse shows and played polo with other army luminaries, including George S. Patton, Jr., Adna R. Chaffee, Terry de la Mesa Allen, and Lucian K. Truscott, Jr.

In 1939, again a colonel, Devers became Chief of Staff of the Panama Canal Department. After a year, he was promoted to brigadier general and transferred to command the Washington (D.C.)

Provisional Brigade. Here he atracted the favorable notice of the Army Chief of Staff, General Marshall, who remained one of his warmest supporters. In October 1940 Devers was elevated to major general and assigned to command the 9th Division at Fort Bragg, North Carolina.

In that post he demonstrated a capacity for responsibility and high command, and when Chaffee suddenly became ill the following year and died, Marshall chose Devers to replace him as chief of the Armored Force at Fort Knox, Kentucky.

The U.S. Army at this time was desperately trying to create and shape an armored instrument of warfare that could compete with the German blitzkrieg. In helping to fashion the organization and doctrine of that new combination of arms, Devers played no small part. The tank-infantry-artillery-close support aircraft team that the U.S. Army later wielded so adeptly emerged out of Devers' Armored Force.

In 1943, when the European theater was reorganized to permit Eisenhower to give his undivided attention to operations in the Mediterranean, Marshall selected Devers, now a lieutenant general, to relieve Eisenhower of his burdens in the United Kingdom. Devers went to London and became the commander of the European Theater of Operations, U.S. Army (ETOUSA). His tasks were administrative and diplomatic. When he was in charge of the build-up of American resources for the future cross-Channel attack, he synchronized vast programs of training and equipment. As the senior American officer in the British Isles he served as Marshall's representative in dealings and decisions involving the British allies.

Eisenhower came to London in January 1944 to head up preparations for the Normandy invasion and Devers went to Algiers. There he assumed command of the North African Theater of Operations, U.S. Army (NATOUSA), and served as Deputy Supreme Allied Commander to General Wilson.

He arrived in the theater just as plans were being completed for the Anzio landings, which were designed to propel the Allies in southern Italy directly into Rome. Although he approved the final blueprint, Devers had little to do with the actual planning. Tactically, General Alexander was running the two Allied armies in Italy, and Clark, under Alexander, was commanding the U.S. Fifth Army.

Devers' role was to make sure that the operational forces were receiving the available resources in the amounts needed and using them to advantage. This required close supervision to make certain that joint and combined commanders and forces were pulling their weight and working well together.

In addition to these responsibilities in relation to the fighting front, Devers supervised the wholesale American rearming and re-equipping of French units in North Africa and thus gained valuable insights about forces he would later have to lead in battle. He also kept an eye on logistical and training matters, and was necessarily in close touch with political affairs in French North Africa. Devers carried out his duties with aplomb and success. His was an exacting mission, a job that was as varied as it was demanding.

Beyond Rome, as the citation for the Oak Leaf Cluster to his Distinguished Service Medal has it:

> General Devers' leadership was an important factor in the Italian campaign . . . and the advance to the Gothic Line culminating in the fall of Florence.

Then he had a piece of good luck. For a long time it had been expected that Clark would eventually leave his Fifth Army in Italy and take command of the invasion of southern France. But Anvil, as the landings were called, was alternatively on and off — Churchill and the British wished to cancel it but Eisenhower insisted on it — and Clark decided he would rather stay in Italy. Under Devers' general direction, Patch executed Anvil and took his Seventh Army ashore on August 15, 1944, together with French forces and some British units. When the French First Army was activated under De Lattre, Devers came to southern France as 6th Army Group commander and took operational command of both armies.

Although military historians are still debating the controversial decision to invade southern France, and particularly its effect on the Italian campaign, the strategic decision was outside Devers' authority. Whatever the final verdict — if there is ever one — on the wisdom of that invasion, Anvil, or Dragoon, as it was later called, was a smashing success. A month after the landings, long before anyone had anticipated such results, Devers' troops made contact with Eisenhower's main Overlord forces and turned with them toward Germany.

Devers' immediate objectives were to get through the Vosges mountains and clear the west bank of the upper Rhine. But the swiftness of his advance had outrun the supply line and, like the two other army groups in western Europe, his forces bogged down in the dreary winter fighting.

In November Devers launched what was intended to be a minor supporting attack, but he maneuvered De Lattre's army through the Belfort gap and French troops took Mulhouse and reached the Rhine. Patch's Seventh Army penetrated the Saverne gap, and Leclerc's French 2d Armored Division, which had been given the distinction of being first into Paris, received the honor of taking Strasbourg.

Now at the Rhine, Devers wanted to cross. Instead, Eisenhower ordered Devers to clear the west bank of the Rhine south of Strasbourg to the Swiss border. Devers' forces tried but the German Nineteenth Army resisted in what became known as the Colmar Pocket and held out until February 1945.

Meanwhile the Germans launched their Ardennes counteroffensive. When Patton turned north to relieve Bastogne, Devers extended his thinly stretched troops to take over additional frontage. In this situation, Eisenhower cautioned him against doing too much. Eisenhower wanted Devers to insure the integrity of his army group even if it meant giving up ground already liberated.

The point was that the Colmar Pocket, when considered in conjunction with the Battle of the Bulge, was a threat, and Eisenhower was willing to have Devers withdraw from the low plain between the Vosges and the Rhine. This would enable Devers to hold the critical Vosges passes in more strength. But it also meant giving up Strasbourg, which, if it had little significance for the Americans, meant much to the French. Strasbourg was the symbolic capital of Alsace-Lorraine, the provinces lost to the Germans in 1870 and again in 1940. Devers understood this and was reluctant to withdraw. Beyond this, he believed he could hold the territory his forces had overrun.

When the Germans launched an offensive on the last day of the year, Eisenhower ordered Devers to withdraw to the Vosges. Devers felt that falling back was premature but he prepared to comply. Before he could do so, the French learned of Eisenhower's order. De Gaulle protested to Eisenhower and directed De Lattre to retain

Strasbourg even in defiance of the Allied command. Eisenhower quickly changed his mind, pleasing both the French and Devers. The 6th Army Group turned back the German offensive and Strasbourg remained safely in French hands.

In March 1945, when the Allied forces crossed the Rhine, Devers headed toward the Bavarian and Austrian Alps to forestall a rumored last-ditch Nazi stand in the so-called National Redoubt. During that drive, in April, Devers was confronted by the most serious instance of French intransigence.

He had drawn the army boundaries to give Patch the objective of Stuttgart. But De Lattre wanted the city and his French troops captured it in an imperious display of will. Devers sanctioned De Lattre's act on the basis of the old military axiom: reinforce success. But Devers was shocked by reports and stories of drunkenness, rape, and pillage by French soldiers. Wanting to get the French out of the city and wanting, besides, the Seventh Army to have use of the main road running through Stuttgart, Devers instructed De Lattre to turn the city over to Patch. This was unacceptable to the sensitive De Lattre. He informed De Gaulle, who told him to hold the city despite orders to the contrary.

When Devers heard this, he was outraged by the direct violation of the proper military chain of command. He reported the incident to Eisenhower, terming it "intolerable" to the integrity of the Allied command structure. At the same time Devers sent an American division into Stuttgart to take it from the French by force if necessary. When the Americans arrived, the French received them with open arms but refused to evacuate the city. The next day Devers visited Stuttgart. He discovered that reports of French looting and lack of discipline had been highly exaggerated. His anger cooled and he also saw that Patch could use good roads other than those through Stuttgart. Reversing his instructions, Devers told the French they were welcome to the city.

There was one more instance of disobedience. Late in April De Lattre intruded forty miles into Patch's zone in order to help take Ulm. Quite simply, the French wanted to fly the tricolor again from the city where Napoleon had defeated the Austrians in 1805. Participating with American troops in the attack, they raised their flag over the historic fortress when Ulm was taken, then departed.

There is no question but that Devers had his hands full with his French subordinates. Proud and temperamental, the French also lacked the means to support fully the role they had assumed. They had replacement problems, few organic support units, and were always short of artillery, ammunition, and engineers.

Throughout, Devers retained his equanimity and cheerfulness, qualities to which De Lattre would pay tribute in his postwar memoirs. Devers' method of running his army group was informal and relaxed. For the most part he left the operational planning to his subordinate army commanders. He visited the lower headquarters often, flying in by small liaison plane, making his own observations, making required changes on the spot, judging requests, correcting procedures, encouraging or reproving. Thus he was able to keep his own headquarters relatively small, and his 600 men were half of what Bradley deemed necessary to run his army group.

At the end of the war Devers accepted the unconditional surrender of the German commander of Army Group G. The negotiations and the act were overshadowed by ceremonies of capitulation elsewhere. There was little press coverage of the surrender in Austria.

In the immediate postwar years, after commanding the Army Ground Forces, later redesignated Army Field Forces, Devers retired in 1949. Youthful and rugged in appearance, erect and vigorous, he personified the quiet, dedicated, solid, no-nonsense American.

What characterizes Devers' professional life is his faithful discharge of duty, forthrightly and honestly, without affectation, pretense or self-seeking. What more can be said about a soldier?

Clark

ASK ALMOST ANYONE to name the leading American generals of the European side of World War II, and invariably the answer will be Eisenhower, Patton, Bradley — and Clark.

Mark Clark? Does he really belong in that exalted company of high-ranking commanders? Fighting in a campaign that was termed subordinate and subsidiary to the main action in northwestern Europe, Clark attained a fame that has endured, surprisingly perhaps, for the thirty years that have passed since the end of the war. Was it his gigantic, well-known, and well-oiled personal publicity machine that is responsible for perpetuating a myth? Or was he really one of the great combat leaders of the war? If so, what did he do to deserve his reputation? And why is is that, where there is no hesitation about the others, there is always some about Clark?

Many contemporaries saw him as impatient, imperious, ruthless, and inordinately ambitious. They believed him capable of any action to advance his personal status and enhance his personal stature. Those who know him little remember a tall, thin man who towered above practically everyone, who had a prominent nose and a severe, somewhat strained countenance. To this day, his name is unalterably attached to the United States Fifth Army in Italy. It was he himself who insisted on the term "Mark Clark's Fifth Army," and in many minds that insistence still dogs him.

Those who know him somewhat better recall the incredibly difficult campaigning in a country incredibly difficult for war. They think of the fiascos at the Rapido, Cassino, and Anzio; the near-defeat at Salerno; the heavy casualties suffered in the attacks on the

Winter Line. They wonder whether he made a serious tactical error and deliberately misled — tricked would be the harsher word — his superior during the battle for Rome. They meditate on the fact that the Italian campaign — supposed to grab Italy on the cheap — ended only a few days before V-E Day instead of long before.

Those who know him still better acknowledge the difficulties of the complex coalition effort he personally handled; he had contingents of more nations fighting under him than any other commander in the war. They are aware that when the campaign in Italy began to roll Clark's manpower was sapped to furnish troops for someplace else. They understand that the terrain of Italy offered hospitality to the defender and only obstacles to the attacker.

The truth is that Clark led an army into southern Italy and there performed his tasks so well that his British and American superiors promoted him to the field command of all Allied ground forces in Italy. Long before the end of the war, he was an army group commander who directed the U.S. Fifth and British Eighth armies. He thus reached the high echelon of command exercised by Omar N. Bradley, Jacob L. Devers, and Sir Bernard Law Montgomery. Their equal in the command structure, Clark had the misfortune to be involved in more strategic and tactical controversy than all the others put together. Yet he managed to retain the confidence of his superiors and subordinates, both British and American, in his competence and skill as a professional soldier.

Another aspect of the truth is that Clark was lucky and not so lucky, wise and not so wise, and ambitious to the point of being shortsighted about it; these contradictory strands run through his career.

He graduated from the Military Academy in 1917 and was a captain less than four months later. He served in France with the infantry and was wounded in action. Although he had won honor and promotion quickly, he then remained a captain for sixteen years. A major in 1933, he graduated from the Command and General Staff College and the Army War College. He was with the 3d Division at Fort Lewis from 1937 to 1940, and there he had the good fortune to renew a friendship with Dwight D. Eisenhower that had started at West Point.

After a few months as an instructor at the Army War College and

Italian Campaign, 1943–1945

promotion to lieutenant colonel, Clark joined the staff of Lieutenant General Lesley McNair's General Headquarters. As G–3, he became McNair's right arm. When the headquarters was reorganized into the Army Ground Forces, Clark rose to the position of Chief of Staff. The success of the AGF in training a rapidly expanding army for combat rested in large part on Clark's intelligence, energy, and stamina. In recognition of his unusual ability, he was skipped over the rank of colonel and promoted to brigadier general and shortly after that got his second star.

His work brought him to the favorable notice of General George C. Marshall, Army Chief of Staff. It brought him into contact again with Eisenhower, who was then chief of Marshall's Operations Division. When Marshall sent Eisenhower to England in the spring of 1942 to arrange for the reception and training of American troops, Eisenhower asked for, and received, permission to take Clark with him. They worked well together and quickly established the organizational framework for what was intended to be a cross-Channel invasion force.

After the two young generals returned to Washington, Marshall asked Eisenhower to recommend someone to head the European Theater of Operations, U.S. Army, soon to be activated. Eisenhower unhesitatingly proposed Clark. Marshall instead chose Eisenhower himself, who then selected Clark to accompany him to the United Kingdom as commander of the II Corps. A month later, Eisenhower appointed Clark to command the United States ground forces in the European theater.

The United States presence in the European war was still smaller than that of Britain, and the Americans soon found themselves pulled into the Mediterranean. The decision to invade North Africa in November 1942 sent Clark on a risky voyage by submarine to meet secretly with friendly French officials. His personal daring and good common sense in this agonizing diplomacy facilitated the Allied landings in North Africa. For the amphibious operation and subsequent campaign, Clark was promoted to lieutenant general and named deputy Allied commander in chief. Tough, capable, and hardworking, Clark contributed much to the invasion. In his dealings with Admiral Jean François Darlan and General Henri Giraud and other French officers and administrators, he served Eisenhower and the Allied forces extremely well.

Thus it was that in January 1943, when Eisenhower organized the U.S. Fifth Army in North Africa, the first American army headquarters formed overseas, he put Clark in command. Clark had chafed for an independent operational post. As Eisenhower later noted, Clark was "very anxious to have that command instead of his then title of Deputy Commander-in-Chief." Eisenhower could hardly refuse the reward. Besides, the Fifth Army was to be nothing more than a training organization for several months, and Clark's prior experience with McNair made him admirably fitted for the task.

To have pressed for that command was probably a mistake on Clark's part. It separated him from Eisenhower, and it was about this time that the influence of Walter Bedell Smith on the latter began to grow. It is understandable that a man of Clark's aggressive temperament should want an independent command, a show of his own, a place where he was the boss. Yet he soon found the role unsatisfactory. Fearful that the war in North Africa would end before he could lead his army into combat, he began, as Eisenhower said, to "plague" him for action.

Eisenhower soon gave him an opportunity — and was turned down. This has not heretofore been revealed, and is not generally known. According to Eisenhower, who recalled the incident shortly before his death, what happened was this.

In February, when Marshal Erwin Rommel defeated the Americans in the battle of Kasserine Pass, Eisenhower brought Major General Ernest Harmon out of Morocco and sent him to Tunisia to help Lieutenant General Lloyd R. Fredendall, the II Corps commander. After the Germans were stopped and forced to pull back, Harmon returned and reported his impressions to Eisenhower. On the basis of Harmon's report, Eisenhower decided to relieve Fredendall. He offered the corps command to Harmon, who creditably refused on the ground that it would not be ethical for him to replace a commander he himself had criticized. Suggesting George S. Patton instead, Harmon returned to Morocco. Before accepting Harmon's recommendation, Eisenhower turned to Clark. Would Clark, he asked, go to Tunisia, relieve Frendendall, and take command of the United States forces in contact with the Germans?

At the head of his Fifth Army? Clark asked. Of course he would. No, Eisenhower said. The French, British, and United States troops battling in Tunisia were under the British First Army, and Eisenhower did not want to insert another army headquarters in the field; it would imply his dissatisfaction with General Sir Kenneth A. N. Anderson, the British army commander, and would threaten the delicate balance of the coalition effort. What Eisenhower wanted was that Clark step down temporarily from his own army command and take responsibility for the II Corps. Clark declined on the ground that an army commander should not be asked to accept a subordinate post.

It was another mistake, for Eisenhower became more disenchanted with his close colleague and friend.

He called Patton, who took command of the II Corps and began his meteoric rise. Patton's success in Tunisia and Sicily might well have been Clark's, for even the genius that was Patton's needed an opportunity.

Instead of fighting these campaigns, Clark spent the summer of 1943 supervising the extremely complex and intricate planning for two alternative amphibious operations: a descent upon Sardinia and an invasion of southern Italy. The decision was made for the latter, and even before the start of the Salerno landings Eisenhower could say of Clark that he was "the best organizer, planner, and trainer of troops that I have met . . . the ablest and most experienced officer we have in planning amphibious operations . . . In preparing the minute details of requisitions, landing craft, training of troops and so on, he has no equal in our Army." But whether he could command in the field was still open.

Salerno was an extremely risky venture, but there Clark proved himself. He displayed self-confidence — perhaps more apparent than real — and he fought through obstacles and discouragements to send a finely balanced force ashore. "Clark impresses me, as always," a senior officer wrote at this time, "with his energy and intelligence. You cannot help but like him. He certainly is not afraid to take rather desperate chances, which, after all, is the only way to win a war."

Superb as a planner, he turned out to be splendid as an executor. Energetic and enthusiastic, he personally helped establish the beachhead and contributed his driving presence to repel a dangerous counterattack. Not only did he take charge of a small antitank unit, turning back at point-blank range eighteen German tanks that came within an inch of splitting the beachhead, but he spread an air of determination and courage among the front-line troops as he visited them. At the end of the landing he was awarded the Distinguished Service Cross for bravery.

And yet to some observers he came close to losing his nerve at Salerno. There was no plan for evacuating the beachhead in case the enemy proved too strong. At the height of the crisis Clark sought to rectify this omission; he ordered his staff to prepare two plans, each designed to extricate one of his corps from Salerno should withdrawal become necessary. Unfortunately, word of this got out at the wrong psychological moment, and some members of his command believed he was ready to throw in the towel. He was not; he was simply being practical and realistic as well as thorough. Had a withdrawal been required, Clark would have had a blueprint for it.

With his forces finally in possession of Salerno, and with the Germans withdrawing northward, Clark pushed ahead, took Naples, set into motion an elaborate effort to restore the demolished port, and sought to get to Rome. The terrain and German tenacity stymied his efforts to such an extent that he, together with his superior, General Alexander, espoused an amphibious enterprise at Anzio.

Eisenhower was leaving the theater to take command of the Allied forces in the United Kingdom assembling for the cross-Channel invasion. Montgomery was going with him to command the British forces slated for Normandy. Had Clark enjoyed the same relationship with Eisenhower he had earlier, he might well have gone to the major theater to command the American forces. Instead, Eisenhower took Bradley.

Clark and General Sir Harold Alexander remained in Italy and worked hard to gain acceptance of the Anzio landings in order to out-flank and loosen the German positions along the Garigliano and Rapido rivers, the Gustav Line anchored on Monte Cassino. Al-together, the Anzio proposal was more risky than the Allied planners and tacticians, used to exercising care and caution, would normally consider. Anzio was too far ahead of the main line to provide a good chance of mutual support and quick link-up; creating two fronts would separate the Allied forces and violate the principles of mass, concentration, and economy of force. The strategic aim of the amphibious operation was fuzzy and ambivalent; no one was sure exactly what it was supposed to accomplish. Finally, guaranteeing the success of the landings required operations on the main front that were a desperate gamble. Despite all these conditions, which argued against success, the concept was accepted. Anzio would go.

Primarily because of Clark's stubbornness, a chain of events took place that resulted in a very bad winter for the Allies. First came the disaster at the Rapido, which was not entirely his fault. Next, there was the unopposed landing at Anzio, which bogged down almost immediately — to some extent at least as a result of Clark's decision. Checked here, the Allies made unsuccessful and costly attacks against Cassino and Monte Cassino, which included heavy air bombardment of the Benedictine abbey. The bombing turned Cassino and the monastery into a virtually impassable maze of rubble. This was not so much Clark's fault as that of Lieutenant General Sir Bernard Freyberg, Major General Francis Tuker, and Alexander — curiously enough, a New Zealander, the commander of an Indian division, and the army group commander. The consequence: a stalemate in Italy that lasted until May 1944.

Clark had been scheduled to head the forces invading southern France, but he preferred to remain in Italy until he captured Rome. Time tricked him again, and this proved to be another mistake. General Jacob L. Devers became the army group commander, the equal of Bradley and Montgomery in the main arena.

Meanwhile, Operation Diadem in southern Italy, launched in May, broke the Gustav Line and propelled troops on the main front into contact with the isolated Anzio beachhead. At that point, Alexander wanted the beachhead forces to break out in the eastward and block the German army's withdrawal to and beyond Rome. But Clark was so tempted by the prize of the Eternal City that he disobeyed Alexander's wish and sent his elements directly into the Italian capital.

He told his troops that they had done what no others in the world had managed to do: capture Rome from the south. He was not quite correct; Belisarius had done so in the sixth century. But the Fifth Army's feat was exceptional nonetheless.

The German army escaped.

Well, what is the legitimate aim of armed forces? Destruction of the enemy army or the capture of geographical features that have psychological value? According to Clausewitz, the former is the valid objective. A year later, in conformance with this concept, Eisenhower would renounce Berlin. Clark chose to take Rome. There are those who say both were wrong.

There is some question about whether Clark could actually have trapped the Germans south of Rome. The issue remains conjectural; we shall never know. In any event, the loss of Rome gave the Germans a distinct psychological shock and the Allies a corresponding lift. Two days later, the Normandy invasion began.

The rest of the Italian campaign was bloody but anticlimactic. The Allies pursued the Germans north of Rome to the Arno. Then Clark made the VI Corps available for southern France. He broke across the Arno and reached the Gothic Line, where winter, terrain, and the loss of his manpower denied him and his troops the clear-cut victory they had worked so hard to gain. In the spring of 1945 the Allies broke through, and by April had reached the southern border of Austria.

By then Clark commanded the 15th Army Group and a variety of national contingents. He held them together, treated them fairly according to their capacities and characteristics, and at the end of the war had attained the qualities of a polished military statesman, qualities he exhibited during the occupation of Austria, which he headed, and later in Japan, where he succeeded Matthew B. Ridgway as commander in chief, United Nations Command.

What, then, were his accomplishments, and why does he deserve to be regarded as one of the great American soldiers of World War II?

He had a flair for public relations, but so did, for example, Eisenhower. He had ambition, but so do all general officers. He was tough and ruthless to an extreme, but war is not for tender hearts. Above all, he was capable of the tasks that were required of the high commanders in that war. He directed a large coalition effort, mastered the complexities of amphibious and mountain warfare, and personified the driving determination that all first-rate commanders embodied: the will to meet, defeat, and destroy the enemy.

Despite the controversies that mark the campaign in Italy, despite the subsidiary nature of the theater, Clark was a respected member of the Allied team who pulled his weight and more. In his area no one ever had to ask who was in charge. He exercised the authority of his position and he accepted the responsibility with sureness, competence, and a high degree of professionalism.

Every man makes mistakes, but Clark's were not fatal. They related more to his personal career than to his military ability. Big, rawboned, energetic, and outspoken, learning and growing as he went, he personified in Italy the power of the United States commitment to the Allied venture.

PART III

Masters of Mobile Warfare

MOBILE WARFARE, a war of movement, is the most exciting kind of all. The drawn-out drama of the siege has its appeal, but the soldier or armchair strategist bogged down in Flanders field will share the frustration of the general and long for the exhilaration of movement and pursuit. Mass multiplied by mobility gives momentum; add the most intriguing principle of war, surprise, and you have the recipe for heady victory.

The great campaigns that have enthralled students have been those that moved. Few episodes of the American Civil War stir more interest than Sherman's drive on Atlanta. In the American Revolution, although the duel between Greene and Cornwallis across the Carolinas was fraught with excitement, the movement of columns to Yorktown and their combination with naval forces won the war and provided the unquestionably great maneuver of that struggle.

Napoleon was pre-eminently the exponent of mobile warfare, as he was of nearly everything else. When he took command of the Army of Italy, he stressed movement. His grumbling soldiers soon came to joke that "he fights with our feet." He surprised his enemies by the speed of his marches.

The strategic preferences of Napoleon were ideally suited to mobile warfare. Occasionally his enemies were so foolish that he had nothing to do except to take advantage of their mistakes. Generally he preferred a strategic offensive combined with a tactical defensive. In 1800, when he came down from the Alps and cut the Austrian lines of communication, he lost contact with the enemy and let his own forces get rather badly dispersed. Yet when he bumped into the

Austrians at Marengo, he accepted battle. Standing tactically on the defensive until he could bring up and concentrate his units, he then counterattacked at the right moment and won.

Much the same pattern emerged at Austerlitz. Napoleon launched a strong drive into territory beyond the Danube, then fought a battle initially on the defensive. At the decisive moment, he made his lightning thrust of annihilation.

Central Europe provided the emperor with the best ground for the kind of war he liked to wage. Northern Italy, southern Germany, the valleys of the Po and the Danube, the Saxon plain, all these were ideal battlegrounds, as their inhabitants over the centuries learned to their dismay. In these territories armies could live and forage and fight; they could also move and maneuver. The Napoleonic army that had learned to live off the country and to carry its supplies on its soldiers' backs was the perfect instrument for the mobile warfare of that time.

It was different elsewhere. When the Grand Army marched into Poland in 1806, it lost its momentum. Napoleon's attempts to bring the Russians to battle foundered. His Heilbronn maneuver got lost in the mud, and his battle at Eylau was a slugfest in a blizzard. Had Napoleon not come to think of himself as unbeatable, he might have learned in Poland that it was not a good idea to go to Russia.

The same was true in Spain. Henri IV is credited with saying that small armies are beaten in Spain and large armies starve there. During Napoleon's short visit in the Peninsula, he performed as masterfully as ever, knocking over the Spanish armies along the Ebro with ease. When he left, never to return, he had failed to recognize that his troops were up against a country and a style of warfare that were beyond even their extensive capabilities.

Defeats notwithstanding, the remarkable French mobility gave them the edge over their opponents, and the Grand Army ranks high in the annals of mobile warfare. Its elemental force is still thought of as Napoleon's "long boots" or as "the seven torrents" dashing from the Channel to the Rhine and the Danube. Murat's handling of those campaigns made him George Patton's ideal of what a cavalry commander should be; first and foremost, the essence of cavalry is mobility.

Not until World War II did a new mobile combination come into being. As Murat was the model cavalry man for one century, Patton himself stood for the next. Instead of cuirassiers and lancers, there were Sherman tanks and P-47 Thunderbolts. The difference, as theorists like Liddell Hart could see, was of degree rather than of quality. Patton and Murat would have worked very nicely together in either century.

In colonial North America the French and Indians made outstanding use of their mobility, which was really their best weapon against the slower, more cumbersome English. The British made notable attempts to follow the example of their enemies, the organizing of Rogers' Rangers being the best known. But they never seemed much more than imitators. The French were like wolves in the forest; Braddock was a bullock.

In the nineteenth century, when the British fought many small campaigns, their greatest problem was to come to grips with the enemy. They became specialists in sending out flying columns to do difficult little jobs at long distance. As examples of mobile warfare, not all bear close scrutiny. Lord Napier of Magdala, who overthrew King Theodore in Abyssinia, is a case in point. Superficially, the campaign looks like a classic war of movement. Actually, it was something of a mess. Before Napier would move inland he insisted on building a port on the Red Sea and collecting six months' worth of supplies. He had so seriously overestimated the staying power of his enemy that most of the supplies were later burned when the British pulled out. Generally, however, the British did well against great odds of climate and terrain.

The United States has its own tradition of mobile warfare, and Americans tend to be impatient with the niceties or nuances of military situations. They prefer to head at once for the main objective. British writers on World War II often comment on the American anxiety to cross the Channel and get to France in order to strike at the heart of Germany, this to the detriment not only of British peripheral strategy but also of British politics and failing manpower. The Australian Chester Wilmot, in his book *The Struggle for Europe,* touched off an argument that still continues when he criticized what he regarded as a naive American approach to military and political realities. But American history and experience, together with vast wealth in human and material resources, made the Americans more willing than the British to accept a head-on grapple.

American operations are always supposed to move. Having had

relatively little exposure to the trench warfare of World War I, Americans found it quite foreign to slug it out at Cassino. Grant's sieges of Vicksburg and Richmond are exceptions in American military tradition. In all of America's wars, there are few static battles worth talking about. Thus, it is not surprising that Americans tend to think of mobile warfare as the most highly developed type of war. And it is probably for this reason that Americans regard its expert practitioners as the greatest masters of the military art.

Iberville

AT THE HEAD of an invasion army, William, Prince of Orange, sailed across the English Channel from Holland, and on November 5, 1688, landed unopposed on the southern coast of England. An ambitious man, a militant Protestant, a political opportunist, and the son-in-law of the English king, James II, William not only took advantage of James's stupidity but also took his throne. The bloodless revolt now called the Glorious Revolution restored a Protestant line of royal succession, the supremacy of Parliament, and the liberties of Englishmen.

Orange Billy was hardly interested in the rights of Englishmen; he wanted their money and their blood. His great aim was to defeat Louis XIV, the Catholic monarch of France, and this he had been unable to do with the resources of Holland alone. Now the British head of state, he inaugurated what was later called the Second Hundred Years' War — a series of wars and campaigns that marked a struggle for European power and overseas empire that ended in 1815 when Napoleon's broken battalions fled down the road from Waterloo.

Incidental in this great contest was the fate for North America. Would it be English or French? Protestant or Catholic?

Neither William and his successors nor the masters of France at Versailles were primarily concerned with the New World. The French settlers produced furs, the English colonists rum. For the Europeans, the sugar of the West Indies and the fur pelts of the wilderness were infinitely more important than the American continent.

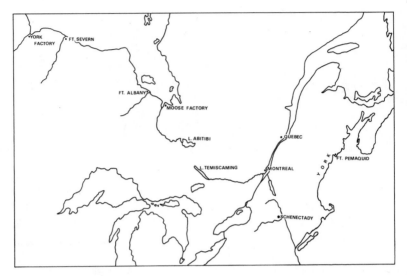

Iberville's America, 1689

Although the narrow and unimaginative European rulers had little interest in the New World, the colonists who lived there had dreams. They wished the land to be settled and developed. They wanted to be securely tied to the destinies of England or France. They were aware of the potential wealth and importance of the continent. Patriots, who shared the sentiments of their countrymen in Europe, they participaed on their own battlefields in the struggles for the potential domination of Europe.

Thus it was that, as armies fought in Flanders and in the Palatinate, men who fished and hunted on the banks of the St. Lawrence and Hudson rivers, separated by hundreds of miles of virgin forest, plotted each other's destruction. Among them was Pierre le Moyne, Sieur d'Iberville, an inveterate English-hater and guerrilla fighter.

Generally known as one of the founders of Louisiana, Iberville was portrayed on a children's series shown on Canadian television several years ago as a combination of Zorro and Robin Hood, a champion of freedom and the common man. Actually, he was a ruthless soldier, motivated not only by a vision of French empire and glory but also by a desire for personal fortune. In that age the two usually went hand in hand; freebooter and patriot were often indistinguishable.

What set Iberville apart was his competence. He was probably the greatest practitioner of long-range hit-and-run warfare in North America. As a soldier, his exploits make those of T. E. Lawrence and of the Long Range Desert Group of World War II look like weekend jaunts in a national park.

Iberville was born in Montreal in 1661, the third son of one of the wealthiest noblemen of New France. Preparing for a naval career, he made several trips to France during his youth, gained a rudimentary schooling, and eventually obtained a commission in the navy. After serving several years as a junior officer, he returned late in 1685 to Quebec — just in time to join the expedition that opened the French struggle to win control over Hudson Bay.

This military venture antedated Europe's War of the League of Augsburg, which initiated the Second Hundred Years' War between England and France. Although the contest in Europe was fought over the issues of dynasty and religion, the Hudson Bay operation had an additional stimulus: a matter of cash.

The inhabitants of New France lived on the fur trade, their only profitable commodity. When some English businessmen formed a company to trade in the Hudson Bay area, they threatened the French prosperity. The French Canadians had already noticed with discomfort the growth of New England and New York to the south. They soon became aware of the British presence in the north.

If the English cut the French out of the fur trade altogether, the results would be disastrous for Canada. According to the prevailing mercantile theory, a colony was worthless unless it could contribute to the economy of the mother country. It deserved no support, no infusions of settlers and funds, no military protection. If Quebec was to survive, if there was to be a French empire in North America, the English had to be eliminated.

It was already difficult to think of driving the English out of New England and New York. The best the French could do, they began to believe, was to hem them into the area east of the Appalachians. In the north, however, the English were vulnerable. Since this territory was becoming the center of the fur trade, this was the place to strike.

It made no difference that England and France were enjoying an interval of formal peace. In the seventeenth century, trade was a kind of cold war. The French would destroy the Hudson's Bay Company, establish control over the country, have the fur themselves, and enhance the glory of Catholic France.

The first expedition against Hudson Bay was led by the Chevalier de Troyes, an experienced soldier from old France. An older brother of Iberville was second in command. Iberville was next in line. A younger brother was also with the party. This, then, was the beginning of a family war against the British.

In March 1686, this military force of thirty regular soldiers and seventy Canadian volunteers left Quebec. On snowshoes, the men moved up the Ottawa Valley. They walked 600 miles to the headwaters of the Ottawa River, Lake Temiskaming. They hiked across a mountain range to Lake Abitibi. After building canoes, they paddled another 300 miles across the lake and down the Abitibi and Moose rivers. It took them eighty-five days — almost three months — of unrelieved hardship and suffering to reach James Bay, the lower extension of the larger Hudson Bay.

The men were sick and hungry, at times near despair and mutiny.

Their officers, notably Iberville, held them together and kept them going. That the force arrived at its objective was a triumph of leadership and of endurance against the unrelenting hostility of the northern wilderness.

A venture of this sort deserved to succeed, and it did. Emerging out of the night of June 11, the 100 Frenchmen surprised the seventeen sleeping English traders at Fort Moose and captured them before they could get out of their nightshirts.

Two weeks later the French appeared at Fort Charles and seized the unsuspecting handful of traders there. They also found and took the English sloop *Craven,* which was supposed to carry a cargo of furs to England. Loading captured furs, guns, goods, and prisoners aboard the ship, the French sailed for the main English station, Fort Albany, in what is now eastern Ontario, on James Bay at the mouth of the Albany River. A short bombardment by the ship's guns persuaded the English garrison to surrender, for the men turned on their officers, saying that they had no guarantee that the Hudson's Bay Company was prepared to reimburse them for limbs they lost in a fight.

As a consequence the English were nearly swept out of the bottom of Hudson Bay. They retained only isolated posts at the mouths of the Hayes and Severn rivers. Why the French did not eliminate the remaining British posts is a mystery. Perhaps they were exhausted. Perhaps they were running low on provisions and ammunition. Perhaps they felt that the British, without further prompting, would realize the folly of staying.

In any event, the French descent on Hudson Bay was the start of a duel that Iberville would carry on for the rest of his life. His unremitting purpose would be to drive the English out of the New World entirely. Had the decision depended on his efforts alone, he might well have succeeded. After spending a year at Hudson Bay, Iberville went to France to expound his ideas at Versailles, to gain acceptance of his imperial vision, to obtain support for his strategic view, to secure help in carrying out his tactical principles.

A man of sound strategic sense, Iberville combined in himself the abilities of the soldier and the sailor. The unusual duality gave him insights into colonial warfare that were lacking in most of the governors of Canada and in their superiors in France.

Iberville realized that the domination of North America rested fundamentally on control of the sea routes between the colonies and Europe. The bedrock of imperial strategy must, then, be maritime. If the French commanded the waters of the St. Lawrence approaches, the routes to Hudson Bay, and the Atlantic seacoast, they would strangle the British colonies, which would surely die. Commanding the sea, the French could launch raids against isolated British settlements and destroy them one by one. The result would be the extinction of the British empire in the New World.

Tactically, Iberville was an exponent of the sudden strike. Whether carrying out an attack by sea or through the forests, he would adopt and adapt the Indian way of war, moving swiftly, silently, cruelly.

He failed to persuade the policy-makers at Versailles to his view. Deciding that he needed no help, he determined to execute his plans anyway. Lack of interest and distance would prevent the politicians and administrators in France and Quebec from interfering with his self-imposed mission.

The expedition to Hudson Bay in 1686 had so stunned the English that they agreed to a treaty of neutrality in that area. This had little effect on Iberville's personal war. In 1688 he was once again on the shore of the bay at the head of a small force, capturing Englishmen, confiscating their furs, preventing them from hunting. When they contracted scurvy, he imprisoned their doctor and kept him from treating his patients. To their protests that he was infringing on their rights, Iberville replied that neither his king nor theirs was worried about what was happening at Hudson Bay. The subsequent outbreak of war in Europe gave his actions a retrospective legitimacy.

War between France and England being formally declared, Iberville accompanied his older brother on a raid down the Hudson Valley. In the dead of winter, 200 Canadians and Indians passed through the classic Lake Champlain–Lake George invasion route. They headed for Albany but changed their minds when they learned that a sizable garrison of Connecticut troops was standing guard. Instead, they struck Schenectady. Appearing at midnight, January 9, 1690, they wiped out the town in two hours, killing sixty inhabitants and burning more than 60 houses. Leaving the aged and the infants to fend for themselves, they started back to Quebec with thirty prisoners.

Two years later, Iberville ravaged the York District in Maine.

Fort Pemaquid, on the Maine coast, managed to hold out against his assault. But Iberville returned in 1696, took it by surprise, and burned it to the ground. In the same year, he sailed to Newfoundland and systematically destroyed the English settlements. He encouraged his Indians to burn and to loot indiscriminately, and he left the ravaged fishing villages helpless in the middle of winter. Only two settlements survived, St. John's and Carbonear.

Iberville pushed hard for a naval expedition against New York, arguing that success would throttle the southern threat to Canada at its source. But to the royal court at Versailles, fortresses in the Netherlands were far more attractive than stockades on the edge of a virgin wilderness.

Frustrated in his larger design, in 1697 Iberville returned to Hudson Bay. He sailed there in command of three ships. Two having become separated from him in the ice and fog, he was alone when he met an English squadron of three small warships. In the ensuing battle, Iberville sank one and captured two. Then shipwrecked himself, he gathered his followers and prisoners, marched overland, and laid siege to Fort York. His other ships arrived during the operations and the British surrendered.

Leaving a French garrison to occupy the fort, Iberville sailed to France to bring news of his victory and to sell 20,000 pounds sterling worth of fur pelts. He disposed of his pelts at a profit and argued that the English were destroyed at Hudson Bay. All they retained was a slender foothold on that rich area. They could be finished off with little difficulty.

He was doomed to disappointment. Europe was subsiding into a peace of exhaustion. Hudson Bay was far away. The peace commissioners made no effort to resolve the uncertainty regarding possession of the territory. It remained in dispute until 1713, when the Treaty of Utrecht concluded another war. At that time France was on the brink of its long slide into bankruptcy and revolution. Hudson Bay went to Britain.

By then Iberville had passed from the scene. He led an expedition to Louisiana in 1698 to found a colony where Sieur Robert Cavelier de la Salle had failed thirteen years earlier. On the outbreak of the War of the Spanish Succession, he took command of a large expedition, sailed into the Caribbean, captured two islands of the West

Indies for the French crown, and spread terror and despair throughout the English settlements. Then, contracting what was probably yellow fever, he died in Havana on July 9, 1706, at the age of forty-five.

One of the first soldiers in the New World to understand and visualize the whole imperial scene, Iberville grasped the fundamental strategic considerations of overseas empire. He showed himself a master of mobile warfare in the immensely difficult conditions of virgin North America. He had a remarkable affinity for the Indians, those always worrisome allies. Though his cause — that of a greater and vital France — was finally lost, his achievements were of lasting significance.

> His exploits illustrated the physical and moral strength, the resourcefulness and adaptability that were required in some measure of the whole colonial society to survive and prosper in the exacting wilderness conditions . . . The fierce patriotism, the bravery, even the savage cruelty, which characterized Iberville's campaigns against the English, were to a lesser degree the qualities essential to all life and progress in early North America.

He had a flair for irregular warfare, the temperament for "distant and dangerous enterprises" that took him and his men to Newfoundland, New York, and the remote regions of Canada. "On each . . . occasion, they showed independent initiative and great physical endurance, and their operations were marked by ruthlessness, speed, elasticity, and good organization."

Iberville made war vindictively.

His later reputation was hurt by charges of avarice, even beyond that which was acceptable according to the loose standards of his time. Louis de Buade de Frontenac, governor of Canada, thought him vain and boastful and believed he had "his interests and his trade much more in view than the king's service." After Iberville's death, his widow was financially ruined by claims against her husband's estate.

The embodiment of New France's efforts against the English for fifteen years, Iberville was as "hardened to the water as a fish"; he was "as military as his sword." Although he won his battles and campaigns, he failed to create a French empire in the New World. The fault and the blame lay at Versailles, where the policy-makers failed to understand his vision.

Crook

AFTER THE CIVIL WAR demobilization, many Union officers resigned, others retired, some took to the bottle, a few to books, and a handful to fighting Indians.

It is one of the ironies of United States history, and perhaps a commentary on the national character, that most people in our country know much about our least successful Indian fighter, George Custer; they know almost nothing about our most successful one, George Crook.

In the quarter century after 1865, the main task of the undersized and undernourished U.S. Army was to keep the peace on the frontier. As Americans moved westward in search of space and opportunity, they filled up the map, destroyed the buffalo, broke the prairie sod, and entered the hostile lands of the southwest. They displaced the Indian who had been there for centuries, and when they did not kill him they ruined the delicate natural balance on which his survival depended. As the ship of state plowed its way to the Pacific, it threw up a bow wave of blood and flame. The Indian would not go the white man's way and the white man would not let him go his own way. Two civilizations were in conflict and the weaker would die. But it died hard.

The American Indian of the west has been called the finest irregular cavalryman in the world. He could live on next to nothing and make his horses subsist on almost the same. By the later nineteenth century he was armed as well as his white opponent, and sometimes better. He was illiterate but he knew every foot of the country he ranged over. His methods of war were sharp and savage. He fought for the most basic cause of human endeavor: his own survival.

Unfortunately for him, he was disadvantaged by the weaknesses of primitive society. Very few of the Indian leaders were able to attain the stature of national heroes. Tribes remained as hostile to each other as to the white man. In discipline, organization, and technology the Indian was inferior to his enemy, and in the end this inferiority would destroy him. He was a magnificent guerrilla fighter but, as modern practitioners of the art have noted, this alone is not enough to win.

For the U.S. Army, the problem of how to cope with guerrilla warfare on the frontier was hardly new. It had often appeared before. The methods of dealing with guerrillas are easily stated: destroy the enemy's bases and communications, isolate him, harass him, give him no rest until he succumbs.

What was difficult was how to do this with a tiny army — and against an enemy who had virtually no bases, no means of communication, and no great material needs. The Indian lived so frugally — he could travel so lightly — that chasing him was like hunting a shadow. The only way to defeat the Indian, it seemed, was to become more Indian than he — to turn his virtues against him and to take advantage of all his weaknesses. To do this successfully, and in addition to win the Indian's trust and honor, was the particular genius of George Crook.

During the first thirty years of his life, there was nothing to suggest that Crook's career would be exceptional. He appeared to be nothing more than the average competent professional officer. He reached his peak during the War between the States, and it could well have been expected that he would subside into a decent obscurity.

Born in Ohio in 1829, he graduated from the Military Academy in 1852, thirty-eighth in a class of forty-three. He was commissioned a lieutenant of infantry and served for several years in the Pacific northwest. There he first experienced Indian campaigning. He also stopped a poisoned arrowhead, which he carried inside him for the rest of his life.

Crook has been described as "about six feet in his stockings, straight as an arrow, broad-shouldered, lithe, sinewy as a cat, and able to bear any amount of fatigue." Despite his imposing stature and bearing, he hardly presented a martial picture as an Indian fighter. A bushy, two-pronged beard covered his firm features. In the field he usually wore baggy trousers, a slouch hat, and a single-breasted hunting jacket with bulging pockets. He rode a mule and carried a double-barreled shotgun across his saddle. His appearance was so nondescript that he was once offered a job as a packer by one of his own mule-drivers. The Indians called him Gray Fox, a tribute to his inner qualities as well as to his beard.

Crook rose rapidly in the Civil War. He earned several brevet promotions, and at the end of the war was a major general of the U.S. Volunteers in command of the cavalry of the Army of the Potomac.

Reverting to substantive rank, Crook became lieutenant colonel of the 23d Infantry Regiment, stationed at Boise, Idaho. For three years he conducted operations against the Indians of southern Oregon, Idaho, and northern California. He finally succeeded in pacifying the area, for which he received the thanks of the Oregon legislature and a letter of commendation from the army.

In 1871, President Grant named Crook to command the troops in northern Arizona. His mission was to end the depredations of the Apache. Ever since the end of the Civil War, when the Volunteer forces departed, the Apache had been on the warpath. They had plenty of justification, for they had been tricked, cheated, and abused by the white inhabitants with what can be described only as fantastic foolhardiness. Now, as usual, the army was being called in to set matters right.

Crook knew neither the Arizona territory nor the Apache, but one of his greatest virtues was the ability to acknowledge his own ignorance. On his arrival at Tucson, he began to question everyone about the situation. He absorbed information like a sponge — facts about terrain, Indians, troops, officers, Mexicans, local conditions. He undertook an inspection trip to test his men and equipment. He enrolled companies of Apache scouts from bands that were antagonistic to the hostiles. He was perhaps the first man in high places to recognize that the divisions separating groups of Indians could be used as a weapon.

After some delays imposed on him by Washington, Crook took to the field. With a well-equipped force supported by mobile pack trains, he hounded the Apache until they conceded defeat. They returned to their reservations.

By 1873 the territory was relatively peaceful, and Crook reported his campaign concluded. This time he received not only the thanks of the Arizona legislature but an unusual reward from the army: he was promoted from lieutenant colonel to brigadier general.

Even more important was the respect he gained from the Indians. An eminently just and honest man, Crook had the vision to see beyond the narrow horizons of his own time and society. He understood what was happening and what was being done to the Indians, and though he was necessarily firm as a soldier he was also fair. He treated his opponents with straightforward directness. He constantly recommended better treatment for the Indians, stepping on many toes in the process — those of traders, politicians, land speculators, and others. His later years were spent in bitter controversy with, among others, Brigadier General Nelson A. Miles over what he believed was the white man's betrayal of the Indians. The Indians, even the Apache, came to fear the Gray Fox as a warrior but to believe in him as a man.

After the Arizona campaign the army recognized Crook as a specialist in Indian warfare. In 1875 he was appointed to command the Department of the Platte. The discovery of gold in the Black Hills of Dakota meant trouble with the Sioux and Cheyenne, whose treaty lands were being invaded by gold hunters. In reprisal, the Indians took to the warpath.

Adopting his former strategy, Crook set three converging columns into motion and headed for the Sioux country. He personally commanded one column of 1200 men, and Chief Crazy Horse fought him to a halt on the Rosebud River. Crook had to fall back to re-equip. The two other columns, led by Brigadier General Alfred Terry and Colonel John Gibbon, planned to link up on the Little Big Horn. It was Terry's dispatch of Custer and 600 troopers of the 7th Cavalry that set the stage for the worst United States defeat in the whole of the Indian wars. This disaster almost brought Crook's campaign to collapse.

Much less known than the Little Big Horn battle was the ensuing pursuit of the Indians by Crook and Terry. Launching an expedition through the winter months of 1876–77, Crook and his men relentlessly drove the Indians before them, breaking them up into little bands and defeating them piecemeal. They chased Sitting Bull and his Sioux into Canada, and in January 1877 defeated the last major group of hostiles at the Battle of Wolf Mountain. By spring, calm in the territory was restored.

In 1882 Crook went back to Arizona, where his greatest exploit came against Geronimo's Apache. Late in 1881 the Chiricahua Apache broke out of their reservations, and by early 1882 the whole territory was in a state of frenzied alarm. Late in July Washington posted Crook to command the department, and he arrived at Fort Apache early in September. His initial actions were as unconventional as his dress. He set himself up in a tent about a mile from the post and apparently withdrew into prolonged periods of meditation, interspersed by occasional hunting trips. Actually, he was going through his usual preliminary process of acquiring information.

Within a month or so he managed to visit most of the tribes, and he took steps to redress their very real grievances. As a consequence, Crook narrowed the rebellion to a hard core of Chiricahua Apache who were centered in the Sierra Madre Mountains across the border in Mexico, led by Geronimo.

While Crook's forces gathered at Willcox, Arizona, he himself crossed the border and gained the assurance of cooperation from his opposite numbers in Mexico. Then, on May 1, 1883, Crook and his command crossed the border, determined to harass the Apache until they gave in. Crook led a numerically unimpressive force. He had a troop of the 6th Cavalry, about 200 friendly Apache and a few civilian scouts, and enough packers to handle five pack trains totaling some 350 animals. If his contingent was small, it was also very tough and competent. Crook had no belief in comfort in the field. Every man carried what he wore and one blanket; nothing more. Each had forty rounds of ammunition. Reserve supplies were in the pack trains. The column was stripped to the bone and ready to remain in the field until it or the Apache collapsed.

In ten days Crook penetrated deep into the Sierra Madres. He lost many mules over cliffs and very nearly a future Army Chief of Staff, the then Captain Adna R. Chaffee, whose horse slid over a bank and took him with it.

In the heart of the enemy country Crook broke up his command. He sent his scouts forward in small parties to track the hostiles, while he followed the most promising lead with his main body. Gradually he ran the Apache into a corner. He first picked up some of their women. He next raided and destroyed their bivouacs and scattered their horses. Finally, in May 1883, Crook forced Geronimo to give himself up.

There was peace then for two years, while Crook administered the territory to the satisfaction of almost everyone. But the unstable equilibrium of reservation and white settler could not be maintained indefinitely. In 1885 the Apache went on a rampage again. Geronimo was once more captured by Crook on March 27, 1886, but two nights later he escaped with part of his band. The War Department failed to understand the conditions that prompted the Indian violence and seemed to question Crook's administration. Stung by the implied criticism, Crook asked to be relieved. (Geronimo's final surrender was engineered by Miles on September 4 after Crook had been relieved.) He never again fought against the Indians.

In the spring of 1886 Crook returned to the command of the Department of the Platte where he remained until April 6, 1888, when he was promoted to major general and posted to the command of the Division of the Missouri, with headquarters at Chicago. He died there on March 21, 1890.

There may appear to be little in common between the horse cavalryman of the 1870s and the helicopter-borne soldier of today. In reality, the same old equation applies. Resourcefulness, intelligence, mobility, and endurance are still the fundamentals of antiguerrilla warfare. Whether by horse or by helicopter, the soldier must isolate the guerrilla, cut him from his bases and his sanctuaries, interrupt his communications, and give him no rest.

George Crook realized all of this a century ago and practiced it successfully. But he was aware of more. He knew that the basic issues would ultimately be settled beyond the battlefield. Justice, fair dealing, and honesty were the weapons in that conflict. In his own life as well as in his campaigns, he exemplified these virtues.

Had there been more Crooks and fewer crooks on the frontier, there might well have been less violence and, today, less discomfort with this aspect of our national heritage.

Wolseley

GILBERT AND SULLIVAN parodied him in *The Pirates of Penzance* as "the modern major-general." The Liberal press admiringly called him "our only general." The Conservative party in England contemptuously agreed. Everyone else, especially the Cockneys, used the term "all Sir Garnet" to mean "AOK."

The subject of these slightly diverse views was Field Marshal Viscount Sir Garnet Joseph Wolseley, who rose from a distressed family of Anglo-Irish gentry to be commander in chief of the British Army. His active service life encompassed such a wide variety of campaigns in so many places that his name crops up throughout the history of British imperialism. His activity as a military reformer moved the British Army out of the nineteenth century and into the twentieth, and transformed a tradition-weighted establishment into a modern, efficient force.

Wolseley was born in 1833, the third son of a major in the 25th Borderers Regiment. His father died young, but his mother, a firm Irish Protestant, did well by her children, and young Garnet, with ambition and his father's example before him, turned to the army to make his way in the world.

After working in a draftsman's office and learning the rudiments of surveying, Wolseley was commissioned a second lieutenant in 1852. He was immediately shipped out for service in the Second Burmese War. Here he was wounded, promoted to first lieutenant, and mentioned in dispatches. He was sent home to convalesce and, upon his recovery, was available for transfer to the Crimea.

During the Crimean War, the British Army was short of every-

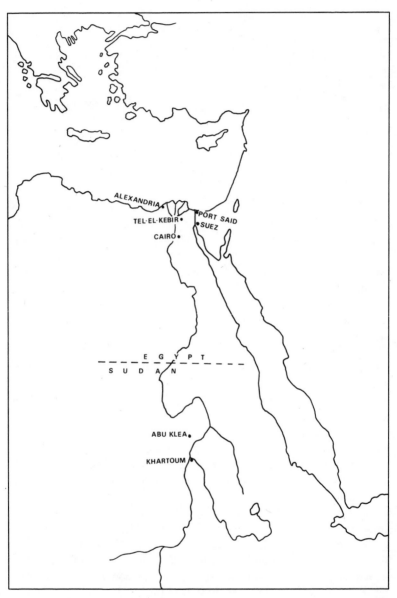

Egypt and the Sudan, 1882–1885

thing, especially talent and brains. Because of Wolseley's knowledge of surveying, he worked as an engineer officer on the trenches. His luck held good, and as the result of high casualties through sickness, injury, and battle — as the young officers' toast had it: "Here's to a bloody war or a sickly season" — Wolseley became a captain before he was twenty-one.

Wounded again and losing the sight of an eye, he was recommended to be a brevet major. Since regulations forbade that an officer be a major until he had six years of service, Wolseley had to wait three years to receive his promotion.

The waiting period was filled with activity. His battalion was ordered to China but was sent to India to deal with the Bengal Mutiny. Wolseley played a distinguished role in the relief of Lucknow and later in the operations in Oudh. By the time the mutiny was put down, Wolseley had been mentioned in dispatches five more times and was a brevet lieutenant colonel. He was twenty-five years old.

Sent off at once to China to undertake the delayed campaign, he participated in storming the Taku Forts and the Summer Palace at Peking. He later watched sadly as the troops were given license to loot priceless treasures. At the end of the campaign he received his substantive promotion to major.

He was now a field-grade officer, and the first phase of his career was over. He had served in four campaigns and had won praise and promotion in all of them. In later years he would say that if a young officer wished to distinguish himself, he could best do so by trying to get killed. Like John Paul Jones, he advised going in harm's way.

Having learned much of the bravery and resilience of the British soldier, he also came to understand how these qualities were relied upon to overcome deficiencies in the army's command and organization. When he left China to return to England, he determined to improve not only his own military competence but also the army's efficiency.

It was a large order for a young man, for the British Army in the 1860s was a peculiar institution. The Duke of Wellington, who had placed his heavy impression on the structure, had died in 1852, and his remarkable influence continued to be strong. This tendency to military conservatism, to preserve the army that had been victorious in previous campaigns, prevented the currents of reform in British civil life from penetrating the confines of the army.

In many respects the army was still a private club. Officers purchased their commissions, which guaranteed that control of the army would remain in the hands of the upper classes. Men who did not have appropriate social status, family connections, and wealth were thus restricted, no matter what their ability or experience, to the lower commissioned grades. Wolseley was an exception. It was his conspicuous gallantry in combat, in addition to an extraordinary run of luck, that enabled him to mount the ladder of promotion despite the lack of personal wealth.

The mixture of private ownership and public service made it tremendously difficult to change this aspect of the army. Interfering with a man's commission or his unit was an infringement on the sacred right of private property.

Above the regimental level, military organization and direction were chaotic. The supporting services were always starved for funds, and what little money they received was devoted to preparing for a war in the classic European manner. Yet the army seemed never to fight a European war, but rather to be engaged in the odds and ends of imperial campaigns. For these, the ancillary services were remarkably ill fitted.

At the same time the demands of imperial and colonial garrisons required the army to be dribbled out here and there in little penny packets around the empire. Central training and control were hardly feasible. When an emergency arose the army operated on the "fire brigade" concept, which the British thought was new in the 1960s. The only difference a century earlier was that they then had neither transports nor reserves.

Later in his career, in 1882, when Wolseley asked for six battalions to be sent to Egypt, he was informed that the dispatch of such a large force "woud leave England absolutely defenseless." If this remark suggests certain shortcomings in the high command, it does no more than reflect the obvious fact of an almost nonexistent national policy.

There were actually two high commands. One was the War Office, where the secretary of state for war tried to run the army as directed by Parliament. The other was the Horse Guards, where His Royal Highness the Duke of Cambridge, Queen Victoria's uncle, tried to run the army as his personal plaything. Rarely did one command take cognizance of what the other was doing. As a consequence, the army was a collection of separate units, each proud of its individual achievements, rather than a unified whole. It was in this period that a British general remarked that soldiering was always a hazardous business; but, he said, soldiering in the British Army involves rather more peculiar hazards than in any other army. These were some of the conditions that Wolseley hoped to change.

Before he could do so, the American Civil War prompted a British build-up in Canada, and in 1861 Wolseley was transferred there as Assistant Quartermaster General. Having little of an official nature to do, he studied his profession, wrote a book, toured the Civil War battlefields, and met some of the leading military figures on both sides. He was especially impressed by Stonewall Jackson. Wolseley remained in Canada for several years, receiving his colonelcy in 1865.

Four years later, still in Canada, he published a slim volume that made him financially comfortable for the rest of his life. His *Soldier's Pocket Book* was a military landmark. Up to this time, drill and administrative manuals had been solely concerned with peacetime soldiering. Wolseley's work was the forerunner of the modern field-service regulations, and it ran through many editions. It told the young soldier and the new officer what they needed to know in order to survive on active service.

Command of a field expedition came at last to Wolseley in 1870. On the Canadian frontier the advance of national sovereignty into Hudson's Bay Company territory touched off a rebellion by French Canadians and Indians led by Louis Riel. Wolseley marched with 1200 men to put down the disturbance. It was mostly a matter of transport and supply, moving his force 600 miles, by water and portage, from Lake Superior to Fort Garry near Winnipeg. Wolseley was completely successful. His quick and decisive operation dispersed the opposition without bloodshed. Returning to England, he received a knighthood for this accomplishment.

His next fight was quite different and much tougher. He was assigned to the War Office as Assistant Adjutant General, and he became a leading figure in the struggle to update the army. Allying himself with the Liberal politicians, he was the foremost military man involved in the now famous Cardwell reforms that abolished the purchase system of commissions, set up an adequate army reserve, and adopted the short enlistment term. These were considerable advances over the old army system; as such, they made a name for Wolseley, and they made him enemies. A slim, neat figure who gave the impression of being a small man, precise in attitudes, a bit of an intellectual snob, he did not conform to the popular army picture of an officer, and many resented him for it.

Active campaigning beckoned him in 1873, and he proceeded to West Africa with an expeditionary force. British colonial activity on the Gold Coast had impinged on Ashanti lands and prompted Ashanti raids and eventually a major uprising that placed the small British garrisons in jeopardy. Wolseley was appointed governor of the colony and instructed to end what was known as the Ashanti War.

He marched into the interior, burned the Ashanti capital of Kumasi, and withdrew his forces before they could be contaminated by fever. By his determination and dispatch, he avoided protracted warfare and restored peace. The most notable military feature of the campaign was Wolseley's employment of a group of bright, young officers, many of whom had served with him previously and been marked for future honors. This was an informal, incipient staff system. It was fiercely resented by nonmembers and referred to as Wolseley's "gang," his "ring," or "the cabal." However distasteful to others, it was, nonetheless, the way the army would have to move in the future.

Again Wolseley came home to a grateful Britain. He received further honors, a promotion to major general, and an outright grant of 25,000 pounds sterling, a substantial sum.

Although the Franco-Prussian War, the decisive Prussian victory, and the birth of Germany had awakened Englishmen to the dawning age of "Blood and Iron," the Liberal government was economy-minded. It was unwilling to spend much money on revamping the military services. Wolseley the reformer found himself in the strange position of being used by his political friends who held up his campaigns as examples to show that reform was unnecessary. He was, in effect, hoist on his own petard. Despite the new technology, organization, and doctrine being developed in Germany, the British Army lagged behind the modernizing efforts of other leading European powers.

To restrain his work in favor of reform, the government sent him to field service in Natal and Cyprus. He then participated in operations against the Zulus and in what is sometimes called the first Boer War.

Home once more, he engaged in political battles. As Quartermaster General of the British Army, he fought the Duke of Cambridge, the Queen, the Conservative party, and the stand-pat elements in the army on the issue of modernization. His enemies regarded him as an egotistical, pushy upstart who had no respect for traditions. He insisted that he respected tradition but could not allow it to impair efficiency. The outcome of this struggle was inconclusive. Much work remained to be done.

Meanwhile, in 1882, Wolseley embarked on the most famous of his campaigns. There was a rebellion in Egypt, one that resembled in many respects the typical twentieth-century nationalist movements. The British and French agreed to move in jointly, to restore order, to protect their nationals, and to safeguard the Suez Canal. But the French government fell as a result of "being distracted from the Rhine to the Nile," and the British went in alone.

The Royal Navy bombarded, then occupied, Alexandria, and Wolseley set out to meet the Egyptian insurgents. After seizing the Canal, he marched overland and handily defeated the Egyptians at Tel-el-Kebir. The rest was a mopping-up exercise, which Wolseley performed with his usual economy and dispatch. He went home to become a baron, to be promoted to full general, and to receive a grant of 30,000 pounds sterling.

The British occupation of Egypt was proclaimed to the world as being merely temporary. As soon as order was restored, the British would leave and let the Egyptians govern themselves again. But this was easier said than done. Instead of getting out in the 1880s, the British were drawn increasingly deeper into administration. They would, of course, remain there until after World War II, and they would be sorry even then to go.

A year and a half after Wolseley departed from Egypt, he was back again. This time it was a revolt in the Sudan, nominally held by Egypt. The British had sent Charles "Chinese" Gordon to supervise the evacuation of Egyptian military forces from the Sudan. Gordon disobeyed his orders, and he and his small force of Egyptians were trapped in Khartoum. British newspaper pressure finally forced the government to send a relief expedition. Wolseley was called upon to command it.

Doubting that his large infantry force could reach Gordon, who was besieged for nearly a year, in time to rescue the garrison, Wolseley sent ahead a detachment of about 1200 men. These relatively few troops, Wolseley hoped, would stiffen Gordon's garrison and enable him to hold out until the arrival of Wolseley's main body. At the wells of Abu Klea, in January 1885, Wolseley's advance detachment met 10,000 Arabs and defeated them after a fierce fight. Proceeding then to Khartoum, the British forward elements arrived two days after Gordon and his garrison had been overrun and massacred. Wolseley had failed, but barely.

This was his last field command. After returning home and being made a viscount, Wolseley spent the rest of his career in administrative posts, trying to complete the work of army reform. The reconquest of the Sudan would be carried out by Kitchener in the late 1890s, and he would become a national hero as a result.

The foremost figure in the British army, Wolseley was made commander in chief in 1895. His attempts to build a powerful army responsive to central policy direction ran afoul of the parsimony of the politicians. Despite endeavors to hinder his efforts, Wolseley improved the army's state of readiness to the point where it was able to react relatively quickly to the outbreak of the South African War. The actual field operations would show up deficiencies in training and organization, in weapons and mobility, in logistics and administration that Wolseley had long inveighed against.

But Wolseley had by then retired. He left the service in 1899, and was soon eclipsed by Roberts and Kitchener, who rose to fame in the Boer War. When Wolseley died in 1913, he was virtually forgotten.

He was, above all, a military politician. The reforms that he so ardently championed redressed the glaring defects that had become obvious in the Crimea. That war is now regarded as one of the major examples of military incompetence. Yet in the 1870s and 1880s, many officers and political leaders held it up as an example of how the British armed forces triumphed over all obstacles and how, therefore, the army required no changes in its structure, techniques, and procedures. They forgot, of course, that these handicaps were of their own devising. When juxtaposed with this kind of attitude, Wolseley's role in reform is more readily appreciated.

Although Wolseley never had the opportunity to show himself a battle commander of genius, he remained in the front rank of British military affairs for nearly half a century. In that half century, the army that had fought at Waterloo and in the Crimea in much the same mode was transformed into the army capable of winning in the different conditions of the South African War.

The difficulties and the problems exposed in the conventional and counterinsurgent operations against the Boers illuminated clearly the value of the reforms that Wolseley had sponsored. Although he had nothing to do with the reorganization of the British Army that permitted it to play its role in World War I, Wolseley's calls for alterations in structure, direction, and technology shaped the course of that modernization. Much of the distance between the charge of the Light Brigade and the operations of the British Expeditionary Force can be measured in terms of Wolseley's career. His impact on his profession was unmistakable and important.

Liddell Hart

YOU LEFT LONDON and, after leaving the highway, drove along leafy lanes through some of the most beautiful countryside imaginable. About an hour from the city and a million miles away, you rounded a bend and there was the unmarked driveway, which rose gently and emerged into a clearing.

If they were expecting you and if the weather was sunny and mild, they would be standing near the house: Sir Basil, a tall, slender man, probably with pipe in mouth, and lovely Lady Kathleen, smiling in welcome.

Their home was large and comfortable, with books seemingly everywhere, even though a wing had been specially built as a library, with a small bedroom and bath for visitors, mostly young, who wanted to spend several days in his military history collection and, at tea time, in conversation with him. He was extraordinarily kind and helpful, and he freely made available to military writers and academicians who were working on books and articles all sorts of materials: notes he had transcribed, papers he had gathered, talks he had had with the great and near-great men of the world.

Many persons came to see him, whatever the stated reason or excuse, simply to pay their respects to a man who had become a legend in his lifetime. He must have been pleased and gratified by the stream of visitors, the bushels of mail, the requests for advice, and the honors that were part of the growing recognition of and admiration for his achievements. But he must also have wondered occasionally whether all of this was sufficient compensation for the bitter frustration he had suffered during several decades.

Some prophets are ignored or neglected, others are castigated and abused. The essential tragedy of Basil Henry Liddell Hart was that he was understood, appreciated, and followed, but only by the enemies of his nation.

Born in Paris on October 31, 1895, of English parents, Liddell Hart attended St. Paul's School in London and Corpus Christie College of Cambridge University. He served as an officer in the King's Own Yorkshire Light Infantry in World War I. Wounded seriously, he was invalided in 1924, and in 1927 retired as a captain.

His career as a writer started immediately after he was wounded on the Somme in 1916. In a hospital back in England, he amused himself by putting down his impressions of the battle and of the generals who directed it. His observations were not so unfavorable as they would later become, even though he had at one point been, as a lieutenant, the ranking surviving officer in his battalion.

Recovered from his wounds and returned for light duty, he wrote occasional articles on the war. Then he became caught up in revising the infantry training manuals. This led him into deeper tactical studies. From there he proceeded to his theories of warfare. Liddell Hart's first concern was with infantry tactics. His study of the German methods of 1918 brought him to several conclusions: that war need not be static and linear, that infantry could break through a defensive system, and that mobility could be restored to warfare. He embodied these ideas in the training manuals he wrote and edited after the war.

In 1920, after meeting Colonel (later Major General) J. F. C. Fuller, the tank advocate, he quickly appreciated the possibilities inherent in tank operations. The perfect complement to Liddell Hart's vision of infantry pouring through a gap in the enemy's line, the tanks provided the mobility and the firepower to keep the infantry going. This, in essence, was his idea of the "expanding torrent." It was the genesis of blitzkrieg. The twin principles of opportunism on the battlefield and of feeding in reserves against the line of least resistance were translated by the U.S. Army, more than twenty years later, into the brief, direct axiom: "Exploit success."

As early as 1922, he proposed a New Model Army, an appropriate analogy with Cromwell's Ironsides. Impressed by General Sir Edmund Allenby's use of cavalry in Palestine, about the only place where horse cavalry had been successfully employed in World War I, Liddell Hart suggested replacing the independent cavalry divisions with tank battalions as integral parts of the infantry divisions. He wanted two tank battalions with every three of infantry, the tanks to perform the cavalry functions. Initially, his tanks were to mount eighteen-pounder (84-mm.) guns, eventually sixty-pounder (127-mm.) guns. The infantry was to move in armored half-track personnel carriers and be supported by self-propelled artillery. These divisions were to have close tactical air support. They were to be supplied by air.

It was all highly visionary in 1922. It was less so in 1940, when the Germans put a slightly less advanced version of it into practice. Liddell Hart, in the last sentence of his memoirs, conveyed his helplessness in the face of the reality he had done so much to create: "For me in that spring of 1940, there was a tragic irony in having to watch, as a mere onlooker, my ideas being applied to pierce the defense of France, my birthplace, and put in extreme jeopardy my own country."

Helplessness and frustration were to be constant companions for the fifteen years between the wars when he devoted all his time to working out and publicizing his theories. He became military correspondent for the *Daily Telegraph;* later he moved to the *Times* of London. He wrote innumerable articles and the first of more than thirty superb books on history, biography, tactics, and strategy. His studies of the lives of great captains, notably Genghis Khan, Sherman, Morgan, Forrest — men who had not been tied to railroads and masses — led him to develop fully his ideas of mobile warfare.

The railways, mass production, and the mass army, he wrote, had strangled military art. It was not strategy to throw away millions of men in muddy battles of attrition, but rather the negation of it. The more his thought evolved, the more critical he became of the men responsible for 1914–18, and the more certain he was that the tank and the airplane were the keys to a new military freedom.

Tank warfare to him was not war as in 1870 or 1916 plus tanks. It was, instead, the use of armored formations operating independently from the rest of the army in long-range raids to break the enemy's lines of communication and his rear-area installations.

What an army needed, he reiterated, were:

tanks able to sustain themselves for relatively long periods of time;

infantry and other elements — engineers, artillery, and the rest — to help the tanks, for example, to demine roads, to build bridges, and the like;

tactical aircraft to scout and reconnoiter, to support by fire, and to confuse the enemy;

all contributing to surprise — in attack, direction, and time — to gain the decisive exploitation of a penetration and to develop it into a pursuit of disrupted and demoralized enemy forces.

From this idea of the expanding torrent of units of combined arms built around tanks and operating independently, it was only a short step to the concept of the indirect approach at high speed into the enemy's rear where the vital and vulnerable organs of command and supply were located. He summed up this thesis by saying that the closer the front, the more immediate the effect; the farther back, the more profound.

For several years, Liddell Hart enjoyed a considerable cooperation from the War Office. He had many friends in uniform, and the younger reformers in particular were willing to work with him. But in 1927 he became completely frustrated by the lack of progress toward establishing an experimental armored division. He lashed out in anger and contempt against the Colonel Blimps in the high command. The result was costly. His channels of information began to dry up. He was suddenly unwelcome. As long as he had served as a sounding board for contemplated projects and as an unofficial though influential spokesman for army reform, he received assistance. But when he went faster than the army was prepared to go, he came close to destroying his own usefulness.

During the late 1920s and early 1930s Liddell Hart fought a lonely battle to get his ideas accepted by the public and incorporated into the British Army. Constantly, in public and private, through books and articles, speeches and letters, he endeavored to speed the adoption of his views on war and to bring about changes in the military establishment. He was in these years the prophet in the wilderness.

Events conspired against him, for this was the period of disarmament and lack of interest, war-weariness and pacifism, and economic depression, all topped by unimaginative political and military leadership. Here and there he won a disciple — a few men in the United States and France who listened, a few in Germany and Russia. But no one in Great Britain who mattered. While Sir George Milne and Sir Archibald Montgomery-Massingberd were Chiefs of the Imperial General Staff, the army was hardly disposed to be taught lessons by a retired captain of infantry.

It was at this time that Liddell Hart produced some of his best historical writing. In the campaigns of the past he found the principles he expounded applying to the future. As his ideas took more concrete form, he became more outspokenly critical of the generalship of World War I, and this only reinforced the distaste with which he was regarded by the War Office.

The British Army was now being run by men who had made their reputations in 1914–18, and they were hardly known as inspired innovators. It was not pleasant for them to be reminded that Genghis Khan had lived in an age when "merit and not seniority was the key to advancement." Scipio and Saxe had known many things of which the current British leaders were ignorant, and Liddell Hart took bitter satisfaction in pointing this out. Bitter satisfaction was all he got.

These were the bad years for him, and yet there was one place in officialdom where they listened to Liddell Hart and accommodated him to a certain extent. Lord Trenchard, marshal of the Royal Air Force, and some of the senior permanent civil servants recognized the validity of what Liddell Hart was preaching, and they gave him support, most of it covertly. When Sir Samuel Hoare was secretary of state for air he privately solicited Liddell Hart's views and assistance. These ties encouraged Liddell Hart in his long uphill battle to gain for Britain a modern defense posture. They also led him to see airpower as the dominant weapon of the future, and he wrote of its vast potential for sudden, overwhelming attack. These ideas made him defensive-minded in the late 1930s, and his writings on this subject may well have contributed to the overestimation of German air might that helped to paralyze British will in 1938.

Gradually, as World War I receded and World War II approached, Liddell Hart's voice began to be heard again. In 1935 he left the *Telegraph* for the *Times,* and from this influential platform he continued his battle. It was not his own genius, however, but another, more sinister one, that created a more receptive climate for his work. The rise of Adolf Hitler in Germany at last made Englishmen look to their moat, and they were alarmed by what they saw. Liddell Hart's countrymen were ready to give him a hearing, if no more than that.

Late in 1935, Alfred Duff Cooper, the secretary of state for war, invited Liddell Hart to lunch. He said he would welcome informed but unofficial suggestions and criticisms of the military programs. What Duff Cooper was looking for, in effect, was knowledge to balance the views of his service chiefs. Liddell Hart agreed to serve in that capacity and the two decided to keep the arrangement confidential. They worked fairly well together but the results were slow in the face of British military traditionalism. (For example, the Chief of the Imperial General Staff believed that officers of the Royal Tank Regiment should be required to fox-hunt in order to improve their decision-making power.)

When Duff Cooper left the War Office in May 1937 and moved to the Admiralty, he turned Liddell Hart over to his successor, Leslie Hore-Belisha. At this point, Liddell Hart became a true gray eminence at the War Office. An undercover general staff all by himself, he tirelessly suggested changes in training, in tables of organization and equipment, in mobilization plans, and even in personnel assignments. Within six months, the War Office was in a state of near panic, and otherwise kindly old men nearing retirement came to loathe the military correspondent of the *Times*. Hore-Belisha pretended he knew Liddell Hart only casually, but the deception fooled no one.

Natural resistance to innovation was compounded because the suggestions were those of an outsider. So much pressure built up that it was impossible to consider proposals solely on their merits. Finally, in 1938, Liddell Hart could stand the tension no longer. He broke with Hore-Belisha over what he considered to be the utter inadequacy of Britain's antiaircraft defenses. Resuming his independent role with the *Times,* he criticized the military hierarchy and the drift of his country, unprepared, toward war.

Ironically, he was attracting attention elsewhere. A handful of devoted enthusiasts in the U.S. Army were talking of motorization and mechanization and armored warfare. Russian soldiers were experimenting with combinations of armor and aircraft and carrying out airborne maneuvers. A few Frenchmen listened, among them a virtually unknown major with a bent for writing, Charles de Gaulle, whose book, *Vers l'armée du métier* (*Toward a Professional Army*), was almost pure Liddell Hart in thesis. De Gaulle called for armored mobility even though all the French generals knew positively that defense was dominant and that the next war would be like the last, except that this time France would be snugly dug in and ready. Publication of De Gaulle's book had two results: he was struck off the promotion list for 1936 and he excited the admiration of Paul Reynaud, an outspoken advocate of rearmament. But French doctrine, like that of the British, lagged. They had the best tanks in the world, but they distributed them sparingly as infantry support weapons. France would enter the war with only a few armored formations, and these would be half-formed.

But Liddell Hart's theories bore fruit in Germany. With an army restricted by the Versailles peace treaty until Hitler tore up the document, Germany had to look ahead and innovate. The armed forces consequently had open and inquiring attitudes. And there, in that country, the new doctrines were applied. Although the Germans never quite carried Liddell Hart's theories to their conclusions — it would take the mobilized industrial capacities of the United States and of the Soviet Union to do that — the Germans nevertheless created panzer formations, the type of armored forces Liddell Hart had urged. They practiced his idea of tactical air support, and the Condor Legion tested the concept during the Spanish Civil War.

General Heinz Guderian clearly acknowledged the debt when he wrote:

> It was Liddell Hart who emphasized the use of amored forces for long-range strokes, operations against the opposing army's communications, and also proposed a type of armored division combining panzer and panzer-infantry units. Deeply impressed by these ideas I tried to develop them in a sense practicable for our own army. So I owe many suggestions of our further development to Captain Liddell Hart.

General Fritz Bayerlein, Rommel's chief of staff in North Africa and later commander of the Panzer Lehr Division, said much the same thing:

> During the war, in many conferences and personal talks with Field Marshal Rommel, we discussed Liddell Hart's military works, which

won our admiration. Of all military writers, it was Liddell Hart who made the deepest impression on the Field Marshal — and greatly influenced his tactical and strategical thinking. He, like Guderian, could in many respects be termed Liddell Hart's "pupil."

By 1938 and 1939, Liddell Hart was advocating a defensive strategy for Britain, at least partly because he realized that Britain was incapable of any other. Arguing that Britain should accept only a limited liability in its military obligations if Hitler opened a campaign of continental warfare, he pressed for a return to the traditional British policy of blockade and economic warfare. The small expeditionary force, he said, should be held as a strategic reserve capable of great mobility. Foreseeing the advent of German blitzkrieg, he believed that the British Army should be committed only for counteroffensive action in the Low Countries or in the Middle East.

In sum, he envisioned Britain's concentration on waging moral and economic warfare to bring about internal collapse of the enemy. (It was therefore, no accident that the Allies' COSSAC [Chief of Staff to Supreme Allied Commander] in 1943 developed two plans along with Overlord, both predicated on the possibility of German collapse.) The function of the outnumbered British forces should be, he said, to launch operations on the enemy flanks in accordance with a peripheral or indirect strategy (which was later embodied in operations launched against Norway and in the Mediterranean area).

The course of World War II more than justified Liddell Hart's prophecies. Instead of being held in reserve, the British Expeditionary Force, sent upon the outbreak of war to France, assumed responsibility for a portion of the Allied front. When the Germans, using Liddell Hart's concepts, ripped through the Allied defenses in the spring of 1940 and prompted France to surrender and Britain to retract its ground forces through Dunkirk, the British were forced on the defensive. Subsequent British offensive strategy was peripheral and indirect in nature, with major reliance placed on seapower and air might.

Not until the United States was able to contribute sufficient resources to the coalition could the Allied forces, which had swiftly been upgraded and modernized, set into motion in northwestern Europe — first across France, then across Germany — a blitzkrieg that brought the earlier German technique close to perfection. General Omar N. Bradley's Cobra attack in July 1944, and its subsequent development in the race across France to the German border, illustrated beautifully the function of the "expanding torrent" and the exploitation of a breakout into a pursuit; and General George S. Patton, Jr., better than anyone, practiced the technique.

In the way that the carrier task force dominated the war in the Pacific, the close coordination of tanks, motorized infantry, self-propelled artillery, and tactical aircraft — Liddell Hart's intellectual creation — reigned supreme in the European theater.

Enjoying a vastly growing reputation, Liddell Hart continued to write after World War II. Hardly content to rest on his laurels, he applied his vision to problems of a future obscured by nuclear weapons. What he wrote in 1954 is relevant in 1975:

> We have moved into a new era of strategy that is very different to what was assumed by the advocates of air-atomic power . . . The strategy now being developed by our opponents is inspired by the dual idea of evading and hamstringing superior air-power. Ironically, the further we have developed the "massive" effect of the bombing weapon, the more we have helped the progress of this new guerrilla-type strategy . . .
>
> The common assumption that atomic power has cancelled out strategy is ill-founded and misleading. By carrying destructiveness to a "suicidal" extreme, atomic power is stimulating and accelerating a reversion to the indirect methods that are the essence of a strategy — since they endow warfare with intelligent properties that raise it above the brute application of force.

It is difficult to select the books that best represent the output of Liddell Hart's inquiring mind. Perhaps the following bear rereading: *The Rommel Papers; The Other Side of the Hill* (entitled in the United States *The German Generals Talk*); *A History of the World War, 1914–1918; Strategy;* the biographies of Ferdinand Foch, T. E. Lawrence, and William T. Sherman; *The Tanks;* and his memoirs.

Presented the honorary degree of doctor of literature by Oxford in 1964, made an honorary fellow of Corpus Christi College in 1965, he was knighted in 1966. Military editor of the fourteenth edition of the *Encyclopaedia Britannica,* generally regarded as the best edition for military matters, he was also distinguished visiting professor of history at the University of California at Davis, in 1965–66. Having lectured on strategy and tactics at the military institutions of many countries, he had agreed to come to the Naval War College in Newport during the spring of 1970.

But he died on January 29, 1970, "the captain who teaches generals," as the Israelis called him, and the departure of this kind and generous man was a sorrowful loss.

Barrie Pitt, one of his friends and disciples — and there are many of them, relatively young men who are now in the forefront of the thinkers concerned with and writing on military operations, principles, doctrine, strategy, and history — wrote in a letter from England:

> You were doubtless as saddened as all of us by the death of Basil Liddell Hart — though there is no doubt that he went exactly as he would have wished. He had just come back from three weeks at Bournemouth, spent in a superb hotel with Kathleen to look after his every need and [Field Marshal] Montgomery to argue with. Apparently both old gentlemen were in great form . . . On Thursday morning Basil got up and began work in his usual fashion, fell down with a stroke at about 10 o'clock and never regained consciousness. He died about 8 o'clock in the evening — and since the announcement on British radio, telegrams and letters from all over the world have not ceased to flow in. The funeral was yesterday morning at the little village church at Medmenham which was, needless to say, crowded. The British Army Staff sent a Major-General, but there were only two other uniformed personages present. You will be pleased to know they were both U.S. colonels, one from the Army and one from the Marine Corps.

Patton and Montgomery

IF ONE WERE ASKED to select the outstanding American and British field commanders on the European side of World War II, he would surely choose George S. Patton, Jr., and Bernard L. Montgomery. They are generally regarded — and justly so — as the best leaders of combat troops in that part of the war. Their instinct for warfare was sure, their grasp of military operations was superb, and their handling of large units was expert. Each captured the imagination of the world, and each has become a folk hero.

To compare Patton and Montgomery would, at first glance, seem to be simply a matter of cataloguing distinct differences in appearance, character, personality, and methods of operation. Such are the instant impressions.

In World War II at least, Patton was large and loud, outspoken and blunt, a blusterer and braggart, a highly flamboyant type, a profane man and an athletic type. He was a general who acted on impulse, who roared, who projected the warrior figure, rough, tough, and direct, whose basic method seemed to be one of smashing and overwhelming the enemy forces on the battlefield.

Montgomery, on the other hand, was smaller and quieter, diplomatic and devious, reflective and soft-spoken; an ascetic person who neither smoked nor drank and who had no apparent interest in women. Mild and deliberate, he projected the figure of the military intellectual, the general who outsmarted the enemy as the result of careful study, rumination, and preparation.

Summarizing these impressions, we might say that one general was overplayed, the other understated. Yet the contrasting qualities described are so superficial as to be meaningless for any real appreciation of these two soldiers. In actuality, despite the popular legends, they were very much alike.

The evident differences in behavior and in the impressions they imparted were deliberate projections of carefully cultivated characteristics that they displayed for public consumption. The war masks they showed — not only to the troops under their command, but also to the folks back home — corresponded with national stereotypes, exaggerations — caricatures, if you wish — that were highly effective in both cases.

In private both were quiet and studious. They were in essence contemplative. Yet the demands of leadership, as they saw them, made them assume certain poses and postures, and each was extremely efficacious as the battlefield leader he portrayed.

Patton's way with his soldiers, his ability to stimulate them to give their utmost, needs no elaborate documentation here. Known as Gorgeous Georgie in North Africa and Old Blood and Guts in Sicily, Patton may have provoked as much distaste as admiration among his troops, but he moved them emotionally and they performed magnificently for him. As one doughboy said, "That SOB, I would follow him to hell and back." In the thousands, men still say proudly, "I rolled with Patton." The rapport that he established with his troops was immediate and positive, for the personal image he created appealed to the essential motivations of combat soldiers. He was a consummate actor, and the role that he played in his dress and action was consciously adopted and vigorously demonstrated with marvelous effect.

So, too, Montgomery. Like Patton he had his highly visible trademarks. Instead of the ivory-handled pistols, he affected a beret and a sweater. Yet who can doubt the deep and very real affection he inspired among his troops. Anyone who saw the mad and pell-mell rush of men to throng about Monty's jeep in response to his invitation to gather round must be impressed by the emotional pull he exerted.

The point is that both generals, in their different manners, acting consciously in response to the contrasting demands of leadership for American and British peoples, compelled their troops to identify with the Old Man. It has long been a truism in military life that when soldiers imitate their commander, leadership and morale are first rate and high. The close affinity that existed between Patton and his troops, and between Montgomery and his, is a mark of the superb generalship that these leaders personified. Both men inspired confidence, admiration and affection.

Despite the surface differences in manner, both men were very much alike in their military qualities. They were lifelong students of the art of war. Their knowledge of military history was enormous. They were voracious readers, and each aspired to, and acquired, a thorough-going professionalism. They were technically expert in the various manifestations of their craft — in logistics, tactics, operations. They had mastered weapons and weapons systems. They were proficient in matters of doctrine and alert to innovations in methodology. What each cultivated for his public relations was an image that met the characteristics required by his respective people.

As for their methods of operation, they too are more alike than contrasting. An example is their use of their staffs. Although Patton liked to pretend that he made instantaneous decisions, and although Montgomery liked to isolate himself for hours in his van to work out his operational problems and plans, they both relied on the brilliant staff work of men they had hand-picked to assist them. Here again each conformed with national prejudices in appearance. A man of studious demeanor or habit would hardly have gone over with American troops. An apparently impulsive and reckless man would hardly have been right for the British, who remembered, and were conditioned by, the heavy casualties of Passchendaele in World War I.

If Patton seemed to prefer the direct smash and the lightning thrust, it was because this was the American way. The basic American approach to strategy in the European theater was the desire for a massive thrust along the most direct path to the heart of the major enemy. This concept derived from the relative abundance of United States resources in manpower and matériel.

The British were constrained by the relative scarcity of their human and material resources, and they preferred an indirect approach, one more flexible, taking advantage of opportunity. Whereas Patton and the Americans could afford to spend the coin of warfare, Montgomery and the British had to be thrifty, prudent, even cautious. Witness the extreme care with which Montgomery pursued Rommel across the length of Libya, and compare it with the reckless abandon with which Patton expanded the exploitation in Normandy into pursuit.

Yet to say that Patton steamrollered over his opponents and that Montgomery outmaneuvered them is far from the truth. In Sicily it was Montgomery who sought to overwhelm the German defensive line at Catania by butting against it; Patton, going the long way through Palermo, entered Messina first. In Sicily Montgomery, urged to do so by his naval friends, finally mounted a single amphibious end run to outflank the German line on the east coast; Patton, without urging, launched two on the north shore, one of which, as it is turned out, was unnecessary.

There were, then, contrasting styles. Montgomery is commonly regarded as master of the set-piece battle, as at El Alamein, Caen, Arnhem-Nijmegen, and the crossing of the Rhine. Patton is usually considered the slasher, the master of the ad hoc operation. So it would seem that tactically each general ran contrary to his nation's strategic outlook — the American strategy was direct and massive; it was the British whose strategy was flexible — the reverse of Patton's and Montgomery's tactical habits.

The easy generalization is, of course, all too easy. Let us not forget that during the pursuit of the defeated German armies in Normandy, during August and early September 1944, the British and Canadians under Montgomery went just as fast and just as far as the Americans under Bradley, more specifically, under Hodges and Patton. We must therefore qualify the real differences, which in fact there were. But these differences did not result only from national characteristics and requirements; they stemmed in large part also from the professional upbringing of both men. Patton was basically a cavalryman and Montgomery was essentially an infantryman.

Let us briefly trace their careers. Patton was born in November 1885; Montgomery two years and six days later. They were both Scorpios, whatever that means. Patton's family was a mixture of romantic Virginia aristocracy and terribly pragmatic California pioneer. Montgomery's family was of the clergy. Both men adored their fathers. Patton had a happy childhood; Montgomery an unhappy time. The difference lay in the affection of Patton's mother and the lack of affection in Montgomery's. Patton never sought to understand the motivation of his drive, what made him run; Montgomery constantly tried to comprehend what made him tick.

Montgomery went to St. Paul's School in London, then to Sandhurst, and entered the army in 1908. Patton went to Dr. Stephen

Cutter Clark's Classical School for Boys in Pasadena, then to the Virginia Military Institute for a year, and finally took five years to graduate from West Point, which he did in 1909.

Montgomery was assigned to India; Patton to Fort Sheridan, Illinois, Fort Meyer, Virginia, later to Fort Riley, Kansas. Patton participated in the Olympics at Stockholm and traveled to some extent in Europe.

Montgomery went to France with the British Expeditionary Force in 1914, and in October, as a lieutenant in command of an infantry platoon, led an assault near Ypres, was badly wounded, and was awarded the Distinguished Service Order. Patton was taking the cavalry course and also giving instruction in the use of the saber; he had the magnificently impressive title of Master of the Sword.

Montgomery recuperated from his wound in England, and in 1915 returned to France. He served for the rest of the war as a staff officer and at the end was a lieutenant colonel. To what extent Montgomery absorbed the lessons of the static war on the western front is conjectural, but there is no doubt that the enormous casualties that were finally senseless became an indelible part of his experience. He resolved that if ever he commanded large units there would be no battle, if he had his way, until careful calculation and preparation made certain that troops would never be sent into a forlorn assault, an attack that had little chance of success.

Patton went into Mexico with Pershing in 1916, became a national hero for about a week by killing three members of Pancho Villa's army, and learned much of his military craft by observing and studying Pershing, upon whom he consciously modeled himself. He accompanied Pershing to France in 1917, was the first United States officer assigned to the Tank Corps, became the leading American tanker, and led his brigade at St.-Mihiel and in the Meuse-Argonne offensive, where he was wounded. He received the Distinguished Service Cross for gallantry and ended the war as a colonel, one grade above Montgomery. If Patton carried with him a single impression from his experiences, it was the importance of mobility.

For Montgomery, it was a long war; for Patton, a relatively short one. Montgomery probably had no significant relations with Americans or French, but rather a more normal wartime duty, perhaps a more parochial experience. Patton came to know a variety of people who were the great and near-great. He was, of course, close to

Pershing, a friend of Billy Mitchell, James Harbord, Hugh Drum, Malin Craig, and a host of others. He met Clemenceau, Pétain, and knew General Eugène Estienne, head of the French tanks. He came to know many British officers, including Haig, Trenchard, Elles, Fuller, and also the young Prince of Wales, later King Edward VIII — Patton once rolled dice with the prince and, because no women were present, danced with him to the phonograph.

Montgomery went to the Staff College at Camberly in 1920, spent three years there as an instructor, and later became the chief instructor at the Staff College at Quetta, then in India, now in Pakistan. Patton took the advanced cavalry course, was an honor graduate of the Command and General Staff College at Fort Leavenworth, and a distinguished graduate of the Army War College. Both men thus acquired the requisite military education for the practice of their profession and for the exercise of high command.

Montgomery married at the age of forty and was widowed after ten years of very happy married life. Patton married at twenty-five and had a long and very happy married life.

In 1939 Montgomery was a major general in command of the 3d Division, which he took to France at the outbreak of the war. Patton was a colonel in command at Fort Meyer and was performing ceremonial functions in Washington. By July 1940 Montgomery had fought the fierce Battle of France through the evacuation of Dunkirk and was a corps commander; Patton was still a colonel, but was now assigned to command an armored brigade at Fort Benning, Georgia.

In August 1942 Montgomery took command of the Eighth Army in Egypt. Patton was in command of the I Armored Corps. In October Montgomery won the Battle of El Alamein and started pursuing Rommel across Libya. In November Patton took his Western Task Force ashore at French Morocco, one of three simultaneous assaults in Operation Torch.

The North Africa landings made instant heroes of Patton, Eisenhower, and Mark Clark, who became the darlings of Americans everywhere. At that time Montgomery was becoming more than a British national hero; he was attaining the rank of a global star. El Alamein, his greatest victory, made him known to the world, and the subsequent pursuit of Rommel into Tunisia increased his heroic stature.

In March 1943, after the American disaster at Kasserine Pass,

Eisenhower moved Patton from Morocco to Tunisia, where Patton took command of the battered II Corps. He revitalized this command, retrained the men, gave them confidence, led them in battle, and triumphed at El Guettar. Then, after turning over the corps to his deputy, Omar N. Bradley, Patton left to work out the preparations for the invasion of Sicily.

It has been said — by a British author — that Prime Minister Churchill deliberately built up Montgomery's reputation in the interest of stimulating civilian and army morale. The British had their air and naval heroes by virtue of the Battles of Britain and of the Atlantic. Montgomery became the ground-force hero and received the utmost support and publicity from Churchill as well as from Alan Brooke, Chief of the Imperial General Staff.

Although Patton had no such high and obvious support, he had several influential people in his corner. Henry L. Stimson, Republican secretary of war in Roosevelt's Democratic administration, was an old friend. Pershing was an old friend. So too, but in more reserved form, was Marshall. And so, too, Eisenhower.

Patton and Montgomery met professionally sometime between the end of the North Africa campaign in May 1943 and the invasion of Sicily in July. Both were involved in the planning for Sicily, and they met personally during that period of time. In the Patton papers is a printed brochure prepared by Montgomery, who wrote up his appreciation of the lessons learned in the desert campaign. His observations of warfare received wide distribution. Montgomery's lessons were very much like an exegesis on the principles of war, with examples to illustrate certain undying truths — truths like the necessity to gain surprise, concentration, and all the rest. Patton had a copy of his manual, and he wrote in the margins, "Excellent," "Agreed," "He is right." All of Patton's reactions to Montgomery's strictures indicate a remarkable similarity of outlook. Both generals were wedded, at least in principle, to very similar methods of operation.

It was in Sicily that each commanded an army and Patton stole the glory. He began to equal Montgomery as a living legend. For it was there that Patton proved that American troops were as good as British troops, an issue in some doubt since the Kasserine Pass disaster. It was in Sicily too that Patton's career almost ended because of the slapping incidents. Montgomery took his Eighth Army across the Strait of Messina into the mainland of Italy and fought alongside Mark Clark's Fifth Army. Patton made conspicuous appearances in the Mediterranean in order to deceive the Germans about Allied future plans. If there was little glory for Patton during the final months of 1943, there was little for Montgomery either. Southern Italy turned out to be a bitter battlefield and, contrary to Allied expectations, Rome remained in enemy hands.

Early in 1944 Montgomery went to England to head the British forces in the invasion of Normandy and Patton to take command of the Third Army, the follow-up American force. Montgomery was pro-tem commander of the Allied ground forces during the first three months of the invasion and looked less than spectacular at Caen, which he said he would take on D-Day and which he finally captured forty-two days later. He looked none too good in Operation Goodwood, where he failed to break through. He appeared less than masterful in directing the drive to Falaise.

Patton entered the campaign on August 1 and immediately broke open the operation. He expanded a local breakthrough into a theater-wide breakout and pressed home the defeat of the two German field armies in Normandy. The subsequent pursuit across France to the German border, in which everyone participated, was of Patton's making.

At least part of Montgomery's insistence on launching Operation Market-Garden, an attempt to cross the lower Rhine, stemmed from his desire to regain the ascendancy. Although the rationale of Market-Garden was sound, the operation was uncharacteristic of Montgomery. It was not the kind of thing one would expect him to sponsor. It failed for a variety of reasons and mischances, none of which can be ascribed directly to Montgomery.

By this time he was a field marshal, heading an army group and directing three armies, one British, one Canadian, and one American. Patton was two grades below him, a lieutenant general in command of a single army. Yet they had become rivals. The rivalry was at first friendly. For example, they wagered on all sorts of things, small bets like how long it would take Patton to reach Brest. But as they competed for newspaper headlines, the rivalry became somewhat heated. Patton is supposed to have said, as the Argentan-Falaise pocket was being closed, "Let me go on to Falaise, and I'll drive the Limeys into the sea."

He never said this, but he never denied it; it was too good a remark. But there was a statement that resembled it, and this was probably the origin of the wisecrack. What happened was this: Patton was halted at Argentan and prohibited from going on to Falaise and having a head-on collision with the Canadians, who were closing the pocket from the other side. Several days later Montgomery and Bradley decided to let Patton go ahead and meet the Canadians, not at Falaise but at a place called Trun. Patton was at Bradley's headquarters when the decision was made, and he phoned his chief of staff to get the operation started at once. Since the wire might be tapped by the Germans, Patton spoke guardedly. "When initial objective is taken," he said, "continue to original objective, thence on."

The chief of staff wanted to be sure he understood. "What is meant," he asked, "by 'thence on'?"

Giving authority for an unlimited advance, Patton replied, "Another Dunkirk."

The rivalry that had been building between Montgomery and Patton became positively bitter by the fall of 1944, for by then Patton and Montgomery were competing for supplies, for transport, for the precious gasoline that kept armies moving. This was competition with a vengeance, for at stake was the question of who would win the war; that is, if any hard charger on a white horse was going to have that honor. The rivalry continued through the Battle of the Bulge, at the Rhine River crossings, and across Germany, but in the later stages of the war it involved the entire United States high command, notably Eisenhower and Bradley rather than Patton.

At the end of the war Montgomery was a field marshal and the acknowledged hero of the British world. He would go on to command the British Army of the Rhine, to serve as Chief of the Imperial General Staff, and to play an important role in NATO matters. He has received marked adulation from the British public and from British historians, such as Chester Wilmot, C. P. Stacey, L. F. Ellis, H. Essame, and Ronald Lewin, all of whom have interpreted the war from what might be called the Montgomery point of view. Even R. W. Thompson, who is somewhat dubious about Montgomery's claim to fame, follows the Montgomery line.

The American point of view, best exemplified by the official volumes in the U.S. Army series and in the works of Charles B. Mac-Donald and Stephen Ambrose, interprets events from the Eisenhower outlook. In that continuing battle of the books the focus is really on the Eisenhower-Montgomery disputes. Patton, an army commander, has an inconspicuous place in that debate.

At the end of the war Patton was a four-star general and soon afterward fell into disgrace for having said that members of the Nazi party were little different from Republicans and Democrats. Patton died as the result of a freak automobile accident and immediately attained, if not sainthood, then at least a well-deserved enshrinement as one of America's and the world's great captains.

Patton and Montgomery were so very different, so very much alike. It is no coincidence that the British Eighth Army and the U.S. Third Army were quite similar: the troops confident to the point of cockiness, highly motivated, highly effective, professional, and veteran. Both men were extreme egoists. Both suffered terrible anxieties and insecurities. They generated a highly charged emotional intensity toward themselves, feelings that have been extremely polarized, whether favorable or hostile.

They were prisoners of their experience, captives of their national histories and attitudes. Yet to say that each was little more than the product of impersonal forces is to overlook the driving will power that motivated both, that made them excel in their profession, that drove them to fame and glory and to a large share of the credit in the winning of World War II.

PART IV

Coalition Warfare: The Soldier as Diplomat and Politician

THE HIGHER IN COMMAND the soldier goes, the further removed is he from operational routine. For many officers, command of a division is the pinnacle of a career, because at that point the commander still has direct contact with the troops who wage the war. The division is the largest unit that a commander can handle as a fighting entity. He is still captain of his ship. Beyond that, the immediacy of warfare is gone. Commanding on levels above the division has its compensations. In modern war, from the corps up, the leader has a chance of becoming famous.

The successive echelons of the higher command structure — division, corps, army, army group — go back to the French. They initiated the modern regimental system at the end of the seventeenth century, and they originated the divisional establishment at the end of the eighteenth. During the revolution they developed the idea of separate armies — Army of the Rhine, Army of Italy, Army of the Sambre and Meuse — which were, in reality, corps consisting of several divisions. When Napoleon appeared on top of the heap, the corps organization became the Grand Army. Thus, Napoleon's marshals were his corps commanders, and these are the men who are talked about in the Napoleonic saga. For example, Davout had the I Corps, and is well known; the three division commanders who served under him, Gudin, Friant, and Morand, are largely forgotten. In Napoleon's army, the corps was the natural unit.

A century later, societies and armies had grown so big that the unit of discussion in World War I was the field army. The Schlieffen

Plan dealt with the armies of Kluck, Bülow, and Hausen. At that time, when the war started, the small British Expeditionary Force was composed of two corps that together made up a single small army fighting alongside five French armies. Later, when the British were drawn fully into the morass, they too had their armies — Plumer's Second, Byng's Third, Gough's Fifth, with several intermediate corps headquarters under each army directing twelve, nineteen, and eighteen divisions respectively.

In actual fact the expansion went beyond this. For practical purposes the national commanders of World War I were army group commanders, each commanding his national field army. The British commander in chief, Haig, was in effect performing the function exercised by Montgomery in 1944–45, and various French generals, notably Joffre and Pétain, were essentially doing what would be Bradley's job. Pershing too operated on that level as he directed the two American field armies in the latter weeks of the war.

Although the army group was a logical extension, given the size of the forces engaged, the arrangement on the Allied level was less than perfect. The national interests of the commanders and of their governments often led to clashes with the fundamental military requirements of the battlefield. All limped along, however, as best they could until the German offensives in the spring of 1918 brought them to the edge of collapse. Then, under the pressure of imminent defeat, the Allies agreed at last to appoint a Supreme Allied Commander in order to give unity to their activities. Marshal Foch was named to that command.

Foch's mandate as a commander was extremely limited. He was less a commander than an advisor, less a director than a pleader for cooperation. His role was defined in a note scribbled by the Allied representatives meeting at Doullens at the end of March. "General Foch," the paper read, "is appointed by the British and French governments to co-ordinate the action of the Allied Armies on the Western Front. To this end he will come to an understanding with the two generals-in-chief [Haig and Pétain], who are requested to furnish him with the necessary information." Later, the American government too agreed to subordinate Pershing's operations to Foch's wishes.

If Foch hardly received a clarion call to leadership, the Supreme

Allied Command served its purpose. Foch gave a certain overall consistency to the operations that the Allies needed desperately to coordinate in order to win the war.

This weakness is probably true of coalitions generally. Of them as of religions, it may be said that nothing fails like success. The great coalition wars in modern history have all resulted from one condition, the predominance or threatened predominance of a single state. Between 1689 and 1815, the coalitions were anti-French, for France had the most powerful government, the largest homogeneous territory and population, and the capacity to upset the balance of power. The exception in the period resulted from the rise of Prussia, and the anti-Prussian coalition during the Seven Years' War had France, Austria, and Russia ranged together to defeat the upstart Frederick the Great. They failed because of ineptness and jealously. At least twice Austria or Russia might have taken Berlin and overrun Prussia; they held back because each felt its ally was not pulling his weight.

After 1815 Germany menaced the continental balance. Thus the two coalitions of the twentieth century were anti-German. The second effort, the Anglo-American partnership in World War II, has been called the most successful example of coalition warfare ever waged. It may not have seemed so to the participants, as the acidulous Alanbrooke diaries, King memoirs, and Patton papers indicate; but compared with earlier groupings, it was a marvel indeed. The fact that it took half a dozen so-called coalitions to defeat Napoleon makes the Allied effort in the mid-twentieth century look remarkably harmonious and effective.

In a coalition effort, the commanders at the top of the scale are in a never-never land between the political and military realities. Below them military forces are usually organized in separate national armies. Above them are the civilian politicians who have their own domestic interests and their own interpretations of foreign policy. The military high command is the point of contact between political and military aspirations and activities; because of this, the coalition commanders must function as superb artists.

During World War II, the political leaders of the United States and Great Britain, Roosevelt and Churchill, were both interested in the conduct of military operations. They concerted their objectives and agreed to a large extent on their policies. Differences of view about the shape of the postwar world were never allowed to become serious enough to disrupt the primary aim of the coalition: defeat of the enemy. Eisenhower as Supreme Allied Commander was fortunate that his political superiors enjoyed a rare degree of unity.

By contrast, in 1813–14, when the allies finally defeated Napoleon, they managed to do so only by adhering very loosely to their agreements on who would do what. They never achieved a supreme military command, though they somehow coordinated their actions. Nor did they ever reach unanimity on exactly what they wanted in Europe afterward. Within a year of the French defeat, the allies were so deeply embroiled in dividing up the spoils that they were threatening each other with war and courting France as a key power.

The same kind of divergence on war aims appeared after World War I. As soon as Germany collapsed, the Allies found themselves desiring vastly different and nearly incompatible settlements. France wanted Germany ruined, and to this end soon began playing separatist politics in the Rhineland. Britain wanted a return to prewar business prosperity, and to that end advocated rehabilitating Germany, which was completely at variance with the desire for reparations and for punishing Germany as an aggressor. The United States was not at all sure what it wanted, and the difference between President Wilson's view and his country's outlook went a long way toward destroying any settlement at all.

With this kind of record for coalitions, it is hardly surprising that the Allies of World War II also fell to squabbling soon after the war. In retrospect, it is obvious that only a massive dose of willful self-deception allowed the western Allies and the Russians to form a team in the first place, but at that time the overriding necessity was to defeat Germany, and that could be done only in concert.

The soldier who can run a coalition is a rare figure. To reach that stratospheric position and remain there, he must be aggressive, bold, ruthless, and enterprising — in short, he has to possess all the traditional military virtues. He is then told to do a job that requires tact, tolerance, forbearance, and patience — qualities that had little to do with his previous advancement.

There is something of Jekyll and Hyde about it, and it is probably significant that neither of the two greatest American exponents of cooperation in World War II, Marshall and Eisenhower, had the kind of reputation as a combat leader that, for example, Patton did. What is more surprising is to see Patton performing very well in a similar situation in North Africa with the French, generally agreed to be among the more prickly of allies. Who will ever forget Churchill's growl that the heaviest cross he bore in the war was the Cross of Lorraine?

The coalition soldier thus steps out of what has to that point been his natural milieu, and the man who can do so successfully is one who has indeed proved his versatility. Defeating one's enemies while placating one's allies calls for the remarkable characteristics of the soldier-statesman.

Rochambeau

Jean Baptiste Donatien de Vimeur, Comte de Rochambeau, known to his troops affectionately as "Papa" Rochambeau, was no kindly, paternal, slightly fussy commander who carefully husbanded his soldiers. He was, rather, a crisp, spare, incisive tactician and field commander. Simple in his tastes, dignified in his behavior, without ostentation or airs of self-importance, he was also a military statesman who successfully managed the difficult Franco-American alliance under the trying circumstances of the American Revolution.

Born at Vendôme in 1725, the third son of a noble family, Rochambeau was destined for the Church. From the age of five, he received an education appropriate to such a future. On the point of accepting his tonsure when his elder brother died, he was, at age seventeen, abruptly snatched from the Church and handed over to the army.

His first taste of combat came in the War of the Austrian Succession, which someone called "as unreasonable in its object as it was disastrous in its consequences." True for the war, it was hardly that for young Rochambeau. He began as a junior officer in the cavalry regiment of Saint-Simon, and he so distinguished himself in Bohemia, Bavaria, and along the Rhine that he came to the favorable attention of several of the royal princes. They suggested that he buy himself a regiment, the only way to get a respectable command in those days. Though his family was relatively poor, it managed to scrape up the price of an infantry colonelcy. In March 1747, when he was not quite twenty-two, Rochambeau became colonel of the Regiment de la Marche.

Leading his regiment in combat, he was severely wounded in the butchery at Laufeldt. He was sufficiently recovered to take part in the siege of Maastricht, the last great event of the war.

After the Treaty of Aix-la-Chapelle, Rochambeau might have joined the court at Versailles, but intrigue and gossip were never to his liking. He retired to Vendôme, where he married and lived as a country gentleman. His pastoral existence was broken by occasional tours of garrison duty.

The outbreak of the Seven Years' War gave him the opportunity for further active service, and he distinguished himself again in a number of engagements in Germany. He also took part in the amphibious expedition to Minorca. He became noted for his unusual attention both to discipline and to the well-being of his men. By the end of the war, he was a brigadier general. Appointed Inspector General of Cavalry, Rochambeau served again with his old army, and was then transferred to command a military district in the south of France. He thereby acquired intimate knowledge of the higher levels of army organization and broadened his competence.

Two years later, when France became the ally of the United States in its revolt against Great Britain, Rochambeau was a veteran soldier, tried in battle, skilled in administrative practice, and at home in the different aspects of his career. Not only had he the requisite background for high command, but he also combined with this what was remarkable in the officer class of his day, a knowledge of the motivations of his men and a concern for the military proficiency of his troops.

None of this explains why he was given the command of the expeditionary force sent to America. In the *ancien régime,* command often went to those who stood in highest favor at Versailles, and the talents required for advancement at the court were scarcely those that fitted a man for military service.

The French had already dispatched an expedition under Estaing to assist the Americans. He sailed fruitlessly around the western Atlantic, doing little harm to the British but much to the alliance. The Americans were impatient for action; in addition, they resented his high-handed ways with them.

In 1779, with the alliance in danger of dissolution on the working level, Lafayette persuaded the French government to send a second

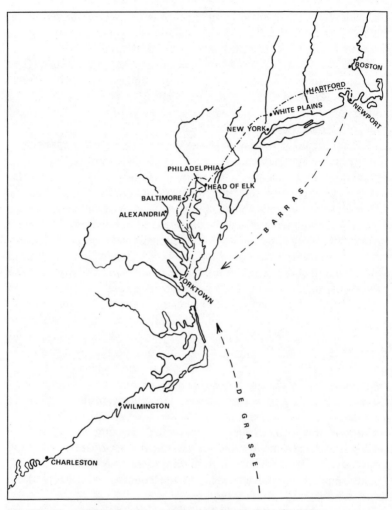

The Yorktown Combination and Rochambeau's March, 1781

force to America. He himself, whose military talents were inferior to his own opinion of them, hoped to command. He was disappointed when the task went instead to Rochambeau. The choice turned out to be wise, for the young Lafayette would probably have lacked the experience and maturity to overcome the traditional incompetence of the Ministry of War and the proverbial stupidity of the Ministry of the Marine.

Rochambeau, now fifty-five years old, had just been promoted to the grade of lieutenant general. He had also been granted indefinite leave because of the death of his father and his own affliction with inflammatory rheumatism. Despite his poor health, he set out for Brest to assemble and train a force for transportation to America.

That any joint and combined operations succeeded in the eighteenth century is a wonder. In Rochambeau's case, the Spanish allies refused to cooperate with him. The treasury made endless difficulties about funds. The navy dragged its feet. Time passed.

It was necessary for Rochambeau to exert all his tact, skill, and persistence to get his force afloat. Resolving his problems, he had 7600 troops at Brest ready to embark in April 1780. He then learned that the navy transports had room for only 5500. He made the best of that reality, and the transports, escorted by warships, took his reduced ranks aboard and sailed on May 1. They anchored off Newport, Rhode Island, on July 11.

Lafayette accompanied the expedition in a junior capacity and assisted Rochambeau as best he could. Rochambeau would need all the help he could get, for he was short of practically everything — weapons, ammunition, supplies, and, since France was already drifting toward bankruptcy, especially money. In addition, Rochambeau could speak no English.

Immediately blockaded by British naval forces, which prevented French reinforcement and resupply, Rochambeau and his men camped in Rhode Island for ten months. It took all of Rochambeau's ingenuity to hold his organization together. Instructed to act under Washington's orders, he had also been told to preserve his force in being, to remain in contact with the French fleet, and to await reinforcements. To a certain extent these instructions were contradictory and even impossible. Washington wanted the French to help him take New York. Although Lafayette urged action, Rochambeau politely insisted that active campaigning was, for the moment at least, out of the question. He was hoping for the promised reinforcements. He had lost touch with the navy. He was without funds.

To the ragged Americans it often appeared that the French, who seemed to have everything, were willing to do nothing. Rochambeau, who felt abandoned by his government and who once paid his officers out of his relatively meager private capital, felt doomed to inaction.

An added difficulty was Lafayette, who acted as interpreter in his correspondence with Washington. Lafayette tried to minimize the obstacles faced by both allies. As a result, each commander sometimes had the impression that the other had promised more than he actually delivered. Rochambeau at last chided Lafayette in a fatherly way and requested him to confine his efforts to translation only.

Washington and Rochambeau met at Hartford in September 1780 and the American proposed his pet project — a joint and combined operation to take New York City. Rochambeau quietly demurred. He pointed out that unless they had command of the sea the undertaking was impractical. This was something that Washington should have known, for he had, in 1776, nearly lost his army there because of British seapower.

The spring of 1781 came, and still the French were in Rhode Island. American visitors often remarked that they could be trusted to camp in apple orchards without stealing the fruit, but this hardly offset the increasing frustrations on both sides of the alliance.

In May, Rochambeau learned that he was to have no reinforcements, although he was to be sent some money. And another French fleet, de Grasse's, was to sail for the West Indies, then come north to assist the allies.

Upon receipt of this news, Rochambeau met with Washington again, this time at Wethersfield, Connecticut. They talked about plans. Washington still favored New York; Rochambeau still hesitated. Yet they agreed that if de Grasse did in fact show up, wide strategic vistas would be opened for consideration. The allies might even do something in the south, where Cornwallis was giving the Americans a difficult time.

Rochambeau broke camp on June 10 and marched his troops to White Plains, New York. There were some skirmishes around New York early in July. And then events took place that drew the attention of the allies southward.

Cornwallis had moved into Virginia, placing the middle states in jeopardy, and Lafayette, now commanding Franco-American troops in that area, was hard pressed. At the same time, information arrived from de Grasse. He was sailing from the West Indies for the Chesapeake Bay. As it became obvious to Washington and Rochambeau that the British in New York were too strong for them, they looked toward, and were drawn to, the south.

The Yorktown campaign was something of a miracle for eighteenth-century warfare. The skill required to bring widely separated fleets and armies together at the right place and time can be appreciated only if one knows how often such combinations failed miserably. Luck was the prime factor. This time everything went right. Lafayette pinned Cornwallis into Yorktown. De Grasse arrived from Haiti late in August, landed 3000 troops, and put to sea just in time to intercept and chase away a British relief squadron coming to help Cornwallis. Barras arrived with his naval squadron, bringing siege artillery from Newport on September 10. Washington, Rochambeau, and their troops, after a march that did credit to the stamina of the soldiers, the organizing capacity of their commanders, and the logistical support from the middle colonies, came to Williamsburg during the next ten days.

All in all, the allied descent on Yorktown was a remarkable strategic concentration, and those who brought it off — out of the depths of despair and near bankruptcy — deserved to win. They formally opened the siege early in October, and on the nineteenth, Cornwallis, trapped against the sea and deprived of naval assistance, could only surrender.

The best of the King's Army in North America — British, Germans, and Loyalists — marched out between the ranks of French and Americans and laid down arms and colors. Reports of the event are curiously somber. The clink of weapons, the shrill of fifes, the beat of drums seemed only to accentuate the silence. The world was turned upside down, and everyone seemed to sense dimly that this was a day beyond jubilation.

Rochambeau, the perfect ally, remained in the United States more than a year afterward. His troops eventually marched north to Boston and sailed home from there. After receiving the thanks of the Continental Congress, he himself departed from Anne Arundel, as

Annapolis, Maryland, was then called, and arrived at St. Nazaire in February 1783.

In France he was poorly recompensed for his services. In private, Louis XVI told Rochambeau that the allied victory was largely his achievement. In public, Lafayette was the hero. Rochambeau was hurt by the failure to acknowledge his triumph, but he was the kind of man who continued to serve despite the absence of plaudits and praise.

It is customary to forget that historical figures live beyond the pages of history they illuminate. Rochambeau, who had come home from America sick and tired, looked forward to retirement in the countryside he loved. Although he lived twenty-four years more, he had little of the repose he sought.

In 1784 he took command of the military district of Picardy. In 1789 he assumed command of the Rhine frontier in Alsace. Retiring later that year because of ill health, he was recalled the next to command the northern military district. In 1791 he was finally offered the baton of a marshal of France, the highest mark of military distinction.

Old and in poor health, he was involved in the disastrous campaigns of the early French Revolution, but he acquitted himself well. During the Terror he spent some time in prison, but escaped the guillotine. He was at last allowed to retire permanently.

In 1801 Rochambeau was invited to a meeting with Napoleon, then First Consul, and several of his officers. Among them was Berthier, Napoleon's chief of staff and a former member of Rochambeau's headquarters in America. At Rochambeau's entry into the room where the others were waiting, the greatest soldier of the age, who could be charming when he chose, announced to him, "General, here are your pupils."

Rochambeau quietly replied that his pupils had far surpassed the master.

Still later, Rochambeau was made an officer of Napoleon's Legion of Honor. Whatever Rochambeau as an old royalist thought of it, the motto on the star of the Legion's insignia, *Honneur et Patrie* — Honor and Country — pretty well summed up his life.

He died at his chateau in 1807.

Rochambeau was an example of the best type of soldier of the old monarchy. The worst were unspeakable, but the best were very good indeed. Like many aristocrats, Rochambeau was thoroughly a soldier. One of his distant ancestors had died while with Saint Louis on a Crusade to the Holy Land. His own son would be killed at the battle of Leipzig. His eldest grandson would receive praise for his combat exploits from Marshal Davout, who was sparing in his approbation.

The peculiar distinction of Rochambeau was that he was both a fine combat leader and an astute military statesman. He was equally outstanding on the battlefield and at the council table. Having discharged the details of his profession at all the levels of military administration, he never lost his critical faculties or his initiative despite the demands of routine.

When he went to America he was at the peak of his mental powers despite his declining health. He recognized intuitively the difficulties of the coalition. He represented France, a world power, yet worked faithfully under Washington, who led the relatively poor forces of a nation in the pangs of birth.

Realizing that the French had supplied much of the money and matériel and that the Americans had done nearly all of their own fighting, he maintained, by his tact, patience, and consideration, an alliance that could easily have broken apart. Unlike Estaing, who had jeopardized the partnership, Rochambeau held together not only his own people but also his allies, who must indeed have seemed strange to this soldier from the formal fields of Europe.

The coup at Yorktown was a stroke of genius. Much of the success was a happy compound of wind, weather, and de Grasse. More of it was Washington. But ultimately the achievement was Rochambeau's, for it was he who doggedly sustained the cooperation that in the end won the War of Independence.

Few endeavors are more trying than coalition warfare. In the eighteenth century, when doctrine was lacking and experience was scarce, Rochambeau mastered the art of military diplomacy as he had mastered the other elements of his profession. Lafayette became the popular hero, but it was Rochambeau, with his wisdom and dedication, who sparked the Franco-American friendship that, whatever its subsequent vicissitudes, has endured to the present day.

Patton

THE STEREOTYPED PORTRAIT of General George S. Patton, Jr., shows him as a brutal, driving commander on the field of battle, an aggressive leader who used a calculated flamboyance and a hard-nosed profanity to motivate his men in combat. To most Americans he personified action, and in many quarters he is still seen merely as impulsive, impetuous, little given to thought and reason. Riding roughshod over sensibilities, slapping soldiers in hospitals, embodying the fetishes of the martinet, he is supposed to have cursed his way across the battlefields of the European theater, leading his soldiers from victory to victory by the sheer power of violence.

Perhaps this caricature of a great soldier that exists in the popular mind can never be entirely changed. But in French Morocco, as commanding general of United States troops from November 1942 to March 1943, George Patton fulfilled a very different function, operated in a very surprising manner. During those four months his activities as a military leader were largely political and diplomatic in nature.

George S. Patton, Jr., a diplomat? Contrary to what Ladislas Farago and Kenneth Pendar have written, Patton turned in a superb performance as a diplomat-soldier. The evidence lies in his diary and his letters home, which indicate how he visualized the tasks he undertook and how he understood their meaning.

The invasion of Morocco by troops under Patton was one of three simultaneous landings made by Anglo-American forces in French Northwest Africa. The entire undertaking was known as Operation Torch and was under the command of General Dwight D. Eisenhower. Patton's force sailed directly from the United States and headed for Casablanca. The other two forces left the United Kingdom to come ashore at Oran and Algiers in Algeria. The main idea behind the venture was to persuade the French to join the Allies in the fight against the Axis. With French cooperation, the Allies hoped to expel the Axis forces from North Africa and there to establish a base from which to launch an invasion of the European continent.

Torch was hazardous for a variety of reasons. It was the first time that American troops would be engaged in the European side of the war. It was the first combined Anglo-American operation. And it was militarily risky because Allied amphibious equipment and techniques were rudimentary.

Patton's invasion was particularly dangerous because of the difficult Atlantic tides and storms offshore. In addition, no one knew how the French would react. They had pledged the Germans and Italians that they would fight to repel any force that sought to come ashore. But the Allies hoped that the French were awaiting the opportunity to turn against the Axis.

On October 22, 1942, the day before he boarded the cruiser *Augusta* at Norfolk for the voyage to Morocco, Patton recognized the magnitude of his task. In his inimitable fashion, he sounded as though he were blowing his horn. But he was, in reality, appalled by the challenges ahead. He wrote in his diary, "When I think of the greatness of my job and realize that I am what I am, I am amazed, but on reflection, who is as good as I am? I know of no one."

His military mission, stated simply, was to get his troops ashore and stay, and this would demand the forceful leadership that came to be characteristic of Patton. He planned three landings — at Safi, Fedala, and Port Lyautey — then a movement to take Casablanca from the land side. With that port in his possession, he was to be ready to defend against a potentially hostile incursion into French Morocco from Spanish Morocco. He was also to be prepared to furnish troop units for a subsequent Allied attack eastward from Algeria to secure Tunisia.

Patton's political mission was somewhat more delicate. He was to bring French Morocco under Allied control without disturbing the French control over a restless native population. This would require some rather nice manipulation of French and Moroccan sensibilities.

The French would have to be defeated in battle or brought to surrender, but their authority over the Moroccans would somehow have to be maintained. Morocco, a protectorate of the French, was under the nominal authority of the sultan, but a host of regional and local leaders called pashas traditionally challenged his supremacy.

In both military and political missions, Patton was under General Eisenhower, General Mark W. Clark, the Allied deputy commander in chief, and the Allied Force Headquarters located temporarily at Gibraltar. But given the distances, the state of communications, and the uncertainty of developments in Operation Torch, Patton would, in fact, have a reasonable degree of freedom of action.

According to Patton's diary, he went ashore at 1242, November 8, hit the beach at 1320, got very wet in the surf, and went to Fedala where he inspected the town and the port. There he performed his first political act. "All the French soldiers, except the marines," he wrote, "saluted [me] and grinned. We put on mixed Military Police, half American and half French." In other words, he saw to it that the United States military authority was in evidence without displacing the French military presence.

There were, during the three days of hostilities in North Africa, attempts to negotiate with the French, not only in Algeria, where a cease-fire was finally arranged with Admiral Jean F. Darlan, but also in Morocco. Meanwhile, on November 10, Patton wrote in his diary, "An important Frenchman came and suggested that I write the Sultan. I did. Doubt if it does any good."

What he wrote to "His Majesty the Sultan of Morocco" was a flowery but firm letter explaining "the purpose of the American operations in Morocco." Stressing "the ancient and traditional friendship of the Government and People of the United States of America for the Person of Your Majesty and his People, as well as for the Government of France," Patton said that the Americans wanted "to protect your Throne and your Country, and the people of France in Morocco, against the enslavement by our common enemy — the Nazis, and to maintain your authority and the French civil authority." Patton demanded nothing except friendship; he guaranteed respect for "your religious institutions, your customs, and your laws." He was careful to identify the French armed forces as "my friends" and the shedding of French blood as "painful sentiments." The tone of this letter set the stage for later relations between Patton and the sultan, relations characterized by mutual respect and trust, even personal liking.

As for the French, General Auguste P. Noguès, the resident general, and Admiral François Michelier, commander of the naval forces in Morocco, came to Patton's headquarters at 1400, November 11, in order to discuss the terms of a cease-fire. Patton's diary reads: "I had a guard of honor [for them]. No use kicking a man when he is down. I had written a set of terms along the lines Ike had sent me. They were so different from those used in Algiers that I decided to have a gentlemen's agreement [with the French] until I found out what Ike had done. The French don't want to fight [us]."

Patton received the French officers with great dignity and complimented them on the combat effectiveness of their forces. He had two prepared sets of terms, but neither was relevant, so Patton dismissed both arrangements and said that there would be an informal understanding. The Allies would depend on the continued French capacity to control the natives and protect the sultan. The Americans were to occupy areas they needed for security and future operations, prisoners of war were to be exchanged, French troops were to be temporarily confined in barracks but not disarmed, and the French were not to punish any Frenchman who had helped the Americans come ashore.

These were generous arrangements for the French, and the French officers were genuinely pleased. They were suddenly anxious when Patton insisted on an additional requirement. He proposed a toast to the liberation of France by the joint defeat of the common enemy. To say that the Noguès-Michelier-Patton conference ended on a note of cordiality would be a distinct understatement.

It is important to remember Patton's experience with the French in World War I. He had been a member of General John J. Pershing's staff in France and, because Patton was close to Pershing, he was present at ceremonial meetings with such high-ranking French military as Marshals Joseph J. C. Joffre, Henri P. Pétain, Ferdinand Foch, and others. He attended the French tank school at Chamlieu in 1917 and became a close comrade of French combat officers. He had French tankers serving under his command during the St.-Mihiel and Meuse-Argonne offensives. He knew the French, had great respect for them, spoke the language — ungrammatically but fluently. He could and did make much of the personal bond of affection between the officers of both nations.

Yet Patton was aware of political undercurrents and crosscurrents on the French scene. On the day after he met with Noguès and Michelier, he recorded in his diary, "Chief of Civil Staff for General Noguès came in and tried to get me committed on politics." Patton was having none of this.

He was also somewhat torn by American disharmony. On the same day, he wrote, "a bunch from Ike's staff tried to put me on the spot for not disarming the French . . . To disarm or discredit the French meant an Arab war which would demobilize 60,000 [American] men as a starter. All agreed with me at last"

Two days later, on November 14, Generals Alfred M. Gruenther and James H. Doolittle flew from Algiers to give Patton the news of the political arrangements in North Africa. Darlan was to head the civil government, General Henri Giraud the military, and Noguès would remain governor of Morocco. Patton immediately sent two staff officers to Noguès with the message. It said in essence, that Patton expected Noguès to keep things quiet and orderly in the new state of affairs, as before. He also expected Noguès to stabilize the franc at seventy-five to one, which Noguès announced on the following day. On learning that, Patton sent him a letter recapitulating in detail what he understood Noguès had agreed to do.

With French cooperation buttoned up, Patton was ready to tackle the sultan. On November 16, Patton went to Rabat to call on Noguès and to accompany him to the sultan's palace. The 2d Armored Division had an escort at the edge of town waiting to take Patton to the residency. Compared to the French units, which were armed with obsolete weapons and equipment, the escort was a modern and powerful force — tanks, infantry, and artillery. But according to the diary: "I felt it [the escort] would just rub it in on the French, so I dismissed it." He drove to Noguès' residence with a small party.

Patton and Noguès then went to the palace. There was a colorful ceremony, which Patton obviously enjoyed: exotic warriors, prancing horses, strange music, medieval pageantry which he noted, remembered, and described in detail. Inside the palace in the throne room, the sultan made a ceremonial speech of welcome. "Then I made a speech, laying down the law with due respect. It pleased the French and Keyes [Patton's very level-headed deputy commander, General Geoffrey Keyes] thought it good. . . . A deputation from General Clark arrived with a letter for the Sultan from the President [of the United States]. It was patently not apropos, so I took the liberty of holding it. I will see Ike at Gib[raltar] tomorrow" — to tell him why Patton had withheld the letter. His reason for keeping the letter was that it failed to mention and support the French authority in sufficiently strong terms.

Later that day he recorded, "A captain from Giraud's staff reported to test out sentiment" — meaning, apparently, to see who was really running things in Morocco. "I told him he must first see Giraud. I intend to play it straight even if the French do not."

At this point, Patton distrusted Noguès. But as Patton came to appreciate the extent of factionalism among the French authorities — there were those who were Gaullists, pro-Axis, pro-Allies, pro-Darlan, pro-Giraud, and so on — he came to depend on Noguès, who kept the native population in hand and the French friendly.

On November 17, Patton flew to Gibraltar and saw Eisenhower. He wrote, "Ike backed me up about letter to Sultan."

Back in Morocco on the following day, Patton went to Rabat. He accompanied Noguès to the sultan's palace to celebrate the fifteenth anniversary of the sultan's accession to the throne. The ceremonies were again outstanding and exotic. More to the point:

Noguès read a long prepared speech . . . When the Sultan had replied I felt that the United States should be heard, so without asking anyone's permission, I stepped into the middle of the room and made a very respectful but pointed speech which was well received by both the Arabs and French; in fact the Sultan said that the fact of my being present and having spoken would have a profound effect on the entire Moslem world.

Later that day the good will spread by Patton ran into difficulties. He recorded: "The President's press conference [in Washington], in which he practically repudiated Ike and Darlan, had a bad effect. I told Noguès it was only a trial balloon and not to worry. People should not try to settle things by radio."

On November 19, Patton sent a letter to Eisenhower to sum up the situation as he saw it. He assured Ike that

The French were most cordial and helpful . . . The French position in Morocco rests almost entirely on the mythical supremacy of France, which at the present time is represented to the Arab mind by Darlan as a direct emissary from the Marshal [Pétain]. Anything which is said in the United States to destroy this mythical French authority could have and probably will have a very adverse effect on the Arab. I am convinced that the Sultan . . . is wholly for us but he has not the authority or the means of controlling the Arabian tribes whereas the French prestige, nebulous as it may seem to us, can and will maintain order.

Patton sent word to Noguès on November 20 to stop unfavorable broadcasts by Radio Morocco and to make the press in Morocco "come across." He had the first band concert in front of his American headquarters. There was much applause by the French. He made sure that the band played the "Marseillaise" as well as the "Star-Spangled Banner."

On the tenth day after the armistice in North Africa, Keyes, Patton's deputy, presented the sultan with a telegram from President Franklin D. Roosevelt. This message was in line with Patton's thoughts on maintaining the French authority. Relations had been regularized to such an extent that Patton told the French to go ahead and man their traditional coast artillery and antiaircraft artillery batteries.

On November 27: "Was quite sick all day with a stomach ache, but had to go to a large dinner given by Mr. Poussier, Chief of Civil Affairs." The diplomatic life can sometimes be hell too. "Admiral Michelier and the Pasha of Marrakech were present. I sat next to the Pasha, whose French being almost as bad as mine, understood me very well . . . I sent him home by airplane and gave him a ride in a tank. He came here especially to meet me."

A week later at a lunch with the French governor of Dakar, together with Noguès and Michelier, Patton was pleased by the demonstrations of friendship he received. He did not forget to be attentive to the sultan's grand vizier and the chief of protocol, who were also at the luncheon.

Patton kept in close personal touch with the French and Moroccan officials, always making certain that they appreciated the power of American arms and the unobtrusive stability that American arms brought. When the pasha of Safi called and tried to get Patton committed to a free Arab state in Morocco after the war, Patton recorded, "I sweet talked him but said nothing."

Early in December, Patton issued 152,000 gallons of gasoline to permit farming machinery to be employed. He was duly thanked by the chief of the farmers' union.

When German planes raided Morocco, struck an Arab town, and killed eighty-five Moroccans early in January, Patton immediately sent a letter of condolence to the pasha, along with 100,000 francs for distribution to the bereaved families.

Patton attended many ceremonial functions — *diffas* or feasts given by the sultan or by a variety of pashas, all-day boar hunts. He exchanged gifts — a United States carbine made a fine impression. He went to dinners and luncheons, parades and band concerts, all in the interest of promoting a personal diplomacy that stressed stability and the status quo, friendship and good will.

He had had much experience directing ceremonial shows of one sort or another. He had been stationed at Fort Myer several times during his career, and there he had escorted funeral corteges and visiting royalty. During 1939 and half of 1940, in command of Fort Myer, he staged the magnificently impressive horse shows that were the army's showcase, designed to make friends and influence the influential. He believed in pomp and circumstance, in the efficacy of the social occasion. And nowhere did he better display his social presence and charm, his personal ebullience in the interest of diplomacy, than in Morocco.

It was not his job, he felt, to be interested in the political, social, racial, and religious problems of Morocco. He saw his duty as the task of maintaining order and stability in the country so that his military forces would not have to be drawn into what he regarded as a diversionary mission. His American forces were in Morocco not to reform the state, not to improve social conditions, not to change restrictive laws, but rather to be ready to fight the war against the Axis.

The culmination of his career as a diplomat came during the Casablanca Conference, attended by President Roosevelt and Prime Minister Winston Churchill and their highest personal and military advisors. Patton was responsible for the billeting and security arrangements; and he hosted innumerable luncheons and dinners for the great Allied names of World War II. As he wrote to his brother-in-law: "I was sort of a stage manager and had quite an interesting social season." To his wife, he wrote, "My guest book, had I kept one, would be an envy to all lion hunters."

It was during the Casablanca Conference that presidential advisor Harry Hopkins asked Patton an interesting question. In his diary Patton recorded the conversation as follows: "Hopkins asked me how I would like to be an ambassador. I said I would resign if I got such a job. He said I had shown such ability that they needed me. I still said I would resign and go fishing rather than take such a job."

One can suppose that Hopkins was not entirely serious. But Patton thought he was, so Hopkins was complimenting Patton generously. Yet Patton was right to turn him down. He could have been successful, no doubt, as Admiral William D. Leahy had been as ambassador to Vichy. But how correct Patton was to refuse the possibility became more than clear in the following months when he returned to the battlefield and carved out his rise to military glory.

No one would insist that Patton was uniquely qualified to handle the situation in Morocco. Any number of United States officers were equipped to be effective as soldier-diplomats. But in his use of veiled threat, ceremonial skill, and personal charm, Patton maintained the political power of the United States in Morocco without disturbing French control and native susceptibilities.

Anything but slapdash, George Patton was thoughtful and accomplished. He was far more versatile than he is generally regarded, far more perceptive than he is usually given credit for, far more self-controlled than the public image he displayed.

Command at Kasserine

EISENHOWER desired a truly Allied command in North Africa, with a real unity of direction and a centralized administrative responsibility. What he had in Tunisia was a loose coalition.

"Alliances in the past," he wrote after the war, "have often done no more than to name the common foe, and 'unity of command' has been a pious aspiration thinly disguising the national jealousies, ambitions and recriminations of high ranking officers, unwilling to subordinate themselves or their forces to a commander of a different nationality."

Had he been a bitter man, he might have thus described the situation in Tunisia during the winter and spring of 1942–43.

He erased national distinctions in his own headquarters by creating an integrated and close-knit Anglo-American staff and by insisting that its members, his own official family, work in harmony.

But the field commanders grappled with insoluble problems — problems over which they had little control. Perhaps partially because of their frustration, some commanders began to squabble among themselves. In part their clashes stemmed from differences in national interest and outlook. More significantly, some personality conflicts originated from a simple diversity of character and behavior. For the exercise of command is not only a matter of structure, doctrine, and authority; it is also a matter of personality — each commander commands in a personal manner. In times of tactical success, frictions among men are apt to be overlooked or minimized; in times of operational adversity, annoyances develop into irritations and exacerbate a deteriorating situation. This is essentially what happened during the battle of Kasserine Pass.

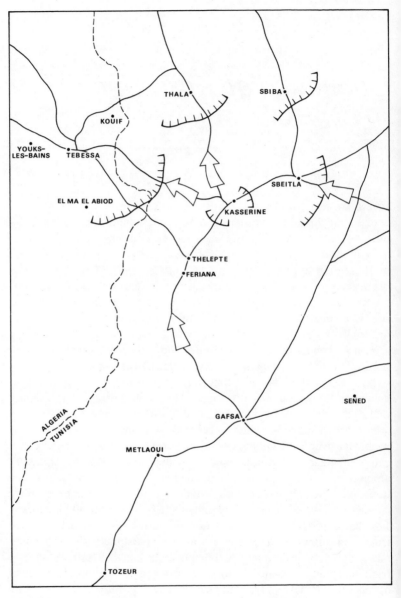

Sbeitla

Preinvasion planning had projected Tunisia as a British theater of operations, and this alone produced a measure of grief. The entire line of supply was British in concept, organization, and control. Since both British and United States officers were generally unfamiliar with the methods of their comrades-in-arms, American units employed with the British First Army encountered unexpected difficulties in getting support.

Some United States commanders believed that the British were being favored in the choice of missions, equipment, and supplies and some Americans, who were inclined to be less reserved and more outspoken than the British, rubbed their cousins the wrong way.

When the French joined the team, the complexities grew. Political considerations provoked some difficulties, but most came from the comparatively strange procedures, national characteristics, and interests of the French, differences accentuated by the barrier of language.

Lieutenant General K. A. N. Anderson, commander of the British First Army, had the impression that the French were unduly sensitive and suspicious and he also had reservations about their possible performance in battle.

When Eisenhower proposed that the French forces, like the Americans, go under Anderson's command, General Henri Giraud, commander of French military forces in North Africa, refused. With the French unwilling to serve under British command, Eisenhower and Giraud formulated a vague, oral agrement that hardly solved the problem. Eisenhower himself would exercise direct command of the three-nation force in Tunisia even though he was in Algiers, 400 miles from the front, too far for effective direction and control.

To facilitate his exercise of command, Eisenhower established a forward command post at Constantine. He appointed Major General Lucian K. Truscott, Jr., his deputy chief of staff and personal representative for operations. Through Truscott, Eisenhower planned to coordinate the parallel activities of the three national forces.

Truscott, though extremely competent, was a relatively junior officer, and at Constantine he would be 200 miles from the front. No matter how rapidly, accurately, and completely he learned about developments and transmitted the information to Eisenhower he would be unable to regulate affairs effectively, particularly in an emergency. Furthermore, regulation or coordination was hardly the same as command.

Anderson, commander of the British First Army, was Eisenhower's "advisor" for the entire Tunisian front. In effect, he was monitoring and coordinating the combat forces. But he never quite took hold. Though personally bold and fearless, he inspired Americans with little confidence, he was too reserved and reticent. And he usually took a a dark view of operations. His chief of staff was even more dour, silent, and pessimistic. Both officers believed in wide margins to compensate for error and chance, and they looked with disfavor on the movement of United States forces into southern Tunisia. They believed that the resources being shifted there distracted from the more important job of building up the First Army for the eventual and decisive drive to Tunis.

The insertion of the United States II Corps into the command structure dislocated the command arrangements, and part of the trouble came from the character and personality of its commander, who did little to simplify the problems of interallied cooperation and command.

The commander was Major General Lloyd R. Fredendall, an Anglophobe who disliked Anderson in particular. He had no confidence in and little patience with the French. He never understood the pathetic nature of their mule-drawn carts, ancient trucks, and obsolete guns, or the wretched condition of their battered light tanks. Nor did he appreciate the frustration of men who were denied the weapons they needed to fight. Had he observed the scene, he would have dismissed its significance: French soldiers who stood in delight at a road junction as United States tanks passed and who watched in the way that children gape at fire engines.

At the time of the North African invasion in November 1942, Fredendall was fifty-nine years old. He looked younger because of his unlined face and vigorous movements. Of medium height, he was solidly built, almost chunky. He spoke loudly and had a firm opinion on every subject.

He had entered the Military Academy in 1901 and stayed for one semester. He returned in 1902 for another half year. Commissioned in 1907, he had the usual assignments of the time and gathered broad experience from a variety of tours. He served along the Mexican border, trained troops in France during World War I, completed the course at Leavenworth as a "distinguished graduate," graduated from the Army War College, and was a brigadier general in 1939.

A division commander in 1940, Fredendall took command of the II Corps in 1941. In the following year, when Eisenhower went to England to take command of the European theater and the II Corps headquarters moved there also, Major General Mark W. Clark replaced Fredendall as head of the corps because Eisenhower was unacquainted with Fredendall and wanted Clark to be his right-hand man. But when the North Africa landings were projected with Eisenhower as Supreme Allied Commander and Clark as Deputy Supreme Allied Commander, someone was needed to head the II Corps.

General George C. Marshall, Army Chief of Staff, suggested eight officers who, he felt, were capable of commanding a corps and of directing one of the principal landing forces in the North Africa invasion. Among them was Fredendall. Because he had previously commanded the II Corps and knew the staff and because he was familiar with the invasion plans, Eisenhower chose him.

Fredendall arrived in London a month before the operation and, as was customary, reported promptly to Eisenhower, the theater commander, who happened to be a rather junior officer. Eisenhower had become a brigadier general two years after Fredendall.

During the invasion of North Africa, Fredendall commanded the troops that landed at Oran. They performed superbly and seized their objectives in less than three days — the only Allied units to win a decision wholly by force of arms. Though Fredendall had remained in his command post aboard ship offshore, he gained his reputation as a forceful commander who had succeeded. In an army lacking experienced leaders, success was a virtue highly esteemed.

When he went ashore on November 10, the third day of the invasion, it was to confer with the French on an armistice. Yet the citation for the Distinguished Service Medal awarded by Eisenhower spoke of his "exceptionally meritorious service," his "brilliant leadership and resolute force," and his having "demonstrated the highest qualities of leadership."

Concerned solely with the military features of the operation, Fredendall was uninterested in the politics. He dismissed political matters as irrelevant, permitted all civilian officials to retain their positions no matter what their party affiliation, made no effort to identify and restrain Axis sympathizers, or to locate and help those French who had been pro-American, and adopted a policy of what was later generously called "very mild arrangements." Given the complexities of the political situation in French North Africa, it was simpler to close one's eyes to the realities.

Fredendall and his staff moved into the Grand Hotel, the best in Oran, and in that elegant continental establishment the headquarters soon took on the trappings and the pageantry, as well as the spit and polish, of a rather swanky garrison life. Leggings and unbuttoned khaki shirts were definitely out, officers' blouses and pinks in.

When the routine duties began to pall, Fredendall became impatient. The war was going to be won in Tunisia, and he wanted to be in on the kill. Eisenhower could hardly refuse him, for during the landings he had said, "Clean up that situation today and write your own ticket." Fredendall had cleaned it up.

Already Fredendall was known for his picturesque language. It gave his personality a certain flair. The journal of one combat unit recorded the striking contrast between normal military communications and Fredendall's mannerisms. The entries were matter-of-fact, without excitement, completely businesslike in tone. For example, "All Green assault wave is proceeding to final objectives. Your reserves released to you." Or, "Roads and bridges to top of hairpin turn are OK. Beach roadway material urgently required." Suddenly a message came from Fredendall: "Go get 'em at once . . . Go smash 'em." The details be damned.

"Everything is rosy," he had radioed from his ship during the invasion. The troops "went to town."

The commander stamps his temperament on his subordinates, and Fredendall's permeated the command. The password established each day to enable troops to distinguish friend from foe consisted of two words: a challenge by the guard, and a response by the unknown. They were usually innocuous, something like "San Francisco–California," or "Popeye–Sailor Man," and the soldiers were required to know them. The password in the II Corps area one day was "Snafu–Damn Right." Maybe it was good for morale.

This resort to slang deprived Fredendall's speech of precision. What he said was sometimes incomprehensible because it embodied only a half-formed and vague impulse rather than a thoroughly formulated idea. Using slogans as a substitute for thought, he failed to communicate his wishes clearly. If a subordinate asked for clarification, he responded with a hostility that stemmed from an improper assumption: the subordinate was stupid or trying to make him look foolish.

Sometimes the lack of clarity worked the other way. For example, the XII Air Support Command had the task of air support to the II Corps. To insure close cooperation between air and ground components, the air commander set up his headquarters near the corps command post in the belief that men who were in close association would work together better. The theory was fine, but the practice, in this case, was somewhat deficient. He and Fredendall got along so well that Fredendall told him, "Don't wait for us to order air missions. You know what the situation is; just keep pounding them." Although this reflected great confidence, it also represented the abdication of responsibility to make known clearly the requirements of the troops on the ground. Unless the air commander is explicitly requested or directed to carry out definite missions in a changing situation, he can never be fully responsive to ground force needs.

Loud and brassy, Fredendall was outspoken in his opinions and inclined to be critical of superiors and subordinates alike. Somewhat ponderous in action, overbearing in attitude, he often jumped to conclusions. When he spoke, it was with an air of finality. He knew best, and there was little anyone could tell him. His humor was not always funny or in the best of taste. In short, he considered himself a rough, tough customer who was going to let nothing stand in the way of winning the war, even if it took all kinds of flailing of arms and bearing down.

Yet twinges of doubt nagged those who visited his command post near Tebessa. Commanders usually try to establish their headquarters near a road, adjacent to existing communications facilities, and close enough to the combat units for convenient visits. Fredendall's was distant from the front and far up a canyon, a gulch that could be entered only by a barely passable road constructed by his corps engineers. Though towering mountains and wooded hillsides concealed his presence, he had underground shelters blasted and dug for himself and his staff. Two hundred engineers would work for more than three weeks on this project, then abandon it, unfinished, under pressure of the German threat at Kasserine Pass.

The command post was cold, cheerless, even gloomy, despite what one visitor called "exceedingly military" behavior by the staff. Everyone wore helmets and pistols despite the rear-area location, and this gave an unfortunate impression, as someone remarked, of an "excessive emphasis on security and safety." To those who asked, Fredendall explained that German aircraft were active over the area and that they made special efforts to destroy command posts. He had gone underground because he had no intention of having his activities disrupted. Though sixty or seventy miles behind the front was rather far for frequent visits to the combat units, he saw no need to be closer. He would run the battle by telephone and radio.

"Most American officers who saw this command post for the first time," an observer wrote, "were somewhat embarrassed, and their comments were usually caustic." For nothing can take the place of personal visits by a commander to his troops, and nothing can substitute for personal reconnaissance, the actual sight of the ground, which often erases the pessimism created by grease pencils tracing dispositions on a map far to the rear of the action.

Rarely leaving his command post, Fredendall would be impatient with the recommendations of whose who were familiar with the terrain and the other vital conditions on the front, and the units serving under him would come to believe that the corps headquarters was looking out for itself above all and had little interest in, and knowledge of, the real situation as it was known to the troops on the ground.

Rommel put it this way:

There are always moments when the commander's place is not back with his staff but up with the troops. It is sheer nonsense to say that maintenance of the men's morale is the job of the battalion commander alone. The higher the rank, the greater the effect of the example. The men tend to feel no kind of contact with a commander who, they know, is sitting somewhere in headquarters. What they want is what might be termed a physical contact with him. In moments of panic, fatigue, or disorganization, or when something out of the ordinary has to be demanded from them, the personal example of the commander works wonders, especially if he has had the wit to create some sort of legend around himself.

The legend that Fredendall tried to create would soon fall apart.

The principal United States unit that would serve in southern Tunisia under Fredendall's II Corps was the 1st Armored Division. Its commander, Major General Orlando Ward, was fifty-one years old. A graduate of West Point, he had fought under Pershing in Mexico and in France. A "distinguished graduate" of Leavenworth, he completed the course at the Army War College and later served as Secretary of the General Staff in Washington, where his intelligence, competence, and balance were remarked. A spare man who was quiet in speech and manner, with a rose-tinted complexion that caused him to be called Pinky, in his appearance he had something of the ascetic and the intellectual. Methodical and thorough, he had trained his division well. His men held him in high esteem. His dignity and soldierly bearing gave confidence. What he lacked in fire he made up in fairness and integrity.

Between Fredendall and Ward there would soon develop, in one observer's understated words, a "most unusual" antipathy. Fredendall openly detested Ward; Ward, in his quiet manner, had no use for Fredendall. The mutual dislike would have serious repercussions.

When Eisenhower instructed Fredendall in January 1943 to send a suitable force to help the French stabilize the line, he stirred an instant but somewhat irregular response. The normal procedure would have been for Fredendall to consult with Ward, his major subordinate commander. Instead, he by-passed the 1st Armored Division commander in a manner that Ward considered to be a contemptuous disregard of his own prerogatives. Fredendall directly telephoned Combat Command B, one of Ward's two principal subordinate commands.

"Move your command," Fredendall told a staff officer. "That is, the walking boys, pop guns, Baker's outfit and the outfit which is the reverse of Baker's outfit, and the big fellow to M, which is due north of where you are now, as soon as possible. Have your boss report to the French gentleman whose name begins with J at a place which begins with D which is five grid squares to the left of M."

The unmilitary flavor of the order and the eccentricity of the language could be excused only on the ground that Fredendall was endeavoring to guarantee the security of his telephone.

The commander of CCB, Brigadier General Paul M. Robinett, was a short and cocky American who believed that he had a better grasp of the situation, both tactical and strategic, than anyone else in the Allied camp. Having participated in the fighting in northern Tunisia and having thus acquired knowledge of German tactics, he was sure he knew more about combat than Fredendall and Ward. Having attended the Ecole de Guerre and the French cavalry school at Saumur before the war, he felt he knew the French army and its methods of operation. Having been Secretary of the General Staff, he was certain he understood the point of view at Washington. In command of a relatively powerful force of about 3500 men, he liked being separated from his parent organization, welcomed an independent role, and enjoyed dealing directly with the top commanders. An excellent combat officer, he had a well-trained and spirited command, a grasp of terrain that gave him an eerie prescience, and energy as well as thoroughness.

Moving quickly, his CCB performed splendidly and, together with British forces, helped to stabilize the front.

Fredendall, it appeared, was getting the job done. But, in addition to irritating Ward unnecessarily, he had complicated Robinett's mission. By telling him to keep in touch with corps headquarters, he detached him from Ward's control. And Tebessa was too far away for Fredendall to exercise competent direction. During much of his week of combat, Robinett was unable to determine whether he was under the command of Eisenhower, Anderson, Fredendall, Truscott, or the French. Each made his presence, weight, and superior rank felt.

The mixture of Allied units — each with its own distinctive organization, training, doctrine, communications, supply arrangements, and staff procedures — gave each commander a feeling of helplessness, particularly since higher headquarters were too far away to exercise the required control and guidance.

Instructed to perform a defensive mission in southern Tunisia, Fredendall was eager to show his aggressiveness, and he decided to launch a series of hit-and-run raids to upset the Germans and give his inexperienced United States units a taste of combat. Ward protested, and so did the local French commander. Both preferred to have Americans reinforce the poorly equipped French troops who were holding a series of mountain passes.

Frendendall saw no necessity to change his plans.

A small United States force staged a raid that was designed principally as a morale exercise. It was highly successful. Fredendall was overjoyed. Telephoning Eisenhower's representative, Truscott, in the middle of the day, he crowed. "Remember that force I sent toward Maknassy looking for trouble? They ran into some stuff and smeared it. I can't give you the details . . . They were very cheerful about what they had done — our trouble is to get them back. They are coming back tonight . . . Whatever it was, they smacked the hell out of them. I thought you might like to have a little cheerful information from down here."

Later that evening he was flying high as he reported the details. "I told them to go on and get contact," and the troops located the enemy and "ran them all out of town . . . Trump that if you can, damn it! . . . There is a splendid note of cheer down here. We must have killed a hell of a lot but could not stay to find out."

Hoping that he was satisfied with his adventure, French commanders visited him and asked again for troops to bolster the French positions. Frendendall knew better. He now ordered a stronger raid. The result was a confused action complicated by the opening events of what the Germans would develop into the battle of Kasserine Pass.

"Use your tanks and shove," Fredendall bellowed to Ward, but it was no go. Fredendall's hit-and-run raids had been wasteful, and the directive that he issued "to restore the situation" was, unfortunately, based on an inadequate knowledge of the enemy's strength, an incomplete understanding of the Allied dispositions, and an insufficient appreciation of the terrain.

Eisenhower began to question Fredendall's ability. Had he expended men, ammunition, and other supplies in useless operations? Had he broken his units into too many small detachments? Was he exerting sufficient control? Was he being rash?

Fredendall drew up a detailed directive, prescribing exactly the defensive measures he wished Ward to carry out. "You will take immediate steps," he wrote, "to see that the following steps . . . are put into effect." Then he lectured Ward in a tone that was as unflattering as it was inappropriate, covering subjects that all junior officers are supposed to have mastered: the proper employment of patrols, wire, mines, the importance of aerial photography, the function of artillery, and other similar topics. "You will inform me," Fredendall added, "when the instructions enumerated in this directive have been complied with."

There was one more thought — this one contained in a hand-written postscript at the bottom of the paper: "In other words I want a very strong active defense and not just a passive one. The enemy must be harassed at every opportunity. Reconnaissance must never be relaxed — especially at night. Positions [I have] indicated *must* be wired and mined *now*. L.R.F."

These instructions were contrary to normal United States practice. According to United States military doctrine, when a commander assigns a mission, he gives the subordinate the initiative and the authority to carry out the mission in his own way. Fredendall had, in effect, done Ward's job; he had placed Ward's units in definite locations, and he had given them specific tasks to perform.

In part this reflected his lack of confidence in Ward. In part it followed and conformed with Anderson's practice. Since Anderson was giving Fredendall's affairs a rather close and detailed supervision, Fredendall saw no reason why he should not adopt a similar method with Ward.

There were two significant differences. British Army doctrine permitted a far closer command supervision over subordinates. In addition, Anderson moved around the front constantly and knew the situation first-hand, but Fredendall tarried well to the rear and was in no position to challenge Anderson's detailed orders.

Though Fredendall had made only one short visit to the front, he as much as took command of Ward's division. Ward, in effect, became a supernumerary, his headquarters taking on the complexion of a message center that transmitted communications from corps down to the units and informational reports from the smaller units up to corps. Ward's close associates who were aware of the ill-feeling between him and Fredendall appreciated the insulting nature of the instructions. They were amazed at Ward's self-control; he remained calm and cheerful throughout.

Quite apart from the personality conflict, there were defects in Fredendall's scheme of defense. Senior officers in the 1st Armored Division recognized the error of Fredendall's dispositions, but they could persuade neither him nor his staff members to make the personal reconnaissance that would have quickly showed how easily the Germans could take advantage of the unit deployments he had ordered.

Furthermore, Fredendall's meticulous placement of Ward's units froze the defense. Ward would be unable to react quickly in a crisis. He would first have to get permission from a commander who was far to the rear and who doubted Ward's command ability. Ward would lack the freedom to maneuver his units that characterizes the successful management of battlefield tactics. Vague but disquieting rumors of the bad blood between Fredendall and Ward having reached Eisenhower, he decided to make an inspection tour of the American front. With Truscott he drove to Tebessa. The location of Fredendall's command post in the canyon and the tunneling still in progress surprised and dismayed Eisenhower. Yet he found the positions in the II Corps area "as good as could be made."

If responsibility on the corps level was rather well understood, the delineation of command below was not always firm. A French division was spread out alongside Ward's United States units. Despite the closeness of French and United States units, Fredendall had never defined the mission of the French division commander, who, as a consequence, had no definite role in the defense of southern Tunisia. In effect, he was an advisor on the use of the French forces in the II Corps area. In that capacity, he had clearly expressed his predilections. But advice is free and can, of course, be disregarded.

When the Germans attacked in mid-February, Fredendall's reaction was simple: everyone was to hold tight. By the time Fredendall understood what was happening, Ward's division had suffered defeat. When Ward finally prevailed upon him to recognize the danger, it was too late. In grudging acquiescence to what he at first considered to be Ward's excessive concern, Fredendall gave permission for a counterattack. It was unsuccessful.

Fredendall obtained reinforcement to bolster Ward's units. "Move the big elephants . . ." Fredendall radioed Robinett. "Move fast, and come shooting."

It was a chastened and somber Fredendall who telephoned Truscott. "The picture this morning," he said frankly, "does not look too good." He doubted that Ward could hold. "It does not look good," he repeated. And then there was a flash of the old spirit, the indomitable Fredendall who was going to win the war single-handed. Trying to find some semblance of a silver lining, he added, "The worst will be the loss of two battalions of tanks."

He was in some error. Two battalions of tanks — and more — had indeed been lost in two days, but far more was gone: almost a regiment of infantry and at least two battalions of artillery.

Fredendall phoned Ward and told him "to get his division straightened out and to hold defensively." Ward was pleased to go over on the defense. His foremost concern, he admitted candidly, was to preserve his division "as a fighting force."

When Fredendall telephoned Truscott to give him the latest news, he was less than altogether coherent. There was, he said a "tank battle coming up . . . They are coming in with sixty tanks . . . If we get rocked loose from that place, it is going to expose the [whole central area of Tunisia] . . ." But maybe Ward could stand fast, for Robinett's CCB had arrived and was "getting set in behind so that if they come through they can take them."

Things developed better than expected. The Germans failed to press home their attack; they were having trouble coordinating too. As for the Americans, all Ward's troops were accounted for and in place despite sporadic enemy shelling. Though reduced in numbers, the division was finally, for the first time since the opening of the North African campaign, fighting as a single unit. The defenses were good; the troops seasoned. There was every reason to believe that Ward could hold indefinitely.

During the night Truscott telephoned Fredendall for news. The corps commander was asleep and a staff officer answered the phone. Everything was quiet, he reported cheerfully. Everything was in good order. The tank battle had petered out. Everything was under control. Everything looked good. Everything was dandy.

That was just about the time that everything went to pieces.

Fredendall telephoned Truscott to tell him that the situation was "extremely grave." Ward, he said, was "uncertain of ability to hold." The situation was bad. But now he thought that Ward "was doing best he could." Later he told Truscott that "Ward fears we may have lost the First Armored Division." The trouble, Fredendall added, was Anderson's fault. Anderson had failed to accept the gravity of Fredendall's earlier reports.

Around Tebessa, confusion and panic were setting in. Allied troops were blowing up ammunition dumps and destroying supplies, and the smoke rising from forward airfields, along with crowds or Allied soldiers clogging the roads to the rear, brought unrest.

"There is some confusion," Frendendall reported to Truscott, "but we are getting along pretty well."

His statement was somewhat misleading. Though the disorder at Tebessa calmed, Fredendall moved his corps headquarters out of the canyon to a safer place. During the shift he was out of touch with his superiors, who needed information, and his subordinates, who needed direction. Not until five hours later, when his headquarters was somewhat re-established in a mining hamlet fifteen miles from Tebessa did Fredendall telephone Truscott to find out what had been happening.

The II Corps was in a state of shock. A catastrophe had been averted by a small margin, and danger still threatened to deepen the crisis. Badly mauled units were dispersed and intermixed. Many commanders lacked definite missions, and some felt their troops slipping out of control. Everyone was extremely fatigued. But the Germans relaxed their pressure and thus gave the Americans time to restore some kind of personal order that spread cohesion among the men and units.

"We are a little thin," Fredendall told Truscott, "but if they [the Germans] will just reconnoiter for a while, we'll be all set. The longer they let us alone, the better we'll be set." He wanted, above all, more troops — an infantry battalion "worse than hell," for he was holding "a lot of mountain passes against armor" without a "damn bit of reserve." But the 1st Armored Division, he said, still had a "very fine spirit."

Somewhat later, when Fredendall thought of reinforcing the troops holding Kasserine Pass, he alerted the 1st Armored Division. But he sent word to Robinett, not to Ward.

The message that Robinett received was garbled, without punctuation, composed in haste, and transmitted in some excitement. After being straightened out, it read: "General Robinett — Fight going on south . . . In the event of a penetration of the Kasserine Pass, you will be prepared to move a portion of your division" — Robinett was startled; was Ward relieved and was Robinett now in command of the division? — "to counterattack . . . The situation at this time is not serious. This is furnished only for your information and planning."

Robinett immediately alerted his subordinates and checked out the message with Ward's headquarters. So far as everyone knew, Ward was still in command.

It was the old story; Fredendall was by-passing Ward. The relations between the two men had so deteriorated that Fredendall had telephoned Truscott to say that Ward "simply had to be relieved" of his command. Would Truscott talk to Eisenhower about getting a replacement?

Meanwhile, the battle was developing at Kasserine Pass, and Fredendall sent Robinett another message ordering him to march his CCB without delay to the narrows and take command of all units defending the pass. Would he come ahead of his troops and report personally to Fredendall, who was going to be making a personal reconnaissance?

With a less than perfect understanding of the situation, Fredendall expected Robinett to clear the Germans from the narrows before the end of the day. The only question in Fredendall's mind was where to get Robinett started. To resolve the matter, he drove toward Kasserine Pass.

Robinett met Fredendall on the road as the corps commander was returning from his brief inspection tour.

"Head your column off," he told Robinett, "and move . . . and secure the passes . . . Stop enemy advance in that sector, drive him out of the valley, and restore your position in the Kasserine Pass."

It was a large order.

"If you get away with this one, Robby," Fredendall said, "I'll make you a field marshal."

Flattered by Fredendall's confidence, Robinett promised to do his best.

"Good luck!" Fredendall said, and got into his jeep and drove away.

Things were going badly at the II Corps command post. A hectic week of nervous tension and little sleep had made many headquarters people jumpy. They expected the worst, and every sign seemed to bear out their impression of approaching disaster. Convinced that the Allied defenses were caving in everywhere, Fredendall went to see the French division commander in his area.

While he was away, Robinett visited the corps command post to lodge a blunt complaint. To a staff member, he presented a list of inexcusable and unforgiveable blunders. No one was coordinating the units in the battle area, and coordination was sorely needed. No one in the field knew what unit boundaries had been assigned by higher headquarters, and specific areas of unit responsibility were urgently required. No one knew who was on the flanks or in support, and the piecemeal commitment of small units from different organizations was causing untold confusion. No one was coordinating defensive fires or providing military police and transportation to take charge of evacuating prisoners to the rear. Why wasn't corps exercising the proper control?

Soon after Robinett departed, someone at corps headquarters decided that the command post had to move to avoid being overrun and captured. When Fredendall returned, he found his command post half-abandoned, many of its staff officers and troops moving to the rear. He tried to round up and call back the headquarters clerks and raido operators but many had already gone.

Apprised of Robinett's complaint, Fredendall decided that the dissolution of his command post prevented him from taking the requisite control. He gave Ward and Major General Terry Allen, who commanded the 1st Infantry Division, split responsibility to coordinate the units along the front.

Shortly thereafter General Alphonse Juin, French ground forces commander, came to visit Fredendall. He found the corps commander sitting on a box in his empty office.

Was it true, Juin asked, that he was considering making a withdrawal?

Fredendall nodded.

Why withdraw?

Fredendall said he had to be prepared for the worst.

If a withdrawal became necessary, in which direction would he go?

To the north. He could not abandon the British.

To Juin this meant that Fredendall had already as good as renounced a defense of Tebessa. If the Germans took Tebessa, they as good as had Constantine. Juin tried to get Fredendall to reconsider. Leaving Tebessa, he told the American, meant abandoning his base of supply and being cut off from Algiers.

Fredendall made a hopeless gesture.

Judging that technical and military arguments would have little effect, Juin tried a sentimental approach. If Fredendall would not defend Tebessa, he said, the French would fight alone until the death of the last man. The appeal was effective. Fredendall was visibly moved. He swore he would not abandon Tebessa. Juin was hardly reassured.

Though the whole Allied situation in Tunisia seemed on the verge of disintegrating, an American officer was arriving to take hold on the southern flank. No one knew exactly what his place would be in the command structure. Would he take command of the II Corps, become Fredendall's deputy, or replace Ward?

The American about to arrive was barrel-chested Ernie Harmon. He would blow in like a whirlwind, determined to set things right.

Actually, the battle of Kasserine Pass was over; Rommel had decided to withdraw. But no one on the Allied side of the front could know that. While tension remained at a high pitch, Harmon arrived to add a significant and dramatic postscript.

As the relationship between Fredendall and Ward grew worse — the two men were strictly on "official" terms, barely speaking to each other except in the line of duty — Eisenhower and Truscott talked of bringing Major General Ernest N. Harmon from Morocco, where he headed the 2d Armored Division under the overall command of Major General George S. Patton, Jr. When Eisenhower decided to send Harmon to Tunisia, he first thought of relieving Ward and giving Harmon the task of rehabilitating the 1st Armored Division. But when his principal subordinate pointed out that Fredendall had hobbled Ward and had prevented him from commanding the division, Eisenhower concluded that a change in the midst of battle would be, his word, "inexpedient." He determined to send Harmon as "a useful senior assistant" to Fredendall in "the unusual conditions of the present battle." Fredendall was to use Harmon in any way he wished except to relieve Ward. In effect, Harmon was to be Fredendall's deputy commander or Eisenhower's personal representative at the front.

Harmon was a West Pointer, forty-eight years of age. He had served in combat during World War I. He was a graduate of Leavenworth and the War College. Brigadier general in March 1942, major general five months later, he had a reputation as a hard-driving, hard-talking commander. There was nothing elegant about him, nothing subtle, nothing reticent. Completely direct in his approach to all problems, he believed firmly in the precept that a commander belonged up front with his men. No hanging around near headquarters for Harmon.

When he received Eisenhower's summons, he flew to Algiers. Arriving late, he saw the Supreme Commander, who brought him up to date on developments in Tunisia; then Harmon went to a hotel for a few hours' sleep. Early the next day a chauffeur called for him, then picked up Eisenhower and several others who were to drive to Constantine. An air raid over Algiers held up their start and they reached Constantine late in the afternoon.

After a short discussion with Truscott, Harmon left by jeep for Tebessa. All along the road he bucked heavy traffic moving the other way. At Tebessa, he tried to find the II Corps rear headquarters. No one knew where it was. Everyone seemed to be gone, or going to Constantine. He finally found the place where corps rear headquarters had been. A telephone was here and it was working. Harmon bulled his way past several operators to get Fredendall on the wire.

Were they moving? Harmon asked. And if so, where?

They were not moving. They were waiting for him to arrive.

He reached corps headquarters at 0300 in the morning, a few hours after Rommel, on the other side of the front, had ordered his forces to start withdrawing.

Harmon found Fredendall and two of his principal staff officers, he later remembered, "sitting around looking very glum." He thought Fredendall was drunk, but he was only groggy from nervous tension and lack of sleep.

The first thing Fredendall did was to ask whether Harmon thought the command post ought to move. Harmon found that a hell of a question to ask someone just arriving. Instinctively he answered, "Hell, no."

Fredendall turned to the two staff officers. "All right," he said. "That settles that. We stay."

Turning again to Harmon, Fredendall asked whether he had come to relieve Ward.

Harmon answered no to that too.

Fredendall then handed him an envelope and said, "Here it is. The party is yours."

Somewhat startled, Harmon opened the envelope and found a typewritten order placing him in command of "the battle then in progress."

What the hell did that mean?

It meant that he was in direct command of the combat troops and that his mission was to hold the Germans and then drive them out.

The phone rang and Fredendall answered. It was Ward's Chief of Staff, and Fredendall told him to hurry up those diesel tanks he was getting into shape. He had some difficulty getting the message across, for after a while he looked over to Harmon and made a gesture of disgust. He couldn't do a damned thing with Ward, Fredendall said.

What was the trouble?

Fredendall explained. A whole bunch of new Shermans had been sent from the States for the British, and the British had turned some back to Ward, who really needed them. He had formed a provisional tank unit, but the crews had come out of light tanks and were unfamiliar with the Shermans. Ward wanted to give the troops some experience before he committed them.

To hell with that, Harmon thought. The tanks were too good to waste. Their presence on the line would at least raise morale.

"Am I in command?" Harmon asked.

"Yes."

"Well, here, give me that phone."

Harmon told Ward's Chief of Staff to get those tanks in the line by daylight — and that was an order.

"Yes, sir," the Chief of Staff said, but he wanted Harmon to know it was a wrong order.

Harmon answered that he didn't give a damn whether it was wrong or not. The tanks were doing nobody any good if the Germans broke through. He wanted those Sherman tanks there by daylight.

Now, he asked Fredendall, what help could he expect? Fredendall gave him a jeep with a radio and an operator as well as a driver who knew the area, and an assistant operations officer. Turning over to Harmon the job of running the battle, he went to bed.

Harmon drove to Ward's command post. Ward was asleep, but got up at once.

"Ward," Harmon said, "I'm about one thousand files behind you [meaning he was quite junior to Ward on the rolls of the Regular Army] but these are my orders and that's how it is."

Ward was most cooperative. He turned out his staff officers, who quickly briefed Harmon; he said he would get those diesels up as fast as he could; and he issued an order to his subordinate commanders that they were to be ready to move at dawn in any direction except to the rear.

Satisfied that Ward had everything under control, Harmon went on to the most critical place on the front. He found a British brigadier in charge. The brigadier was all right. He was even more profane in his language than Harmon. "We gave them a bloody nose yesterday," he said, "and we'll do it again this morning."

When Harmon learned that Anderson, the British First Army commander, had ordered the artillery to move out to the rear, he countermanded the order. "To hell with that!" he said. He took responsibility for holding the artillery where it was. He figured that if the Allies won, nobody would mind; if they lost, nobody would care.

Harmon waited for Ward's tanks to arrive. He really didn't expect them by daylight. They came around 1000, which was pretty fast. Harmon personally placed the tanks into position. Then he went to visit Robinett, who was glad to see him. He told Harmon there was no question about the ability of CCB to hold. He was sure he could hold.

"We are not only going to hold," Harmon told him, "but we are going to drive them back."

Certain that Robinett had his outfit well in hand, Harmon returned to Fredendall's command post for an hour or two of sleep. He was worn out. But he knew he could bounce back.

Bounce back he did, and he took over Ward's command post, his staff, and his facilities. Fredendall's installation was still being manned by a skeleton force.

Uninformed of Harmon's exact role and believing his own relief to be only a matter of time, Ward moved to Robinett's command post. But he soon learned that he was not to be relieved, so he returned to an active role, ably seconding Harmon's efforts designed to make sure that the troop units remained firmly in place.

It wasn't long before the tide turned, went the other way, and United States troops retook the pass and the village of Kasserine. With Allied troops streaming through Kasserine Pass — this time in the right direction — Harmon returned to the corps command post. He found everyone, he said later, "very jovial and happy" and "pleased about everything." In the midst of the mutual congratulations and back-slapping, Fredendall suddenly asked, "Are you going to relieve Ward?"

"No," Harmon answered. "I think he did pretty well."

"Then I guess we won't need you anymore," Fredendall said.

So Harmon headed back to Constantine. Obviously disappointed because he had commanded "the battle" rather than the corps, he told Truscott he wanted to get back to his 2d Armored Division and teach his troops some of the lessons he had learned.

He stopped at Algiers to see Eisenhower and to give him his impressions of the front. They were brief: Ward was all right, but not Fredendall.

Eisenhower offered Harmon command of the II Corps, but he declined. He could not, he said, take the corps after recommending Fredendall's relief. It would look as though he were motivated by his desire for the command. He suggested, instead, Patton.

Then he returned to Morocco and his division. General Sir Harold Alexander had arrived during the battle of Kasserine Pass to take command of Allied ground troops in Tunisia — Anderson's First Army and Lieutenant General Bernard L. Montgomery's Eighth, which had crossed the border from Libya. Judging Fredendall's performance to have been deficient, Alexander informed Eisenhower that he would welcome a new commander. The recommendation clinched the case that had been building up against Fredendall. His subordinates too had lost confidence in his leadership. Since he disliked and distrusted the British and would never get on well with Alexander and Anderson, and since he had made it quite clear that if he or Ward were retained, the other would have to go, Eisenhower removed him from command of the II Corps.

Ordered home ostensibly because of his ability to train troops, Fredendall received a hero's greeting, command of the Second Army — a training organization — and promotion to lieutenant general. Few suspected that his performance at Kasserine Pass had been less than adequate. Eisenhower's aide reported to President Roosevelt. "I explained to him," he later wrote, "the reluctance Ike had in relieving Fredendall, and his hope that . . . Fredendall's fine qualities, particularly for training, would not be lost to the army."

For his new corps commander in Tunisia, Eisenhower chose

Patton, a man he termed a "tank expert." Catapulted into the spotlight when the American public needed a hero, Patton captured the imagination of the world and started toward fame. If Harmon, who displayed many of the same military virtues and characteristics, had accepted command of the II Corps in Tunisia, would he have become the Patton of World War II?

Harmon returned to Tunisia, this time to take command of a unit rather than, as before, a battle. He replaced Ward at the head of the 1st Armored Division, for a cloud had gathered around Ward. How much Ward was to blame for the defeat at Kasserine Pass was difficult to determine. By ignoring Ward, Fredendall had deprived him of his proper place in the command structure and thereby excused him of fault or blame. But would Harmon, for example, have accepted such treatment?

Finding Ward somewhat pale for his taste, preferring the colorful exuberance of Harmon, Patton gave Ward a virtually impossible battle assignment. Ward personally led the assault, was slightly wounded, and failed to capture his objective. Patton relieved him. Ward returned to the United States. But his relief had been manifestly unfair, and he received command of another armored division, which he trained, took to Europe, and led with distinction during the closing months of the war.

Harmon and the 1st Armored Division sat out the Sicily campaign, then went to southern Italy. The terrain was ill-suited for armor, and the division and Harmon were largely wasted, though they performed well at Anzio. Returning to the United States for rest in the summer of 1944, Harmon took command of a corps. But he elected to go to Europe late in the year to take command of his old outfit, the 2d Armored Division. In January 1945 he was given command of the XXII Corps, which he directed for the remaining months of the war with his usual vigor and competence.

The tangled command channels and personality clashes that surfaced during the battle of Kasserine Pass brought reforms in training, in doctrine, and in command and staff procedures. But the most fruitful result was the formation of a team of individual leaders who were able to work together in mutual cooperation and confidence. One of the important consequences of the troubles at Kasserine was the emergence of the men who would lead the Allies to eventual victory: Eisenhower, Patton, Bradley (who came to prominence first as Patton's deputy); Alexander and Montgomery; and Juin (who led French troops in Italy with distinction).

As disappointing as the Allied command was at Kasserine Pass, the performance of the Axis commanders was even worse. Unlike the Allies, who mastered the complex art of coalition warfare, the Axis nations of Germany and Italy failed to learn their lessons. As suspicion, resentment, and intrigue marred the combined Italo-German operations at the topmost levels of command, mutual antagonism and recrimination plagued the commanders in the field. Though the Allies lost the battle of Kasserine Pass, the Axis commanders, by their bungling, failed to win.

Eisenhower

A SURPRISING NUMBER of professional soldiers and military historians give General of the Army Dwight D. Eisenhower failing grades as a commander in World War II. They say he was hardly adequate as a wartime leader of troops. The number of critics is surprising because of the general's immense popularity. Rarely has any American received the confidence and affection that were tendered to him as Supreme Allied Commander.

What do they say against him?

He was lucky, his critics maintain, rather than expert. His greatest asset was a ready smile and a likable personality that enabled him to win friends among influential men and admiration from the common people. He lacked battle experience, his detractors claim. He never heard a shot fired in anger. He never commanded a unit in combat except, of course, all the forces in the European Theater of Operations, and there he was blessed with splendid subordinates: Bedell Smith as his chief of staff to run his Allied Force Headquarters in the Mediterranean and later his Supreme Headquarters in Europe; Alexander, Bradley, Tedder, Montgomery, Spaatz, Devers, Cunningham, Patton, and others to conduct the fighting.

His job as Supreme Allied Commander permitted him to act as if he were a chairman of the board, presiding over deliberations and directing a vast enterprise by remote control. He hated to make decisions, hesitated to take action on the battlefield, disliked interfering with his combat leaders. He was, they tell us, no more than a glorified message center between Washington and the field, keeping his immediate superiors, General George C. Marshall and the Combined

Chiefs of Staff, informed of developments and transmitting their instructions to his subordinates. His function was primarily ceremonial. His most effective performance was to visit troop units in the interest of bolstering and sustaining morale.

His reputation thus rests, they argue, on certain nonmilitary qualities. Photogenic, amiable, and easy to get along with, Eisenhower was Supreme Commander, they say, because he had no firm military convictions, was amenable to suggestion, and would bring little harm to projects determined by his superiors and executed by his subordinates.

This portrait of General Eisenhower has rarely appeared in print. It emerges, rather, in private conversations and discussions among retired generals and in casual exchanges of ideas among military historians.

For example, a retired general tells the story of what he considers to be a typical illustration of Eisenhower's inability to make up his mind. A division embarking for an invasion was already aboard its ships when an air force officer, over the protests of navy and army officers, insisted on adding to the overcrowded vessels a cargo of aerial bombs. Since this would require unloading some of the ground force equipment regarded as essential for the landings, representatives of the three services went to Eisenhower for a resolution of the problem. Unwilling to rule, Eisenhower sent the three officers to another room with instructions to return in five minutes with a recommended solution. In the adjoining room, the air force representative was quick to realize he was outnumbered two to one, and this was the decision reported to Eisenhower, who accepted it.

A judgment worthy of Solomon? Not at all, the narrator says. On the contrary, Eisenhower's behavior was unmilitary, for he was reluctant to make a decision, and making decisions is what generals are paid for.

One of the most unflattering characterizations of General Eisenhower appeared in Ralph Ingersoll's book *Top Secret,* published in 1946. According to Ingersoll, Eisenhower was a pawn of the British, a front-office stooge, a yes-man who took credit for the battles won by his subordinates.

"By nature a conciliator and an arbitrator [Eisenhower] had nothing whatever to do with leading the invasion [of Normandy]," Ingersoll wrote. Instead, "he backed up the powers of attorney he had given his three British Commanders-in-Chief" — General Montgomery, Admiral Ramsay, and Air Chief Marshal Leigh-Mallory — while he remained "almost wholly occupied in England with the statesman's part of the role of Supreme Commander. He visited the field forces for official inspections only."

The sole purely military responsibility left to Eisenhower, according to Ingersoll, was his function as a go-between — keeping his three subordinate service commanders in touch with his own superiors, the Combined Chiefs of Staff. Though he bore the public responsibility, he did little more about the invasion than pace the floor and listen to the weather prophets who told him when to proceed. His headquarters, Ingersoll continues, was designed to coordinate the Anglo-American war effort rather than to command actively in the field and to win battles; to be informed of decisions — on strategy by the Combined Chiefs and the heads of the two Allied states, and on tactics by his field commanders — instead of making decisions.

In sum, Ingersoll argues, Eisenhower left the actual management of the war to those with more experience. Instead of maintaining a strong hand at the helm, Eisenhower was nothing more than "a chairman — a shrewd, intelligent, tactful chairman" — who had been "especially selected for his ability to conciliate, to see both points of view, to be above national interests — and to be neither bold nor decisive, and neither a leader nor a general." Eisenhower, in other words, failed to fit Ingersoll's conception of a military leader.

Eleven years later, in 1957, Arthur Bryant wrote a history of the war, *The Turn of the Tide,* an excellent account with a pronounced British point of view, for the book was based on the diaries of Field Marshal Lord Alanbrooke, Chief of the Imperial General Staff and the British counterpart of General Marshall. Alanbrooke's view was much like Ingersoll's.

Alanbrooke wrote:

Eisenhower had never even commanded a battalion in action when he found himself commanding a group of Armies in North Africa. No wonder he was at a loss as to what to do, and allowed himself to be absorbed in the political situation at the expense of the tactical. I had little confidence in his having the ability to handle the military situation confronting him, and he caused me great anxiety . . . He learnt a lot during the war, but tactics, strategy and command were never his strong points.

At the Casablanca Conference in January 1943, when the Combined Chiefs decided to unify the North African theater under Eisenhower's command, Alanbrooke recorded his private thoughts as follows:

> [Eisenhower] had neither the tactical nor strategical experience required for such a task. By bringing Alexander over from the Middle East and appointing him as Deputy to Eisenhower, we were . . . flattering and pleasing the Americans in so far as we were placing our senior and experienced commander to function under their commander who had no war experience . . . We were pushing Eisenhower up into the stratosphere and rarefied atmosphere of a Supreme Commander, where he would be free to devote his time to the political and inter-allied problems, whilst we inserted under him one of our own commanders to deal with the military situations and to restore the necessary drive and co-ordination which had been so seriously lacking.
>
> Where he shone was his ability to handle Allied forces, to treat them all with strict impartiality, and to get the very best out of an inter-Allied force . . . He was uncommonly well served by his Chief of Staff, Bedell Smith, who had far more flair for military matters than his master. In addition Ike was blest with a wonderful charm that carried him far; perhaps his great asset was a greater share of luck than most of us receive in life. However, if Ike had rather more than his share of luck we, as allies, were certainly extremely fortunate to have such an exceptionally charming individual as Supreme Commander. What he may have lacked in military ability he greatly made up for by the charm of his personality.

Alanbrooke's judgment is surely an acerbic and back-handed compliment.

Another book that attempts to measure generalship is Colonel Trevor N. Dupuy's *Combat Leaders of World War II,* published in 1965. Dupuy concisely sums up the case against Eisenhower without accepting it entirely:

> Eisenhower's detractors claim that he had no real combat command experience and was merely a genial "chairman of the board"; a political general who could get along well with the British and who leaned over backward to avoid interallied and interservice controversies; a man

who preferred to settle disputes and to solve problems by compromise rather than by decision; a soldier who failed to understand the basic strategical issues involved in the defeat of Germany. He has been criticized by his subordinates Montgomery, Bradley, and Patton, not only for having failed to make a strategic decision for a truly decisive main effort in Western Europe but also for hesitancy in carrying out the more cautious decisions which he did make.

Given General Eisenhower's extreme popularity, both during and after the war, how can one explain such caustic characterizations of one of America's greatest wartime heroes? Jealousy? Politics? Or something more substantial?

Jealousy there doubtless was. Eisenhower was outranked by many of his subordinates. Promoted over a host of officers who were senior to him on the rolls of the Regular Army, Eisenhower had the difficult task of asserting his primacy over those who remembered him as a rather junior officer during the pre–World War II period. At least one of his division commanders was a brigadier general when young Major and Mamie Eisenhower came to call.

Some contend that Marshall sent Eisenhower to England in 1942 to hold the command of the cross-Channel invasion for Marshall himself. The events between June 1942, when Eisenhower arrived in England, and June 1944, when the Allies crossed the Channel, demonstrated clearly Eisenhower's capacity to command the complicated aspects of what was probably the most complex military operation in history. If he was, indeed, sent to hold the fort for Marshall, he soon outgrew the role, for his quickly increasing maturity made him no one's man but his own.

Was politics responsible for some of the castigation of his wartime performance? Undoubtedly, and particularly after his entry into domestic politics. Operating in the unfamiliar field of national politics in the 1950s, General Eisenhower could put his foot into his mouth with incredible ease. His befuddled sentences muddled by foggy logic became classic. His critics assumed that his military utterances had been much like his presidential pronouncements.

What they failed to realize was his mastery of the military area. At a briefing for a group of VIPs in Paris while he was commanding SHAPE in the early 1950s, Eisenhower spontaneously took the pointer and made the presentation himself. At the end of his extemporaneous talk his audience of hard-headed politicians and business men stood and cheered — literally. They were impressed by his grasp of realities and his translation of them into comprehensible English and dazzled by the clarity and force of his expression. He was at home in the military field.

Does something more substantial explain the criticism of his role as a commander? His critics point to several crises during the Mediterranean and European campaigns in which he manifested less than a crystal-clear direction of events.

For example, what about the inability of the Allied troops to seize Tunisia before the arrival of Axis forces late in 1942? What of his failure to close the Argentan-Falaise pocket firmly in August 1944? How about the debate in the fall of 1944 between those who advocated a broad-front strategy and those who wished to concentrate the Allied resources for an exploitation on a narrow front? And Berlin — would not a great military figure have grasped the strategic significance of the German capital and have driven vigorously to capture it instead of being diverted uselessly in quest of what turned out to be a phantom German redoubt?

These are the most serious issues, the salient points in the indictment of Eisenhower as less than adequate as a military commander. How valid is the charge?

The thirty years that have passed since the end of World War II are surely enough time to make possible a dispassionate examination of the case for and against General Eisenhower as a soldier, to "place" him among the galaxy of American military men. In this connection, two questions are worth considering. Can the charges leveled by General Eisenhower's critics be supported? And how does he rate and rank with the great American figures of military history?

Answering these questions is as difficult as measuring quality. Emotion enters the process of judgment, colors evaluation, and renders conclusions a matter of opinion. Disregarding the honors that came to him after the end of World War II, let us consider his merit as a military commander. Was he, as is sometimes alleged, not really very good? Or will the reputation he acquired and enjoyed during the war remain one of his enduring claims to fame?

Let us take the charges one by one and analyze their substance and relevance.

Lucky? He certainly was. All great leaders in any field of endeavor have luck. Without that intangible good fortune of having things come out right in the end, all the expertise in the world goes for naught. It is better to be lucky than wise; an ounce of luck is better than a pound of wisdom. These are only two of many sayings that illustrate what has long been observed: luck is an indispensable asset of those who succeed.

Patton, without question one of the great combat leaders of all time, was serious when he code-named his Third Army headquarters Lucky and thus came to be known as Lucky 6. Superstitious? He was an avid student of military history, and he appreciated the importance of luck as an ingredient of success.

Eisenhower's decision about D-Day discloses the marvelous good fortune he enjoyed. The date for the invasion of northwest Europe having been set, the incredibly complicated machinery for launching the greatest amphibious operation of the war having gotten under way, everything was in readiness for the attack when the weather, on which the whole operation depended, turned bad. Worsening weather would bring disaster.

Should the invasion go, or should it be postponed? After a postponement of one day, the weather still looked threatening, but Eisenhower decided to go. Intuition, foolhardiness, or luck — it was the correct decision. The invasion went as scheduled, all the better for the poor weather because the Germans on the other side of the English Channel doubted that any man would have the nerve to launch an invasion at that time.

Was he a military expert? Look at his professional background. Graduate of West Point, tank school, Command and General Staff College (with honors), Army War College, Army Industrial College; he had all the schooling the army had to offer.

For six years, between 1929 and 1935, he served at the top level of the army — in the offices of the assistant secretary of war and of the Chief of Staff. He commanded tank battalions in the 1920s, served at regimental level, then held posts successively at division, corps, and army echelons — all before the United States entered World War II.

His promotions during World Wars I and II amply argue his case as an expert, for his rise in rank during both wars was exceedingly rapid, even for a West Pointer. In 1915 he was a second lieutenant;

three years later a lieutenant colonel, the second man in his class of 164 graduates to reach the rank. In 1941 he was a lieutenant colonel; three years later he had five-star rank.

To say that these promotions were based on a smile and a personality is an affront to a system that is ruthless in preventing the inefficient from reaching and remaining in places of great responsibility. Despite claims by the disgruntled, the nonexpert has little chance to advance to high rank in the army.

Was he blessed with the ability to impress influential people? Absolutely yes. For almost five years, from 1935 to 1940, he was General MacArthur's assistant in the Philippines. General MacArthur was not notably tolerant of the inefficient. In June 1941 Eisenhower was General Krueger's Third Army chief of staff. Krueger too, a hard-boiled old pro, recognized Eisenhower's abilities and helped push him up the ladder to greater responsibility. In early 1942, as chief of the War Plans Division of the War Department General Staff, then as chief of the Operations Division in the Chief of Staff's office, Eisenhower impressed General Marshall sufficiently with his capacity and capability to win appointment in June of that year as commanding general of the European theater.

An impressive record? One can be sure that MacArthur, Krueger, and Marshall were hardly taken in by a pleasant smile, an engaging personality, or soft-soap. To have impressed these generals is a recommendation of the highest kind.

What did impress them? Quick and bright, Eisenhower had a capacity for learning, an ability for assessing complicated situations, a facility for striking to the heart of a problem. He usually came up with just the right solution. In sum, his judgment was sound, his balance excellent.

Add an ability to get along with people and you have a rare person — sharp, smart, and persuasive, one fitted by intelligence and temperament for high command and for the association with persons of high rank that responsibility requires.

What of his battle experience? True enough, he never commanded a small unit in action. Except for the sound of artillery and air bombardment, except for the distant chatter of machine guns or a far-off fusillade of musketry, he probably never heard a shot fired in anger.

Whether this disqualifies a soldier from holding high command is a moot question. It is interesting to note that General Bradley first exercised command in combat at the corps level, a rather high place to break into the occupation of combat leader. Yet this hardly hindered him from becoming the most brilliant practitioner of grand tactics in the European theater. General Marshall, the strategic architect of World War II, who more than any single person was responsible for the overall direction of the war, never had a field command in wartime.

In some respects Eisenhower was much like Marshall. He had an intuitive ability to surround himself with capable advisors and subordinates. And he was able to call upon them and receive from them the utmost in loyalty and effort.

Twice during the war Patton's indiscretions brought him close to dismissal: the slapping incidents in Sicily and a security breach in England. Though a lesser man would have fired Patton, Eisenhower gave him a severe tongue-lashing and kept him. Appreciating Patton's combat leadership, he was convinced that American troops would win more rapidly with Patton in the field.

Walter Bedell Smith, his chief of staff, exemplified Eisenhower's happy facility for having the right man in the right job. Eisenhower without Smith, his critics aver, would have been lost. But Smith did what Eisenhower wanted. He frequently acted as Eisenhower's hatchet-man and performed some of the unpleasant duties that are an unavoidable part of command. No one has ever questioned who was boss.

Ah, yes, some would say, but it was really Marshall who sent Smith over to keep Eisenhower on the straight and narrow. Smith was Marshall's man. If he was at the beginning, he soon lost any split allegiance he might have had. During the negotiations for the surrender of Italy in the summer of 1943, Smith, who played the most important role in the military diplomacy, carried out Eisenhower's wishes, not Marshall's, which were in some discord with the policy that Eisenhower enunciated and executed. For "Eisenhower," according to Alanbrooke, "wanted to offer the Italians an easy and honourable way out . . . in return for immediate use of their airfields and strategic strong points" — and he had his way over the objections of the politicians and strategists in Washington and London.

Was Smith particularly useful because Eisenhower was unable to be tough? It seems more likely that Eisenhower rarely chose to play that role. Yet he could, when he had to, be ruthless, firm, and resolute. Montgomery, who wanted desperately to be the ground-forces commander in northwest Europe, harassed Eisenhower throughout the summer and fall of 1944. Eisenhower was extremely patient, but finally put him in his place. At the end of the war, Montgomery's tribute to his commander, recorded in his book *Normandy to the Baltic,* is somewhat touching and even slightly pathetic.

Nor did Eisenhower hesitate when it came to weeding out inefficient officers. Some thought him rather heartless. One corps commander in North Africa and two in southern Italy got the ax — to say nothing of the division commanders who were relieved.

The famous Eisenhower temper was one of the better-kept secrets of the war. But many associates can testify to the astringent and explosive — almost choleric — reaction he had to evidence of inefficiency. The men he selected usually worked out beautifully. Those who were sent to him were the ones who were more likely to perform beneath his expectations.

Eisenhower's brilliance in selecting and working with his American colleagues was matched by his success with the British. Assisted in the Mediterranean by Alexander, Cunningham, and Tedder — who commanded, respectively, the Allied ground, sea, and air forces — Eisenhower welded them, as well as his Anglo-American staff, into a well-balanced team. It was the same in northwest Europe. "Thanks to Eisenhower," even Alanbrooke had to admit, "there was remarkably little friction" between the officers of the two nations.

Commanding a coalition effort, Eisenhower — and perhaps only he could have done it — made it work. He did it so naturally that American purists called him pro-British, and British extremists accused him of being pro-American. In one instance, when certain influential British officers urged him vainly to get rid of Montgomery, they charged Eisenhower with being too British. What they failed to recognize was his ability to combine skillfully the best characteristics and procedures of both nations.

Some Americans think he gave up certain prerogatives of command because he conducted the war in the British fashion of commanding by committee. To the degree that he accommodated himself to this British practice he showed not weakness but rather a measure of his flexibility. He consulted his subordinate commanders more than Americans are apt to; he called frequent conferences; he asked often for expressions of opinion. Without these amenities, it is doubtful that he would have secured, at least at first, the cooperation and, ultimately, the devotion of his non-American associates.

It is significant that he maintained his relative independence and freedom as theater commander. His rejection of interference by higher authority is an American rather than a British characteristic. The British on occasion sought to exert over him the close supervision normally exercised over British theater commanders. He resisted gracefully. Despite Churchill's enormous pressure, for example, to call off the invasion of southern France, Eisenhower was convinced that the landings were necessary, and he brought them off. There was never any question about who was the Supreme Commander in the Mediterranean or in northwest Europe.

It is interesting that Churchill's insistence on and his eventual engineering of the Anzio invasion occurred at the time when Eisenhower was leaving the Mediterranean theater to assume command of the Overlord forces in England. Had Eisenhower remained in the Mediterranean, it is possible that Churchill might have been unable to bulldoze aside the objections of the professional soldiers who advised against the Anzio landings.

Even Alanbrooke acknowledged on at least two occasions "the moral courage" of Eisenhower and on a third occasion his "good sense." To name another instance of Eisenhower's brilliance, Alanbrooke characterized his handling of Darlan and his military agreement with the French in North Africa as a master stroke for which Eisenhower "took full responsibility" and deserved it. "Eisenhower never flinched," Alanbroke noted; his "firmness was rewarded."

Was Eisenhower in constant contact with his superiors in Washington and in London? Of course. Many messages, quite a few of them personal communications for Marshall's "eyes only," flashed from his headquarters, and a great many were received. Marshall often asked for recommendations, explanations, and clarifications, frequently offered guidance and advice, but never told Eisenhower what to do. Most of Eisenhower's messages to his chief were informative in purpose, nature, and content. In a war of global proportions, all parts of the whole had to fit into the overall concept and plan. Since the Combined Chiefs set objectives and allocated resources, they had to remain in closest touch with the commanders who ran the theaters of war.

What of the substantive issues? How about his inability to thrust eastward from Algiers to Bizerte and Tunis in November and December of 1942 before the Axis forces managed to build up a formidable opposition? The eastward thrust from Algiers came to an unhappy end as a consequence of the onset of the rainy season and the inability of the slender Allied logistical system to support a prolonged drive. Calling off the offensive was an unpleasant decision — as Alanbrooke noted, with admiration of Eisenhower's fortitude — but Eisenhower faced up directly to the stalemate that had developed. A lesser man might have persisted, and the only result would have been a higher Allied casualty rate.

Was Eisenhower to blame for permitting the escape from Normandy of two German field armies that were virtually, but not quite, surrounded at Argentan and Falaise? There is some justification for feeling that Eisenhower let events slip out of his control. Montgomery was then — in August 1944 — ground forces commander, and though Bradley encircled the German troops who had pushed their heads into a noose at Mortain, Montgomery failed to remove the army group boundary that halted Bradley at the edge of complete success. Only Eisenhower could have intervened; only Eisenhower could have ordered Montgomery to eliminate the restriction that held back the Americans. Eisenhower preferred to observe instead of interfering. He left the conduct of the battle to his subordinates. Though he made no excuse, his reason for remaining aloof was the fact that his own headquarters was not yet established on the continent. He lacked the staff facilities — the signal, intelligence, and other information — that would have permitted him to reach a sound decision on a matter that required detailed and timely knowledge. As a consequence, though 50,000 German troops were destroyed, the two field armies that were almost encircled were able to breakout and retreat to the German border, their headquarters and staffs in the main intact.

What of the broad-front–narrow-front controversy during the pursuit phase of the European operation, in the latter days of August 1944 and the early days of September, when four Allied armies were streaming across the Seine and heading toward the Siegfried Line on the heels of the fleeing Germans? Should Eisenhower have allocated the bulk of his resources to one of the pursuing forces instead of spreading them among all?

The debate is usually discussed in strict military terms: mass, objective, and economy of force. These military issues were important, but the fundamental question was political and related to the proprieties of coalition warfare. Eisenhower had many obligations — to his troops of various nations, to those directing the war, and to the British and American publics. How could he slight a British commander in favor of an American, or vice versa? The stability of any coalition force rests on delicate conditions, and the broad-front strategy, a compromise adopted by Eisenhower over Montgomery's vehement protests and Bradley's quiet reservations, fulfilled the conditions for equilibrium better than any other course of action. Neither Montgomery nor Bradley — or Patton for that matter — received favored treatment at this stage of the campaign or any other.

"Eisenhower," Bryant writes, giving Alanbrooke's thoughts in quite another context that has relevance to this situation, "might be without experience of war but he had precisely the qualities — of character, selflessness and good sense — to knit the staff officers of two nations into an integrated organization in which national differences and jealousies were forgotten. His insistence that Anglo-American rivalry was the unforgivable sin created in his raw headquarters a new conception of inter-Allied unity."

In addition, the logistical organization in the European theater, by virtue of the great and unexpected speed of the advance across France, had been outstripped in its capacity to serve the combat units, and this fact was probably appreciated more clearly by Eisenhower than by any of his subordinates. Montgomery claimed he could drive all the way to Berlin, and Patton bemoaned the lack of gasoline that prevented him from cutting the German forces to ribbons; but Eisenhower knew — perhaps intuitively — that the logistical apparatus established in Normandy and expanding slowly behind the combat units was unable to support even a single, concentrated thrust in the decisive strength required to bring the Germans to their knees in the latter months of 1944. This has become crystal clear in historical perspective.

The failure to take Berlin? Berlin was simply not in the cards. Given the political guidance Eisenhower received from the United States, given the strict military aims enunciated by the Anglo-American alliance, and given the American insistence on the Constitutional principle of civilian control over the military, it was impossible for Eisenhower or anyone else in his position to go beyond the Elbe River. The participants who work within the confines of a policy structure framed within the context of a particular time period are, unfortunately, deprived of the clarity that is the undisputed possession of the Monday-morning quarterback.

Much more important, however, is the fact — usually overlooked — that the Russians could have taken Berlin as early as February 1945. Though Berlin was at most a week's drive away, the Russians chose to procrastinate while their armies moved forward on other fronts. They were reluctant to deliver the *coup de grâce,* dispatch the crumbling Nazi structure, and finish off the war until they had overrun eastern Europe. Even if the Allied forces had made a move toward Berlin, there is little doubt that the Russians could have gotten there first.

The fact is that Eisenhower's superb accomplishment in World War II was his management of the complex establishment that won the war in northwestern Europe. The machinery he directed contained ground, sea, and air contingents manned by Americans, British, Canadians, French, Poles, Belgians, Dutch, Czechs, and others.

If his function resembled on occasion the behavior of a chairman of the board, it was because the warfare of his time and place required it. In addition to the responsibility for winning battles, Eisenhower had duties that were, from a narrow and old-fashioned point of view, somewhat nonmilitary. He was concerned — and had to be — with civilian relations, fiscal policy in liberated countries, political problems, and what might be called miltary diplomacy: how to deal with the French in North Africa, how to negotiate the surrender of Italy, how to regard the status of the Free French during the liberation of France. If he interfered little with the tactical decisions of his subordinate commanders, it was because he was sometimes too busy with other matters and, more frequently, because he had confidence in their abilities.

Yet he had no hesitation in settling disagreements on the tactical level. Pantelleria, an island in the Mediterranean, fell easily to Allied troops because Eisenhower, over the arguments of subordinates, insisted it could be softened by air bombardment. Over the protests of Leigh-Mallory he ordered the airborne drops in Normandy. He showed no reluctance in changing the whole plan and course of the Normandy campaign in the early days of August when he swung the bulk of his forces eastward toward the Seine and away from Brittany. He faltered not an instant in deciding to cross the Seine instead of pausing there in accordance with all prior planning. He had no hesitation in capping the unexpected capture of the Remagen bridge by pushing immediate exploitation. And during the Bulge, over the objections of some of his closest advisors, he placed Montgomery in command of American troops on the northern shoulder in order to fulfill the precept of unity of command. There are many such instances of his direct personal influence on the battlefield.

More often than not Eisenhower's decisions reflected a compromise. The very nature of his command position, as well as the strength and closeness of the coalition, required tact and discretion. Whereas General MacArthur in the South Pacific could run the show in a rather high-handed manner because the Americans were contributing the overwhelmingly preponderant strength in that theater, the case was different in Europe. British strength exceeded American commitments in the early part of the war, and not until the final year of the struggle did the American resources pull ahead.

Part of Eisenhower's great strength as a commander lay precisely in his popularity. There was a quality of humanness about him that stemmed from his directness and simplicity. Much like President Truman, who gained sympathy by his humility when he was forced to step into the shoes of a giant, Eisenhower had the common touch that brought understanding. He imparted the impression that he was an ordinary human being doing the very best he could in a situation fraught with danger and difficulty. He leveled with the press, took the news correspondents into his confidence, and made it clear always that he was responsible for whatever might or did go wrong. At Kasserine he took the blame though he was obviously not at fault. During the few hours before the D-Day invasion he scribbled a note taking full responsibility in the event the landings failed. He insisted he had been wrong about the Bulge. He had no need to assert his responsibility for what went right, for the people of the Allied nations stood solidly behind him.

In his "rapid grooming for high office," Chester Wilmot wrote in 1952:

There was not time for Eisenhower to go through the mill of command and gain battle experience. On the other hand, the ten years in Washington and Manila had given him intimate knowledge of politico-military problems on the highest level and a breadth of outlook unusual in a regular soldier. This training stood him in good stead when he rose to be Commander-in-Chief for Operation TORCH. In this post the personal and political integrity of the man was more important than the professional ability of the soldier. Others could — and did — provide expert and experienced leadership in the field, but nobody else revealed Eisenhower's remarkable capacity for integrating the efforts of different allies and rival services and for creating harmony between individuals with varied backgrounds and temperaments. From the outset he demanded "immediate and continuous loyalty to the concept of unity" . . . Because he remained true to this principle, Eisenhower was to become the most successful commander of allied forces in the history of war.

Are any predecessors and contemporaries comparable with Eisenhower? General Pershing comes to mind despite real differences in the circumstances. Pershing commanded only American troops in Europe. No other theaters competed for American resources. And the imperfect state of communications, making close touch between France and Washington impossible, required virtually complete independence on Pershing's part.

But perhaps the most important difference was the role of the United States in world affairs. In 1917 Britain and France were the leaders. The United States had yet to prove its strength, its military know-how. Convinced that the inexperienced American troops would perform better under French and British leadership, the Allied nations wanted to use them to stiffen existing formations along the front. Under instructions to retain the national identity of the American commitment, Pershing had to be tough and uncompromising. On the defensive until American units proved their worth near the end of the war, Pershing was the exponent of the "hard sell."

In the 1940s, the United States was the leader of the Allied coalition, and Eisenhower's appointment as Supreme Commander symbolized the status. Eisenhower could be, and was, affable, amiable, relaxed. The soft sell.

General MacArthur? When war came to the United States in 1941, MacArthur had already made his mark. He had a brilliant World

War I record, and he had reached the pinnacle of army advancement as Chief of Staff. A distinguished figure, he commanded his theater in what seems like splendid aloofness. Marshall suggested that MacArthur organize a coalition theater command structure along the lines established by Eisenhower. But MacArthur retained a staff that was completely American. Perhaps MacArthur was not so flexible as Eisenhower. In a sense MacArthur represented an earlier tradition, the heritage of Pershing. Eisenhower inaugurated a broader framework of operations more in tune with the nature of modern coalition warfare.

What if MacArthur had commanded the European theater? Would he have been so successful? Would he have been able immediately to impress the British to such an extent as to gain an entirely free hand in running the show alone? It seems doubtful. The British had too much at stake.

Would MacArthur, if faced with the necessity to do so, have been able to create and make work a close coalition effort like Eisenhower's? This too seems doubtful. During the Korean War, MacArthur had a unique opportunity to create a real United Nations command. By a brilliant stroke he could have organized a headquarters symbolic of the Free World's aspirations. Instead he maintained the traditional American organization, no different from that of World War I, from his own World War II experience. He might have established on the military plane, somewhat in the manner of SHAPE, the leadership of the United States in a Pacific coalition of Free World nations.

Younger in outlook, a figure firmly rooted in his own times, Eisenhower maintained the ascendancy of American arms with an unparalleled ease and graciousness. Not only did he make a complex coalition effort work superbly, but he also remained a heroic figure to the troops of all the allied nations under his command.

Not a Patton, a Bradley, or a Montgomery, Eisenhower directed them and engineered victory in Europe. In so doing, he became an American hero worthy of his nation's praise and adulation.

America's greatest field commander in World War II, Eisenhower represented more than anyone else the new leadership and the new American role in the world history. His achievement was great. His military stature is assured.

Coalition Command

DURING THE BATTLE for the Anzio beachhead in February 1944, among the various messages sent by Prime Minister Winston Churchill to the commanders in the Mediterranean was a peculiar wire to General Sir Harold Alexander. Alexander, who commanded the Anglo-American land forces in Italy, was recognized everywhere as one of the war's outstanding leaders. Yet Churchill, in this particular instance, chose to question Alexander's methods of exercising command.

Churchill's message was spawned by disappointment. He had expected swift victory and quick capture of Rome as a result of the Anzio landing. But a quite different situation had developed. Instead of hurling a wildcat ashore — to use Churchill's words — the Allies had put aground a stranded whale.

In searching for the reasons why the Anzio operation had failed to produce the desired effect on the Germans, Churchill wondered whether at least part of the explanation lay particularly in the area of Alexander's command control. Had General Alexander been decisive enough? If not, had he been hampered by the fact that he commanded a coalition force?

There was no way for Churchill to know for sure, but he had a hunch. "I have a feeling," the prime minister wired Alexander, "that you may have hesitated to assert your authority because you were dealing so largely with Americans." And just in case his intuition was correct, Churchill decided to leave no doubt on that score. "You are quite entitled," he added, "to give them orders."

The advice was gratuitous and obvious. No one questioned

Alexander's right, despite his British nationality, to command American troops. After all, the War Office had placed the British troops participating in the North Africa invasion more than a year earlier directly under an American, General Eisenhower. What applied to the one applied equally to the other.

Yet Churchill had put his finger on the basic difficulty of coalition effort: the constant tug-of-war that goes on between the opposing forces of nationality and alliance. No one would dispute the necessity that made Alexander command American troops in a manner different from the way he handled British troops. The essential difference was a requirement of coalition war. Because Alexander was a quiet commander, not a swashbuckling one, Churchill suspected that he had been too much the gentleman, hesitant to take a strong stand for fear of disturbing the harmony of the coalition.

Whether Churchill was right, whether this made General Alexander less effective as a commander, and whether this had any bearing on the Anzio battle are debatable propositions despite Churchill's guess. Yet the fact remains that coalition warfare imposes certain restrictions on commanders. In a sense, allied warfare compels commanders to act in accordance with a set of manners somewhat different from what is usually expected on the battlefield. In addition to the normal attributes of a commander, a coalition commander needs understanding, tact, and sensitivity of a special sort. If he is lacking in these and cannot change his behavior patterns, if he is not inclined to respect a point of view valid to one of his allies, he is not likely to gain cohesion and combination in his forces in the degree normally required for success.

Volumes have been written on coalition warfare, most of them about problems at the highest echelon. Relatively few writings deal with the problems of coalition warfare on the battlefield. In most instances, perhaps, the difficulties stemming from the coalition itself are dismissed as nothing more than bickering. And some, of course, reflect only temperamental resentment and jealousy on the part of individuals. But many situations are worth looking into for the subtle interplay of national interest and pride with coalition goals.

In this age of perpetual crisis, when alliances are so important in our national life, commanders on all levels may find themselves directing the members of more than one national group. A survey of some past experiences might prove useful to those who will lead in the future.

The essential fact of any coalition is that it is formed by and composed of independent members who have joined freely in search of a common objective. In pursuit of the common goal, each member renounces, usually tacitly, some of its prerogatives of independence. It can no longer act alone, but must coordinate its action with its allies. When the colonies in the New World banded together to win their independence, they were combining in the interest of attaining an end too large for the individual capabilities of each member but within the realm of accomplishment if all acted together. Their success as a larger entity notwithstanding, each state still retains some vestiges of its early sovereignty.

A coalition is not so very different. The independent members have temporarily merged their capabilities and submerged their differences in the interest of the common goal. Yet in a coalition effort involving nations, each retains the right to determine the extent of its participation. Consequently, to keep a coalition from shaking apart, its leaders must be delicate in handling members who may have somewhat disparate aims despite their overriding interest in the central issue that made the coalition possible and desirable in the first place.

During World War I, the coalition of the Allies was very loose. Each nation did not do much more than cooperate with the others. The national military commanders had equal status, and Sir John French, who led the British Expeditionary Force, and General Joffre, who led the French armies, coordinated their operations. The personal antipathy each felt for the other often prevented close coordination. But more important, each commander was responsive only to the wishes of his own government.

The appointment of an Allied generalissimo in the spring of 1918 did not materially change the coalition concept. For Foch, the Supreme Commander, had such limited authority that he chose to fulfill his role by persuading the national commanders — Haig, Pétain, and Pershing — to a common course of action. What was lacking was a higher authority — a single coalition body on the political level — which could give direction and meaning to Foch's military position. In the absence of a combined authority, unity of command was embodied in Foch's person, and he never established a large headquarters. What he was able to do was provide in his person a focal point for what might be called better coordinated co-operation — not a true unity of command — among the nations engaged in their common pursuit: defeat of the Germans.

A potentially disturbing incident concerning the capture of Sedan illustrates how the coalition worked. Sedan, occupied by the Germans during most of the war, came to have a value to the Allies far beyond its real worth. American and French units fighting alongside each other during the Meuse-Argonne offensive in 1918 were both in position to take Sedan, and both wanted to. To the Americans, their capture of the town would represent the symbolic culmination of their newly mobilized military strength. To the French, Sedan would in part erase the distasteful memories of the Franco-Prussian War.

Though Sedan lay within the French zone of advance, Pershing directed the Americans to disregard the military boundaries. Two United States corps therefore ignored the neighboring French and engaged in an intramural contest for glory, their troops rushing pell-mell toward the town.

Before the Americans reached Sedan, French authorities made known their displeasure. Though Foch issued no order, Pershing canceled his previous direction. The Americans held back in favor of the French. Assured the honor of liberating Sedan and their national aim thus satisfied, the French graciously invited the Americans to send a token force to accompany their troops into the town.

Loose coalition or not, good sense prevailed at Sedan when Pershing respected a matter of national pride that was very important to the French.

In World War II the coalition among the Allied powers of Great Britain and the United States reached a degree of closeness and maturity in political and military matters never before attained. Even this combination of powers respected the fundamental right of each nation to take exception to coalition decisions.

When the British placed their invasion forces under General Eisenhower for the North Africa campaign, they were explicit on this point in their instructions to their national commander, General Anderson. "In the unlikely event," the War Office directed, "of your receiving an order which, in your view, will give rise to a grave and exceptional situation, you have the right to appeal to the War Office." National aims, the War Office was saying, come first.

But there was an important addition to these instructions. Anderson had the right to appeal to his War Office, but only if his appeal had no adverse effect on coalition operations: "provided that by so doing an opportunity is not lost, nor any part of the Allied Force endangered." Furthermore, before appealing any order from General Eisenhower, Anderson was first to inform the Supreme Commander of his intention to protest and also to advise him of the reasons why an appeal was deemed justified.

In this way the national commander was made more subordinate to the Allied commander than any national commander had been during the previous world war.

An interesting example of this sort of subordination occurred in Sicily, where Alexander, who commanded the 15th Army Group, controlled two armies: Montgomery's British Eighth and Patton's U.S. Seventh. Comparing the successful advance from El Alamein by Montgomery's veterans with the setback suffered by the relatively inexperienced Americans at Kasserine Pass, Alexander gave Montgomery what amounted to a free hand in planning the invasion. The result was not only the assignment to Montgomery of the main effort but the relegation of Patton's army to what was virtually a security mission: protecting Montgomery's left flank and rear.

This was not in accordance with the niceties of coalition warfare. For assignments must be made in terms of maintaining an equitable division of effort and a proportionate share of the sacrifices and glory to each national participant. Alexander, of course, was thinking only of how to gain victory in the shortest possible time. But the Americans, and particularly Patton, resented Alexander's disregard of the more recent United States military achievements in Tunisia. The subordinate role Alexander projected in Sicily for the Seventh Army seemed to the Americans unjust, and it rankled. Despite the urgings of his close associates, however, Patton refused to protest Alexander's directive. An American commander was subordinate to Alexander, and the fact that Alexander was British made no difference. The Allied command structure stood, and in Patton's view had to stand — unchallenged.

The result of the assignment had, in the execution, an ironic overtone. Montgomery was halted by the Germans, and Alexander had to permit Patton to undertake a more important offensive mission. The Sicily campaign then took on, in some respects, the aspect of a fierce rivalry between Americans and British, with both engaging in a race to Messina, the final objective. By reaching Messina first, Patton established the proficiency of American arms to the satisfaction of the alliance partner. Never again would Alexander overlook the importance of national pride in his management of coalition warfare.

A particularly delicate coalition problem of this sort arose in the spring of 1944, when the Indian 4th Division was assigned the mission of attacking Monte Cassino. In order to insure the success of the assault, the division commander, a British officer, requested a bombardment of the abbey atop the mountain. He made his request to his superior, the corps commander, General Freyberg of New Zealand. Freyberg passed on the request to his superior, General Clark, an American, who commanded the Fifth Army.

Clark did not believe a bombardment of the Benedictine monastery was warranted, and he told Freyberg so. But when Freyberg insisted, Clark transmitted the request to General Alexander, the next higher commander, explaining that if his immediate subordinate, the corps commander, were an American, there would be no bombardment. Because of the delicacy of coalition warfare and the sensitivity of the national participants, Clark explained, he felt compelled to seek higher authority.

Alexander might have sought still higher authority, but time was growing short and he made the decision. For the same reason that Clark had sought his advice, Alexander granted Freyberg's request. The abbey was bombed, though, as Clark had foreseen, the air strike did not prompt success in the ground attack.

The same good manners were applied in northwest Europe during the initial months of the Overlord invasion. Montgomery was temporary commander of Allied ground forces and acted in that position until September 1, when Eisenhower took over. During the summer months Bradley was senior American officer on the continent, at first as commander of the U.S. First Army and after August 1 as head of the 12th Army Group. In both positions Bradley was subordinate to Montgomery. Yet in the interest of effective coalition warfare, Montgomery permitted Bradley a latitude of action that went beyond the norm, for Dempsey, commander of the British Second Army, never had the freedom of choice accorded Bradley. Montgomery kept Dempsey, a British officer like himself, under much closer supervision concerning boundaries, plans of attack, and unit assignments.

A consequence — perhaps not so fortunate — of this fine balance took place in August 1944, when the Allied ground forces had almost surrounded the German forces in Normandy. Montgomery, commander of Allied ground forces, also headed the 21st Army Group and controlled the Canadian First Army and British Second Army. These forces, generally speaking, were putting pressure on the Argentan-Falaise pocket from the north. As commander of the 12th Army Group and in control of the U.S. First Army and the U.S. Third Army, Bradley was applying pressure on the Germans from the south.

While Montgomery's forces attacked southward toward Falaise, Bradley's troops were fighting northward toward Argentan. In the process of heading toward Argentan, American troops crossed the army group boundary, which ran generally east-west in that area, and thereby impinged on the British-Canadian zone. His troops having reached the southern outskirts of Argentan and by then gone several miles across the boundary and into British territory, Bradley halted the attack on August 13. The Canadians, attacking toward Falaise since August 8, did not reach their objective until August 16. Through the fifteen-mile gap between Argentan and Falaise, the Germans started on August 16 to escape from the pocket. On the following day Montgomery ordered the Allied troops to continue their attacks to a meeting point in the Trun-Chambois area, where closure of the pocket was finally made on August 20.

For four days, between August 13 and 17, Bradley's forces had remained immobile at the southern shoulder of the pocket near Argentan. Had Eisenhower, Supreme Allied Commander, chosen to intervene, he could have ordered the pocket closed earlier. Eisenhower chose not to interfere, though later he admitted that the opportunity for a great battle of annihilation had been lost. His probable reason for not taking positive action was that he was not free in coalition warfare to question the actions of a subordinate — in this instance Montgomery, a British officer.

The French too were members of the Allied coalition, and one of the most troublesome situations of World War II — that is, from the point of view of the disparate national aims concerned — took place at Paris in late August 1944.

In the interest of pursuing to and into Germany the enemy armies defeated in Normandy, and in the hope of ending the war immediately, Eisenhower decided to by-pass and encircle Paris. His reasons were military, and they were sound: he wished no diversion of troops and supplies from the pursuit, no necessity to bring coal and food to the civilian populace, no great battle with consequent harm to the inhabitants and destruction of the city's historical monuments. Once encircled and isolated, the German garrison would eventually surrender. A political motive buttressed Eisenhower's military reasons: by marching into the city, the Allies would, of necessity, bring with them General de Gaulle, head of the French resistance, who might thereby be placed in political power by the force of Allied arms rather than as the result of a national electoral decision.

Contrary to Eisenhower's plan, De Gaulle wished the capital's liberation at once. To Frenchmen, the liberation of Paris meant the liberation of France. The spiritual capital, Paris was also the hub of national administration and politics, the center of the railway system, communication lines, and highways. In addition, Paris in August 1944 was the prize of an internal contest for power within the French resistance movement; in general, a struggle between Gaullists and the resistance factions of the Left.

A spontaneous insurrection within the city brought matters to a head. As French resistance fighters seized important public buildings in a surge of emotion, they challenged not only the German garrison but also Gaullist plans. It was not clear which of the resistance political parties had seized power in Paris — an important matter in view of the collapse of the Pétain government. And it seemed apparent that the German garrison could, if it wished, put down the insurrection with brutality, destroy the city, and bathe the inhabitants in blood.

Only the immediate entry of regular troops into the capital promised to dissipate the dangers, and to this end the Gaullists tried to get Eisenhower to change his mind in favor of an immediate liberation. A French division, commanded by General Leclerc, was part of Eisenhower's forces for the particular mission of liberating Paris, and De Gaulle went so far as to threaten politely that if Eisenhower did not send these troops into the capital he would have to do so himself. De Gaulle could make this kind of threat, for as potential chief of the French government he was a political leader, and like Roosevelt and Churchill stood above Eisenhower, the military commander.

Leclerc, whose division had been engaged in the battle of the Argentan-Falaise pocket about 100 miles from Paris, was impatient to get to the capital, and upon the conclusion of the battle on August 21 he dispatched a small force toward the city. Fearful that the Allied command might not be able to honor its promise of permitting French troops the glory of liberating the capital, Leclerc instructed the small force to be ready to enter the city in case Eisenhower decided to restore order in Paris by means of an Allied force.

Leclerc's superior, General Gerow, who commanded the United States V Corps, ordered Leclerc to recall the troops moving toward Paris. Refusing to do so, Leclerc sought higher authority. He went to see General Bradley, who, he discovered, was by then conferring with Eisenhower on the possibility of changing the plans for bypassing and avoiding Paris.

Pressed on all sides — by the French who wanted the capital, by the British who favored De Gaulle's political aspirations, and by his own wish to preserve the city from harm — Eisenhower found a military reason to change his mind. If it were true, as reported, that the French resistance — the French Forces of the Interior — controlled parts of the city, Eisenhower could send help. He could dispatch an Allied force of French, American, and British soldiers to march into Paris, and he did so. At the same time, he reserved the honor of initial entry to the French. This Allied force was placed under Gerow's V Corps headquarters. But no British troops showed up for the march to Paris, apparently believing that the liberation was strictly a matter for the French.

When Leclerc's troops alone seemed unable to penetrate into Paris on August 24 — a failure due to faulty attack dispositions, German strength, and swarms of civilians who greeted and blocked their liberators — the American command decided to send a United States division into the city. French and American divisions entered Paris on August 25 and officially liberated the capital.

Wishing a military parade in Paris to symbolize the culmination of the resistance — a political motive — De Gaulle asked Leclerc to furnish the troops. Gerow, Leclerc's superior, protested on military grounds: he felt the city was still not secure. The parade was held, and there was scattered shooting along the route of march.

Several days later, when Gerow, the senior Allied commander, formally handed over responsibility for the city to the French authorities, the military governor flatly told him that the French had handled the administration of the city from the moment of its liberation.

The long, traditional Franco-American friendship was by then strained to the disagreeable point where there was real hostility between these two allies. The French had wanted to liberate Paris themselves in order to expiate their defeat in 1940 and to make the act of liberation part of their heritage and history. They resented the imposition of American comrades.

If there was no necessity for liberating Paris on military grounds, there was perhaps little point in sending a United States division into the capital and little justification for placing the action within the framework of an American corps. More flexible command arrangements would have allowed the French to liberate Paris as they wished.

For the Americans, who felt that part of the glory and prestige of liberating Paris was small repayment for their countrymen lost between the Normandy beaches and the gates of the capital, the French were guilty of bad faith and poor manners, politically unreliable and militarily untrustworthy. For the French, who even before the liberation felt that they owed the Americans too much, the Americans were inexcusably naive and uncomprehending of Gallic aspirations.

A final example, the controversy over the broad front versus the narrow front, may also be instructive. In the fall of 1944, as the Allied armies drove from the Seine River toward the German border in pursuit of the enemy forces defeated in Normandy, a debate developed between Eisenhower, Supreme Allied Commander, and Montgomery, senior British officer on the continent. The question at issue was how the Allies ought to make what was then regarded as being their final culminating effort against Germany.

Partly because Eisenhower on September 1 had just taken command of the ground forces and partly because pursuit warfare by its very nature is fluid, the drive beyond the Seine was relatively uncontrolled. All the armies pushed forward against minor, sporadic resistance, the only limiting factor being a developing shortage of supplies, particularly gasoline, which by early September was starting to curtail motor transportation, then essential to the pursuit. The shortage resulted from the inability of the Communications Zone supply apparatus to keep up with the spectacular speed of the breakout, launched out of the hedgerow country in late July.

Characteristically more cautious than his American counterparts, and also endowed with fewer resources, Montgomery had immobilized one corps behind the Seine, distributing its vehicles and gasoline to the pursuing elements. Bradley, on the other hand, preferred to let all his forces go as far as they could toward the German border. Yet since Eisenhower had designated Montgomery's advance as the main Allied effort, and since in compliance with Montgomery's request Eisenhower had instructed Bradley to make his main effort with the U.S. First Army so as to assist the neighboring British, Bradley in late August gave greater amounts of gasoline to Hodges' First Army than to Patton's Third. This action was logical also because Hodges and Montgomery were heading toward the Ruhr, the major Allied objective, while Patton was advancing toward the Saar, an area much less important when judged in terms of how best to destroy the German capacity to resist.

The 6th Army Group, controlling one French and one American army, was by this time approaching Germany from southern France. On September 15 it would join Eisenhower's forces and come under his command. At that time the three army groups constituting Eisenhower's land forces would be stretched more than 300 miles across Holland, Belgium, and France from the North Sea to the Swiss border.

Late in August Montgomery initiated what became a strategic debate when he suggested that the shortage of supplies, particularly gasoline, ought to make the Allies think of concentrating their resources into a single major blow against the Germans. He envisioned a steamroller of forty divisions plunging across the Ruhr, the center of German industrial power, toward Berlin, heart of the enemy state. By virtue of the location of the Allied forces and his own seniority, it would, of course, be Montgomery and his British troops who would lead this attack. This became known as the narrow-front strategy.

Eisenhower, preferring what became termed the broad-front strategy, wanted all the forces along the line to advance, in order, as he said, to stretch the enemy's defenses and make them more vulnerable at all points of entry into Germany. He did not think that Allied logistics could support a single massive thrust to Berlin — a belief borne out as being correct by logistical studies after the war. And he thought that the Germans could concentrate enough forces to halt a single drive whereas they did not have the strength to stop advances all along the front.

These were good reasons, but there were two additional ones in Eisenhower's mind. He could not permit Montgomery to forge ahead at the expense of Patton, for he felt the American public would neither understand nor condone this decision. A thrust led by Montgomery, if successful, would have become a British victory rather than an Allied triumph. Furthermore Eisenhower could not in good conscience entrust Montgomery, who had a reputation for caution and prudence, with a mission requiring the slashing, aggressive tactics of Bradley or Patton. Yet to replace Montgomery by an American would have broken the ties of the coalition effort.

Eisenhower's broad-front strategy prevailed. In view of the fact that the miraculous resurrection of enemy strength at the border (the Germans called it "the miracle in the west") — an event coinciding with the lowest ebb of Allied logistical fortunes — stopped the Allies at the Siegfried Line (along the German border), it seems probable that a single offensive advance would have met the same fate. It seems probable also that part of Montgomery's motivation in seeking a single thrust was his desire once again to be the commander of the Allied ground forces, a position he had held temporarily during the initial part of the invasion until he was replaced, as had been originally agreed, by the Supreme Commander, Eisenhower.

The fact that the British Chiefs of Staff supported Montgomery's proposal gives additional color to the coalition debate. Eisenhower received no overt support from the United States Joint Chiefs of Staff, though they were sympathetic to his viewpoint, for he needed none — he was, in fact, Supreme Allied Commander. The debate between him and his British subordinate continued for more than a month. The reason for the long duration of the argument was the fact that national partners in a coalition effort were involved. Given the niceties of coalition warfare, Eisenhower could not peremptorily cut short the argument.

Alliances at work exhibit from time to time the conflict between national interests and coalition aims. There are no pat solutions on how to reconcile the differences; only good sense and understanding, which lead to perception and wisdom.

P A R T   V

Some Related Problems

"Theirs not to reason why,/Theirs but to do and die" was once thought to be the supreme expression of military virtue. The traditional soldier's creed could be summed up in three words: discipline, obedience, loyalty. By definition, no army can exist without these qualities.

The professional soldier has always had, or at least has aspired to have, a more especially developed sense of honor than the civilian. In some eras, particularly when he was underpaid, it was almost his only compensation. The fundamental difference between the soldier and the civilian is that the soldier is ready to die for his employer — his country, government, or state; that is what he has engaged to do, if necessary. The uniform is the symbol of that pledge. It proclaims that the wearer is the king's man or the state's man or the country's man; uniforms originated as distinguishing marks for members of royal bodyguards.

In the armed forces of the early modern period a soldier's honor was altogether personal. It derived from his class origins and from his sense of self. Before nationalism was fully developed, this individual honor was portable. A soldier could serve where he wished. For example, one of the most famous American colonial soldiers, Colonel Henri Bouquet, was born a Swiss, fought in the Dutch and the Sardinian armies, and then accepted a British commission. His honor required him to give loyal service to his employer of the moment, and his behavior was typical of the soldier of the seventeenth and eighteenth centuries.

Indeed, in the seventeenth century a man's honor was likely to be consecrated more to the religion of his choice than to the country. The English Catholic Duke of Berwick, a bastard son of James II, became a marshal of France. Marshal Schomberg, born a German, won a French field marshal's baton but left France during the persecution of the Huguenots, and died leading the Protestant forces of William of Orange at the Battle of the Boyne in Ireland. General Ligonier, a French Protestant by birth, commanded the British infantry at Fontenoy. When he was taken prisoner and brought before Louis XV, he thought he might be accused of treason; instead the king congratulated him on the performance of his troops and invited him to dinner.

The nascent nationalism that was a consequence of the French Revolution changed all that. Henceforth, soldiers served the country of their birth or naturalization, and their nationality, together with their honor, became fixed and inalienable. Loyalty to one's country exceeded all other claims. "My country, may she always be in the right. But right or wrong, my country!"

Such a credo worked well in a simple age, and most of the time still does. But what happens in more complex situations? Take a Czechoslovakian officer whose country was partitioned out of existence in 1938 and 1939. Did his loyalty then belong to the Germans who took over the greater part of his land? Or to the Poles who took the rest?

An even more painful case in point is France in 1940. The country had fallen before an enemy that was regarded as undisguised tyranny. Yet the government of France had made peace with that enemy and was trying to collaborate with it. Where did duty lie? Everybody had to answer that question in his own way, but one set of loyalties was likely to conflict with another. If each soldier is allowed to make his own decision the military organization is eliminated, for the essence of service is that the military man has abrogated the right to his own choice.

Perhaps the most anguished lot was that of the French garrison of 20,000 men in Indochina during World War II. Isolated and all but forgotten, they continued a twilight existence under Japanese direction for most of the war, for they decided their duty lay in preserving the French presence in that part of the empire. In 1945, after the Japanese massacred or imprisoned many, the survivors, about 6000, fought their way to Nationalist China. The reward for their efforts was to be interned and eventually disgraced as adherents of the Vichy regime, which had disappeared and of which they knew practically nothing.

The classic case, of course, is that of the Germans. Nowhere was the sense of military honor more highly developed, almost to the point of caricature, than in the Prussian-German military system, and nowhere was it more thoroughly perverted. In the early 1930s the German army planned to use Hitler. Instead he used them. In the name of military obedience and honor, officers were made parties to crimes that will forever be a black mark on the history of their time and their nation. Yet Hitler knew his men. When he required them to take a personal oath of allegiance to himself, he put up an obstacle few of them could bring themselves to overcome. An oath was a sacred promise, even when given to a man who believed that honor was nothing more than a trap for fools.

The problem was by no means resolved at Nuremburg. The passage of a generation since then has provided sufficient perspective for the victors to be less sure of their rectitude than they were in 1945. Other people besides the defeated Germans have wondered why Russians who murdered Poles should sit in judgment on Germans who murdered Poles.

For Americans, the agony of Vietnam provided startling dilemmas. That such complicated issues might someday arise was recognized in the armed services long before the United States became involved in Vietnam. The military regulations and codes of justice, rewritten in the late 1940s, tried to deal with the kind of obedience required of servicemen. But the proviso that a soldier is not obligated to obey an unlawful order hardly leads to precise definition. What, after all, is an unlawful order? Who decides, and at what point?

These questions illustrate some of the fundamental tensions that are part of the military heritage. They are intrinsic in the profession of arms. If the problem of clashing loyalties between the civilian and military virtues and prerogatives was solved one way in Spain in the 1930s and in Greece thirty years later, there is no reason to suppose that American military men will follow that path. The rather vague West Point precept of Duty, Honor, Country, has served American soldiers well for almost two centuries. It is only when citizens begin to question the exact meaning of long-cherished notions that they betray their lack of faith in the present and future.

The point is that the military profession is far from being an uncomplicated trade. It imposes subtle strains on its members. A man who would be a master of the art of command must not only deal with the ever-changing nature of warfare; he must also find his place and his peace in the sometimes conflicting calls of duty.

Military Obedience

DISCIPLINED OBEDIENCE — the habit of following orders — is a soldierly virtue and a military necessity. But in times of great national upheaval and confusion, conflicting orders may lead a soldier as easily to dishonor as to glory. This is what happened in Tunisia shortly after United States and British forces invaded French North Africa in 1942.

General Georges Barré, who commanded the French army in Tunisia, and Admiral Louis Derrien, who headed the French naval forces, wanted to give instant and unquestioning obedience to their superiors. Both wished only to serve their country. Yet their paths diverged. Judgment, conscience, and circumstances separated them. Here is the dilemma they faced and the choices they made.

After the German lightning campaign of 1940 and the defeat of France, French North Africa became almost a forgotten corner of the earth. Except for frantic refugees from Hitler's Europe who crowded the coastal cities, life continued as aimlessly as usual. The war had passed it by, and so, apparently, had the world. No German or Italian soldiers were present to disturb the quiet.

The French troops, who conducted training exercises and retreat parades as though nothing of importance had happened for half a century and nothing would happen for half a century to come, sank into desuetude. Their outmoded casernes decayed for lack of repairs. Their uniforms, once stirring to the sight, seemed old-fashioned and seedy. With limited responsibilities and curtailed means, they waited — like extras on a movie set — for the action to start.

The armistice of June 1940 set all the conditions. In France, the

Germans occupied the northern part of the country and for the other half Marshal Henri Philippe Pétain established a governmnt at Vichy. The French army was reduced to a skeleton police force of about 100,000 in metropolitan France and the same number in the North African territories. The Germans promised to leave the powerful French navy and the African possessions undisturbed so long as France respected the armistice. Pétain abided strictly by the armistice terms, though General Maxime Weygrand issued secret instructions to conserve and conceal weapons and military stores for the day the French army would fight again.

A clandestine resistance movement soon arose, sponsored and controlled in large part by political parties that regarded Vichy as defeatist or — worse — pro-German. The British assisted these underground forces and eventually the Americans helped supply ammunition, equipment, radio operators, and instructors in sabotage and guerrilla warfare.

Four days before the armistice had been signed, General Charles de Gaulle issued his radio appeal from England. Urging the people of France to continue the battle, he asked all able-bodied men to join him in a fighting force to be organized for action against the Germans. In August 1940 Prime Minister Winston Churchill recognized De Gaulle as the "head of all free Frenchmen, wherever located, who rally around you to the support of the Allied cause."

About a year later the Free French in London formed a National Committee under De Gaulle's presidency. Widely regarded as the legitimate successor, in embryo and in exile, to the defunct Third Republic, the committee received formal recognition from most Allied governments and active British support. The Americans gave only indirect assistance in the form of lend-lease supplies.

Authorities in several French overseas possessions, who saw Pétain's Vichy government as a fascist impostor, a puppet of the Germans, announced their allegiance to De Gaulle. By the end of 1942 these included French Equatorial Africa, the Cameroons, Syria, and others. Not French North Africa — not French Morocco, or Algeria or Tunisia. They remained faithful to the Vichy government of Marshal Pétain. The Axis governments promised to send no armed forces there if the French themselves would guarantee to keep all foreign powers out. Pétain's Vichy government made the pledge, and the military chiefs set out to rehabilitate the restricted forces they were authorized. Their avowed purposes were to control restless natives and to defend against invasion from any quarter by any nation. Secretly they hoped to fight the Axis again.

Most officials in North Africa, like the bulk of the people, followed a policy of unity behind Marshal Pétain. They regarded Vichy as the legitimate government and they opposed De Gaulle. They had profound faith in Pétain and admired his authoritarianism. They felt that he held the Germans closely to the armistice terms and had the best interests of France at heart.

Devotion to Pétain was particularly strong among the military. The great majority of professional soldiers, with little interest in politics, saw De Gaulle dividing and further weakening France, undermining the national leadership. At the instigation of Admiral Jean François Darlan, commander in chief of the armed forces and Pétain's deputy and designated successor, the Vichy government replaced civilians with high-ranking military officers in almost all the leading administrative positions in French North Africa.

An Allied invasion of French North Africa would, therefore, meet a dedicated force pledged to defend French soil: *"Défendre l'Afrique contre quiconque"* — ("To defend Africa against anyone"), as Weygand had put it. Even with their limited and outmoded weapons, the French were capable of putting up a good fight.

Actually, whatever their personal predilections, the French had little choice. Failure to resist an invasion — any invasion — would invalidate the armistice and bring swift Axis retaliation. The Germans would have no compunction about overrunning the defenseless unoccupied zone of metropolitan France, taking the Vichy government prisoner, seizing the bulk of the fleet at Toulon, and holding, in effect, the entire populace hostage.

The Allied governments were well aware of the understandable French reluctance to break the armistice provisions. But surely, the Allies figured, the French had more to gain from an Allied victory in the war. And in that case, resisting Allied landings in conformance with the armistice terms would be a useless, costly sacrifice contrary to the best long-range interests of France. Here, then, was a dilemma in the making.

To facilitate the invasion, Allied leaders sought the help of a small group of pro-Allied elements in North Africa, hoping that a few bands of daring men might capture key military installations along the shore. This was why General Mark W. Clark traveled secretly by submarine to a hazardous rendezvous on an African beach a few weeks before the landings.

They also enlisted the help of General Henri Giraud, a national hero who had twice escaped German prison camps — once in World War I and again in World War II. Affiliated with neither De Gaulle nor Pétain, he might unify North Africa behind his martial presence, form and head a new government dedicated to active Allied support, and initiate military operations against the Axis. The Allied planners decided to land only in French Morocco and Algeria. Tunisia was too close to the Axis-held islands of Pantelleria, Sicily, and Sardinia and too vulnerable to Axis planes based there and in southern Italy. After the troops were firmly ashore, Allied forces would thrust eastward, drive toward Tunis, and seize Tunisia.

The invasion of northwest Africa on November 8, 1942 (Operation Torch), was a quick success, and the triumph was aided by the accidental presence in Algiers of Admiral Darlan, Marshal Pétain's deputy. While Pétain in Vichy insisted that the armistice of 1940 be honored and the Allied invaders repulsed, Darlan made contact with the Allies, agreed at once to a local cease-fire, began to negotiate with the Allied commanders for a broader understanding, and on November 10 ordered all resistance to stop.

The contradictory statements of Pétain in Vichy and of Darlan in Algiers, the apparent clash of authority between Pétain, head of the state, and Darlan, his deputy, brought perplexity to the people of North Africa. Caught in the middle, the French military forces became passive.

Events moved swiftly. At midnight of the tenth, the day that Darlan halted opposition against the Allies, more than ten German divisions crossed the demarcation line in metropolitan France and six Italian divisions marched into eastern France. Overrunning the free zone governed by Vichy, they disarmed and disbanded the armistice army, occupied the entire country, and took Corsica. When the Germans attempted to seize the warships sheltered at Toulon, French naval authorities scuttled the vessels.

On the thirteenth, Darlan established a provisional government in

North Africa with himself at the head. On the fourteenth, he appointed Giraud commander in chief of French ground and air forces in North Africa. On the fifteenth, Giraud issued his first directive, instructing the French military forces to take up arms against the Axis. A week later Darlan signed an agreement that brought French North Africa into the Allied camp. Now there were three distinct governments, each claiming to speak for France: Pétain's in Vichy, the legal body; De Gaulle's in London, anti-Vichy and professing legitimacy; and Darlan's in Algiers, offering simply to fight alongside the Allies. Which government should be obeyed?

While Frenchmen debated the question — the practical choice lay between Pétain and Darlan — Allied forces started an eastward march from Algiers toward Tunis. Though they moved almost 500 miles in a week, their hope of reaching the northeastern corner of Tunisia without meeting Axis opposition turned out to be a cruel disappointment. Sicily was too close — less than a hundred miles away — and the ports and airfields of Bizerte and Tunis were too valuable for the Axis to accept passively the Allied eastward move overland. Planes could transport Axis soldiers to Tunisia in a few hours; ships in less than a day. Only the French military forces in Tunisia could prevent Axis troops from entering the country freely. Would they do so? Or would they let Axis contingents pour in? The answer was soon evident. The French offered no resistance. Mental anguish and agonizing doubts had begotten a paralysis of will.

This is the story of Barré and Derrien.

Vice Admiral Jean-Pierre Estéva, the Resident General in Tunis, the supreme French official in Tunisia — in effect, the governor — learned around midnight of November 7 that Allied forces were about to invade Morocco and Algeria. He wasted no time informing his chief military subordinates, Barré and Derrien.

Derrien, who commanded the naval base at Bizerte, immediately put his coastal batteries on combat alert, issued orders to call up reservists, and prepared to defend against what he termed Anglo-Saxon aggression.

Barré, who commanded the ground forces, did nothing. His troops were dispersed and difficult to assemble. He saw no way to offer effective opposition during the hours of darkness. And he wanted more information.

The information he wanted came at 0945, November 8, in a message from the Pétain government: "Profiting from our disarmament and from intelligence hypocritically obtained, the Anglo-Saxons have just attacked French North Africa . . . The Marshal of France, Chief of State, has replied in the only way the interest and honor of France permit: 'We are attacked. We shall defend ourselves. This is the order that I give.'"

Barré then issued an order to his troops: "The Marshal confirms our mission: defend the empire against no matter who will try to gain a foothold. Our duty as soldiers is simple and clear: execute the order of the Marshal."

By evening the northern coast of Tunisia was prepared for defense against United States and British incursion. At midnight the German High Command informed Vichy that it was indispensable to oppose the invasion by having Axis air forces based in Tunisia and in the Constantine area of Algeria, and by having permission in exactly an hour and a quarter. Estimating that it was unable to deny what the Germans could take by force, the French government acceded.

A message received in Tunis early on November 9 announced the imminent arrival of German planes: "The French Government has had to accept the use of air bases in Constantine and Tunisia by German air forces destined to act against our aggressors. Technical discussions [a French request that only German aircraft, no Italian planes, be sent] are in process at Wiesbaden."

From Algiers, Darlan sent confirmation: "The Americans having invaded Africa first are our adversaries and we must combat them alone or with help." He meant Axis help.

That morning the German theater commander, Field Marshal Albert Kesselring, from his headquarters near Rome, sent two German officers to North Africa by plane. Landing at an airfield in Algeria between Algiers and Constantine, they tried to reach Darlan by telephone in order to regulate the use of French military air bases. Unable to get in touch with him, they flew to Tunis, where Barré received them. He asked them to delay the arrival of German planes until he had explicit instructions from Vichy. They agreed.

While he solicited instructions, the German officers called on the Resident General, who supported Barré's action. At 1230, before he had a reply to his request, the first German planes landed at Tunis. By 1500 that afternoon 103 aircraft were on the field.

As the initial planes were touching down, Barré telegraphed Vichy: "I have the duty to inform you of the emotion that is already being caused by this occupation . . . and the disturbing commentaries it is provoking among the majority of officers whose loyalty I will soon be unable to account for."

Derrien also made known his indignation and concern: "I have been told that tomorrow, November 10, a convoy should arrive at Bizerte for the purpose of supplying the Axis air units. I inform you that these movements are of a nature to produce in the army, air, and navy of Bizerte, which I hold perfectly in hand for the moment, an emotion of which I cannot forestall the results." What needed immediate rectification was the noxious presence at Tunis of German aircraft parked beside French planes.

"I understand your sentiments," Vichy replied that evening of November 9, "but it is impossible after the Anglo-Saxon aggression to prevent the German planes from coming . . . Neither we nor the Germans carried the war to French North Africa. We can only submit." Then as an afterthought: "Have confidence."

The Resident General received much the same word: "As much as we could refuse access to our territories to all military forces before the Anglo-Saxon aggression, as much now is it impossible to prevent one or the other belligerent from carrying the war to our soil."

Barré had, meanwhile, placed several hundred soldiers around the airfield to guard the German planes. He also instructed his troops to defend the ports against Allied invasion from the sea and to resist forces coming overland from Algeria.

Two messages from Darlan in Algiers on the morning of November 10 changed everything. Announcing his assumption of authority over French North Africa, he ordered all hostilities suspended. All troops were to return to their camps and bases and show "an attitude of complete neutrality toward all belligerents."

That afternoon, when several British aircraft attacked the airfield at Tunis and destroyed six German planes — the first Allied bombardment of a series that would be launched every two or three days — the French units surrounding the air base retired to avoid being struck by bombs. After the air raid, they marched to their barracks. When the Germans announced that planes would land on the following day at Bizerte and that troops would arrive at Bizerte and Tunis, Vichy quickly instructed Barré and Derrien to permit their entry.

But all contacts between German and French troops were to be avoided, and no units were to be intermingled or mixed.

On the morning of November 11 Derrien informed his subordinates: "In several hours sad events for French hearts are going to take place . . . German troops are going to land on Tunisian soil. The government of the Marshal has had to submit to these difficult exigencies. Our duty is to obey him. I count on everyone to keep his calm, his sang-froid, and his dignity." Within minutes came the upsetting news that Pétain had disavowed Darlan's cease-fire. "I have given the order to defend against the aggressor," Pétain announced. "I maintain that order."

Did this mean, Derrien asked the Resident General, that he was to fire on the Anglo-Saxons?

The Resident General thought not, but he telephoned Darlan to find out. Learning that General Alphonse Juin now commanded the army in North Africa, he put in a call to him. According to Juin, Barré and Derrien were free to do as they thought best.

Derrien telephoned Barré. What did he think they ought to do? In his opinion, Barré said, the best thing was to observe an absolute neutrality toward everyone, Axis and Anglo-Saxon alike, and this he ordered his troops to display. Dissatisfied, Derrien cabled Vichy: "My point of view is as follows: (1) According to your message . . . the landing of German troops is authorized. (2) The struggle continues against the Anglo-Saxons. General Barré, after having telephoned General Juin, estimates that the line of conduct to follow is strict neutrality toward all belligerents. I ask you to take all measures to clear up the confusion as soon as possible because it creates a dangerous trouble in all spirits."

The minister of the navy replied. Pétain had repudiated Darlan and had designated General Auguste Noguès, the commander in Morocco, to be his sole representative in North Africa. He added: "My personal advice since the events of this [past] night [referring to the Axis occupation of the free zone of metropolitan France] is passivity vis-à-vis all."

Seeking reassurance, Derrien telephoned the Resident General. Barré was there on a visit, and he came to the phone. He said that, according to Juin, the Germans and Italians, by occupying all of France, had broken the armistice. For that reason, after some discussion, Derrien and Barré decided to open fire on the Axis ships that were due to appear at Bizerte. They would permit Allied ships to enter freely.

Barré had a special request. Would Derrien hold his fire against Axis planes so long as no Axis ships appeared? Barré was moving his troops to the mountains immediately west of Tunis and Bizerte, and during that march they would be extremely vulnerable to air attack.

Derrien agreed. He instructed his subordinates to oppose all Axis landings, to fire against Axis ships approaching the coast, to refrain from hostile acts against the Americans and their allies, and to observe until otherwise notified an attitude of neutrality toward Axis aircraft. Carried away by his feelings, Derrien also issued a rousing order of the day: "After two long days of discussion and confusion, the order has just reached me formally and precisely, designating the enemy against whom you are going to have to fight. This enemy is the German and Italian. Soldiers, sailors, aviators of the defenses of Bizerte, you are now fixed. Go with full heart against the adversaries of 1940, for we have a revenge to take. *Vive la France!*"

Then he telephoned the Resident General and informed him of his action. The Resident General was disturbed. What bothered him was the widespread distribution given to orders of the day. The emotional call, though restricted to military channels of communication, was indiscreet. It could have, he felt, not only serious but disastrous consequences. If the Germans somehow learned of it, they might move immediately against Barré, who was assembling his men in the hills.

It was a chastened Derrien who at once classified his order of the day "secret," thus imposing special handling procedures on its dissemination. Forty minutes later, after uncomfortable indecision, he annulled he order. Neutrality was to be the order of the day. But the message had already been read to the soldiers, sailors, marines, and airmen in the Bizerte area, and the call to arms had engendered great enthusiasm. The annulment brought consternation and heartbreak.

Six German ships and one Italian vessel that arrived at the port of Tunis with troops, weapons, and ammunition found no impediment raised against unloading.

During the night a message from Vichy informed Derrien that Pétain was continuing the struggle against Anglo-Saxon aggression.

"You should let pass without interference the Italo-German forces landing in Tunisia," he was instructed. "Follow the order of the Marshal." Unable to bring himself to quite this position, Derrien ordered a strict neutrality toward all foreign forces.

About fifty miles west of Bizerte and Tunis, Barré was concentrating his ground forces. He awaited what he judged would be an inevitable opening of hostilities against the Axis. After a last visit with the Resident General, who raised no objection, he set up his command post about seventy-five miles west of Tunis on the main road to Constantine.

Derrien spent a sleepless night. He was unable to obey Darlan, whom Pétain had repudiated. He had no instructions from Noguès, whom Pétain had appointed. And he estimated that his position at Bizerte was untenable without the support of Barré's troops. Telephoning Algiers for help on November 12, he found only confusion. Darlan would make no decision. Juin considered himself unqualified to exercise command. Everyone awaited Noguès, who was expected that afternoon. Completely discouraged and depressed, Derrien told a colleague, "I have seven citations and forty-two years of service, and I shall be known as the admiral who delivered Bizerte to the Germans."

Derrien had two alternatives: open hostilities against the Germans scheduled to debark at Bizerte — but this was against the orders of his government and also seemed contrary to the Resident General's frame of reference; or take his naval garrison to join Barré — but this meant abandoning the base, the arsenal, and the ships.

German planes landed at Bizerte that morning, bringing antiaircraft guns to defend the airfield. Then, all day long, air transports disgorged and deposited troops and matériel. When two German officers announced the arrival of ships and asked Derrien to make available the port's unloading facilities, he inquired of Vichy: "Discharge of their cargo requires accord of the Navy; should I accord it?" Yes, came the reply.

That evening Barré had a telephone call from Juin, who said that an immediate state of hostility against the Germans was desirable. Barré demurred. The Germans in Tunisia were too powerful, his own troops too vulnerable. Let the Germans open hostilities.

It was a helpless and harassed Derrien who set out by automobile on the morning of the thirteenth to meet with Barré along the road to Constantine. Was there some way out of the mess? Halfway to the meeting place, he was overtaken by a messenger. Urgent orders had arrived in Tunis for him. Returning, he learned that the urgent orders were from Darlan, who had consolidated his authority in Algiers and who wanted Derrien to throw the Germans into the sea, bottle up the harbors of Bizerte and Tunis, and withdraw his naval forces overland to the southwest, to the Algerian border area near Tebessa and Kasserine. He no longer had the strength to do all that.

On the following day, November 14, a message from Pétain to Darlan was transmitted to Tunisia for information: "You must defend North Africa against American aggression. Your decision violates my orders and is contrary to your mission. I order the army of Africa to exercise no action and in no circumstances against the Axis forces and to add nothing to the difficulties of the Fatherland."

The words struck home with Derrien. He made his decision. So far as he was concerned, Barré had passed "into dissidence." For while the influx of Axis troops at Bizerte and Tunis continued, Barré was deploying his troops across the interior of Tunisia, along a line from north to south, to bar an Axis advance to the west.

An emissary from Vichy arrived in Tunis on the fifteenth to reinforce the authority of the Marshal of France, Henri Pétain. He spoke with the Resident General and with Derrien, but he wished also to see Barré. The Resident General sent a letter by a navy captain, who reached Barré's command post late in the afternoon. Would Barré come to Tunis for a conference? Barré said he was unable to leave his troops. The official from Vichy sent a second messenger that evening. "I beg General Barré," he had written, "to come see me immediately no matter what the hour of the night." Barré confirmed in writing the response he had already made. He added that the official could come to see him if he wished.

Pétain's emissary drove out on the morning of the sixteenth. When he approached the line of French troops and saw them turned facing the east, he decided to go no farther. He feared he might be seized and held, so he turned back. At the first village that had a post office, he sent Barré a telegram: "General, I have the honor to confirm to you the order of the Marshal, Chief of State, to defend the territory of the Regency against the Anglo-Saxon invader." Barré disregarded the message. His troops, who occupied a defensive line about forty-five miles west of Tunis and Bizerte, were under orders to oppose by force any Axis units that might approach.

Derrien, in contrast, was issuing another order of the day: "Foreign or dissident propagandists are trying to trouble our spirts. Conscious of my responsibilities, faithful to my vow to the Marshal of France, assured of the authenticity of his messages, I confirm to all troops placed under my command . . . (1) oppose by force all American attacks. (2) Abstain from all hostile action against Axis force."

Despite a personal letter from Darlan — *"Tu ne vas tout de même pas faire tirer des Français contre d'autres Français"* ("Just the same, you are not going to make Frenchmen fire against other Frenchmen") — Derrien was too far committed to change course. On his own initiative, at his own suggestion, accepted eagerly by the Germans, he signed an agreement with the German commander of Bizerte, promising to defend with his forces certain sectors in the Bizerte area. He would, he assured the Germans, repulse all attempts of Anglo-American forces to debark.

With Derrien in their pocket, the Germans set out to get Barré. On the afternoon of November 18, the German minister at Tunis sent his deputy to Barré's command post. Traveling by car, he was stopped about forty-five miles west of Tunis by French troops, who telephoned that a delegate of the German command wished to see Barré. Barré sent a subordinate general officer, but the German insisted on seeing Barré personally. Agreeing, he fixed a rendezvous at a farm near the French line. Around midnight, as Barré was driving toward the farm, he met the general who had seen the German and who gave him a letter.

The letter, written that day, was from the German commander in Tunis, who reminded Barré that the governments of Germany and France had decided to repulse Anglo-American aggression against the French empire. To that end, it was necessary to have contact with Barré and his staff to regulate their collaboration. Could he have an immediate decision? What he wanted particularly was to have all the routes cleared of obstacles that might obstruct a German advance to the west — toward Algeria and a meeting with the Allied invaders. Would Barré therefore order his troops to treat the Germans as allies? It appeared indispensable that they have an immediate talk in Tunis to straighten out the details.

There seemed little point in conferring with the German delegate. But he was waiting and Barré had agreed to see him. So he continued to the farm and met the deputy minister as arranged. It was then 0100, November 19. The German insisted that the fate of the French people depended on whether Barré rallied to Pétain and removed all obstructions in the path of the imminent advance to the west. Barré said he would need first to confer with his chief, Juin, who was in Algiers. This would take several days at least. That would be too long. Unless the German commander had a favorable response by 0700 that morning — in six hours — he would have to take action. Barré made a gesture of regret. The meeting broke up. The deputy minister returned to Tunis; Barré to his command post.

At 1100 that morning German planes bombed the French positions and the farm where the meeting had taken place. Twenty minutes later German artillery opened fire and infantry approached. When French soldiers returned the fire and drove off the Germans, they committed the army in North Africa to active oppositon.

Marshal Pétain tried to reverse the course of events. "Frenchmen," he declared, "some general officers in the service of a foreign power have refused to obey my orders. Generals, officers, noncommissioned officers, and soldiers of the army of Africa, do not obey these unworthy chiefs. I reiterate to you the order to resist the Anglo-Saxon aggression. We live in tragic hours; disorder reigns in our spirits. You hear news which has no other aim but to divide you and weaken you. But the truth is simple: failure to hold to the discipline which I require from each of you puts your country in danger . . . Union [between France and Africa] is more than ever indispensable. I remain your guide. You have but one duty: obey. You have but one government: that which I have been given the power to govern. You have but one country, which I incarnate: France."

The rhetoric had no visible effect. The French forces in North Africa, with the exception of those trapped behind the German lines in Tunisia, had opted in favor of the Allies.

Little more than two weeks later, on December 7, at 1800 in the evening, a German liaison officer visited Derrien at his home. The German commanding the Bizerte sector was convoking a meeting of the important French officials. Would he be so good as to repair, with all his high-ranking staff members and commanders, to the tent of the Bizerte area commander at 0930 the next morning? Yes, of course. But Derrien decided to take only three principal subordinates.

At the appointed time and at the designated place, Derrien reported. As he entered the German compound, he noted the presence of what seemed to him an inordinate number of heavily armed guards. As he stepped into the tent, he noticed the arrival overhead of four squadrons of JU-88s, which continued to fly menacingly over the camp during the conference. The German commander presented Derrien to General Alfred Gause, who had been sent by Hitler. After bowing stiffly, Gause handed Derrien a paper. It was an ultimatum that Derrien read in silence.

The policy of collaboration with the enemy had reached its logical conclusion. Hitler had ordered the French forces in Tunisia to be disarmed. All troops were to be demobilized immediately. All weapons, military buildings, depots, mobile installations, radio stations, and other facilities, including vessels, were to be handed over intact. The scuttling of ships or the destruction of equipment would be considered an act of sabotage, and the perpetrators would be tried by a German tribunal and executed immediately. Peaceful acceptance would mean repatriation to France for all or, if they wished, eventual reconstitution into new units to fight alongside the Germans. Refusal would result in immediate attack by the Germans, who would take no prisoners but would kill all troops to "the last officer and soldier."

Derrien had thirty minutes to make up his mnd. "To you, Admiral," the paper concluded, "the decision! Free return to France or death."

Derrien and his three colleagues left the tent. Between lines of armed guards standing at attention they walked a hundred steps. What could they do? Resistance was impossible. Opposition would serve no useful purpose. Why sacrifice lives hopelessly? He would have to give up the coastal batteries, the arsenal, three torpedo boats, nine submarines, two dispatch vessels, some artillery, and the weapons of 7000 Senegalese and 5000 other troops.

He waited until twenty minutes had passed. Perhaps he needed time to compose himself. Then he returned and informed Gause of his submission.

At ten minutes before 1100, Derrien issued his final instructions: "Total demobilization order given in France has just reached me by German authorities. By terms of his order, all military matériel must be turned over intact to Axis troops. Axis troops will take all measures without pity against attempts to resist, to sabotage, to scuttle. I ask all to obey this sad order to avoid spilling useless blood. This order to be executed without delay."

In contrast, Barré's soldiers, under the command of their own military leaders, were fighting proudly beside the British and Americans.

When a nation and its military forces are torn between conflicting loyalties, as were the French forces in North Africa in 1942, there are rarely any winners.

Admiral Derrien, who chose to remain loyal to Pétain, remained in North Africa and attempted to protect civilians who were threatened with deportation by the Germans. After the Allied liberation of Tunisia, he was tried by a special tribunal in March 1944 and was absolved of the charge of having surrendered Bizerte but was held responsible for not having scuttled his ships. He was sentenced to dismissal from the navy and imprisonment for life. Released from prison in 1946, he died twelve days later and was buried with full military honors.

General Barré, who chose to side with the Allies, fought throughout the North African campaign and in May 1943 was accorded the honor of making the first entry into Tunis at the head of French troops. But the Gaullist Committee of National Liberation excluded him from the Regular Army and filed charges that he had collaborated with the Axis. He was never brought to trial and retired from active service after the war. Thus the man who courageously chose to stand up to the enemy tasted the bitter dregs of political ostracism and public distrust.

Hitler versus His Generals

IN THE YEARS since World War II some German generals have declared that Germany lost the war because Hitler insanely meddled in military affairs of which he knew nothing. If only, they sighed, Hitler had not interfered with the conduct of military operations . . .

This thesis not only exonerates the German generals of blame and establishes Hitler as the scapegoat for the military disaster; it also restores the prestige of the German army.

Americans find it rather natural to accept this point of view. Hitler had personified the enemy, and a mad dog seemed more detestable than an evil one. The professional officers of the German army, in contrast, had the reputation of being well trained and efficient soldiers. It was inconceivable that in the campaign of western Europe during 1944 and 1945 they could have made the blunders that had led so irresistibly to defeat. The explanation must be that they had had to carry out orders from Hitler, who had stupidly intervened.

There is no disputing the fact that Hitler took an active part in military matters. The master of Germany, he exercised military command. He directed the formulation of military plans, both strategic and tactical, and he supervised their execution. His system of personal dictatorship, the pyramid of command that culminated in him, his claim to legendary omniscience for public consumption, his diminishing confidence in his subordinates' abilities, all made his close control of the military perhaps inevitable.

Hitler's commander in the western theater, Field Marshal von Rundstedt, was one of the most respected officers in the army. But Rundstedt did not have the virtual *carte blanche* for the conduct of operations that his opponent, General Eisenhower, enjoyed. Rundstedt functioned under the close inspection of Hitler. He had no authority over air force and naval units. He controlled no theater reserves. He did not have a unified command. He shared responsibility wth one of his subordinates, Rommel.

Field Marshal Rommel, who commanded an army group and controlled the tactical forces that were to oppose an Allied invasion, was also an eminently respected officer. He took orders from Rundstedt, but he had the direct access to Hitler that was a privilege of all field marshals. Although responsibility for defense against an Allied landing might logically have belonged to Rundstedt as theater commander, Hitler had charged Rommel specifically with repelling the expected invasion.

The lack of cohesion in the German command structure in the west reflected an absence of coherence in defensive planning. Despite this condition, the three commanders in the west acted in unison when the Allies assaulted the Normandy beaches. Rommel gave battle on the coast, Rundstedt began to prepare a counterattack, and Hitler commenced to think of moving reserve divisions toward the battlefield. As they directed the war in tactical terms, concerned with parrying the Allied efforts to establish a beachhead on the continent, the German commanders searched for a decisive action that would destroy the Allies in a single blow of strategic importance.

The traditional thought and training of the German military establishment stressed the ideal of defeating the enemy by a decisive act of annihilation. Such a philosophy of war rejected the idea of a gradual and cumulative strategy of attrition. Thus oriented, the German military leaders, although fighting essentially a defensive war, were thinking offensively. Their reaction against the Allied landing was ultimately to be a counterattack that would obliterate Allied hopes forever.

The accord that had unified the commanders in the west did not last for long. Five days after the Allied invasion, Hitler and his generals were in disagreement. Their point of departure was Cherbourg. The differences of opinion among them revealed a divergence of thought and of concept that was to characterize the entire German campaign in western Europe.

The port of Cherbourg had a significant place in Allied intentions.

A basic feature of the Allied invasion plan Overlord was the postulated needs for securing major ports in France. Without ports, the Allies would not be able to remain on the continent; they would not be able to receive quickly enough the troops and matériel in the quantities required to defeat Germany. The first mission assigned to American troops, therefore, was to take Cherbourg.

The city and its marvelous harbor lie at the northern tip of a peninsula. American soldiers had landed on the east coast of the peninsula near the base. As a preliminary action to capturing Cherbourg, the Americans planned to thrust across the base of the peninsula to the west coast. The result would isolate Cherbourg from landward reinforcement. Holding a line across the peninsula near the base, the Americans would then drive north and capture the port. The Germans had long recognized Cherbourg as an obvious Allied objective, and they had prepared to defend the port with three divisions fighting from fortifications around the city. But five days after the Allied landing on the Normandy coast, it appeared to Rundstedt and to Rommel that Cherbourg had little importance. Two facts were more significant.

First, the Allies had gained a firm foothold in France. Experience in Sicily and Italy demonstrated that once Allied landing troops succeeded in digging in on shore, it was impossible to dislodge them. Thus, the German anti-invasion plans of meeting and repelling the Allied assault on the beaches had failed. Second, the headquarters that Rundstedt had activated to prepare the German counterattack was bombed out of existence by a lucky Allied air strike.

The effect of these events, realization of the successful Allied landing, and the shock of having the counterattack headquarters destroyed seemed to paralyze the field marshals. Suddenly bereft of hope, they appeared to be destitute of ideas. They sought only to consolidate the front. As for Cherbourg, they agreed to leave light forces in the city and thereby sacrifice only a few troops. The units saved from what they considered a useless defense of the port would establish a strong defensive line south of the American drive across the base of the peninsula.

Hitler, however, was still thinking of an attack to destroy the invasion forces. To further his plan, he ordered a crack SS panzer corps from his eastern front to Normandy. But while these troops were in transit, he wanted to deny the Allies Cherbourg. He was not interested in conserving several thousand soldiers in the Cherbourg peninsula when he could, by expending them, keep the Allies from gaining a major port. He was not willing to yield cheaply an important link in the projected chain of Allied logistics. While his commanders prepared the master counterstroke, for which they needed about a month's time, Hitler wanted them to hold on to Cherbourg. When he learned that they had decided to abandon the port, he interfered with the conduct of operations.

At a meeting with Rundstedt and Rommel eleven days after the invasion, Hitler pressed his commanders for a counterattack. Prodded by Hitler, Rundstedt suggested the British portion of the front near Caen as the critical sector. He recommended an attack there, an action that might eventually split the Allied forces on the beaches and that in any case would deny the Allies easy access to the Seine River and Paris, objectives that must be of prime importance to the Allies. Although Hitler seemed little concerned about Paris at the moment, he accepted Rundstedt's choice. But he warned that Cherbourg must be defended in accordance with the original plans.

While Hitler was speaking, news came that the Americans had cut the base of the Cherbourg peninsula and were about to turn toward the city. Hitler immediately authorized the withdrawal of German troops into the fortification. He added several important qualifications: at least three divisions must fall back on Cherbourg; they must make Americans fight for every inch of ground; and they must hold the port for no less than a month.

A simple error balked Hitler's wishes. Before he added his qualifying remarks, a subordinate left the conference room to telephone instructions to the troops in the field. These instructions authorized a withdrawal into the port. Consequently, only one division and confused elements of two others managed to reach Cherbourg, a force so small that it was inadequate either to fight strong delaying action or to man fully the defenses of the city. Later, but too late, frantic efforts were made to reinforce the garrison by air and by sea. But no airborne troops were prepared to execute such a mission, and demolition of the Cherbourg harbor had already progressed too far to permit troops arriving by water to debark.

Cherbourg thus slipped through the fingers of the field marshals.

Disheartened by German troop confusion, by inadequate provisioning of the port fortifications, and by the vigor of the American attack, the commanders virtually abandoned Cherbourg and concentrated their efforts to mount against the British the decisive counterattack that might throw the Allies back into the sea. They reckoned without Hitler. A week after the conference Hitler intervened again to order the proposed attack shifted west and against the Americans in order to relieve pressure on the Cherbourg garrison.

By then, Allied action had developed the situation beyond German control. On the following day the British commenced a large-scale attack toward Caen; a day later Cherbourg fell to the Americans. With Cherbourg gone and the British threatening Caen, the Germans had no alternative but to commit reserves to hold the persistent British attack. The only reserves available were the troops preparing to launch the German counterattack. These had to be committed defensively. Forced by Allied initiative, the Germans reluctantly abandoned their offensive concept for one of defense.

Hitler's interest in Cherbourg had been strategic, not tactical. His basic strategic desire had been to hold the Allies and hamper their build-up until the Germans could launch the countermeasure that would change the course of the war. Hitler's commanders, on the other hand, had been thinking tactically. They had not grasped Hitler's willingness to give ground to the British in order to strike indirectly at Cherbourg. They had not seemed to understand Hitler's desire to prevent the Americans, and thus eventually the Allies, from improving their logistical situation. Even the German air force command in the west, forced to choose between supporting ground troops in the Cherbourg or the Caen regions, had on its own initiative selected the latter.

From the Allied point of view, Hitler was correct. Cherbourg was the important immediate Allied objective, not Paris. The French capital was far from Allied minds in June 1944; in fact, Allied plans for the distant future called for troops to by-pass Paris.

With the German counteroffensive forces dissipated in defense against the British, Rundstedt came to the conclusion that the Germans could neither drive the Allies from their beachhead nor hold the Allies in Normandy. For him there were two alternatives: capitulation or withdrawal across France to the German border. Either course of action reflected a defeatist point of view, an attitude that Rommel had demonstrated as early as several days after the invasion.

Hitler in contrast had not abandoned the idea of launching a decisive offensive action some time in the future. With the army temporarily on the defensive, he ordered the air force and the navy to perform two functions. They were to disrupt Allied logistics and also permit the German army to regain a freedom of movement that would allow Hitler to launch his decisive act. Whether Hitler believed that the feeble forces of Goering and Doenitz could bring about the conditions he desired, he proceeded on the assumption that they might. In the meantime, while the principal effort took place on the sea and in the air, the ground troops had to stand fast to prevent the expansion of the Allied beachhead.

Hitler's insistence on holding a defensive line in France stemmed from two facts. Withdrawing troops always lost not only morale but also personnel through stragglers and equipment through abandonment; Germany could afford neither. On the eastern front the vastness of space made limited withdrawals or a Russian breakthrough matters of little importance, but on the western front such an event could well be disastrous. Believing it more dangerous for the German army to attempt to withdraw across France and through its hostile population, a withdrawal that was sure to be harassed by Allied air, Hitler attempted to hold.

Convinced that the situation had disintegrated beyond repair, Rundstedt requested relief at the end of June. At about the same time a report from a subordinate headquarters, transmitted through the chain of command and endorsed at every echelon, seemed to imply criticism of Hitler's direction of the war. Profoundly disturbed, Hitler relieved Rundstedt; he sent a cryptic message to Rommel telling him to learn to take orders.

Hitler needed about a week to realize that Goering and Doenitz were unable to fulfill his requirements for a decisive offensive act on the ground. He fell back on his minister of production, Speer. Hope for victory, Hitler decided, lay in the speedy manufacture of jet aircraft, more tanks, munitions, and fuel. Until such weapons could be employed against the Allies, the German ground troops, still performing a secondary mission, had to continue to hold the line and delay the Allies.

By this time many German generals, both on the eastern and western fronts, had become convinced that defeat was inevitable. The Russians had instituted a gigantic offensive that menaced the German position in Scandinavia. There was danger of defection in the Balkans. In the west, the Allies had become capable of breaking through the shallow German defensive line in France and of driving immediately into Germany. A conspiracy reached its climax on July 20 with an unsuccessful attempt on Hitler's life. Smashed immediately, the *putsch* had no direct effect on military operations in the west. Yet Hitler began to have tormenting thoughts that he was surrounded by traitors.

Three days after the *putsch* Hitler agreed that a German withdrawal from France had become necessary. But the Allies moved too fast. Two days later the Americans launched the attack that developed into the breakout. The success of the Americans was accelerated by inefficiency on the part of the German army commander opposing them, Hausser. By the time that Field Marshal Kluge, Rundstedt's replacement, who had also assumed Rommel's duties, could gather together in his hands the reins of tactical control, American troops were at Avranches.

As American units streamed south of Avranches and turned simultaneously westward into Brittany and eastward toward the Seine, Hitler acted strategically again, rather than tactically. Thinking in terms of strategic logistics, Hitler continued in Brittany his policy of denying the Allies major ports. He had transformed these ports into fortress cities. He had placed ruthless and determined men in command of them, and he had ordered them to defend "to the last man, to the last cartridge." Cherbourg had taught Hitler a lesson. He had been disappointed there because his field commanders had failed to grasp his strategic conception. But he had also been embittered by the tactical defense of Cherbourg. Instead of conducting the final resistance in the city as he had wished, the last defenders had fought a vain action on the extreme point of the peninsula where the Americans had ultimately taken some 8000 prisoners who might, according to Hitler, better have fought within the city and thereby delayed the Allied capture of the port. He had then resolved that the Brittany ports would not be lost so easily as Cherbourg, and he had taken measures to implement his resolution.

Satisfied that the Americans would not gain Brittany and its ports quickly, Hitler acted against the breakout forces streaming through Avranches by ordering a counterattack that was essentially strategic in nature. The counterattack, to be launched westward through Mortain to Avranches, a distance of twenty miles, was to cut the American supply lines. Success would separate American forces north and south of Avranches, sever the American troops in Brittany from their supplies coming from the invasion beaches and from Cherbourg, and place the Americans in a state of confusion.

Admittedly, such action was a gamble. But in the belief that the Allies were capable of more mobility on the ground than the Germans and could therefore beat them in a war of movement, and in the belief that Allied air and the French movement would continually harass a German withdrawal, Hitler decided that the gamble was worth the risk.

Kluge and most of the field commanders, despite misgivings, carried through the Mortain counterattack. But the attack was halfhearted, imperfectly prepared, and incorrectly timed; it also miscalculated by a scant thousand yards a point on the American front so weak that the attack if made there would quite certainly have carried the Germans to Avranches. Furthermore, refusal of a division commander, Schwerin, to attack, an instance of flagrant disobedience, seriously impaired whatever chance the Germans had had of success. The tenacity of the American defense at Mortain, the speed of American reaction to the attack, and the efficacy of Allied air and artillery sealed the doom of the German effort. Although a failure primarily because of the tactical incompetence of his commanders, Hitler's counterattack had caused the Allies extreme concern and had threatened to nullify at least temporarily the Allied advance.

Failure at Mortain was followed by the familiar events of the Argentan-Falaise pocket. The dire prophecies that German generals had muttered came true. The defeated German army streamed in retreat across France, smashed en route in Normandy and at the Seine, unable to turn and fight until it reached the Siegfried Line at the German border.

Meanwhile, although his generals had frantically recommended that all the troops be recalled to Germany, Hitler insisted that the Brittany fortress ports be held. From a tactical point of view, defense of these coastal cities was an inexcusable waste of resources. Strategically, their temporary retention by German garrisons caused the Allies to divert a sizable force into Brittany and indirectly resulted in partially preventing, on logistical grounds, the Allies from surging forward in strength against the Siegfried Line.

The tenacious German defense of St. Malo delayed the liberation of Brittany for two weeks. At the successful completion of the American siege of St. Malo, three hundred German soldiers still held a tiny island several thousand yards offshore, and they continued to do so for two more weeks against combined air, sea, and land bombardments.

The defenders of Brest engaged more than three American divisions and kept them occupied more than a month. Each American soldier in Brittany and each round of ammunition expended there meant so much less available to be used against the German homeland.

In a move that was similar but more significant because of its vital importance, Hitler denied the Allies the port of Antwerp on the Channel coast. Despite the pleas of Field Marshal Model, who had replaced Kluge, Hitler refused to withdraw his troops along the Scheldt estuary, which connects Antwerp to the sea. In contrast to Cherbourg, which functioned as an Allied port from the middle of July, the port of Antwerp was of no use to the Allies until the end of November, three long months after the German retreat from France.

Without the major ports on which they had based their invasion plans, the Allies outran their logistics as they swept across France. Having lost the momentum of their drive at the German border, they prepared for winter battle. By then, Hitler had scraped together a force to defend Germany.

During this interval, despite his disastrous defeat in France, Hitler continued to search for the mighty blow that would crush the Allies in one decisive act. In September he found it. In December he launched it — the Ardennes counteroffensive called the Battle of the Bulge. Little more than two weeks after the Allies began to employ the port of Antwerp, Hitler threatened to take it back.

Perhaps the Ardennes counteroffensive was a mistake. Certainly the attack wasted German resources, and its failure clearly revealed German bankruptcy. But Hitler had no alternative. A cautious policy would have served only to prolong a conflict already lost, lost unless a daring act changed the entire course of the war.

Possessing an active and bold imagination, as astute grasp of geopolitics, a highly developed ability to estimate and appraise, Hitler could coordinate his military goals and his political objectives far better than anyone else. Fighting a defensive war with limited resources, he could afford no error. Everything was important, and in view of Allied superiority in men and matériel, everything was more or less a gamble. Since he alone had access to all the information available from all the fronts, he alone was capable of correct decisions. Feeling that he needed to give his personal attention to all matters, he assumed areas of responsibility usually relegated to subordinates.

By 1944 he had delegated to his henchmen by default much of his governmental activity. He did not dare do so on the critical field of battle. But the burden of his commitments prevented him from being everywhere at once. Hitler was not a superman.

As long as Germany was victorious, most German generals were content to regard Hitler as a genius. When German fortunes declined, Hitler's interference seemed nefarious, and professional officers began to resent the spectacle of a political figure, a former corporal, meddling in military affairs.

For the most part from a social class historically more European than national, the officer corps began to question a war that by 1944 had begun to appear inconclusive if not hopeless. When they discovered that Hitler sometimes oversimplified or disguised situations to inject courage into subordinates, they lost faith in him. Interpreting his close supervision, correctly, as lack of confidence in their abilities, they became indifferent or mutinous. "You demand our trust," Rommel once told him, "but you do not trust us."

In an organization permeated by distrust and suspicion, deceit and falsehood replaced candor. As the split between Hitler and his military commanders spread, concealed facts and incomplete reports became commonplace. Information on military operations, on armament production, on personnel figures departed increasingly from reality.

Worse, the pyramid of command was no longer a hierarchy of commanders filling positions in accordance with military efficiency. It had become a collection of personalities in which personal ambitions and suspicions ran counter to precepts of command. To a lesser extent, Hitler's subordinates reflected him, and each commander became his own strategic planner, each convinced that he alone was right.

Hitler's strength lay in the fact that he had no alternative but resistance. His weakness was the fear that all dictators suffer, the possible disloyalty of disillusioned hero worshipers.

Disillusioned by the prospect of defeat, many German generals lost the blind faith that holds together a dictatorship. In that moment and for that reason they failed to comprehend Hitler's conduct of the war. Lamely, and later, they protested his orders to continue to fight. His strategic concept was beyond them. Their fear of failure had perhaps unnerved them. Perhaps, too, they had suddenly become aware of the dishonor that awaited them for having helped Hitler ascend to the place of *Führer*.

Despite overwhelming Allied power, despite an entourage of defeatists on the one hand and a handful of unrealistic flatterers on the other, Hitler waged effective war in the west. That he was able to do so with Germany in such weakened condition indicates that he had a firm grasp of strategic reality, a capability beyond the capacity of his tactical commanders. It would appear that the military ability of the German generals suffers in comparison, that their efficiency was overrated, and that their military reputation was perhaps more publicized than real.

This is not altogether true. The ingredient that might have prevented the split between Hitler and his generals was the cementing bond of faith. Subordinate commanders seldom know all the reasons for decisions at higher headquarters. If they trust their superior officers, subordinates will follow instructions even though those orders may appear to be irrational. If they lose confidence, they will interpret apparent irrationality as madness. While *"Sieg Heil!"* had meaning, the military machine ran beautifully. But when the generals became frightened by the prospect of defeat, they balked, and thus they accelerated the Allied victory.

Stone

WHEN YOU MEET General Stone the first thing that will strike you — perhaps a moment after you notice how loud his voice is — is his unabashed bluntness. He is a hard man and he pulls no punches.

"I was the best division commander in Vietnam," this gruff retired major general will tell you, and then go on to explain, directly and emphatically, with no false modesty, why he thinks so.

When he has finished you'll have to believe him, for what he says is not idle talk or bluster. He is smart, knowledgeable, articulate, and convincing, but not at the expense of others. General Stone doesn't tear anyone down to build himself up. His perception, sense of logic, and ability to think are as obvious as his commanding bearing, and they more than support his supreme confidence in himself.

As a young instructor at the Command and General Staff College after World War II, he proclaimed to his students, many of them with more rank and experience, that he knew more about the subject he was teaching than anyone else in the army.

A general officer challenged him from the floor. "More than General Eisenhower?" he asked. General Dwight D. Eisenhower was then Army Chief of Staff.

"Yes, sir. I said more than anyone," he replied. "General Eisenhower is far too busy with more important matters to have the time I have taken to become the best-informed officer in this particular subject. And before we are through here, everyone will agree."

Eventually everyone did.

The officer who tells this story was in that class, and he remembers the occasion with a grin and with a slight shudder of discomfort.

"Imagine the nerve of the guy, the" — he searched for the right word — "gall of the youngster." He shook his head regretfully. Then his eyes lit up. "But you know," he said, "he was right, absolutely right. He proved what he said. And you can't help liking a guy like that."

Well, you'll either like him at first blush or heartily dislike him. If you admire men who are intelligent, and outspokenly honest, you'll find him easy to take. On the other hand, you might find him abrasive. Many do. He is not lovable or concerned with being a nice guy. Except for an occasional special kind of boyish smile that suggests the existence of a warm and sensitive human being beneath the rough exterior, he is a tough man and fearless.

The point is that Charley Stone is a maverick. The word comes from a nineteenth-century Texas rancher named Samuel Maverick who, unlike his contemporaries, left his cattle unbranded. Gradually the term came to mean a person who acts independently. It signifies today a person who doesn't always go along with "the system," someone who remains within the establishment and who fights complacency.

All organizations try to perpetuate their methods of operation and the form of their concerns. Most members go along with the system — which is why, to a large extent, there is a system in the first place. They do their jobs in the same old ways because these are the accepted procedures. Sometimes it is because it is safer and better for self-advancement. Yet what gives any system vitality is its ability to modify its practices in order to adjust to exigencies and new conditions. This often is the function of the mavericks, who are usually few in number. They shake things up and make evolutionary and beneficial change possible. "Somebody has to be a catalyst" is the way Stone puts it.

Some mavericks do their work quietly. Others are noisy and become controversial because they rock the boat. Stone belonged in the latter category and admits it freely. The essence of being a maverick, according to him, is the gift of imagination. There are, he says, a few people who think hard about their jobs, who ponder and reason things out, and who look ahead to change the system in order to improve it. There is always room for improvement, there are always better ways to do the task, to perform the mission.

He regards the security of the United States as our most important task. Believing thoroughly in his profession and all that it stands for, he is genuinely and seriously concerned and active in its betterment.

For example, late in July 1967, at the height of the Detroit rioting, he was sent by General Harold K. Johnson, then Chief of Staff, to assess the capabilities and operations of the 46th Infantry Division, a Michigan National Guard unit on duty there. The next day he was appointed deputy commander of Task Force Detroit, with his original mission continuing as an additional task.

After a week of fifteen- to twenty-two-hour days spent talking with hundreds of people in the Army and Air National Guards, Regular Army, and police force, and to other citizens in the embattled area, he wrote a comprehensive and frank report. It stated clearly and objectively that the National Guard needed more training in such things as riot control and military discipline. When he was called to Washington to testify before a congressional committee, he repeated his opinions candidly and publicly. The report didn't exactly make him popular, but, again, he was not interested in being a nice guy. He was concerned with the security of the United States and the improvement of its military forces, and by being honest and outspoken he helped bring about improvements.

His opinions may have earned him some enemies, but what happened was good for the Guard, the army, and the country. "Another part of being a maverick," Charley Stone says, "is being inquisitive and being inquisitive makes you obnoxious."

Whether as a commander or as a staff member, throughout his career he made it a practice to check everything he could. Once he was assured that a subordinate had, as ordered, placed fifteen men in a certain position. When he checked, he found only five. His subordinate hadn't lied; he thought he had stationed the required number of men there and, in fact, would have sworn that he had.

Why did Stone check? Because he understands the fallibility of man. Despite the best of intentions, things can go wrong — and usually do unless the person responsible understands the responsibility of his position.

A more significant example occurred when he was commanding the 4th Division in Vietnam and discovered that his artillery was shooting a tremendous amount of ammunition. Were the expenditures effective? No one could tell him. If all the firing wasn't doing much good, he figured, there wasn't any point in continuing what was a fantastic waste, particularly since it was difficult to get ammunition forward. After studying the matter, he concluded that the construction of the enemy bunkers was the key to the problem. How could he know what effect the artillery was having on them?

There was, it turned out, a simple solution, but no one had thought of it. He had some bunkers built similar to enemy shelters that had been overrun and captured. Then he had every type of shell and each kind of fuze used against those bunkers. Next he assessed the effects of that fire. He discovered some astonishing things: small-caliber rounds had little effect and high-explosive shells and delayed fuzes were no good — unless of course, enemy troops were outside their bunkers. Only then did a time-on-target (TOT) concentration bring results. But there was no point in continuing to fire, because after the first volley the enemy scrambled back into the bunkers where they were safe except from eight-inch or, to a lesser extent, 155-mm. armor-piercing shells.

Based on what he had learned, Stone drew up an SOP (standard operating procedure) for firing artillery against bunkers in the 4th Division area. Ammunition expenditures declined drastically. At the same time, more rounds were on hand for firing against other vulnerable targets.

He is proud of that demonstration. It illustrates his belief in the application of intelligence in the solution of problems. Intelligence and imagination, added to the virtue of being reasonable, are the key words that describe his way of doing things.

As a student at the Army War College, he stimulated much argument and controversy, particularly over a solution of problems that would accompany the introduction of a large number of Allied divisions into a certain country and the development of a military campaign. This, he thought, was a lot of nonsense. The premise itself had no validity. The condition of the country, the state of its communications, and the existing logistical facilities made a situation of the sort that had been propounded patently impossible.

Why, he asked his fellow students, waste time on a problem of no practical consequence?

Wreck your own career, they told him, not ours.

Nevertheless, he challenged the instructors. In the uproar that followed he stood his ground and in the end earned the respect of staff and administration. That particular problem was deleted from the course.

When he was in Korea in command of the 19th Infantry stationed along the demilitarized zone, he constantly questioned premises and procedures in letters to the division commander, Major General Russell L. Vittrup, a giant of a man whose gentle manner did not obscure the authority of his actions. General Vittrup came by to visit Colonel Stone one day to impart some information. Of the three regimental commanders in the division, one had written no letters to division headquarters, the second had written one — and the commander of the 19th Infantry had dispatched 134.

Charley Stone got the point. He was monopolizing the attention and energies of the division staff. That wasn't right, so he quit sending letters. But he didn't stop thinking creatively. He simply made his ideas known in other ways.

There is no use doing anything, he feels, unless one does it as well as one can. He believes that in the challenging times of the mid-twentieth century, every man owes the army the very best he can offer.

He was once known as the best poker player in the army and one who played for high stakes. "Gentlemen," he would announce at the beginning of a card-playing session, "let's get something clear from the start. I'm not out to pass a pleasant social hour with you. I'm out to win your money." He usually did, and quite a bit. But suddenly he quit. He discovered he was getting a reputation for being a poker player, hunter, and fisherman. Everyone was forgetting the hard work he was putting into his profession.

How does he see himself? He'll tell you frankly: smart — meaning highly intelligent; brilliant — meaning articulate; dedicated — meaning hard-working; interested — meaning seriously concerned; energetic — meaning willing to work long hours; egotistical — meaning self-confident; and ambitious — meaning desiring to do the job well, not for the sake of self but for the sake of the service. "I can do any job in the service," he says, "and I think I have proved that I can."

Where did Stone come from? How did this maverick, with all the enemies he must have made along the way, manage to reach two-star rank? He will tell you that he has no enemies. He might admit that he has provoked jealousy among a few — not many — of his colleagues, but his subordinates admired him because he was always concerned with their welfare and his superiors liked him because he always did a superior job.

He was born in New York City, and to this day he carries a trace of New Yorkese in his speech. He graduated from the College of the City of New York, a fount of radicalism and pacifism in the 1930s. He had lost his father when he was very young. The strongest influence in his life, except for his mother, was his grandfather, who was known as the maverick of the New York City police force. His grandfather was also a naturalist, and he inculcated in young Stone a love for plants and flowers. Everywhere he has been stationed he has planted flowers and trees for relaxation and because he loves to see things grow.

When he graduated from high school in January 1933, he, along with all Americans, was in the depths of the Great Depression. Consequently, he went to CCNY because tuition was free and his high grades gave him entry. He first arrived on campus the day after the midyear graduation when an ROTC parade had provoked a student demonstration and an assault on the college president, who, in the press of the mob, had swung his umbrella to clear an escape lane.

The event received widespread press coverage, and freshman Stone read the story in a newspaper as he rode the subway to college to register. He was upset; he thought the disorder unwarranted and the assault shameful. When he arrived, he found students gathered before the registration tables chanting "Don't join the ROTC!" and threatening violence against those who did. He had no idea what the ROTC was, but because some students were trying to inhibit the free choice of others, he decided to join it, whatever it was. He persuaded two companions to do likewise, and all three signed up.

He enjoyed the ROTC, though his heart was set on becoming a landscape architect. But the family lacked money, and just the year before he graduated the Thomason Act of 1936 went into effect. United States Representative Robert Ewing Thomason of Texas had thought it wrong that only officers who entered the army after 1926, except for some engineers and other specialists, were West Pointers. He felt it was bad to isolate the army officers corps from the American public. He therefore sponsored legislation authorizing fifty second lieutenants to be commissioned in the Regular Army each year from colleges other than West Point. His scheme would allow the thousand top ROTC graduates to serve a year of active duty on a competitive tour. At the end of the year, fifty were to be selected for Regular Army commissions.

This appealed to Charley Stone. He had a job to start immediately after graduation, even though jobs were scarce in 1937. He had won the prize as the best pupil-teacher in the New York City school system and was scheduled to teach in Roslyn, Long Island, a pleasant suburban community. But he opted for the army. His friends told him he was crazy. He was wasting his time; he'd never get a Regular Army commission. The odds were too heavy.

That challenge provided even stronger motivation. He would, he vowed, make it anyway. He did. Forty-one of the thousand ROTC graduates serving a competitive tour in 1937–38 were chosen, and young Stone was among them.

Throughout his career Stone has had many challenging and fulfilling assignments but he counts nothing as more rewarding than the command of a division in combat. There are two major reasons: it is the ultimate test of an infantry officer's professional skill and it is the highest position in which a personal relationship can exist with the troops. Commanding a division in combat, he says, means you have to solve problems — "problems that are for real." You have solved them previously only in theory and you never knew then whether your solutions were right or wrong. In combat you know at once because the results are right there.

His most important tactical accomplishment as commander of the 4th Infantry Division, he feels, was defense of the Central Highlands of South Vietnam during the monsoon season. The area was large and close to major bases. His prime advantage was the high mobility of his combat elements. The trouble was that the monsoons would ground the planes and helicopters for many days. At these times the strong points he had positioned to block enemy invasion routes were vulnerable.

He assessed the overall situation, then planned in detail to cover the contingency that air transportation might be unavailable at intervals. On that basis, he selected a series of fire support bases to cover the area; they were different from the geographical locations normally used when the choppers could fly. He changed the logistical structure and constructed new bases to help the flow of supplies. He decided where to put his airmobile forces, including gasoline and repair parts, in order to get the best effect.

"It sounds easy to say it like this," he said. "But it took many long hours of patient work and a whole series of subsidiary but nonetheless important decisions. For example, I had to decide where to make my main engineer effort in the face of conflicting claims on a limited resource."

In the end he could see the results of his preparations. The enemy came in as expected in main force contingents rather than small guerrilla detachments, and they were clobbered.

"Our work proved us right," he said proudly. "Our people were not killed, our forces were not trapped, our supplies were where they were supposed to be, and the enemy was soundly beaten."

What distinguished the fighting in Vietnam, the general believes, was what he calls the "fantastic mobility" of the American troops coupled with outstanding communications. "As the division commander," he said, "I knew everything that happened in my area five minutes after it happened. I could react to it at once."

Mobility permitted him to move his troops swiftly from one threatened point to another in order to gain local superiority, not necessarily in numbers but in firepower; it allowed him to move fire support bases from hill to hill in quest of the commanding ground. Sometimes his troops occupied a hill for several days to frustrate enemy movements; sometimes they held a hill for several weeks to inhibit an enemy build-up. In a typical month, the number of battalions in the 1st Brigade at Dak To fluctuated from two to five to three. Nothing in Stone's scheme of things was tied to passive waiting. No one was bogged down to defend bridges, roads and villages. Rather he employed the opposite of static warfare; his people were on the move to locate and fight the North Vietnamese and Viet Cong.

Did his tactics pay off? During the Tet offensive in the spring of 1968, the highest kill ratio registered was in the three highland provinces on the Cambodian border — Charley Stone country — where the enemy lost nearly 3000 troops, the United States fewer than fifty, and the ARVN about 145.

When the time came for Stone to leave Vietnam, he had some leaflets printed in Vietnamese distributed through airdrops to the enemy troops. Carrying a photograph of "Thieu Tuong Charles P.

Stone," it is entitled "A Letter to the Officers and Men of the B-3 Front." It said, in part:

> Upon my departure from the 4th Infantry Division I want to take this last opportunity to speak to you. As I return home to join my dear family, I take many memories with me. There are the pleasant memories of the South Vietnamese people . . . I also take with me sad memories. I recall seeing thousands of North Vietnamese sent to their death by the stupid tactics of their leaders . . . If your leaders continue their wasteful practice and stupid tactics, my successor will also have a successful tour . . . I should thank the commander of the B-3 Front for making my command tour successful, but his poor leadership has resulted in many of your friends and comrades being killed . . . Why has he permitted so many to be killed and crippled? . . . Your leader has sacrificed many members of the 66th, 95C, 101D, 24th, 320th, 32d, 33d, and 174th Regiments.

An unprecedented gesture of scorn for poor leadership and compassion for troops badly led, Charley Stone's message expressed his conviction that the enemy was third-rate.

"I fight him on that basis," he told a reporter in Vietnam toward the close of a typical eighteen-hour day. During that day he had written to his wife, attended seven briefings, planned two tactical operations, flown 150 miles in his helicopter, mailed notes to the families of fifteen soldiers, played volleyball, planted lilies by his trailer, sipped a brandy Alexander instead of his usual tomato juice at a staff cocktail party — and never let anyone forget who was boss.

"They say," he told the reporter, "I'm the most confident commander in Vietnam, and I think they're right.'

How had he dealt a series of crippling blows to the 40,000 communists in the 4th Division area of operations?

"I fight differently every month," he answered. "Three NVA divisions came down here in April and May. They did not capture a single hill or fulfill a single objective."

Keeping his 18,000 soldiers constantly on the move, deploying them in a fleet of 131 helicopters to intercept and destroy the enemy, Stone won from General Creighton W. Abrams the "highest esteem for the professional way in which you have led and directed the 4th Division . . . You have no peer."

His immediate superior characterized his performance as one of "conspicuously outstanding caliber." The officer wrote:

> Capitalizing on his impressive competence, General Stone acquired a firm grasp on his unit, mission and area of responsibility in remarkably short order . . . he succeeded in infusing the division with his personality and *modus operandi* in minimum time without loss of continuity or effectiveness. Aggressive, out-going, self-assured and vigorous, he gives the Ivy [4th] Division a spirited, thoroughly professional "can do" brand of leadership that translates into victory on the battlefield . . . Through timely and penetrating analysis of intelligence and coordination with Government of Vietnam forces he was quick to gain control of each situation and to inflict telling defeat upon the enemy. Though strong-willed and assertive by nature, I have yet to find him less than ideally cooperative nor anything but an enthusiastic contributive team player . . . Stone is an imaginative planner, gifted tactician and talented administrator who is guided by highest standards. I have observed, too, a deep and abiding concern on his part for the well-being of the officers and men under his command . . . I predict that his tour of command will provide the stepping stone to three-star rank, for which I regard him as eminently well qualified.

The endorsement from the next higher headquarters read, in part:

> He is a very strong, positive, aggressive leader who provides the type of tough, bold and imaginative leadership required in a division on the battlefield. He inspires confidence, boldness and the spirit of the offensive among his officers and men . . . General Stone is very definitely 3-star caliber.

But Charley Stone never got his third star, for a reason that is comprehensible only within the context of his own personality.

When he was given the 4th Division, he made it clear that he wanted to come back to the United States after the normal one-year tour. There had been too many separations from his wife and daughter during his career, and he had no wish to prolong what would probably — after more than thirty years of service — be his last overseas assignment. So he told his superiors, firmly as usual, that that was his intention: to remain in Vietnam for a year.

About nine months later, having made his mark in Vietnam, having won the confidence — and more — of his superiors, subordinates, and colleagues, he was unofficially given to understand that he could have command of a corps-size field force and elevation to lieutenant general. Tempting as the opportunity was, it meant he would have to stay longer than the time he had fixed.

Was there any possibility of a promotion in the States? he asked. Was he being contemplated for a post back home that might lead to promotion? The replies, he recalls, were vague, so he telephoned his wife and said he had been offered a chance to stay on longer in Vietnam. Her distress at the news brought him to an immediate decision. The next morning he submitted his request for retirement, effective when his tour in command of the 4th Division ended.

He couldn't quite explain his decision to astounded friends, except to say that he wasn't ambitious for himself. He had reached the apex of his wishes by leading a division in combat. All else, it seemed to him, would be a let-down. Probably most important, he had driven himself too hard in his professional endeavors to have been able to afford the time with his family he and they deserved. It was time now to be with his family, to settle down and build a home, to plant flowers and trees, to rearrange the landscape.

Then came the ironic blow that knocked some of the joy out of his final days of active duty, a blow that left a sour taste. He might have become bitter, but he's not built that way. Besides, to a large extent, it was his own fault. He, himself — Charley Stone, smart, able, savvy, and self-confident — committed a blunder, probably the single error of any consequence in his entire career.

The incident that was to cast a pall over his retirement took place at Camp Enari, the 4th Division base camp inhabited by 8000 men who supported the combat troops manning the so-called forward positions. These, incidentally, were no more "forward" than Enari itself, for Enari too was hit by mortars and rockets and raids. But the camp had more of the amenities of civilian life than the other posts. The men worked a hard and long day but in the evening they had beer, movies, television, post exchange, and other rear-area luxuries.

The general was fond of walking through the camp, and in the course of his walks he found that saluting was poor. There was no saluting elsewhere in the division's area, but there seemed to him no reason why in the base camp, actually a small city of 8000, the customs of the service should be discontinued or observed in a slovenly manner. So, as he walked through the area, Stone often saluted soldiers first in order to get them into the habit. Occasionally he stopped and explained to a soldier the meaning of the salute and why it was expected. The overwhelming number of men he talked with were responsive, he recalls. Very few were recalcitrant or insolent. The presence of these few, he decided, was bad for morale, bad for discipline, and bad for the proper functioning of the base camp.

To make sure everyone knew the rules for saluting in the base camp, Stone mentioned the matter when he addressed newly arrived troops every Sunday. He directed his officers to put out the word and he told his chief of staff to get out a memorandum for unit bulletin boards. The memo said that those who failed to salute properly in Camp Enari would be sent to an area where saluting was not required.

In seven months, just eight soldiers were sent out of Camp Enari for failing to respond satisfactorily when stopped and advised of the rule. Two soldiers went to the 2d Brigade's headquarters, two to the 3d Brigade's headquarters, two to Fire Base No. 3 and two to Dak To. There they performed the same jobs they had done at Enari. There, too, they found themselves at camps numbering 1000 to 1200 men, with movies, beer, and the rest.

The trouble began when an enterprising reporter read the notice on a bulletin board and wrote a story that was picked up and spread far and wide. Charley Stone became fair game, and the newspapers hooted about the general who ordered his men to "salute or shoot." The exaggeration quickly snowballed. As the reporters looked around they dug up other accusations. General Stone, it was said, was unpopular because he had revoked the men's driving licenses.

What had actually happened was that when Stone had discovered that his command had one of the highest vehicular accident rates in Vietnam, he established a new policy and enforced it. Speeders at Camp Enari had their licenses taken away. Ten months later, the 4th Division had the lowest accident rate in Vietnam.

More stories were published that said Stone had taken the guns away from his troops and left them unable to defend themselves. In fact, he had found that his command had an incidence of accidental or self-inflicted gunshot wounds that was nearly double that of any other division in Vietnam, and that most of these accidents occurred in Camp Enari where the men carried their personal weapons. Since the camp was well outposted and guarded and there was always ample warning of an enemy attack, he ordered the personal weapons collected and placed in the bunkers where the troops took shelter and manned defensive positions in time of enemy action. There they would have their weapons at hand. Within several months, the 4th Division enjoyed the lowest incidence of self-inflicted wounds of any comparable unit.

The Stone image would have fared better if the public had been told the stories that didn't get into print. For instance, during the same walk in which he criticized men for not saluting he would also stop and chat for several minutes with soldiers, ask them how they were doing, and so on — perhaps a dozen or so each day. He would always ask the soldier's name and his aide, who was nearby, would jot it down along with a few notes on their conversation. In the evening, Stone would write to the soldier's parents or wife, saying he had talked with their son or husband and assuring them he was all right — or whatever was fitting. Sometimes the families replied. One letter from Evansville, Ind., read:

> Words cannot express the thanks and respect I have for you for writing us about your chat with our son . . . I just couldn't imagine a man of your stature and position to take time out of your busy schedule to assure the parents of one of your men. Although I served with the 34th Infantry — World War II "drafted" — it almost brought tears to my eyes to read your letter. They just don't make generals like you any more. Thanking you again and wishing you the very best of luck and a very speedy and safe victory. Sincerely . . .

From Grand Rapids, Iowa, came a letter that said, "I have a son under your command, and I am glad of it. He is, too."

From Long Island, New York: "Hurrah for General Stone. You kept my grandson safe. God bless you."

Letters like these were never published during the saluting affair, but many other things were. One of the most vicious stories characterized the general "who sent soldiers to the front as punishment for not saluting" as a man who "doesn't want to be remembered as the individual who forced soldiers to salute or go to the field. Yet that is exactly what General Stone is going to be remembered as, unless there is some pretty fast action to make him better known for something else."

It would be a pity if he were remembered for that. He was a maverick, but no martinet.

What bothered Charley Stone most of all, and still does, is not what he regards as a "tempest in a teapot." It is that no one in the Pentagon tried to clarify the basic misconception. No one stood up and said loudly, as *he* would have: "Look here. Stone is responsible for the lives of 22,000 men, twenty-four hours a day. As the commander, he is expected to look everywhere for clues to the responsiveness of his men to orders. Permissiveness in the army, much less insolence and recalcitrance, cannot be tolerated. The military virtues are obedience and discipline at all times so that they can be counted on when absolutely necessary for the security of army units and the success of their missions."

It could have been so simple, he says, but no one spoke up.

He came back to work on the permanent home he never had time to establish in the army. He fixed up and modernized a large old house in the country. It sits along a river in the midst of enough acres to allow a huge azalea garden, a large orchard, and plenty of shade trees. He says he is "resting" now, but he is as active and busy physically as he has ever been.

"It's too bad he retired when he did," a senior officer who had a distinguished record in World War II said when he learned about Stone. "It's a distinct loss for the army. The army needs people like him. The thing about Charley is that he was good for the army."

Despite his claim to a massive self-conceit, despite his loud voice and self-assertiveness, despite his abrasive self-confidence, he turns out to be quite a nice guy, in addition to being one of the finest soldiers the U.S. Army has ever produced. There are quite a few like him. They are not famous, just outstanding.

Relieved of Command

WHAT HAPPENS when the effectiveness of a military unit or an agency fails to measure up to expectations? According to the relevant army field manual, "The situation may dictate . . . a change in command." Meaning, bluntly, a change in commander.

But whose expectations? The superior of the person being judged. Is that the only test of whether a commander retains his command? Is that the system? Can a commander who has worked long and hard to attain a command be removed by the whim of his superior? It would appear so.

Are there no safeguards built into the system to insure that it operates fairly and to the benefit of the service? Perhaps. Let us see how some reliefs have been made and for what reasons.

When a professional baseball or football team has a losing season, the manager or coach stands a good chance of being fired. For, like the military, the goal is victory. A lack of success may require a change in the leadership. Not because it is the easiest thing to do, but because a shift in leaders may change and improve the methods of instruction, the team discipline, the strategy and tactics employed. Because a new leader may inspire a new and greater confidence. And, perhaps most important, because a change indicates to higher authority — whether fans or the nation — that the management is concerned with results and is taking action in the hope of bringing about improvement.

It was for no strange reason that his close associates and protégés refer affectionately to one of the most effective and respected combat leaders in World War II as Coach. Clarence R. Huebner, who commanded the 1st Infantry Division and later the V Corps, was a great teacher, and the surprisingly large number of general officers who learned their trade with the Big Red One attests to the efficacy of his methods.

Anyone who attended the morning staff briefings of the 2d Infantry Division in Korea remembers the trouble and time the commanding general, Clark Ruffner, took to explain to his staff why certain decisions had been made and why others were about to be made. His talk was always stimulating, and he gave to these sessions — which at some headquarters are a routine and somewhat boring ritual — a new and exciting dimension.

Baseball managers and football coaches may come and go to the delight and disgust of their followers. But war is no game, except possibly to armchair strategists, and the relief of a commander is an agonizing decision for those who wield the ax. It is also a moment — or a lifetime — of anguish for the one who gets the cut. Yet the removal of a commander has still another effect often overlooked, and this observation Dwight D. Eisenhower placed above the others. He once wrote:

> The relief of a combat leader is something that is not to be lightly done in war. Its first effect is to indicate to troops a dissatisfaction with their performance; otherwise the commander would be commended, not relieved. This probable effect must always be weighed against the hoped-for advantage of assigning to the post another, and possibly untried, commander. On the other hand, really inept leadership must be quickly detected and instantly removed. Lives of thousands are involved — the question is not one of academic justice for the leader, it is of concern for the many and the objective of victory.

The latter part of this stricture was what he stressed when, after the United States defeat at Kasserine Pass, he assigned George S. Patton, Jr., to command the II Corps in North Africa. "You must not retain for one instant," Eisenhower told Patton, "any man in a responsible position where you have become doubtful of his ability to do the job . . . This matter frequently calls for more courage than any other thing you will have to do, but I expect you to be perfectly cold-blooded about it."

Actually, the records indicate that General Eisenhower himself might have acted more swiftly at Kasserine. One wonders whether expectations of success in North Africa were too low; or whether, simply, no suitable replacements were deemed at hand. In any case, later in the war General Eisenhower showed no want of these qualities of courage and cold-bloodedness. He relieved subordinates instantly upon signs that they had less than a firm grasp of their duties.

What makes the relief of commanders possible, of course, is the principle of interchangeable parts. Any officer who is suitably trained can take over any unit. This is the American belief.

Yet in another army that prided itself on adherence to the scientific method, in a nation as distant from warlordism as Nazi Germany, at least one division commander was indispensable. General Gerhard Graf von Schwerin was relieved for a combination of insubordination (he failed to attack as ordered at Mortain) and suspected treason (some of his activities looked very much like attempts to get in touch with the Allied command to negotiate a private settlement). Despite these serious charges, he had to be reinstated to his command. The members of his division, recruited from Schwerin's home area, had so intense an admiration of their commander that they refused to fight under anyone else.

It is difficult to envision this occurring in the U.S. Army, where commanders come and go, most of them headed up to higher posts of authority and responsibility.

Command has two basic elements: authority and responsibility. A commander exercises authority over his subordinates by virtue of his rank or assignment; he is held responsible by his superior commander for everything done under his authority.

Authority and responsibility operate through the chain of command, the hierarchy or succession of commanders that creates the formal channels through which orders are sent down and reports are sent up. Establishing clear and definite lines of authority and responsibility, the chain of command requires that every commander be aware of his place in the chain, and that he have only one immediate superior who assigns him tasks and holds him responsible for what is done. Authority comes down from a single source through constantly multiplying channels, and responsibility reaches upward from a subordinate commander through a single channel. No commander in the chain of command is ever by-passed.

In the words of scholar Richard M. Leighton, "a superior commander, like a feudal lord, can command only his immediate vassals, the commanders on the next lowest level of authority . . . Disciplinary action by a superior authority theoretically can be exercised only upon the commander immediately subordinate, who in turn is responsible for the transgressions of *his* subordinates."

This is the United States system.

In contrast, for example, the British in World War II acted with far less regard to channels of command. The Imperial General Staff often reached down several levels, by-passing the theater commander, to guide or to discipline a commander.

"It seems impossible," General Eisenhower once said in some exasperation, "for the British to grasp the utter simplicity of the system that we employ."

It is not always that simple. A workable system needs to be flexible to accommodate the diversity and fallibility of human behavior. And there have been United States commanders who have had no compunction about skipping several echelons to exercise their authority.

One of the most curious and celebrated incidents illustrating how the chain of command was by-passed occurred during the Papua campaign. Edwin F. Harding kept insisting that his 32d Infantry Division could take Buna only if he had reinforcements, additional supplies, and more artillery. His superiors kept saying that Harding ought to relieve his regimental commanders, whose competence they felt was questionable. Finally, Douglas MacArthur, the Southwest Pacific Area commander, told Robert L. Eichelberger, the I Corps commander, to relieve Harding and Harding's subordinate commanders or MacArthur would relieve them and Eichelberger, too. Eichelberger went to the Buna area and asked Harding what changes he proposed to make in his commanders to get the troops moving. Harding's answer was short: none. So Eichelberger relieved him. But he could not take Buna either until he had received the resources Harding had asked for and had failed to get.

Jumping a command echelon was in actual practice often traditional in combat during World War II. It was said that a division commander needed to know how the battalions were doing, that a corps commander had to have direct knowledge of how the regiments were doing. For sometimes, particularly on the higher levels, it is easier for an army commander than a corps commander to remonstrate, gently or otherwise, with a division commander. The exchange is likely to be less abrasive, more conducive to good continuing relations between the commanders at division and corps.

Apart from the authority a commander exerts, what is the nature of his influence over his troops? If he stamps a measure of his own personality on the men under him, if everyone in the command wants to be and act like the Old Man, the commander is said to be successful. Imitation by troops in bearing or even to the point of affecting personal idiosyncrasies and mannerisms of speech and dress indicates the identification of men with the desires and mission — which should be synonymous — of the commander.

If the commander becomes — somehow, through personal bravery or a well-planted rumor — a hero figure, he imparts an intangible sense of confidence among his men. The Old Man, they will say, knows what is best; he will get us through this mess; we can trust him. If the commander conveys the feeling that he cares about the welfare of his men, not only their safety but also their comfort, he promotes loyalty. If he teaches them what they need to know, he makes them proficient. If he maintains cohesion and discipline, he creates an instrument for performing the tasks for which he will be held responsible.

In short, a commander binds his men together, trains them, provides motivation, and directs them. Yet how effective he is as a commander will be judged solely by his success in his assigned endeavor. This, at least in theory, is the sole criterion. It is all very well, but success and failure may well be subjective matters. One man's success may be another man's failure.

And what if a superior bungles and tries to make a subordinate take the rap? Several principles are built into the system. First, the military establishment distinguishes between responsibility and accountability in ascribing blame. A staff officer acting for his commander may be at fault for a failure, but the commander is normally responsible for choosing — unless he takes over in an emergency — the men who surround, support, assist, and represent him. He takes the blame.

A second principle is the loyalty that goes upward along with responsibility. A subordinate must give his superior an extremely strong loyalty; it is the superior who judges whether the subordinate is competent, never the reverse.

According to Field Manual 22–100, the subordinate has the duty to "execute instructions from his superior with exactness and thoroughness, regardless of his personal feelings." And this sometimes leads to peculiar situations. Lloyd R. Fredendall, the corps commander, and Orlando Ward, the division commander, were in an almost perpetual state of personal conflict at Kasserine Pass. Yet Ward maintained an impeccable loyalty so ethical in nature that he was unable to tell his superior how wrong Fredendall's tactics and orders were.

A third principle in the American command system is the emphasis on mission. A commander tells a subordinate *what* to do, never how — and rarely why. In other words, he gives his subordinate enough authority and sufficient latitude in judgment to do the job assigned, and that makes him responsible.

Thus, when Fredendall laid out Ward's missions in North Africa, he specified in detail and with exactitude how he wanted them accomplished. He consequently usurped Ward's function, denied him the authority of command at his proper level, and thereby prevented Ward from being held responsible for the reverses suffered at Kasserine. The result, as we have seen, was that Fredendall, not Ward, was relieved.

Certain persons outside the chain of command police the command channels to guard against abuses or attempted cover-ups. The inspector general acts in this capacity, as do observers of one kind or another — officers sent from Washington to the theaters of operations to check on various activities.

Finally, there is a great deal of informal conversation and exchange of information among officers up and down the chain of command. When the officer corps is staffed by a relatively small group of professionals who have known each other intimately throughout their careers, little escapes their notice, attention, and knowledge. Furthermore, loyalties develop very early, and an appreciation of personal weaknesses, together with an appreciation of personal strengths, makes it possible for a wise superior to take the compensating action required to assure success.

Since the chain of command resembles a pyramid, and since all commanders are responsible for whatever is done under their authority, the logic may be extended and the buck passed to the point where the President as commander in chief is responsible for everything. In theory this is so. President Harry Truman had a sign on his desk that read: The buck stops here. President John F. Kennedy took responsibility for the fiasco at the Bay of Pigs.

In actual practice, the buck-passing stops relatively close to the source of error, breakdown, or failure. On the eve of the invasion of Normandy, General Eisenhower, in an instinctive assumption of responsibility, penned a note he intended to issue if the landings failed. "If any blame or fault attaches to the attempt," he wrote, "it is mine alone."

Before then, when he commanded the Mediterranean theater, though he was, of course, responsible for everything that happened spheres of responsibility below him were quite well understood. Mark Clark, for example, was responsible for the performance of his Fifth Army.

In Korea, when the communist prisoners of war staged their violent riots at Koje-do, the camp commander was sacked. It was sometimes said that those higher in the chain of command should have been held responsible.

One of the most complicated issues in the Pearl Harbor investigations was the question of who was responsible for the disaster. The blame was initially fixed on the army and navy commanders at Hawaii for having taken improper precautions against surprise attack. The fault was later extended to include members of the higher military staffs in Washington; specifically, for the army, Generals Marshall and Gerow. They had failed to make certain that Walter C. Short, commander of the Hawaiian Department, had properly responded to their instructions.

Short was confused by the directives he received and was eventually relieved from command. But his superiors in Washington had failed to notice his confusion, and, it was maintained, they should have done so. In defense of his course of action, Short said that he had reported what he was doing, had received no comment from his superiors, and had therefore assumed that he was properly complying with orders.

Gerow, the Assistant Chief of Staff, War Plans Division, working directly under Marshall, the Chief of Staff, took responsibility for sending Short a key warning message, a week and a half before the attack, that Short misunderstood. For failing to clarify his instructions and correct Short's misinterpretation, Gerow admitted his error. But Marshall would not let him take the rap. Making a fine distinction, he pointed out that Gerow had had direct responsibility but that he, Marshall, had had full responsibility for what had or had not been done.

It sometimes happens that a subordinate threatens to make his superior look bad, or actually does. By failing in his mission, or at the very least by indicating in his behavior or manner that a failure is impending or imminent, a subordinate may place his superior in jeopardy. Yet a superior is generally loath to remove a subordinate. Removing a subordinate reflects inevitably on the competence of the superior — on his ability to provide proper guidance, support, encouragement, and supervision. Wholesale reliefs in particular not only look bad for the superior in charge; they also hurt subordinate commanders. Officers who are constantly looking over their shoulders to see whether the ax is about to fall are diverting attention and energy from the more important matters on the battlefield. Conversely, a commander who enjoys his superior's confidence is going to do his utmost to retain it. He wants, more than anything, to measure up to the expectations of his chief, unless, of course, those expectations are set too high. Establishing reasonable standards of performance and accomplishment is also a concomitant of leadership.

The whole business, despite General Eisenhower's claim that the system is simple, is really quite tricky. The fact is, success is not the sole criterion in judging a commander's competence. A variety of factors enters into the judgment — all of them, in the final analysis, subjective in nature.

First, a commander may simply be lucky. Take the case in World War II of Robert C. Macon, who led the inexperienced 83d Division into combat in Normandy. In its initial commitment, the division was not only blooded but bloodied — and there is a distinction. The number of casualties suffered was frightful: 2000 in the first two days, and they continued heavy for more than a week. Furthermore, the division failed to move the short distance required by the corps commander.

Fortunately for Macon, his immediate superior was J. Lawton Collins, who understood that the strength of the opposition, the difficulty of the terrain, and the inexperience of the division were preventing accomplishment of the mission. He decided that the competence of the commander was not in question; there is some evidence that he reached that conclusion after he himself virtually took command of the division for most of one day. As a result, Macon remained in command throughout the European campaign. After the division settled down, it performed well consistently.

Eugene M. Landrum was probably one of the unluckiest of all. He took over the 90th Division, which Eisenhower said had not been "properly brought up" in training and was, consequently, "less well prepared for battle than almost any other." This division performed so badly that Bradley very nearly decided to dissolve it and transform it into a replacement pool. When Landrum took over, the division was manning an active front. He nevertheless began intensive training to improve individual and team tactics. After a very short time in which to get results, Landrum was ordered to attack Mont-Castre near La Haye-du-Puits. In that attack the division suffered 4000 casualties in twelve days and displayed what was judged to be a lack of cohesion and proficiency in offensive warfare. After eight days of rest and more training, all the while engaged in an active defense and the integration of thousands of infantry replacements, the division moved into attack at St.-Germain-sur-Sèvres. This time it fell on its face. Landrum was relieved.

Was his removal warranted? Losses in the 90th Division were no higher and the advances no less than those of the adjacent units — the 79th and 4th Divisions — which were never accused of inefficiency. Despite its deficiencies, the 90th Division under Landrum had actually made a splendid showing that was unappreciated at the time. The division had attacked through the worst kind of hedgerow country in plain view of the enemy and had overrun Mont-Castre, a bastion of defense; it had destroyed the greater part of two enemy divisions; it had forced the commitment of the immediate reserves of the opposing corps; it had made necessary the Germans' hurried dispatch to the area of army reserves.

This was reason enough to commend Landrum. But the achievement was obscured at the time, and the only evidence on how well Landrum was doing as a division commander seemed to emerge when the division fell apart immediately thereafter at St.-Germain-sur-Sèvres.

Why did the division perform badly? Because many of its trained troops had become casualties at Mont-Castre. And because higher headquarters felt that the division required a new leader, Landrum was removed without prejudice. "Nothing against Landrum," Eisenhower reported, adding that he would be glad to have Landrum command a division that he himself had taken through the training cycle.

Landrum's successor, Raymond S. McLain, was far luckier. He took over during a static period that permitted thorough training. When the division was next committed, the Germans in Normandy were falling back in confusion after the United States breakthrough. Given the mission of helping to exploit the breakthrough, McLain entered a mobile situation against sporadic resistance. The division moved fast. It looked good. So did McLain, who went on later to take command of a corps.

This is not to be construed as an attempt to downgrade McLain, a highly efficient and effective commander. Would he have given the division a higher combat efficiency had he been assigned to the command earlier? Who can tell? The point is that he took command in particularly favorable circumstances and made the most of them. He might have bungled his opportunity. Instead, he succeeded — handsomely.

Landrum was unfortunate also — and this is another factor operating in the removal of commanders — because he failed to conform to type. He stayed close to his command post, followed the the battle on a map, usually gave his orders by telephone, and was rarely seen by the troops.

The standard performance is quite the opposite. The deputy or assistant commander or chief of staff is supposed to mind the store, while the commander himself visits his forward — subordinate — elements. A "desk" man is usually doomed. The outdoor type, vigorous, handsome, impressive in bearing — like MacArthur, Ridgway, Collins, and others — is the winner.

This is the legend, the stereotype. Yet there have been exceptions. Leland S. Hobbs, who commanded the 30th Division, was often at his desk — his telephone journal is one of the liveliest historical records of the war — and he ran a good show.

Some commanders have been relieved because they were tired or sick. And sometimes this is the excuse rather than the reason. No question about Troy H. Middleton, who had to leave his 45th Division in Italy; none about Gilbert R. Cook, who had to give up his

XII Corps in France. But others appear doubtful, or at least inconclusive. Charles H. Corlett, who had the XIX Corps in Normandy, was a superb commander, yet lacked fire; he left the theater because of illness. Ernest J. Dawley, relieved after the battle of Salerno was won, made a bad impression on his superiors because his hands trembled and his voice shook. The trouble was that he had had to make do with a skeleton staff for ten days. Having found little time to sleep, he was overworked. Still another factor operated in Dawley's case. He did not belong to the "in group." He was not well known to Eisenhower, who questioned Clark about Dawley's efficiency before the Salerno invasion. Although assured by Clark that Dawley was a capable commander, Eisenhower continued to have his doubts and he communicated his reservations to General Marshall even before Dawley was tested in combat. Succeeding at Salerno under extreme handicaps, Dawley was nevertheless removed.

To a certain extent, Fredendall suffered this kind of alienation in North Africa; Lindsay McD. Silvester, John Millikin, and Leroy H. Watson in Europe. Watson's experience is particularly interesting. Relieved from command of the 3d Armored Division and reduced two grades to colonel, he was sent to the 29th Infantry Division, where, as assistant division commander, he soon earned a promotion to brigadier general.

Commanders are sometimes relieved because their personalities cause personal frictions that prevent their working as closely as required with superiors, subordinates, and associates. This may be seen in the relations of Fredendall and Ward, Collins and Leroy Watson, Walton Walker and Lindsay Silvester, Courtney Hodges and John Millikin, Geoffrey Keyes and Fred Walker.

A close-knit combination is hard to beat. A good part of the reason why the First Army broke out of the hedgerow country in Normandy may be found in the warm friendship and mutual respect that existed between Bradley at army and Collins at VII Corps. No need for long explanations between the two men; no need to clarify instructions or suggestions. One knew what the other was thinking; one knew how the other would react. Enjoying a mutual confidence that generated daring and dash in the actions of both, they pried open the German defenses and transformed a frustrating war of position into a heady chase of exploitation and pursuit. When Bradley moved up to the 12th Army Group and Hodges succeeded him at the First

Army, much the same closeness in outlook and concept continued to operate between the corps and army. No wonder other corps commanders complained that Joe Collins got the choice assignments. But, of course, there was more than personality. Collins produced, he was good, and he made his superiors look good in the process.

Basically, it is impossible to discuss personality. Fredendall and Patton, at least superficially, were very much alike in their behavioral patterns. Yet one was unsuccessful, the other strikingly triumphant. In Europe, the First and Third armies were equally successful. Yet the commander of one was the antithesis of the other, not only in personality but in method of operation. Hodges and Patton were thoroughly different.

Occasionally, commanders are relieved for insubordination. The most celebrated case in recent times is, of course, that of General MacArthur in 1951. Two others deserve mention. John S. Wood and Terry Allen were two of the finest division commanders of World War II. Their units looked bad momentarily, one in Germany, the other in Sicily. Their superiors diagnosed the same malady: over-attachment to their troops, to the point where their professional considerations collided with the more objective judgments of their superiors. Allen went to another division, and he led it with his usual high measure of distinction.

Commanders are also relieved for incompetence, but infrequently. It is hard to say exactly which men were deemed inefficient, for it is always more charitable to ascribe the relief to other reasons; for example, selection for promotion to higher responsibility. Fredendall and Lucas were moved from command of a corps in an active theater to command of an army in the States.

But only few commanders prove to be incompetent. The promotion system is too tough and ruthless on commanders at the lower levels. Advancement requires demonstrated proficiency. By the time an officer reaches the levels of high command, he has been so rigorously scrutinized, tested, and selected along the way that there is little chance of his failing to measure up to the demands of the next higher job. Finally, when things are not going right, the most obvious remedy is to relieve the commander. When no other solutions appear feasible, this may work.

This seems to be so in many cases that have been investigated in the course of historical research. The evidence suggests, very strongly, that, for the most part, relief was unwarranted if not altogether unjustified. In the vast number of instances, the breakdown of an activity or the failure to fulfill expectations cannot, after mature reflection, be ascribed to inefficiency on the part of the commander. Yet this is much easier to say here and now than it was at the times and places of the occurrences. For the relieving officers lacked the information, perspective, and objectivity that are all too apparent now. Their perception was rooted in the crisis and urgency of the battlefield rather than in the calm deliberation of the study.

Like beauty, emergency — not to mention success or failure — is in the eye of the beholder. In critical situations that cried for solutions to pressing command problems, the burden of responsibility carried by the superior commanders made it necessary for them to reach rapid decision. They had no time for introspection or patience. They had to act. And in relieving some commanders, they made them casualties of war.

And what of the near misses — Eisenhower at Kasserine Pass, Clark at Salerno and again at Anzio, Fred Walker at the Rapido, Robert Grow in the Cotentin being told to produce "or else"? And what of those persons, particularly in the lower commands, whose death or injury in combat averted the heartbreak of relief?

Quite a few relatively high commanders were removed in World War II. But it was a large army, and it was a citizen army, quickly raised and trained. The professional soldiers were elevated rapidly, without measured exposure to the authority and responsibility of successive levels of command. Then, too, there was an urgency about the proceedings, a strong desire to get the war over quickly. And there were visible objectives that promised to accomplish that end: Berlin and Tokyo.

In Korea the visible objectives — if indeed they existed at all in fact — were unattainable. The warfare seemed more professional, and the process of relief appeared to become, somehow, less overt, more sophisticated, not so harsh.

To venture a guess, probably relatively fewer higher commanders were removed in Vietnam. The leaders were altogether professional and well trained, and the commanders managed a series of small-unit actions. There were no visible geographical objectives that, once gained, could bring the conflict to an end.

A curious trend seems to have developed that, in the future, may make the relief of commanders quite unnecessary. That is the propensity of intermediate headquarters to become vestigial. In Vietnam, helicopters and planes enabled higher commanders in a matter of minutes to be at the lower units who did the fighting, and they were often there. Of what practical use were the commanders in between? It is sometimes said — facetiously, of course — that the President had a direct telephone line to every foxhole. Will the functional need for intermediate commanders disappear altogether?

Commanders have been and are still removed from command for a variety of reasons. A number of seemingly peripheral factors bear on the decision to relieve. And this is how it ought to be. Officers in the chain of command would be less than human if they were not susceptible to such influences. Yet, on the whole, the rule officially prescribed is followed. Commanders are removed when a unit or an activity breaks down, when it fails to function according to expectations — those expectations being always focused on the need to succeed.

Sacking the commander, whether done with regret or in anger, is the most obvious immediate act to restore vitality and improve performance, particularly in a crisis demanding urgent action. This is how the system is supposed to operate; and, generally, this is how it does.

The United States system is individualistic, subjective, and pragmatic. It establishes the function of command as a precarious, challenging, and risky opportunity for the man who exercises it. Every commander well knows and recognizes that the importance of his responsibility makes him vulnerable to the drastic act of relief. If he cannot measure up — that is, if he fails to inspire confidence among superiors and subordinates alike — he must give way to someone who can.

Index

Index